Professor Keith Dobson's *Clinical Depression: An Individualized, Biopsychosocial Approach to Assessment and Treatment* is an excellent resource for clinicians at all levels of experience and training. Dobson, who has been at the forefront of research on depression for several decades and is a world leader in the field, has provided the reader with a balance of scholarly research and practical clinical guidance. This superb book will help the reader understand the complex nature of depression, the antecedence and vulnerabilities, the underlying risk for depression, and the debilitating consequences of depression. Rather than focus on one approach, Dobson reviews and gives examples of the major models of intervention that have empirical validation. Throughout the book, there are clear clinical examples of application, so the reader will come away with an expanded knowledge of the latest work in the field and a sophisticated practical resource for conducting therapy. Written in an accessible and humane voice, this is a book that I will recommend and I will personally refer to in my own work. Bravo!

–ROBERT L. LEAHY, PhD, DIRECTOR, AMERICAN INSTITUTE FOR COGNITIVE THERAPY, NEW YORK, NY, UNITED STATES

This book brings a biopsychosocial model of depression to life in a way that is comprehensive and yet clinically accessible. From cognition to exercise, if substantial data exists in support of a method for addressing depression, it finds its place in this volume as part of a coherent, step-by-step, personalized approach that will be appealing to students and practitioners from a variety of evidence-based orientations. A clear step forward for the field from one of the masters.

–STEVEN C. HAYES, PhD, FOUNDATION PROFESSOR OF PSYCHOLOGY EMERITUS, UNIVERSITY OF NEVADA, RENO, RENO, NV, UNITED STATES

Written by one of the foremost experts on depression, Dr. Keith Dobson surveys the contemporary literature on the nature and treatment of depression with a particular focus on cognitive behavioral therapy. This is an excellent and well-written book that should be part of every clinician's library. Individuals suffering from this debilitating and common condition will equally benefit. I highly recommend it.

–STEFAN G. HOFMANN, PhD, ALEXANDER VON HUMBOLDT PROFESSOR, PHILIPPS-UNIVERSITY OF MARBURG, MARBURG, GERMANY

Dobson's long and broad immersion in research on depression and its treatment has resulted in an engaging guide for trainees and experienced clinicians alike. His accessible and personal writing style comprehensively describes the many presentations of clinically significant depression, multifaceted risk factors and models, and diverse psychotherapy treatments. He makes the case that today's therapists need to understand how each client's depression is different and illustrates how diverse empirically supported treatment models and interventions may contribute useful components.

This is without question one of the best clinician handbooks ever written on depression and its treatment. If there was only one professional book my graduate student trainees could read on depression, this is the book I would highly recommend. My unbridled enthusiasm for this book is based on its many strengths.

CLINICAL DEPRESSION

CLINICAL **DEPRESSION**

AN **INDIVIDUALIZED**,
BIOPSYCHOSOCIAL APPROACH
TO **ASSESSMENT** AND **TREATMENT**

KEITH S. DOBSON

 AMERICAN PSYCHOLOGICAL ASSOCIATION

Published by
American Psychological Association
750 First Street, NE
Washington, DC 20002
https://www.apa.org

Order Department
https://www.apa.org/pubs/books
order@apa.org

Typeset in Meridien and Ortodoxa by Circle Graphics, Inc., Reisterstown, MD

Printer: Sheridan Books, Chelsea, MI
Cover Designer: Mark Karis

Library of Congress Cataloging-in-Publication Data

Names: Dobson, Keith S., author.
Title: Clinical depression : an individualized, biopsychosocial approach to
   assessment and treatment / authored by Keith S. Dobson.
Description: Washington, DC : American Psychological Association, [2024] |
   Includes bibliographical references and index.
Identifiers: LCCN 2023040331 (print) | LCCN 2023040332 (ebook) | ISBN
   9781433836701 (paperback) | ISBN 9781433841064 (ebook)
Subjects: LCSH: Depression, Mental. | Depression, Mental—Treatment. |
   Depression, Mental—Social aspects. | Cognitive therapy. |
   Evidence-based psychotherapy. | BISAC: PSYCHOLOGY / Psychopathology /
   Depression | PSYCHOLOGY / Movements / Cognitive Behavioral Therapy (CBT)
Classification: LCC RC537 .D633 2024 (print) | LCC RC537 (ebook) | DDC
   616.85/27—dc23/eng/20231222
LC record available at https://lccn.loc.gov/2023040331
LC ebook record available at https://lccn.loc.gov/2023040332

https://doi.org/10.1037/0000398-000

Printed in the United States of America

10 9 8 7 6 5 4 3 2 1

CONTENTS

ACKNOWLEDGMENTS

Like the vast majority of books in the field of psychopathology and treatment, this one could not have been written without the tragic suffering of millions of individuals. Humans have struggled with melancholia and depression since the beginning of recorded time, and innumerable articles, treatises, and volumes have been written on the topic. From the earliest models of the humoral theory of melancholia, so well described by Richard Burton (aka Democritus) in *The Anatomy of Melancholy* (Burton, 1621), and down the ages to our contemporary biopsychosocial models, the understanding of human despair has rested on the untold number of people who have experienced what we now call major depression. I want to acknowledge how deeply those individuals have contributed to our understanding of clinical depression. At its essence, this book is intended for you.

This volume has a fairly extensive set of references, and it incorporates the work of both historical and contemporary writers and researchers. I have had the privilege of working in this field for more than 4 decades, and in doing so I have encountered and interacted with a large number of depression specialists. This book, however, offers many of my own thoughts and opinions, some of which may well diverge from my colleagues. Sir Isaac Newton is sometimes quoted as saying, "If I have seen further, it is by standing on the shoulders of giants," and this position is mine as well. At the same time, although I have offered opinions and conjectures, I am very much open to discussion, debate, and the ultimate resolution of these ideas through data.

It is always tempting when writing an acknowledgments section to simply offer broad thanks to the many experts who have come before. This strategy has the benefit of not missing important or notable people, but it also has the unfortunate consequence of not recognizing those individuals who are most important. As such, and with due apologies to anyone I have missed, I acknowledge the influence of the following people, as they have most shaped my own growth and understanding of the field of clinical depression and psychotherapy. In alphabetical order, these individuals are David Barlow, Aaron Beck, Judith Beck, Claudi Bockting, David A. Clark, David M. Clark, Pim Cuijpers, Robert DeRubeis, Sona Dimidjian, David Dozois, Ian Gotlib, Paul Gilbert, Connie Hammen, Steven Hayes, Steve Hollon, Neil Jacobson, Nikolas Kazantzis, Bob Leahy, Chris Martell, Art Nezu, Christine Maguth Nezu, Jackie Persons, Zindel Segal, Brian Shaw, Pam Sokol, John Teasdale, Ed Watkins, Jeffrey Young, and Yang Fahui. I have read and thought about most of the works of all the people just listed, and I am constantly struck by how much more I have to learn.

I have had wonderful opportunities to travel, lecture, and conduct training extensively over the course of my career. Most of this work has involved conferences and workshops on every continent except Antarctica. These opportunities have provided me with the chance to see and discuss how depression is conceptualized and treated in many diverse cultures. Through these discussions I have been repeatedly struck by how culture shapes our understanding of both normal and abnormal psychology and how foolish it is to ignore the importance of culture and context in our clinical work. I have further had the great fortune to work with an enormous number of undergraduate, graduate, and postgraduate trainees. Each of you in your own way has given me new insights and ideas, in particular as most of you have worked in the field of depression research yourselves. I really must demur to listing all the wonderful contacts I have had over the years and simply thank you all for the opportunity to come into your working and living spaces and to learn from you.

I also acknowledge the importance of the people at the American Psychological Association (APA) for this work. Susan Reynolds, my acquisitions editor at APA, was key in getting the book reviewed and underway, and she deserves great credit for keeping my nose to the grindstone. The development people at APA, notably David Becker, similarly have worked hard to make this book a reality. I also want to give a special note of thanks to Elena ("Ellie") Mineva, who tirelessly worked to help ensure the references were complete and correct.

Finally, in a book like this, I would be utterly remiss if I did not acknowledge the importance of my family to my career and work. My lifetime partner, Debbie Dobson, has provided me with innumerable opportunities to discuss and refine my thinking and to jettison some of my less tenable thoughts. She has read portions of this manuscript and offered her considerable wisdom and experience. As referenced in this book, she and I have published and worked together and much of my current thinking has been honed on the sharp edge of her insights, experience, and knowledge. We have had the incredibly good fortune to have two compassionate, caring, brilliant, and engaged children, Kit and Beth, each of whom has found a life partner with whom they have each had two children. You have all enriched my life, and I take this space to acknowledge as much.

CLINICAL **DEPRESSION**

Introduction

Developing Multifaceted Models and Interventions for Depression

"Depression." The word is so simple, and yet it has so many implications. The term is used to describe the mood of feeling sad, down, despondent, or helpless. It is also common to think about depressed behavior, as in being lethargic, slowed down, or withdrawn. Depression also has a cognitive component that includes negative ideas about the self, pessimism about the future, and potential hopelessness. Quickly it becomes clear that depression is not a simple or monolithic construct but rather has multiple levels and aspects.

Depression is considered a clinical syndrome. Clinical depression, or major depressive disorder (MDD) as it is termed in the American Psychiatric Association's (2013, 2022) *Diagnostic and Statistical Manual of Mental Disorders* (5th ed., *DSM-5*; 5th ed., text rev., *DSM-5-TR*), has nine potential symptoms, and a diagnosis of MDD requires at least five of these symptoms (including one of two key criteria) experienced for a period of at least 2 weeks. This definition is consistent with the one in the World Health Organization's (2019) *International Statistical Classification of Diseases and Related Health Problems* (11th ed., *ICD-11*), which also uses the term "major depressive disorder." In this book, the word "depression" is used as a shorthand term for MDD, even though a single term cannot do justice to its complexity and dynamic nature. Indeed, as this book suggests, it is extremely challenging to reflect the multifaceted nature of depression in either its clinical presentation or the broad array of potentially helpful interventions to address this condition.

Throughout this book, depression is never referred to as an illness. At least for me, the word "illness" is fraught with unhelpful and potentially erroneous

https://doi.org/10.1037/0000398-001
Clinical Depression: An Individualized, Biopsychosocial Approach to Assessment and Treatment, by K. S. Dobson

connotations. It is unhelpful because illness typically is considered to be a state that is a polar opposite to health or wellness. In contrast, depression is a dimensional condition, as individuals can vary in terms of the number and severity of the signs and symptoms they experience. Further, being ill is often considered an enduring condition, which is different from the way depression is envisioned here. It is more helpful to see depression as a typically time-bound condition, which can be attenuated and truncated with sufficient and timely care. Furthermore, the term "illness" is often seen as a stigmatized state. There is ample evidence that depression is also stigmatized (see Chapter 3), but adding the idea that depression is an illness can only compound said stigma. Finally, at least in the Western world, illnesses are typically viewed as biomedical in cause. As I argue strongly in this book, such a causal model for depression is not only unhelpful but, ultimately, wrong. Instead, I argue for a comprehensive, biopsychosocial perspective in the broadest sense possible. For example, biological factors include both genetics and epigenetics as well as current neurological functioning, diet, and sleep. Similarly, social factors do not simply include friends and relations but also include the broad influence of culture and cultural heritage as well as spirituality. As is detailed in Chapter 3, the biopsychosocial perspective has many implications for the conceptualization of risk and resiliency, the ways in which we should think of disorder, and manifold consequences for the provision of treatment.

This book has been written with clinicians as the primary audience. I have used the convention of referring to you, the reader, as if you are a clinician who works with clients who struggle with depression. At the same time, I expect that students in professional programs related to the field of mental health will learn much by reading this text and that individuals who deal with the experience of depression may learn novel ways to think about and manage the challenges.

In writing this volume, I adopted a structure that is, hopefully, optimal for the clinician. I start with discussion of some of the broad issues related to depression before delving into key considerations in assessment and the many potentially helpful ways to assist someone who struggles with clinical depression. As such, Part I discusses the variable presentation of depression, the well-established risk and resilience factors for the disorder, and the ways in which our models have evolved over time. Part II of the book addresses the intake and assessment process and the important issue of client engagement in treatment. The chapters in Part III present some of the major, evidence-based strategies to help clients who present with depression. In that section, I argue that there is no single, "best" treatment for depression. Rather, each case needs an idiographic assessment and case conceptualization that will guide the selection of optimal interventions. Unfortunately, even with experience and excellent knowledge about the range of possible interventions, it may be discovered that what "should" help does not, and so clinicians need broad knowledge about options and ways to shift from one strategy to another. Part IV addresses the process of ending therapy and other considerations in the treatment of depression, and Part V presents future considerations needed in the development of evidence-based care for depression.

Each chapter in this book is structured to facilitate a flexible and idiographic approach to care, beginning with a brief review of the theoretical argument for that chapter and the literature related to the chapter's content. From an evidence-based foundation, the major intervention strategies that can be extrapolated are exposed and discussed. Finally, in an effort to make this discussion more real, two hypothetical cases are presented throughout the book to see how these strategies can be implemented in practice.[1] The cases follow two clients (Michael and Miranda) and their therapists (Dr. Mason and Dr. Morales) from pretreatment to the intake interview, key moments in later sessions, and finally the end of treatment. I recognize that two cases can include only a limited number of elements of the complex presentation of depression, and, as such, they are presented in the knowledge that they typify some common assessment, case conceptualization, and treatment issues that can emerge. As argued throughout the book, the presentation of depression is complex and can vary even within the same client over time, so interventions always need to be carefully titrated against the client's evolving and unique needs.

Metaphorically, this book has been decades in its genesis. I have worked in the field of clinical depression since approximately 1980, and, in that time, I have conducted laboratory-based studies of depression, led and co-led clinical trials for both the treatment and prevention of depression, treated many patients in my private practice and as a research trial clinician, trained and supervised many students and professionals, and conducted training workshops in many countries around the world. It has been my extreme privilege to work with some of the best-known and well-published people in the field. I continue to read the literature as much as possible, although the volume of work in this field is frankly overwhelming. Relative to when I began in the field, the amount that is now known about clinical depression is almost impossible to portray. As just one index, a literature search since 1980 using the keyword "depression" in the American Psychological Association PsycInfo database yields the number of annual publications shown in Figure 1. Although the number of annual publications seems to have reached a bit of a plateau in recent years, it would be a daunting task to try to keep up with the approximately 16,000 published works on depression each year!

Models hopefully evolve as the theories and data themselves grow. My own thinking about the optimal ways to conceptualize and treat depression has certainly changed over time. Thus, while this book reflects a foundational cognitive behavior therapy (CBT) framework and a corresponding model of psychopathology and psychotherapy, many ideas in this book are adapted or simply incorporated from other models. My touchstone has been the research evidence. If a strong conceptual model and an evidence base support a treatment

---

[1]All cases presented in this book are fictitious and represent illustrations drawn from my experience but not any specific person.

FIGURE 1. Annual Number of Depression-Related Publications

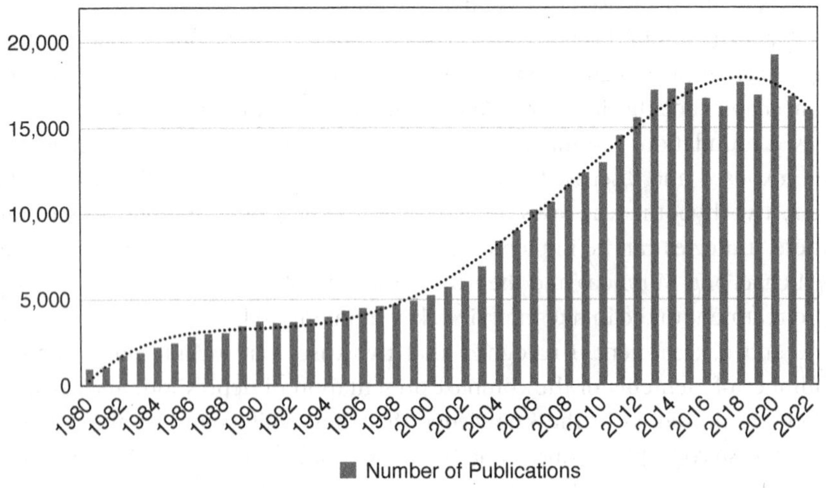

Number of Publications

Note. The data in this figure is from a search of the PsycInfo database. Results show the number of publications per year from 1980 to 2022 that use the keyword "depression."

recommendation, that recommendation is included within this volume. For example, while many professionals in the field of CBT would not consider exercise as a key aspect of the treatment of depression, I argue the evidence is now compelling that regular and modest aerobic exercise is an evidence-based treatment for clinical depression, and so you will find a recommendation for this strategy in this book. As such, the book goes well beyond a standard CBT approach to the topic of clinical depression. I have pushed the literature somewhat and have tried to challenge some conventional ways that clinicians practice therapy. I note in this regard that some treatment recommendations in this book can be provided in diverse fashions, such as with apps or web-based programs, and by a range of clinicians from different professional backgrounds. Although I am a clinical psychologist, I certainly see an enhanced role for many health practitioners in the treatment of depression, optimally working in a collaborative model of care.

A word or two about nomenclature. Throughout this volume I have used the word "client" to refer to any person who receives care or treatment. I recognize that in some settings in which depression is treated the more common term is "patient," so if you work in a medical or health care setting where the common parlance is "patient," I hope you can do that translation. My choice of the term "client" reflects a broader and more inclusive, but hopefully still accurate, term. I have also purposely minimized the used of the adjective "depressed," as in "a depressed client." Depression is most often an episodic and time-limited phenomenon; while a person may experience aspects of depression or even the full syndrome for a time, labeling someone as "a depressed person" is potentially both stigmatizing and inaccurate. Instead, I have tried to use "a person with depression" or some equivalent to indicate this status may end and change over time. Finally, I have avoided wherever possible gendered language, so instead of "his" or "her," you will find "their" in most places. This terminology is consistent with current American Psychological Association publication guidelines and avoids gendered terms where they are not needed or helpful. I note, however, that if the gender of a person is known, as for example in the two extensive cases included throughout the book, or if the gender of an author is known, then specific gender labels are used.

As this brief introduction hopefully suggests, my range of experience is long and broad. I hope that as a reader and practitioner (or potentially someone who experiences depression or has a loved one in this situation), you will find much that is of interest and value in this work. As I noted previously, I have tried to be true to the evidence base, and I take responsibility for any of the expressed opinions. Depression is a significant global health problem that warrants every effort to understand it, to provide compassion to those who suffer, and to provide care and treatment to the maximal extent possible.

UNDERSTANDING DEPRESSION AND ITS TREATMENT

1

The Nature of Depression

It has been said that any road will suffice if you don't know where you're going. One goal of this chapter is to begin to build a road map so you can appreciate some fundamental aspects of depression that should influence its assessment and care. Thus, this chapter includes a description of clinical depression that addresses the critical diagnostic features of this condition. Some of the ongoing debates and discussions about diagnosis and assessment are discussed. Based on this initial understanding, I then turn to issues related to the prevalence and incidence of depression and to some factors that modify our understanding of individuals who experience depression. Finally, the end of the chapter touches on some themes that are built in subsequent chapters and help to provide detail to the road map, such as the ways to consider risk and resiliency in depression and the way to understand empirically supported treatments.

This chapter was written under the assumption that most readers of this book might jump over it and move directly into the chapters related to intervention. I implore you not to take this step. While I recognize that some aspects of Chapter 1 might seem somewhat dry and academic, the content is essential to understand prior to considering models of etiology or potential ways to intervene. With this view in mind, I have tried to keep the chapter as practical as possible, and although essential and recent scholarly references are provided when needed to make a point, I have attempted to limit them to the minimum.

https://doi.org/10.1037/0000398-002
Clinical Depression: An Individualized, Biopsychosocial Approach to Assessment and Treatment, by K. S. Dobson

A CLINICAL DESCRIPTION OF DEPRESSION

What we now call clinical depression has been recognized for centuries. The ancient Greeks and Romans recognized the pattern of malaise, despondency, loss of interest, and low activity that are some hallmark features of the disorder. The knowledge of risk factors was limited at the time, however, and Hippocrates (and later Galen) wrongly attributed this pattern to an excess of one of four suspected bodily humors or fluids. Specifically, they considered that an excess of black bile might explain the condition, which was labeled "melancholia." Their model led to treatments that included diet and exercise as well as bloodletting to reduce the excess of black bile. The humoral theory of depression, as it is sometimes called, survived for centuries and is cited in the classic book of the 17th century, *The Anatomy of Melancholie* (Burton, 1621).

The classic picture of melancholia was largely maintained until the early 20th century. In his groundbreaking study and description of psychiatric patients, Emil Kraepelin (1906) distinguished between what we might call "classic depression" and manic depression (i.e., a pattern that includes an oscillation between periods of depression and excitement, agitation, and potentially undisciplined or risky behaviors), a distinction that survives until today. Perhaps more important in some respects, however, is that Kraepelin introduced organization and standardized nomenclature to the field of mental health. The use of standardized diagnostic criteria to identify a disorder is conventional today, but it was not 100 years ago.

The American Medico-Psychological Association (the forebear to the American Psychiatric Association) adopted an initial set of diagnostic criteria and labels in 1917. Although largely consistent with Kraepelin's work, the manual included diagnostic criteria for 22 forms of "insanity." These diagnoses shifted over time, but it was not until the Second World War that the American Psychiatric Association determined to formalize and publish a definitive list of diagnoses and their associated criteria. The first edition of the *Diagnostic and Statistical Manual of Mental Disorders* (*DSM*; 1952) included 106 diagnoses, many of which were also found in the World Health Organization's (1948) *International Statistical Classification of Diseases, Injuries, and Causes of Death* (6th ed.; *ICD-6*), which was the first edition of the *ICD* to include mental disorders. Notably, both diagnostic manuals included the diagnosis of major depression, although the criteria were somewhat different.

The shift in diagnosis that occurred, which has lasting implications, was the work of a group of psychiatrists who came to believe that diagnoses should be descriptive and not have theoretical assumptions embedded within the criteria. For example, in the second edition of the *DSM* a diagnosis of depressive neurosis was described as follows: "This disorder is manifested by an excessive reaction of depression due to an internal conflict or to an identifiable event such as the loss of a love object or cherished possession" (American Psychiatric Association, 1968, p. 40). This type of diagnosis clearly reflected a theoretical model, and it was argued that diagnoses should instead follow atheoretical and descriptive features only if empirically demonstrated and based on the course and pattern of the disorders (see Kendler et al., 2010, for a description of this history). This work became known as the Feighner criteria (Feighner et al., 1972), published at a pivotal time as psychiatry and mental health were increasingly focused on research. Indeed, the Feighner criteria helped to accelerate this focus, and the 1975 *Research Diagnostic Criteria* (Spitzer & Robins, 1978) adopted the Feighner criteria, as did the highly influential third edition of the *DSM* (American Psychiatric Association, 1980; *DSM-III*). The core Feighner criteria for major depression are still in place today, although the recognized subtypes of depression have evolved somewhat from the *DSM-III* to the current *DSM-5-TR* (American Psychiatric Association, 2022).

The *DSM-5-TR* lists nine possible criteria for a diagnosis of major depression: depressed mood or behavioral expressions of sadness; reduced interest in usual activities or loss of pleasure from usual activities; either increased or decreased appetite and/or increased or decreased weight; sleep disturbance (either reduced or excessive); being physically agitated or slowed down; low energy or tiredness; negative thoughts, including guilt of self-denigration; problems with concentration, making decisions, or thinking; and thoughts about death, suicidal ideation, and/or behaviors. Five or more symptoms must be present for a minimum of 2 weeks and must represent a change from previous levels of functioning. These criteria have not changed much since the Feighner criteria were identified, although the precise terminology has evolved somewhat over time. As such, the estimates of the prevalence of major depression using the *DSM* have been fairly consistent since the mid-1970s. One change that occurred recently relates to the exclusion criteria for a diagnosis of major depression. A person should not receive the diagnosis if medications or another injury or disorder can explain the symptom pattern. Also, to allow for bereavement, the criteria previously excluded a diagnosis within 8 weeks of the death of a loved one. In the *DSM-5* however, this exclusion was removed, with the result that more people are eligible to receive a diagnosis of major depression.

The *ICD* model for diagnosis of depression has also evolved somewhat over time. As with the *DSM*, earlier versions of the *ICD* implied theoretical models that helped to explain the genesis of depression, but current models are descriptive and do not carry theoretical implications. In the *ICD-11* (World Health Organization [WHO], 2019), the major subtypes of depressive disorders are distinguished based on severity (mild, moderate, severe), the absence or presence of psychotic features, and remission status. Variants are also recognized, including recurrent depressive disorder and dysthymic disorder (a more mild but chronic pattern).

The diagnostic criteria in the *ICD-11* for a single moderate depressive disorder (without psychotic features) are as follows:

> Single episode depressive disorder, moderate, without psychotic symptoms is diagnosed when the definitional requirements of a depressive episode have been met, there is no history of prior depressive episodes, the episode is of moderate severity, and there are no delusions or hallucinations during the episode. A depressive episode is characterized by a period of depressed mood or diminished

interest in activities occurring most of the day, nearly every day during a period lasting at least 2 weeks accompanied by other symptoms such as difficulty concentrating, feelings of worthlessness or excessive or inappropriate guilt, hopelessness, recurrent thoughts of death or suicide, changes in appetite or sleep, psychomotor agitation or retardation, and reduced energy or fatigue. In a moderate depressive episode, several symptoms of a depressive episode are present to a marked degree, or a large number of depressive symptoms of lesser severity are present overall. The individual typically has considerable difficulty functioning in multiple domains (personal, family, social, educational, occupational, or other important domains).

Inclusion criteria are symptoms that must be present to diagnose a person with this disorder. A range of possible symptoms can be included, but the key features are a period of depressed mood or diminished interest in activities. These two features are sometimes referred to as *cardinal features*, as one or the other is required for a diagnosis. In addition, though, there are a range of other possible symptoms. In contrast, *exclusion criteria* should obviate a depressive disorder diagnosis. Thus, a person whose symptoms can be attributed to another medical condition (e.g., anemia, hypothyroidism), another mental disorder (e.g., psychosis), or the direct physiological effects of a substance should not be diagnosed with major depression until these exclusions are ruled out. Further, the diagnosis should only be used if the person has never experienced a manic or hypomanic episode because these episodes imply that the person might best be diagnosed with bipolar disorder and because the typical course and treatments of major depression and bipolar disorder are importantly different.

Even a cursory examination of the *DSM-5-TR* and *ICD-11* criteria reveals the possibility of dramatic heterogeneity of symptoms in major depression. Any person requires five of the possible symptoms to receive a *DSM-5* diagnosis, so people will present with five or more symptoms. Further, some symptoms are paradoxical, meaning that you can see either an increase or a decrease in certain symptoms (e.g., appetite, weight, sleep, psychomotor activity), and some are multidimensional (e.g., loss of interest or pleasure in usual activities). When all the various combinations and permutations of criteria are considered, an estimated 935 distinct patterns of symptoms could yield a diagnosis of major depression.[1] Also, while two of the nine symptoms (sad mood, loss of interest or pleasure) are considered cardinal in that one or the other must be present, the variability of symptom patterns allows for two different people to attain the same diagnosis of major depression with only one overlapping symptom. It is also clear that the severity of depression ranges considerably: Someone might experience only five symptoms, whereas someone else might show all nine symptoms. Additionally, some people do not have sufficient symptomatology to receive a formal diagnosis of major depression but experience significant distress from what is termed "subclinical" symptomatology.

The heterogeneity of major depression is greater than the number of symptoms that someone might experience. Although people must show the

---

[1]With thanks to my daughter, who is a mathematics teacher!

EXHIBIT 1.1

Variants of Depressive Disorders in the *ICD-11*

6A70 Single episode depressive disorder
6A70.0 Single episode depressive disorder, mild
6A70.1 Single episode depressive disorder, moderate, without psychotic symptoms
6A70.2 Single episode depressive disorder, moderate, with psychotic symptoms
6A70.3 Single episode depressive disorder, severe, without psychotic symptoms
6A70.4 Single episode depressive disorder, severe, with psychotic symptoms
6A70.5 Single episode depressive disorder, unspecified severity
6A70.6 Single episode depressive disorder, currently in partial remission
6A70.7 Single episode depressive disorder, currently in full remission
6A70.Y Other specified single episode depressive disorder
6A70.Z Single episode depressive disorder, unspecified
6A71 Recurrent depressive disorder
6A72 Dysthymic disorder
6A73 Mixed depressive and anxiety disorder
GA34.41 Premenstrual dysphoric disorder
6A7Y Other specified depressive disorders
6A7Z Depressive disorders, unspecified

Note. From *ICD-11 for Mortality and Morbidity Statistics*, by the World Health Organization, 2023 (https://icd.who.int/browse11/l-m/en#/http://id.who.int/icd/entity/399670840). CC BY-ND 3.0 IGO.

symptoms for a minimum period of 2 weeks to receive a formal diagnosis (to prevent labeling of more transitory depression-like experiences), some people may go into an "episode" of depression that lasts for months or even years. This episode may be a person's first episode (formally defined as a *major depressive episode*, using the *DSM* criteria), but having had one episode of depression increases the likelihood of a subsequent episode much higher than the likelihood of an episode for someone who has never been depressed before. A recurrent episode is defined as a major depressive disorder (MDD), although it has the same diagnostic criteria. In many cases of depression, it is not only the treatment of the current episode of depression that matters, but the development of strategies to reduce the risk, or even to prevent relapse. As seen in Exhibit 1.1., a range of *ICD* depressive diagnoses are possible, which take into account recurrence, as well as some other patterns, which are described further later in the chapter.

SUICIDE AS A RESPONSE TO MAJOR DEPRESSION RATHER THAN A SYMPTOM

This section may anger some of you, as some of my opinion related to suicide is controversial. At the same time, it is likely important to put this opinion clearly before you, as it influences the content of the volume that follows. In short, my opinion is that suicidal thinking, ideation, and actions should not be considered a symptom of major depression but rather a response to it. There is no doubt that some people with clinical depression become hopeless and either engage in self-injury or actually make a deliberate attempt to end their own lives (and sometimes the lives of others, although much less commonly). There is also no doubt that clinicians need to be sensitive to the impulse toward self-injury and to be ready to ask about these issues and intervene if they work with clients with clinical depression.

The issue of assessment and intervention related to suicidal thinking and behavior is discussed further in Chapter 3. Here, I simply want to say that my opinion about suicide comes from two main lines of thought. The first is that the desire to potentially end one's life can emerge for many reasons, but the psychology of suicide most often points to two main factors. One is that the individual is faced with some apparently insurmountable problem, loss, or crisis. This situation could be the loss of a loved one due to death, the sudden termination from a cherished position, social isolation, physical injury from a motor vehicle accident, or a multitude of other circumstances. Across all these situations, the person is highly distressed as a result of the event and tries to overcome it with whatever combination of skills, resources, and supports they have access to. When these efforts fail and the individual becomes hopeless about the ability to overcome the problem, suicidality emerges as yet another—and what one could call the final—way to solve the problem (Van Orden et al., 2010). From this perspective, suicidality is not a symptom of depression but rather is a response to being depressed and the result of being unable to get out of this tragic condition.

The second factor that has affected my opinion about suicidality in the context of depression is that hopelessness can emerge for a variety of reasons. Poverty, victimization, loss, and other circumstances can lead to despondency, discouragement, and despair. The rates of suicide climb in such circumstances as well as after tragedy. Hopelessness also emerges in the context of chronic mental health challenges, such as addictions (Cannon et al., 1999). Indeed, the mental disorder with the highest rate of suicidality is not depression but psychosis (Gill et al., 2015). In this regard, hopelessness and suicidality are not phenomena uniquely associated with depression.

My point is not to diminish the importance of assessing suicidal wishes, impulses, or behaviors that arise when someone experiences depression. In most countries, health care providers have a legal obligation to protect their clients from themselves if the client poses an imminent and credible risk of self-injury or suicide. The onus that health care providers feel for their clients is perhaps most palpable when a client discusses their own death. My point, however, is that while clinicians who work with clients who experience clinical depression need to be comfortable to assess and intervene in this area, the core issue is most often not the suicidal impulse itself. Rather, the perceived reasons for hopelessness that in turn drive the suicidality need to be understood, and the set of unsuccessful resources or coping strategies must be overcome to reduce the risk of self-injury and suicide.

SUBTYPES OF MAJOR DEPRESSION

Given the potential number of presentations of major depression, it is perhaps not surprising that different patterns or subtypes are recognized. Without going into all the variations, several important distinctions are discussed here.

The Reactive-Endogenous Subtype

As discussed in more detail later in this chapter, the longstanding belief in the field is that some clinical depressions have a biological basis, whereas others are psychologically or environmentally based. The *DSM-III* (American Psychiatric Association, 1980) formally identified these two subtypes, and considerable research since then has focused on differentiating *biologically oriented depression*, which might respond better to pharmacotherapy or other biologically focused interventions, from the *reactive* form of depression, which in principle might respond better to psychosocial intervention. Studies have, in some cases, distinguished symptom patterns in diverse samples (Mendels & Cochrane, 1968) and somewhat different courses of development based on this distinction (Kay et al., 1969; Paykel et al., 1974). This said, a differential response to various treatments does not seem to follow from the reactive–endogenous distinction (Malki et al., 2014). Rather, in general, individuals with more physical symptoms of depression respond less well to intervention than others who do not have these features, or they may need more intensive intervention. From my perspective, I think we can conclude that while the precise symptom pattern of a client who presents with depression matters (much more on this topic in Chapter 2), the reactive–endogenous distinction does little to further the treatment of depression. Indeed, the current version of the *DSM* no longer makes this distinction, although it maintains a subtype of *melancholic depression*, with a preponderance of biologically oriented symptoms (e.g., sleep, psychomotor signs). To the best of my knowledge, the presence of the melancholic subtype of depression does not particularly predict treatment response, and so my suspicion is that unless new evidence emerges, this subtype will be found to be unhelpful in treatment planning.

The Anxious Subtype

Based on the wide range of possible symptom patterns seen in clinical depression, it should not be surprising that different individuals appear to have different early signs or symptoms. For example, evidence suggests that sleep disturbance is a clear *prodromal sign*, which means that this symptom can emerge well before the development of a diagnosable major depressive episode. It has been suggested that sleep can be an early warning symptom as many as 10 years prior to the onset of a first episode of depression (Franzen & Buysse, 2008). When sleep disturbance presents in the context of clinical depression, it is important to address this problem directly (for more on this issue, see Chapters 2 and 7).

One clear pattern of symptom onset has been recognized in the literature, the *anxious subtype*. Often, people who develop this subtype are described as shy or nervous children; in their adolescence, they develop clear signs of anxiety and may have enough signs and symptoms to be formally diagnosed with an anxiety disorder. These individuals may present with a good amount of worry, apprehension, negative thoughts, and a tendency to pull away from or avoid challenging situations. In some cases, a trigger event may occur, perceived as a loss or damage that precipitates a depressive reaction, thus leading to a combined experience of anxiety and depression.

Anxiety and depression are considered to be highly *comorbid*, which means that they often present in combination. It has been estimated that as many as 50% of people who have major depression either have or have had a concurrent anxiety disorder (Hirschfeld, 2001). Also, just as people may experience significant depressive symptomatology without having a formal disorder of clinical depression, many people with depression have symptoms of anxiety, even if the anxiety problems do not have the level or pattern to receive a diagnosis. Thus, the anxious subtype of major depression appears commonly and has implications for treatment, as people with this subtype often have strong psychological features (e.g., worry, apprehension, rumination), low self-esteem or diminished willingness to be assertive, fairly strong emotional reactivity, and avoidance patterns. As discussed in Chapter 3, the presence of these characteristics of anxious depression are highly prescriptive for treatment.

Seasonal Affective Disorder

Although the two subtypes of depression discussed in the previous sections are based on symptom patterns, another subtype has been recognized based on patterns of recurrence: the seasonal pattern of major depression, more often referred to as *seasonal affective disorder* or SAD. SAD has been recognized through epidemiological research as a phenomenon that tends to occur in the Northern Hemisphere, predominantly in the winter months. Some evidence suggests that the further north one goes, the higher the rates of seasonal depression, suggesting the phenomenon has something to do with the reduced natural sunlight in the shorter winter days. Models of circadian rhythms and sleep cycles have been implicated, and a form of light therapy that uses full-spectrum artificial light to replace natural light for periods of the day has been shown in randomized trials to benefit people with SAD.

The idea that reduced light and the shortened day result in onset of SAD has been challenged. For example, while SAD is well recognized in the Northern Hemisphere, it does not appear as a regular feature in the Southern Hemisphere, even at a similar degree of latitude where a reciprocal pattern of reduced light emerges. Additionally, SAD does not occur in the only winter months in northern climes. Indeed, the criteria for SAD simply require a recurrent pattern of at least two depression episodes in the same period of the year. Some people have recurrent depression in the summer, for example.

Another challenge to the winter-onset SAD pattern is that factors other than reduced daylight hours for people who live in northern areas affect people's lives. For example, people in northern countries tend to move their activities indoors as their winter approaches; as a result, they tend to reduce their activity, sleep more, and change their dietary patterns to include a higher percentage of carbohydrates. Winters also tend to be the time of year to see increased rates of influenza and colds, which are associated with yet more reductions in activity. So, while light therapy benefits people with winter-onset SAD (Terman et al., 1989), other treatments can also exert a benefit. To my knowledge, there is no reason not to apply the various principles and interventions described throughout this book either alone or in combination with a course of light therapy.

Perinatal Depression

Another pattern of major depression is associated with maternity and child-bearing. Postpartum depression has sometimes been called the "baby blues" in the past, but this term has been discouraged of late because it tends to minimize the potentially severe effects of depression. Further, it is now recognized that some mothers become depressed prior to delivery, and so the current diagnosis is *major depression with peripartum onset*, more commonly called *perinatal depression*. This term reflects a major depression that occurs around birth; it can have its onset at any point prior to the birth and up to several months afterwards. The diagnostic criteria used for major depression are used in this diagnosis, and although the diagnosis can be applied to men, it is most typically used with pregnant women and mothers in the early months of the baby's life.

Perinatal depression has a couple of unique and noteworthy features. One feature is its gender balance. Pregnant women and young mothers face a number of unique issues and stressors, including dramatic hormonal and physical changes, the responsibility for the life of a newborn, and a host of potential relational and personal issues such as the ability to work, changes to partner and family relationships, and more. Stressors of almost any type increase the risk for depression (see Chapter 3), and the importance of childbirth and child-drearing in society can hardly be overstated. Thus, the unique aspects of this experience warrant attention focused on the screening, assessment, and treatment of perinatal depression.

The second aspect of perinatal depression that warrants some notice is its symptomatology. The *DSM-5-TR* allows for the possibility that the negative thought patterns associated with depression can lose contact with reality; this phenomenon is sometimes called *psychotic thinking*. If the disrupted thinking is consistent with the depressive episode (e.g., thinking that one is so evil they need to die), no additional diagnosis would be considered. However, if the thoughts are divergent (e.g., thinking that one can speak with plants), the pattern would be considered an additional problem to be assessed and potentially treated. A greater likelihood of psychotic thinking has been documented in perinatal depression than in other types of depression (Ebeid et al., 2010).

The reasons for this pattern of symptoms are not entirely clear, but it may be associated with the unique hormonal changes or unique pattern and degree of stressors.

THE COURSE OF CLINICAL DEPRESSION

Following discussion of the symptomatology and the range of possible expression of depression, a few other issues need to be added. The experience of depression is rarely static, especially in its early development. Some people have relatively few signs or symptoms, and a catastrophic event leads to the onset of major depression. Others are shy or anxious as children, slowly developing into an anxious adolescents and then slipping into a pattern of avoidance and eventual depression. For some, the onset seems to emerge from nowhere. Often, people have one or two early warning signs that later evolve into a period of depression. Whatever the pattern, at some point the individual slips over the threshold of having a few signs or symptoms and has a pattern that qualifies as a major depressive episode. This point is typically referred to as the *onset* of an episode. Figure 1.1 presents a highly idealized and normative image of the potential course of clinical depression.

As noted earlier in the chapter, the constellation of symptoms must be present for 2 weeks or more for a person to receive a diagnosis of major depression. Thus, some people may have five or more symptoms but for a shorter period of time; they would thus not be diagnosed with major depression. In contrast, others may have an episode that lasts for weeks, months, or even years, with some fluctuation in the pattern of symptoms. Hopefully at some point in time

FIGURE 1.1. The Potential Course of Clinical Depression

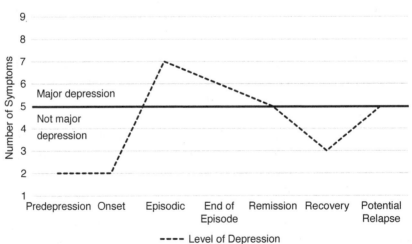

Note. Although the portrayal of symptoms here is linear, symptoms may wax and wane and are unlikely to follow a simple linear pattern.

the symptoms start to abate, either on their own or with treatment, and the individual will transition into *remission*, the point at which the diagnosis does not apply. The person may still have signs or symptoms of depression, however, which are known as residual symptoms. Indeed, "full recovery" is reserved for people who no longer meet the diagnostic criteria for depression and have stayed nondepressed for a period of at least 4 weeks. For people who experience a subsequent episode of depression, the term "relapse" is used to indicate a new episode following remission; "recurrence" is used for an episode that follows prior recovery.

It is well known that people who have a remission from depression are more likely to have a subsequent episode of depression than are people who recover (Paykel, 2008). Thus, it is important that when people come out of an episode of depression, they are treated at least to the point of functioning they had before the onset of the episode of depression. Put otherwise, the goal of treatment should not be remission but recovery and, possibly, prevention of another episode. Prevention strategies are discussed in Chapter 11. Additionally, research suggests that a person who has a first episode of depression is at a higher risk of having a second (or subsequent) episode than are people who have never had a first instance. The estimated rate of recurrence/relapse 2 years following the offset of an episode is about 50%. Further, this risk of relapse/recurrence increases with repeated episodes, and while estimates become somewhat less reliable, it is estimated that the risk of recurrence/relapse is about 75% after a third or subsequent episode and remains at about that level (Klein & Allmann, 2014). Unfortunately, it also appears that the likelihood of a full recovery reduces with subsequent episodes, and in some cases people who experience repeated episodes never fully recover their predepression status. All these notions support the critical importance of early assessment and diagnosis and of sufficiently intensive and prolonged treatment not just to treat the symptoms but to help the client restore optimal functioning and reduce the likelihood of relapse or recurrence.

ESTIMATING THE OCCURRENCE OF DEPRESSION

One positive feature of the depression literature is that the criteria have not changed dramatically in the past several decades. This relative constancy has allowed for the collection of quite good estimates of the occurrence of clinical depression both across different groups and within groups over time. The research about the epidemiology of major depression is robust and reasonably consistent.

It is first important to differentiate between prevalence and incidence, as these two concepts are often confused. In the context of major depression, *prevalence* refers to the proportion of a group that meets diagnostic criteria within a particular time period. Common time periods are *point prevalence* (i.e., the proportion who had the diagnosis at a specific point in time), *annual prevalence* (i.e., the proportion who had the diagnosis during a given year), and *lifetime prevalence* (i.e., the proportion who will have the diagnosis at some point in their lives). These estimates are not independent of each other, although they each provide a somewhat distinct picture of the disorder. The most common estimate is the annual prevalence, but this time frame allows for the possibility that while many people will not experience an episode in the most recent year, for example, others may have multiple episodes. In contrast, point estimates are relatively unstable over time and subject to influences from unusual factors (e.g., a sudden massive unemployment in a particular area), whereas lifetime estimates are influenced by problems of memory and the potential that episodes are missed because they have yet to occur at the time the person is interviewed.

Incidence refers to the proportion of a group of people who develop a disorder during a specific time period. In this context, incidence proportions are rates of depression, although they can again vary by time interval (e.g., one month, one year). Incidence rates are most useful when groups of people encounter a similar circumstance, making it possible to estimate the proportion of that group that has become susceptible to depression. For example, it is possible to estimate the annual rate of depression for all students who enter postsecondary education or for all people who experience an environmental disaster, as these are relatively standard situations that might evoke a depressive response.

Another important point about the research related to the occurrence of depression is the methodology of the study. Although clinical interviews to assess symptoms and estimate prevalence and incidence of mental disorders are considered the gold standard, it is very laborious and expensive to conduct such research. As such, many studies use self-report questionnaires that attempt to standardize questions and can be administered quite efficiently to large samples. There are difficulties with both methods. For example, some symptoms of depression, such as feelings of sadness, are internal experiences, and the only way to assess them is through interview or self-report. Other symptoms may be observable to others but seem fairly normal to the person with depression (e.g., being slowed down in thought and speech), and these symptoms are therefore best assessed by a trained interviewer. In addition, the experience of being depressed may lead to some overstatement of the negativity of the symptoms, resulting in higher reports in self-report questionnaires. In general, prevalence estimates based on interviews tend to yield lower numbers than self-report studies do, and this issue becomes important to consider when thinking about depression.

Rather than provide too much data here, I have chosen to provide a table of estimates of annual prevalence (see Table 1.1). These estimates derive from a number of studies from different regions of the world. When possible, the differences between men and women are reported.

Three patterns are suggested by the data in Table 1.1. First, depression is more prevalent in women than in men. In general, most estimates suggest a 2:1 female–male ratio (see Chapter 2). Second, prevalence estimates are higher when the methodology includes self-reports than when it includes diagnostic

TABLE 1.1. Estimates of the Annual Prevalence of Major Depression From Selected Studies

Study	Country	Methodology	Total %	Male %	Female %
Ettman et al. (2020)	United States	Self-report	—	6.9	10.1
Knoll and MacLennan (2017)	Canada	Self-report	4.7	3.6	5.8
Maske et al. (2016)	Germany	Cross-sectional data analysis	—	4.2	9.9
Vieta et al. (2021)	Spain	Observational study	5.4	3.5	7.2
Lotfaliany et al. (2018)	China	World Mental Health Survey	1.5	1.1	1.9
	India		15.2	12.8	17.7
	Mexico		10.8	3.3	17.3
	Russia		4.8	2.4	6.3
	Ghana		8.3	6.3	10.5
	South Africa		3.7	3.4	4.0

Note. Ettman et al. (2020) and Maske et al. (2016) did not provide total percentages in their studies.

interviews. Whether estimates are too high when people simply fill out a questionnaire or whether estimates are too low when an interviewer does the assessment is impossible to say. Most likely the actual prevalence is in between, even though diagnostic interviews are frequently considered to be the preferred methodology in epidemiological research. From my perspective, as long as the methodology is the same (i.e., the same self-report scale or the same diagnostic interview), rates can be reasonably compared within each methodology.

The third, and admittedly somewhat more tenuous, conclusion from these data is that since the adoption of roughly standardized diagnostic criteria, dating approximately from the *DSM-III* in 1980, the prevalence of depression has not varied too much over time or across cultures. Certainly, some studies suggest increased levels of depression in times of stress (Shah et al., 2021), and some evidence indicates that certain cultures may have lower or higher rates than others, but when the methodology is taken into account, many of these variations become less important. Overall, the annual prevalence of depression can be roughly said to be about 3% to 4% for males and 6% to 8% for females, with a total annual prevalence of approximately 6%.

Major depression is the single most common mental disorder in most cultures, and because of its ubiquitous nature and its serious consequences, the World Health Organization declared that depression is the mental disorder with the highest global degree of burden of illness as of 2020 (Rehm & Shield, 2019), using the concept of disability-adjusted life years (i.e., DALYs; see World Health Organization, n.d.). A DALY is equivalent to the loss of one year of full health; it is a common measure of disability associated with various disorders.

COMORBIDITY PATTERNS IN DEPRESSION

The content of this chapter is focused on clinical depression as a complex but differentiated entity. In fact, clinical depression often presents concurrently with other problems and disorders. As noted in the discussion of the subtypes of depression earlier in the chapter, many people have significant anxiety-related problems or even meet the criteria for anxiety disorder before they develop a first episode of depression. Many people with the mixed anxiety–depression pattern go through a period of significant anxiety as their depression lifts and they begin to face ongoing interactions with life's problems. In some cases, depression may follow other disorders; for example, depression is often a problem subsequent to psychotic episodes. Substance use and depression often have a convoluted relationship with each other, wherein some substances may simulate or even bring on depression (most notably substances that lower the functioning of the central nervous system, such as alcohol, sedatives, and barbiturates), whereas other substances may be taken to control depressive symptoms (most notably substances that increase activity within the central nervous system, such as caffeine and other stimulants). In yet other cases, depression may follow severe medical conditions such as cancer, and the presence of depression in some medical conditions such as chronic pain may complicate reporting and managing the medical condition itself.

The complete assessment of a client who presents with depression must include an evaluation of concurrent problems and comorbid diagnoses. As discussed in Chapter 4, this assessment helps to determine the plans for a given client, the nature of the interventions that are chosen, the prioritization of intervention plans, and possibly the referral of the client for other care.

RISK AND RESILIENCY FACTORS IN DEPRESSION: IMPLICATIONS FOR PRACTICE

As may be gleaned from the material that has been presented so far, clinical depression is a complicated disorder. It can present with variable symptoms, both across different individuals and within the same person over time. It may appear with a clear symptom pattern, as in the mixed anxiety–depression profile, or with other concomitant problems and disorders. First episodes of depression often follow an acute stressful event, although not always. For some individuals, the episode is relatively brief and may never recur, whereas for others a first episode represents the beginning of multiple episodes that become increasingly chronic and debilitating over time.

Further complicating an already complicated situation, the study of depression has focused incredible resources on potential causes. Much of this literature is well beyond the scope of the current volume, but some of the major results are included here because potential causes become the focus of assessment and intervention. Chapter 2 summarizes much of what is currently known about the factors that confer risk for depression as well as factors that provide resilience or reduce the risk. The model presented does not strictly follow a particular theoretical model of depression but rather includes biological, psychological, and social factors (including contextual and cultural factors). From my point of view, this biopsychosocial framework is the most comprehensive and defensible model of depression that can be adopted, as it enables consideration of the broadest array of evidence-based interventions possible, thereby increasing the prospect that depression can be successfully treated.

While much of the literature focuses on factors that increase risk or onset or relapse/recurrence of clinical depression, a relatively newer body of research examines factors that reduce risk and increase resiliency. Some of these literatures are reciprocal, by which I mean that the inverse of a risk factor has been named as a resiliency factor. Perhaps the best example of a reciprocal literature is in the area of social support—data suggest that low social connection and support is a risk factor for depression, whereas strong social support is a protective or resilience factor. The assessment of risk and resilience factors in clients who present with clinical depression is an essential ingredient of optimal care (see in particular Chapter 2 and Chapter 5).

FINAL THOUGHTS ABOUT THE NATURE OF DEPRESSION

This chapter has provided an introduction to the complexity that is clinical or major depression. As discussed, clinical depression is much more than "the blues" or "being down," which are common experiences, but instead represents a long-lasting or chronic syndrome of at least five and up to nine symptoms, based on the *DSM-5-TR* criteria. Clinical depression can be life-threatening, and its prevalence requires that clinicians are ready and willing to assess and intervene appropriately.

In a certain way, the field of depression research and treatment is fortunate that the criteria for clinical depression have been relatively consistent in recent decades. This consistency has permitted the development of an enormous database about the correlates, consequences, risk factors, and treatments for this disorder. The field knows so much, and although it is absolutely impossible to impart this knowledge in a single book, what is presented here reflects my effort to be current and inclusive. Chapter 2, for example, presents a summary of the vast literature on risk and resilience factors for clinical depression, as knowledge of these factors is essential for case planning and effective intervention. Chapter 3 deals with the range of evidence-based therapies that have emerged, in part based on emergent models of risk and resilience. Part II of the book turns toward clinical issues. Chapter 4 focuses on assessment and intake considerations and suggests some skills to evaluate the symptoms and risk/resilience factors for an individual client, which in turn influence the development of case formulation. That case formulation then directs the selection of interventions and the ways in which they are delivered, so the main aspect of the book details this broad array of interventions and provides some data to support different treatment methods as well as the many ways that these interventions can be used in clinical work with clients diagnosed with depression.

CASE ILLUSTRATIONS OF MAJOR DEPRESSION

This section introduces two case examples, each following a different client (Michael and Miranda), that will recur across Chapters 2 through 11. This chapter provides important background details about Michael and Miranda;[2] later chapters expand on their case formulations and follow their therapy processes from beginning to end.

The Case of Michael

Michael is a 63-year-old divorced, cisgender man with two adult children. His parents are deceased, and he has two siblings who live some distance away. He has been generally healthy throughout his life. He had no major illnesses growing up and was quite active with swimming and soccer as a youth. He broke his right leg quite badly in a bicycle accident when he was 17, requiring extensive surgeries; the accident left him with a slight limp and somewhat limited ability to engage in sports and physical activities. He was moderately popular growing up and had a series of intimate relationships, marrying a woman at age 25. At that time, he was already working in sales, which has been his career. Michael originally worked in someone else's insurance company but eventually bought his own agency, which has been quite successful. He prides himself on being an independent businessperson and a "self-made man."

Michael's marriage ended after 14 years and the birth of two children; the couple decided to divorce because they had become distant from each other. The divorce was amicable and mutual, and Michael confided to his wife that he had just ended a relationship with a man. At that time, he became despondent and unsure of himself, so he immersed himself in his work until he regained his sense of self. He began to date and has been in a monogamous relationship with Jon, also a successful businessman, since he was 46 years old. Over the years, in a pattern similar to that of his early marriage, he and Jon have become increasingly distant from each other and are very involved in their work.

Michael has been slowly falling into a depressive state. He sees himself growing older and possibly being alone. His physical status has suffered; he has had worry and sleep problems for many years, and he is increasingly self-medicating with alcohol in the evening and caffeine in the morning. He is self-critical of some of his life choices and feels regret for some decisions he could have made but did not. For example, he entered the work force without much

---

[2]All cases presented in this book are fictitious and represent illustrations drawn from my experience but not from any specific person.

advanced education, and while he has succeeded in many respects, he thinks he could have been more successful if he had more education. His appetite has grown fickle, he tends to eat without much thought or planning, and he has gradually gained weight over the past few years. Lately, he has been forgetful of the details of insurance claims at work and has made some mistakes that others have noticed. As a result, he has withdrawn from making some decisions and has been self-critical and disparaging of his perceived underperformance. He is uncertain if forgetting is the harbinger of cognitive decline but stays quiet and reserved so that others don't see his poor functioning. He also questions whether he should "put himself out to pasture" but has no real sense of what retirement might consist of and has made no plans. He has not discussed either his depression or his thoughts about retirement with his partner. He worries that Jon might leave him if he shares his fears and vulnerabilities.

Recently, Michael made an appointment to see his family physician, Dr. Norton, who declared that his physical status was fairly good, although she noted that he could benefit from healthier eating patterns, improving his sleep hygiene, and losing weight. She suggested that he attend an exercise class in a nearby gym. Dr. Norton diagnosed major depression with melancholic features and prescribed an antidepressant medication. She also recommended that Michael take some time away from work for rest and relaxation. He noted that he seldom took his designated vacation days as he worried that his sales output would suffer. Later, Dr. Norton referred Michael for treatment at a community clinic, which is described in more detail in Chapter 4.

The Case of Miranda

Miranda is a 40-year-old cisgender woman. She has been married to her husband, Jules, for 15 years, and they have two children, aged 9 and 6 years. Miranda's family were originally from Latin America, although she met and married her husband in the United States, where they now live. Although she is physically well, she has had a series of at least three depressive episodes in her lifetime. The first, in her early adulthood, lasted for about a month, whereas the latter two were subsequent to the birth of her children, and each lasted for about 2 months.

Miranda recalls being a shy girl with numerous self-doubts, although she had two good friends growing up. Her mother also had "nerves" and likely experienced depression has well. Her father was largely absent from home, as he worked in a sales position that required considerable traveling; she recalls he was supportive but distant in her childhood. Miranda did well in school but never excelled. She completed schooling at the usual age and after a year of working in retail positions, she took a 2-year program in office administration and began full-time work as an administrative assistant in a legal practice, which she has maintained.

Miranda's first episode of depression happened soon after the sudden end of her first major romantic relationship with a man named Thomas. She was

19 years old and was living at home with her parents. The breakup was not mutual—the man involved simply told her that he had been unfaithful and was leaving her for the other woman. Miranda was devastated and retreated quickly into a shell. She quit her retail job, withdrew from most of her activities and social connections, and disengaged from the world. Her appetite became very limited, and she started to lose weight. She engaged in considerable rumination and vacillated between blame and anger toward Thomas and self-denigration and self-recrimination about what she had done "wrong." She alternated between bouts of sadness and tears and periods of sullen silence, withdrawal, and reduced activity. This episode ended as her parents insisted that she return to work. As she slowly came out of her shell, she decided to obtain administrative training. It took her a long time to trust others again. When she met Jules a few years later and he expressed interest in a relationship, she was reluctant, but she eventually fell in love and agreed to marry.

After marriage, Jules and Miranda set up a home, and both worked in their careers. Miranda's second episode of depression began before the birth of their first child, Cassandra, but was not recognized until after the birth when she was diagnosed with postpartum depression. This episode included sadness, crying, withdrawal, considerable worry before the birth and rumination afterwards, self-critical ideation, and decreased appetite and weight loss, some of which Miranda thought of as a good way to reduce the weight that she had gained during pregnancy. She also experienced sleep dysfunction, especially related to worries about her child, and middle-of-the-night awakening associated with nursing her child but also at other times. This episode was recognized and treated at the time with a low-dose antidepressant medication and some extra childcare support. It took about 2 months to resolve, but even after its conclusion, Miranda reported some residual issues such as sleep problems.

The third episode of depression largely replicated the second episode and took place during the pregnancy and after the birth of the second child, Amanda. This episode of depression was not as severe as the second episode but took longer to resolve. Medications were again prescribed, including antidepressants and sleeping pills, and Miranda saw a therapist for about 2 months to help her cope as a mother of two young children. As the depression resolved, she decided to end treatment and eventually stopped taking the antidepressants, although she still takes a sleeping pill from time to time. Her mood is relatively flat in general, and she continues to demonstrate intermittent worry and rumination, especially when experiencing a stressful event within the family. Changes in her appetite and sleep are the primary indicators that she is not doing well. Her relationship with Jules has changed somewhat, as he has taken on more responsibilities in his work and is somewhat less engaged at home; in addition, the intensity of their relationship has changed with her periods of depression. Overall, she feels her life has gone well and that things are "good." However, this positive feeling did not last, and she eventually sought psychological treatment, as described in Chapter 4.

2

Risk and Resiliency for Depression

The development of any prevention or treatment program requires an understanding of both the factors that influence the disorder and the optimal strategies to modify these factors. The field of depression is fortunate that the risk factors that increase depression are fairly well known (K. S. Dobson & Dozois, 2008). In part, this understanding has been helped by the fact that the criteria for major depression have not changed significantly since the 1970s, as discussed in Chapter 1. The rates of depression and its devastating effects are also significant reasons to devote efforts to understanding the factors associated with depression and to help build intervention models. This chapter includes discussion of the major approaches to the study of risk and to the study of resilience in depression because both aspects can affect our theoretical models and intervention strategies. Chapter 3 then includes a discussion of the ways that risk and resiliency have been built into our major intervention models. In that chapter, I argue that we need to move beyond models that emphasize one or another risk or resiliency factor and instead to consider an integrated model of depression.

THE NATURE OF RISK AND RESILIENCY

For any given health condition, some factors may increase the likelihood a given person will experience that condition, whereas other factors may reduce likelihood. So it is with clinical depression. The research in the field has progressed

https://doi.org/10.1037/0000398-003
Clinical Depression: An Individualized, Biopsychosocial Approach to Assessment and Treatment,
by K. S. Dobson

remarkably in recent years, and we are able to name many factors associated with the degree or severity of a current state of depression and in some cases may predict the future onset of or relapse risk for depression. Researchers have been able to quantify the extent to which certain factors increase the risk for depression. Such quantification may take the form of an odds ratio, typically defined as the increased likelihood of developing the disorder with or without the presence of the risk factor (Szumilas, 2010). For example, an odds ratio of 1.0 for any given factor indicates that the risk of depression is the same whether or not the person has a particular factor. In contrast, an odds ratio of 2.0 indicates that someone with that particular risk factor has double the risk compared to someone who does not. As a third example, an odds ratio of 0.5 indicates that someone with that risk factor has only one half, or 50%, of the risk of depression compared to someone not having that factor. As in this last case, an odds ratio of less than 1.0 indicates that the factor is associated with reduced risk of depression.

In reciprocal fashion to risk indicators, we can now begin to name and quantify demonstrated resiliency factors for depression. These factors, when present, may be associated with lower likelihood of depression. For example, an odds ratio of 0.5 could be used to demonstrate that the likelihood of depression is only .5 or 50% of what it might have been if the resiliency factor were not present. Often, the studied resiliency factors are the inverse of risk factors (e.g., social connection instead of social isolation; resiliency instead of vulnerability). Further, we have less data about the treatment benefits associated with the enhancement of resiliency factors than we have for the benefits of targeting risk factors for change. Given these considerations and the fact that our understanding of resiliency is not as well developed as that for risk factors in depression, the focus in this chapter is on recognizing and ameliorating risk. It can be expected, however, that new interventions to prevent depression, based on the development of resiliency, will increase in the future.

It would be remarkably simple and convenient if depression had a single clear risk factor. We could fully devote attention to that factor, understand its determinants, evaluate its consequences, and develop interventions that are precise and likely effective. Unfortunately, just as the various ways depression can present itself are complex, the models of risk and resilience are complex. In the remainder of this chapter, some of the major established risk and resiliency factors are named, and their relative importance for understanding depression is discussed. Prior to this review, however, it may be helpful to consider the nature of risk and resiliency and the ways in which these concepts are studied.

METHODS TO STUDY RISK AND RESILIENCY: CORRELATION AND CAUSATION

As with many issues in mental health, there are different ways to conceptualize and measure risk and resiliency (Davydov et al., 2010). The simplest method is to measure two constructs and see how they associate with each other. If they are associated, they may actually influence each other. For example, in the context of depression, we know people who are depressed tend to be less active. So, there is clearly an association, or correlation, between the construct of depression and activity. We can even quantify this association through correlational analyses to see the strength of the association, but the degree of correlation cannot tell us if a low degree of activity causes depression, if depression causes inactivity, or if both are somehow caused by a third unknown variable. In statistical theory, correlation does not mean causation.

It is unfortunate in some respects that the simplest way to show a relationship between any two variables or constructs is through correlational analyses. Such patterns show us that something is occurring between two variables, but not the precise pattern. One method to try to separate the relative importance of several variables is to correlate them simultaneously with depression and to examine the relative strength of the correlations. This method is helpful to determine relative associations but cannot determine causal pathways because several factors may all have an influence on depression, or depression may influence several other outcomes at the same time. However, to build our models, it can help to identify the risk or resilience variables in which to invest research time and energy.

Yet a third way to look at risk and resilience is to examine correlations across time. For example, a given risk factor can be measured at one point in time, and its ability to predict later depression can be assessed. This type of *prospective research* can often be done within groups of individuals: It is possible to see if a given risk indicator at Time 1 is more or less predictive of depression at Time 2. If multiple competing risk factors are measured at Time 1, it may be possible to assess their relative ability to predict later depression. Although this type of research is more difficult to conduct than correlational studies at a single point in time because the researcher needs to follow research participants over time, it helps to tell a story of possible risk or resiliency factors. But even with prospective research, it remains possible that the associations may be due to one variable causing the other or the influence of some third unknown and unmeasured variable.

One of the most compelling methods to demonstrate the importance of a risk factor is to assess a group of people at a given point in time and then randomly assign them into one subgroup for which the putative risk factor is simply monitored or another in which the risk factor is manipulated. Perhaps needless to say, it would not be ethical to purposely increase a risk factor for depression or another disorder to see if more people suffer as a result, so almost all of this research uses interventions to reduce the effect of a suspected risk factor. For example, if the hypothesis were that activity is a risk factor for depression, one group's activities could be monitored while the level of activity could be purposefully increased in the other group, and the outcome on depression at a later point in time could be ascertained. This randomized trial methodology provides evidence that the risk factor has a causal impact on later depression. If different versions of the intervention are attempted (e.g., simply encouraging more activity, providing exercise equipment, paying participants to increase their levels of activity), the strategy can be optimized to have the greatest possible benefit.

Not surprisingly, as the rigor of a given investigation increases, so do associated issues such as time to do the study, complexity, cost, and statistical requirements. For these reasons, randomized trials are less frequent than correlational studies, but their importance to the field is greater. When considering the evidence for any given risk or resiliency factor, it is important to consider the quality of the research from all sources. In this and later chapters, I try to make clear whether the data is more or less compelling, in part based on the research design of different studies.

DISTAL AND PROXIMAL RISK AND RESILIENCY FACTORS

Not all potential risk and resiliency factors are equivalent in their ability to influence depression. One important consideration is the timing of the factors. For example, imagine someone who has a first episode of clinical depression at age 24. It is probable that more recent issues in their life have more influence over their current status than factors that are further in the past. Indeed, evidence suggests that recent life events have a major influence especially for a first episode of depression (Kendler et al., 2002) and become somewhat less important if the person has recurrent depression. At the same time, it is well established that certain early experiences are associated with sustained risk for later life depression. Within the field of risk and resiliency, the distinction is often made between *distal* (i.e., further away in time) and *proximal* (i.e., closer in time) risk factors, with the assumption that proximal factors may be more important for the genesis of depression (Paykel, 2003). The relative importance of distal and proximal factors for depression needs to be evaluated through well-conducted research (cf. Bloch-Elkouby et al., 2020; Brown et al., 2008).

The concepts of distal and proximal factors overlap to some extent with another consideration in risk and resiliency: whether a risk factor is fixed/static or modifiable. Within this literature, it is often assumed that potential risk factors such as gender, ethnicity, familial heritage, and genetics are relatively fixed. In a similar vein, early life experiences are literally immutable once the person passes early life. In contrast, variables such as coping skills, interpersonal behaviors, substance use, and activity levels can be changed at any point in time with the appropriate interventions, at least in theory, and so are modifiable.

Choi et al. (2020) examined the association of 106 modifiable factors with depression in a sample of 123,794 adults in the United Kingdom. Their sample was drawn from the UK Biobank, which provided depression self-report assessments at intervals between 6 and 8 years. The researchers identified participants with low levels of depression at Time 1 ($n = 11,378$) and then examined the modifiable factors in the prediction of what they termed "incident depression" (i.e., a likely clinical depression) at Time 2. Through a series of complex analyses in which they statistically controlled for several variables, they computed the odds ratios associated with the factors. Evaluating only the predictive properties of those factors measured at Time 1, they found four factors most associated with increased risk of depression and their approximate odds ratios: lack of dairy in diet (1.5), vitamin B supplements (1.4), daytime napping (1.3), and the use of multivitamins (1.2). In contrast, factors most associated with lowered risk of depression, and their odds ratios, were exercise (0.7), joining a gym or sports club (0.75), moderate or vigorous walking or activity (0.75), and other walking (0.8). Social contact and increased nighttime sleep were also resiliency factors.

The study by Choi and colleagues (2020) provides an excellent glimpse into the world of risk and resiliency. The study included many participants, and the measurement of constructs was good. The statistics were appropriate. Some of the identified risk and resiliency factors involving activity and social contact make perfect sense and could become the focus of interventions. On the other hand, it seems unlikely that taking vitamin B or multivitamin supplements confers risk for later depression; it is possible that another variable explains these associations. For example, it is possible that individuals who often have colds take increased multivitamins, and their history of colds is actually the risk factor for depression, rather than the taking of multivitamins per se. It is impossible to say. As a further study, another group of investigators could randomly assign people to a course of vitamins or no vitamins and observe later onset of depression. Indeed, this study has been done several times with vitamin B, and a review of these studies suggests that although vitamin B appears to reduce stress, it does not affect the onset of depression (L. M. Young et al., 2019). In contrast, a meta-analysis of four randomized trials suggested that vitamin D has a moderate preventive relationship with later depression (Vellekkatt & Menon, 2019). And yet, in another study that was the largest randomized trial to date ($N = 18,353$) but was not included in the Vellekkatt and Menon review, Okereke et al. (2020) failed to find a preventive benefit for vitamin D_3 for either new incident or recurrent cases of depression. Hopefully, you can begin to appreciate that the science of risk and resiliency is challenging and continues to evolve.

It is perhaps not surprising that the focus of the therapy movement for depression has been on modifiable risk factors. These factors are more likely to be amenable to intervention, and changes in these factors can be measured with respect to their outcome on depression. Different therapeutic models tend to focus on one or another aspect of depression and to develop and test interventions within that area (see Chapter 3). This selective focus and attention may unfortunately limit the benefits that clients with depression might otherwise enjoy. Indeed, my perspective is that clinicians who work with depression should broadly conceptualize risk and resiliency and deploy interventions that strategically seem optimized for a given person.

DIMENSIONS OF RISK AND RESILIENCY: THE BIOPSYCHOSOCIAL MODEL

The discussion in this chapter has so far not stipulated much about the content of risk and resiliency factors. In part, my reluctance results from the fact that multiple fields of study often examine risk factors in isolation. Further, investigators (myself included) often develop methods to study risk or resilience and then use and reuse these methods in multiple studies, sometimes to the detriment of a comprehensive understanding of how multiple factors interplay. Further, the relative importance of different risk and resiliency factors likely varies as a function of depression presentation. For example, different risk or resiliency factors may be more or less important for the different symptom patterns of depression described in Chapter 1. Thus, different clusters of symptoms, levels of depression severity, and different patterns of chronicity may all have an impact on the various causal factors for depression.

In addition to the direct risk of any given risk factor, it is likely that some of the risk factors interact with each other. For example, it has been well established that women experience higher rates of depression and that female gender is one of the most consistent risk factors for depression across cultures (Kessler & Bromet, 2013). Many studies of depression risk have, as a result, either focused on gender-specific risk (e.g., studying only females) or separated the results for males and females to see if gender interacts with the other risk factors being studied. In this regard, many of the factors discussed in this chapter have been examined as a function of gender, and a number of risk factors show a stronger association with depression for one gender than another (most of the extant research treats gender as a binary concept, although this approach is likely to change over time). Interactions among risk factors imply that our models of risk and resiliency need to be more complicated and nuanced than simply naming major factors and that our models of intervention need to be commensurately more complex.

It was not so many years ago that leaders in the field of mental health tried to apply the dominant biomedical model in medicine to depression and other mental disorders. The field is fortunate that a competing and more inclusive model was identified and promoted (G. L. Engel, 1977). The *biopsychosocial model* (G. L. Engel, 1981) was an explicit effort to broaden the conceptualization of health and illness and to consider a diverse set of factors in the life of patients that could help to understand the onset of disorder as well as the factors that could be used in treatment and recovery. The biopsychosocial model has been in existence for many years and has been discussed and reviewed for its strengths and limitations (Borrell-Carrió et al., 2004; McLaren, 1998). For example, simply identifying a list of factors related to health and illness is not an actual conceptual model. Further, as noted previously, a broad consideration of biological, psychological, and social factors does not necessarily help the field to know which factors are potential causes of depression, correlates, or perhaps the consequences of having been depressed. At the same time, the biopsychosocial model has pointed the field in directions to investigate and has led to a wide variety of risk factors for depression being studied (K. S. Dobson & Dozois, 2008). The following sections review and highlight some major risk factors that have emerged in this literature.

Biological Risks for Depression

The literature related to the biology of depression has increased dramatically, in part because of biological models of self-regulatory mechanisms (e.g., related to activity, sleep, and mood). Increased funding for neuroscience research and innovative technologies such as functional magnetic resonance imaging (fMRI) have also supported a resurgence of neuroregulatory models for many forms of psychopathology, including depression. Within this general perspective, we can discern the following risk factors: genetics, biochemistry, disrupted self-regulation systems like sleep and diet, and substance use.

Genetics

Genetic background confers a risk for major depression. For example, twin studies have compared the concordance rates of depression in identical and fraternal twins, and the best evidence from a major meta-analysis is that the odds ratio of a first-degree relative having depression if a family member does is 2.84 (Flint & Kendler, 2014). Heritability estimates for major depression are in the range of 38%, which is moderately high but leaves considerable variance for other environmental, social, and personal influences on risk for depression. I recommend consulting the Flint and Kendler (2014) review, as it not only addresses the overall pattern of heritability; it also points out several concerns with the genetic information. For example, it notes that the existing data fail to substantiate any particular genome-wide or candidate genes in major depression. The authors suggest that this result may be partly due to the extremely large number of participants needed to find some effects, but they raise the possibility that the variability in the expression of depression or the existence of depressive subtypes makes the ability to find genetic links more difficult. As they note, "The data we have summarized so far are compatible with the hypothesis that the genetic basis of MD [major depression] arises from the joint effect of very many loci of small effect" (p. 491).

Three other results from Flint and Kendler (2014) are noteworthy. One is that repeated studies have found that the genetic heritability of depression is larger for women than for men (e.g., Kendler et al., 2006). Although the reasons for this difference are not clear, this effect may in part explain the higher rates of depression in women relative to men. The second comment they make, almost in passing, is "Surprisingly, no high-quality adoption study of MD has been performed, so our evidence of the role of genetic factors in its etiology comes solely from twin studies" (p. 484). Adoption studies include twins who were adopted to the same or different families, and so the influence of the environment can be estimated. The lack of such studies makes the estimate of heritability difficult.

The third point is that the heritability estimates make it difficult to know if what is being passed in genetics is specific to depression: "We can conclude that genetic and phenotypic classifications concur in identifying considerable overlap between anxiety and MD" (p. 496). In summary, while twin studies suggest that clinical depression is in part heritable, the precise mechanisms remain elusive at best.

Biochemistry

The science of brain activity and biochemistry is currently many times more complicated than it was when the field emerged. In a now-classic paper, Schildkraut (1965) proposed the catecholamine hypothesis of depression, the essence of which was that "depressions are associated with an absolute or relative decrease in catecholamines, particularly norepinephrine, available at central adrenergic receptor sites" (p. 509). This model was associated with studies to validate the hypothesized deficiency in norepinephrine (NE) and the development of drugs to stimulate NE activity.

Although NE continues to be studied in relation to depression, the neurotransmitter serotonin has become more frequently studied, and other neurotransmitters such as glutamate are under investigation. Further, the models of neurotransmission difficulty have become increasingly complex (see Kim, 2019) and focus less on deficiencies in neurotransmitter production than on receptor sites and neurotransmitter regulation through enzymes. The neural structures within the central nervous system where neurotransmission problems may occur has become a focus of more recent work, with an emphasis on the regulatory mechanisms for mood and behavior in the hypothalamic–pituitary–adrenal (HPA) axis. The development of magnetic resonance imaging (MRI) and functional MRI scanning has also substantially increased the work on specific pathways and neural circuits that may be involved in depression and has emphasized work not just in the HPA axis but also in the frontal lobes of the brain. The role of cortisol as a general stress response that may be common to anxiety and depression has been studied (Nandam et al., 2020), and some evidence suggests that the gut microbiome may be implicated in dynamic mind–body relations coincident with or causal in depression (Limbana et al., 2020).

It is a fair but significantly understated comment that enormous amounts of research, theory, and clinical investigation have attempted to validate biological and biochemical risks for major depression. These approaches have yielded a wide range of drug therapies. Some drugs are thought to be depression specific, including the selective serotonin reuptake inhibitors (SSRIs), which hypothetically help to restore levels of neurotransmission, specifically for serotonin. Other drugs are thought to primarily affect the enzymes that interfere with neurotransmission or to increase receptor site sensitivity. Some drugs are used alone, particularly for mild to moderate depression, whereas others are sometimes used in combination for treatment-resistance, complicated symptom patterns, or for situations in which depression presents with other disorders. Other treatments include electroconvulsive therapy, transcranial magnetic stimulation, and surgical procedures such as deep brain stimulation.

The current volume is not intended to cover the range of biological interventions for major depression, as the field already has excellent reviews (Arroll et al., 2016; Dupuy et al., 2011; Linde et al., 2015; Thase, 2003). Even more, these reviews have been synthesized into clinical practice guidelines (CPGs), which include reviews of the literature by experts and recommendations based on the reviews. These CPGs typically reflect international research but are often written to influence policy directives within different countries. Thus, while one might expect considerable consistency in guidelines, a systematic review of six CPGs (Gabriel et al., 2020) revealed only one major commonality. As the authors stated, "We conclude that, although CPGs converged in some recommendations (e.g., SSRIs as first-line treatment), they diverged in cardinal topics including the absence of recommendations regarding the risk of suicide associated with pharmacotherapy. Consequently, the recommendations listed in a specific CPG should be followed with caution" (p. 1). Their review noted that the development and standards for CPGs themselves have been the matter of debate and evolution (Johnston et al., 2019; Molino et al., 2019; Saddichha & Chaturvedi, 2014). Individuals interested in the use of antidepressant medication or other biological treatments for depression with a client may choose to refer to the CPGs described in Gabriel et al. (2020) and consult with the client's family physician or psychiatrist for specific treatment recommendations.

Physical Dysregulation: Sleep and Diet

The human body is a remarkable system that encompasses a variety of homeostatic regulatory mechanisms. These self-regulating systems include thermoregulation, sleep–wake, hunger–satiation, thirst–hydration, activity–rest, acid–base, oxygen–CO_2, and more. Three regulatory mechanisms are particularly relevant to depression: sleep, diet, and activity. Sleep and diet are discussed here; activity is discussed later in the chapter in the section on behavioral patterns.

The American industrialist E. Joseph Cossman is quoted as saying, "The best bridge between despair and hope is a good night's sleep," and he may have been more prescient than even he knew. Sleep is a natural and most often daily behavior. In its positive form, it is associated with consolidation of daytime learning, creative problem solving, and physical renewal. Sleep normally occurs in stages, including an early deep and restorative stage and a later and lighter stage of rapid eye movement, often associated with dreaming. The typical pattern is for a person to sleep more heavily at the beginning of the sleep cycle and to move to less intense patterns as the sleeper approaches waking. The need for sleep varies among humans: Infants need multiple short sleep periods in a 24-hour cycle, healthy adults require between 7 and 9 hours of maintained sleep, and older adults require perhaps only 7 hours of nighttime sleep for restoration.

Sleep is also influenced by two other issues. One is the circadian rhythm. Most humans experience alertness in the morning, an increase in arousal and activity toward midday, a decrease in arousal in late afternoon, and fatigue and tiredness in the evening, prior to sleep. While the circadian rhythm is normal in many animals, humans can perturb this cycle through behaviors such napping, staying up late, or traveling across time zones. A second issue is that any unusual pattern of arousal can affect sleep. For example, a person who is affected by stress or who worries or ruminates can increase their physiological arousal to the point that sleep becomes disturbed or difficult. As another example, the occasional use of caffeine or other stimulant in the evening can increase nocturnal arousal and inhibit sleep onset or maintenance (Carney & Posner, 2016).

Sleep disturbance is a symptom of major depression, but it can occur in its own right. Indeed, sleep disturbance has been recognized as an early warning signal, or *prodromal sign*, of depression for some time (Ford & Cooper-Patrick, 2001; Perlis et al., 1997). Not only does sleep disturbance often precede the onset of major depression, but sleep disturbance can also remain as a vestige or residual symptom after the conclusion of an episode (Carney et al., 2006), and this residual symptom of sleep disturbance can serve as a predictor of future episodes of depression. Sleep disturbance and depression are highly comorbid, and depression often presents as a secondary problem in sleep clinics.

The relationship between sleep and depression is further complicated because depression is associated with reduced sleep or insomnia in some people but associated with excessive sleep or hypersomnia in others. Sleep is referred to as a paradoxical symptom because of this varied pattern. Most often, though, a third variable helps to explain this paradox: anxiety. People who present with concomitant anxiety and depression often worry about upcoming events and are also prone to ruminate about past events or perceived failures. These patients may have a difficult time falling asleep, or they may wake in the night or early morning and find it difficult to return to sleep because they worry and ruminate. The other pattern of hypersomnia usually reflects more of an unadulterated pattern of depression, that is, without comorbid anxiety. In this case the client is likely to report fatigue, may wish to nap during the daytime, and may sleep for longer than their normal time period. As may be expected, clients with these different sleep problems benefit from different interventions, as described in Chapter 8.

The evidence has long demonstrated diet can both influence and be influenced by depression (cf. Murakami & Sasaki, 2010). The association between dietary patterns and depression has been studied, particularly focusing on the intake of fatty acids, carbohydrates, and simple sugars as well as on various diet plans. There is an obvious logic to the idea that food intake may be related to depression. For example, carbohydrates are a potential precursor of serotonin, a neurotransmitter implicated in depression. It also makes sense that a person might increase their intake of either simple or complex sugars to obtain short-term stimulation if they are feeling low or lethargic. In a similar manner, people who struggle with depression might increase their caffeine intake to stimulate mental activity.

The literature includes many reports of associations between diet and depression. For example, Lai and colleagues' (2014) meta-analysis indicated that a healthy diet comprising high intake of fruits, vegetables, fish, and whole grains had a modest but significantly lower odds ratio for depression (0.86) relative to a diet without these factors. On the other hand, another review and meta-analysis

(Askari et al., 2022) suggested no association between a vegetarian diet and depression or anxiety. The meta-analytic report from Grosso, Micek, Martevano et al. (2016) suggested that dietary consumption of n-3 polyunsaturated fatty acids (n-3 PUFA) mainly derived from eating fish also leads to reduced risk of depression, in the range of 0.78, relative to low or no n-3 PUFA intake. In both of these meta-analyses, the odds ratio was only significant when contrasting high vegetarian or enhanced n-3 PUFA intake to low intake; contrasts with moderate intake were not significant, suggesting that a moderate intake of the n-3 PUFA confers equal benefit to supplemented diets, at least as regards risk of depression.

The literature related to diet and depression is fraught with many claims of causal relationships although most published studies are correlational. In a review of narrative reviews, systematic reviews, and meta-analyses in the area of diet and depression, Thomas-Odenthal et al. (2020) suggested that narrative reviews are most likely to overstate associations and that empirical meta-analyses yield the most conservative estimates of an association. One of their most telling comments was that "In fact, no single meta-analysis came to a strong conclusion regarding the supposed effect of diet on depression" (p. 11). They also cautioned that, compared to other types of review, narrative reviews often had fewer primary papers included in their literature and were more likely to be written by authors with "potential allegiance bias" (p. 11) than other forms of reviews. They and other authors have noted that much of the literature is based on correlational work or cohort studies and that few randomized trials, of the type that might substantiate causal claims, are available for review.

One dietary pattern that seems to be consistently related to depression is the intake of caffeine. As one example, Ruusunen and colleagues (2010) conducted a large prospective cohort study in Finland and found that the intake of larger amounts of coffee reduced the risk of later depression, relative to no coffee drinking. Surprisingly, they failed to find a similar association with tea consumption or caffeine supplements. A meta-analysis of the larger literature (Grosso, Micek, Castellano, et al., 2016) also found that coffee consumption was associated with a relative risk of depression of 0.76 compared to no consumption, with optimal caffeine intake in the range of 400 mg/day (about four cups of brewed coffee). The relationships between tea consumption and caffeine tablets and depression were again marginal in this meta-analysis.

As noted earlier, Choi and colleagues (2020) evaluated the relative risk for developing later depression associated with 106 modifiable risk factors. Four of the top five factors associated with onset of depression were dietary, including (from highest to lower risk) low rates of dairy products in diet, the intake of vitamin B supplements, the use of multivitamins, and increased salt intake. The association between increased vitamin use and later depression is in particular confusing; it may be possible that participants in the study had noted some emotional or other symptoms and begun vitamin use as a preventive strategy, or a third polygenic factor may be involved in the relationship between vitamin intake and depression, but at the least, these data suggest that claims of a preventive benefit from taking vitamin B should be viewed with caution. As the authors noted, "Despite popular views of vitamin B as a mood-boosting supplement, our findings align with a current lack of randomized trial evidence supporting beneficial effects on depression risk" (Choi et al., 2020, p. 951).

Taken as a whole, it appears that sleep has a potent effect on the risk for depression and that sleep disturbance is often a sequalae of having been depressed. Sleep disturbance in the context of depression, whether it is reduced or excessive, needs to be addressed directly. We are fortunate that several effective interventions exist; they are discussed later in this chapter. As for diet, the literature is more tenuous. It appears that a vegetarian and whole grains diet (one with fewer simple sugars or carbohydrates) and a diet high in polyunsaturated fatty acids and coffee confer a modest preventive effect against depression, but only as compared to poor or deficient diets. However, most of the literature is correlational, and while it may establish associations between depression and other factors, the number and quality of studies that support causal inferences is very low. Additionally, most of this literature examines variables in isolation; how these different factors may work together either to synergize or to inhibit each other's effects is for the most part unclear.

Alcohol and Other Substances

Most cases of depression are marked by a suppression of functioning, including lower mood, lower activity, lower desire for food, and more desire for sleep (although a person with the anxious subtype may experience increased activity, agitation, a higher desire for food, or other changes). Depressive symptoms that involve behavioral suppression can look like the same reaction one can have to central nervous system (CNS) suppressants. In many countries, a commonly used CNS suppressant is alcohol, and myriad studies have examined the relationship between alcohol use and depression. In a major meta-analysis, Conner et al. (2009) reported a significant, although small, contemporaneous association between alcohol consumption and depression. They also reported that depression was predictive of future alcohol use and general impairment, although the relationship again was modest. They did not report the potential predictive power of alcohol use on future depression, but a prospective cohort research study of almost 60,000 participants in 19 countries suggested that both occasional and heavy drinking were associated with higher risk of depression relative to moderate drinking (Keyes et al., 2019). These effects were moderated by country of study, gender, and smoking behavior. An unusual finding of this study was that although increased alcohol use was associated with later depression, the strongest drinking pattern associated with later depression was long-term abstinence. Moderate drinking was associated with the lowest hazard of future depression overall, leading the authors to recommend that health care professionals and therapists inquire about alcohol consumption when individuals present with depression to ascertain if the drinking pattern is potentially problematic. This recommendation is consistent with others in which clinicians are advised to assess the range of CNS depressants, such as alcohol, cannabis, opioids, anxiolytics, and sleeping medications used by patients with clinical depression (cf. Nunes & Levin, 2004).

Psychological Risks for Depression

Psychological factors have long been recognized as correlates of depression, and evidence suggests that many of these factors are causal as well. Much of the literature can be traced to the dominance of the cognitive therapy of depression (A. T. Beck, Rush, et al., 1979), which exerted an early influence on theory and research. The literature has been reviewed many times, with one of the best organized reviews coming early (Clark et al., 1999). Although other formulae are possible, the current review is organized around the conceptual clusters of behavioral and cognitive patterns in depression.

Behavioral Patterns Associated With Depression

Depression is primarily associated with reductions in activity and often with decreased appetite and energy. One behavioral pattern that may coincide with these reductions is avoidance. A good number of studies have documented an association between behavioral avoidance and depression (Leventhal, 2008), and avoidant coping (as opposed to problem-oriented or approach coping) may be both a precursor to and a consequence of clinical depression. Thus, when faced with life's challenges, people with depression may procrastinate addressing the problems or may simply not engage with them. In this regard, the association between anxiety and depression makes sense, as anxiety is also often associated with avoidance and/or escape (Ottenbreit et al., 2014).

A longstanding literature also associates depression with reduced rates of positive reinforcement, such that even if the person who is experiencing depression approaches difficult people or situations, they may not obtain satisfaction for their efforts (Carvalho & Hopko, 2011). The hypothesis that reduced pleasure or achievement may result from attempts to solve problems would certainly explain why a client who is depressed might engage or persist less in problem-solving efforts. The behavioral model of depression, which has existed for a long time (Lewinsohn, 1975), states that both reduced activity and lessened positive reinforcement for completed activities are reasons that some people become depressed.

It has been suggested that people who are vulnerable to depression have relatively poor social skills compared to others who do not have this vulnerability. A laboratory study by Libet and Lewinsohn (1973) suggested that people with depression have several measurable interpersonal deficits relative to nondepressed counterparts, including reduced activity levels, a limited range of interpersonal behavior, a low rate of positive reactions, and increased action latency. In a review of the issue, Tse and Bond (2004) concluded that depression is significantly correlated with impaired social perception, cognitive patterns that interfere with social functioning, and social performance. Further, they noted that studies that induced a temporary negative mood in research participants documented social impairment as a consequence. Their conclusion was that social skill deficits were likely correlates of depression and "likely to remit with effective treatment" (p. 260).

Cognitive Patterns Associated With Depression

Given the predominance of cognitive behavior therapy as a psychological treatment model for depression, it is not surprising that cognitive features of depression and cognitive patterns as a vulnerability factor for depression have been extensively studied. An early book on the topic documented strong evidence for the presence of negative cognition as a descriptive feature of depression (Clark et al., 1999), and more recent reviews suggest that people who experience depression tend to have more negative content in their thoughts and selectively process information in a negatively biased fashion (Hammen, 2018). Researchers have used a variety of self-report and naturalistic measures of negative thought as well as laboratory tasks that measure the tendency of people with higher depression scores and clinically depressed people to attend selectively to negative information more than their nondepressed counterparts do, to process negative information more efficiently, and to remember more of this information.

One challenge with much of the research on cognition in depression is that it includes samples of convenience, such as university students or community samples, rather than clinical samples. Another is that much of the research is correlational in nature, which makes tests of risk and vulnerability very difficult. Prospective research does exist, but it tends to include regression analyses to examine long-term correlations rather than risk in terms of odds ratios. A further consideration is that the cognitive model of depression posits that focused situational cognitive processes are involved in depression (such as selective attention to information in the environment) and that stable, trait-like beliefs make the person vulnerable to these situational cognitive processes. The model also proposes that depressogenic beliefs lie dormant until they are activated by relevant stressors or events (Alloy & Riskind, 2006).

Given these considerations, it is fair to say that while the field has very strongly shown that depressive cognitions correlate with overall depressed state, the evidence for a causal role of negative core beliefs has been more elusive (Ingram et al., 1998), with some exceptions. For example, in a large student-based prospective study of the hopelessness model of depression, Alloy and colleagues (2006) followed 347 students for 2.5 years and demonstrated that students with high negative cognitive styles had a significant elevated odds ratio of developing either a first episode or recurrence (ranging from 3.5 to 6.8) relative to control participants with a low level of the same style. The definition of negative cognitive style in this study was somewhat complex, including elevated scores on both a measure of negative attitudes (similar to beliefs) and a measure of attributional style (i.e., the tendency to blame oneself or to draw negative inferences for negative events). In a related study, participants who were already depressed at the initial assessment period and demonstrated a negative cognitive style had more episodes of depression, more severe episodes, and a more chronic course of disorder than low-risk participants did (Iacoviello et al., 2006).

As noted earlier, the cognitive theory states that the cognitive vulnerability to depression is hypothetically latent until activated by life stressors. An early student-based study showed that negative attitudes interacted significantly with reported life stress to correlate with depression levels (Olinger et al., 1987). A similar longitudinal study (Klocek et al., 1997) added social support to the list of predictors, indicating a somewhat more complex model of risk, but the interaction between negative attitudes and life events remained a strong predictor of later increased levels of depression in the student sample.

Yet another cognitive factor implicated in depression is rumination (Abela et al., 2002; Fresco et al., 2002; Nolen-Hoeksema, 2000; Nolen-Hoeksema et al., 2008). Rumination is a reactive set of cognitions following stressful life events, and the characteristic negative attributional style seen in depression is internal (focused on the self, as opposed to external), stable (emphasizing long-term causes, as opposed to unstable or temporary factors), and global (emphasizing broad factors, as opposed to specific factors related to a unique event). Put otherwise, after a negative event, individuals who are depressed make an attribution to some stable and broad attribute of the self to explain the outcome (i.e., they blame some aspect of the self). Importantly, however, not all repetitive thinking is problematic. Indeed, problem-solving a life issue may require concerted attention and planning, but it is possible to differentiate patterns of constructive thinking from less helpful repetitive thinking (Watkins, 2008), and it is possible to show that problematic ruminative thinking is associated with deficits in effective problem solving in people with depression (Watkins & Baracaia, 2002). A specific set of interventions has been developed and tested for ruminative thinking (Watkins, 2016).

One emergent issue in the study of cognition in depression is the relationship among the various cognitive patterns. To address this issue, Hong and Cheung (2015) conducted a meta-analysis of six cognitive patterns associated with anxiety and/or depression to examine their relationships. The patterns in depression were pessimistic inferential style, dysfunctional attitudes, and ruminative style. The authors extracted 159 effect sizes from 73 articles and, based on these results, estimated the mean correlations among the risk factors. The results indicated moderate to strong correlations, and a one-factor model best fit the meta-analytic data. Their conclusion was that although the various scales and measures of cognitive vulnerability may hypothetically evaluate distinct constructs, some common etiologic factor may underlie the constructs.

Behavioral and Cognitive Patterns as Intervention Targets

To summarize this section, it seems clear that distinct behavioral and cognitive patterns are associated with depression. While some patterns are perhaps correlates or consequences of becoming depressed, some are modifiable risk factors and therefore become targets for intervention. As discussed throughout later chapters in this book, a plethora of interventions focus on negative behavioral and thought patterns in depression, and in this volume I present those that seem most relevant and helpful for clients who seek help with depressive experiences.

Social Risks for Depression

To some extent, the preceding section related to cognitive risk for depression has already introduced the idea that life events are risk factors for depression, in particular with respect to the interaction between depressogenic attitudes or beliefs and major life events. As highlighted in following review, social risk factors figure into the risk for depression in several ways. Much of this evidence has existed for some time, but the evidence is certainly compelling.

Adverse Childhood Experiences

One clear social risk factor for depression is childhood adversity. Adverse childhood experiences (ACEs) have been studied in various fashions, and studies typically focus on issues related to child abuse, child neglect, and family dysfunction (e.g., mental illness in the home, parental separation). In a hallmark study, Chapman and colleagues (2004) examined the relationship between ACEs and adult depression in a sample of 9,460 American adults and found that high levels of ACEs increased the odd ratios of adult depression by 2.7 in women and 2.5 in men, relative to individuals with low levels of ACEs. They also reported that as the number of ACEs increased the risk of depression did as well, although the relationship was difficult to study with very high numbers of ACEs; because the number of participants was small, patterns were more difficult to establish. In a similar large community study in Canada, we found a significant association between ACEs and adult depression, with a similar increasing effect of higher numbers of ACEs (Dobson, Allan, et al., 2020). This relationship was found only until four ACEs, however, as the sample size precluded the effective study of the relationship beyond that point.

Multiple other studies in many countries have examined specific patterns of childhood adversity and later depression (cf. T. R. Miller et al., 2020). Adolescent and/or adult depression has been specifically associated with parental separation (Bohman et al., 2017), family disruption (Gilman et al., 2003), father absence (Culpin et al., 2013), and childhood sexual assault (Nelson et al., 2002; Saunders et al., 1992; Weiss et al., 1999). Other studies have addressed childhood experiences and parenting patterns as well as later adult health problems (see Hammen, 2018, for a review).

One challenge for the literature on childhood adversity and adult depression is that the different forms of family dysfunction tend to co-occur. Thus, families with lower socioeconomic status tend to also have more family disruption, and families with more disruption tend to have more caregiver disputes, separations, childhood neglect, economic problems, and so forth. It therefore becomes hard to differentiate the precise patterns among different childhood adversities and later mental health challenges such as depression. This said, studies of factors such as child abuse have controlled for potential confounding variables such as education, socioeconomic status, and current depression, and the effects of past abuse often remain.

A second challenge for this research is that the outcomes of ACEs are varied. Thus, while adolescent and adult depression rates are higher in people who experience more childhood adversity, rates of anxiety, substance use, and other mental disorders are also higher, as are rates of physical disorders (Dobson, Allan, et al., 2020; Dobson, Pusch, et al., 2020). Thus, the risk is not specific. Equally important and related, the precise mechanisms by which childhood adversity confers increased risk for later problems are unclear. Some potential mechanisms include increased sensitization toward life stress, socialization of children into social problems, social impairments in children who experience adversity, difficulties in interpersonal attachment in children who experience high ACE rates, and the development of negative beliefs and schemas, especially as regards interpersonal relationships (Hammen, 2018). It should not be a surprise to learn that researchers have also attempted to build and study more complex models of multiple factors (Abela et al., 2005; Barker et al., 2012; Harkness et al., 2008; Reising et al., 2013). Such studies are often complex and rely on large samples, strong measurement, longitudinal data, and sophisticated statistical methods to study relationships among variables. Taken as a whole, however, it is clear that there are intergenerational aspects of the transmission of depression and that adverse early life experiences substantially increase the risk of later depression.

Negative Life Events

Negative life events have been studied as a risk factor for depression for many years. In some respects, this literature can be connected back to the pioneering work of Freud (1917), who differentiated the psychological processes involved in mourning and depression and in particular the potential responses to loss events. The life events that often trigger depression were further highlighted in early research (G. W. Brown & Harris, 1978), and it has been reported that social events such as interpersonal conflict, separation, and social isolation are all important risk factors for depression (Paykel, 1994). In particular, social isolation and loneliness have been extensively studied and are demonstrable risks for depression across the life span (Cacioppo et al., 2006; Loades et al., 2020; Malcolm et al., 2019). For example, the study of modifiable risk factors cited earlier (Choi et al., 2020) clearly identified lack of social engagement as a risk factor and social engagement, such as having a confidant, as a preventive factor for future depression.

Studies of various major life events have confirmed relationships between depression and loss events such as social isolation, loss of status, loss of relationships, and major challenging events in general (G. W. Brown & Harris, 1989; Kendler et al., 1999). Strong evidence also suggests that small life events and daily hassles (i.e., minor inconveniences of daily life such as crowds, traffic jams, requests and demands from others, and time pressures) are related to risk for depression (Bouteyre et al., 2007; DeLongis et al., 1988). Importantly, it appears that the interpretation of daily hassles as well as the absence of social support are important mediators, so while major life effects may confer a direct risk for depression, minor stressors may need to interact with other variables to increase risk substantially.

Stress Generation

Although both major events and daily hassles may emerge unbidden and without encouragement, it is well recognized that people who are depressed also interact with the environment to sometimes, unwittingly, create more stress for themselves. The stress generation hypothesis (Hammen, 1991) has been extensively studied and supported in the literature (e.g., Hammen, 2018; R. T. Liu, 2013). Evidence suggests that people who become depressed may select or create challenging social circumstances, may interact in ways that drive others away, or may simply disengage from contexts (e.g., a difficult work situation) in ways that then create future challenges (Hammen, 2018; Joiner & Metalsky, 2001). As one example, a person who struggles with depression may withdraw from their usual social relationships and begin to experience loneliness and isolation as a consequence, which in turn generates more depression. Thus, stress generation is a critical variable in the development of depression, in part as depression seems to increase the likelihood of processes related to stress generation, but once enacted these processes increase the risk for later depression in what may become a vicious cycle. Disentangling this longitudinal process is challenging in research (Vanhalst et al., 2012), perhaps even more so with individual clients. Some evidence suggests that first episodes of depression are more frequently precipitated by major life events, but recurrence may require less of a trigger or precipitant (Kendler et al., 2000), perhaps in part because the person themselves unwittingly begins to act in ways that perpetuate a depressive sequence.

Culture

A final social factor that deserves attention with respect to depression is culture. A considerable amount of research has been done to study the different rates of depression in diverse countries (cf. Andrade et al., 2003; Kessler & Bromet, 2013; Moussavi et al., 2007; see also Chapter 1). In one review (Kessler & Bromet, 2013), researchers concluded that although prevalence estimates vary across countries, methodological variance among the published research articles accounts for much of the reported variability. Still, rates of depression are often lower in those countries with higher incomes as compared to low- and middle-income countries. In a study conducted in Germany, immigrants, especially those with relatively low levels of acculturation to the dominant society, were at higher risk of depression than were other individuals (Janssen-Kallenberg et al., 2017). This effect may be related to the personal and economic hardships associated with the immigration experience rather than acculturation as such, but similar effects have been reported elsewhere (Gupta et al., 2013; Yoon et al., 2013).

An important study (Li et al., 2021) examined a variety of sociocultural, ecological, and economic correlates of depression in 195 countries. This study took advantage of a 2017 Global Burden of Disease study (Q. Liu et al., 2020), which provided estimates of the annual prevalence of depression in these countries. The authors cross-referenced these data points with a global database that examined a variety of 27 sociocultural and environmental factors (Kirby et al., 2016). The Li et al. (2021) study revealed that significantly higher rates of depression were associated with more individualist societies (Hofstede, 2001; Minkov et al., 2017) and with higher divorce rates, higher gross domestic product (GDP), and more health care workers. In contrast, lower rates of depression were seen in countries with longer levels of daylight sunshine in winter, wetter climates, and higher levels of power distance, defined as the acceptability of inequality in power differences in relationships. When examined using multiple regression, the one variable that remained a significant correlate of depression was individualism, as countries higher in individualism had higher rates of depression (or, if you prefer, countries with more collectivism had lower rates of depression).

Another interesting aspect of the Li et al. (2021) study was the set of variables not correlated with depression, including a number of factors that might be suspected to be related to depression, such as malnutrition, unemployment, pollution, conflict, and violence. As the authors noted, the quality of some of these indices is perhaps suspect in some countries because the surveillance may not be ideal, but nonetheless, the study provides a unique look at international factors that appear to be correlated with depression. Whether these variables are predictive or the result of depression cannot be discerned with the method of this study, and the study is limited to the variables included in the global database (Kirby et al., 2016).

A challenging aspect of the relationship between culture and depression is that the very conceptualization of symptomatology and its social construction as a disorder varies around the world. This observation has been made for some time (cf. Kleinman & Good, 1985) and remains relevant. Cultural beliefs vary, as do culturally based behaviors and practices. The labeling of and attributions for diverse affects have cross-cultural variations, as does the conceptualization of "abnormal" (Tanaka-Matsumi, 2019). In part predicated on these cultural factors, the recommended approaches to the assessment and treatment of depression also vary. Cultural beliefs, practices, and observances are key components of the life of any person with depression, and as such they should be carefully considered by the therapist when conducting an assessment, case conceptualization, or treatment plan.

THE BIOPSYCHOSOCIAL MODEL REVISITED

In light of the review conducted in this chapter, we can now revisit the biopsychosocial model for depression and fill in the model with a variety of named, evidence-based risk factors. This summary can be found in Figure 2.1, which highlights the major research-based risk factors for depression. As shown in the

FIGURE 2.1. The Biopsychosocial Model for Clinical Depression

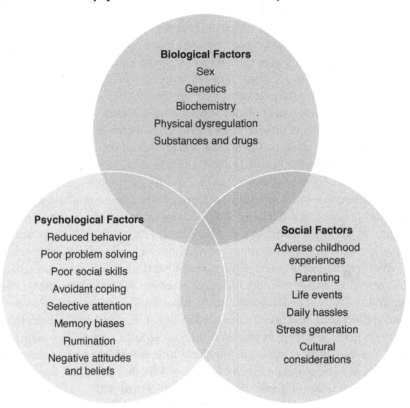

figure, the field has grown remarkably in recent years, and we are now able to stipulate a large number of risk factors for the onset, maintenance, and recurrence of clinical depression. Although the quantity and quality of the data for some risk factors is longer and more substantial than for others, all factors require consideration in prevention and treatment programs. It is also clearly the case that some risk factors are distal and unlikely to be modified once in place (e.g., genetics, ACEs), whereas other risk factors are relatively easy to conceptualize as modifiable and therefore potential targets of intervention.

IMPLICATIONS FOR ASSESSMENT, PREVENTION, AND INTERVENTION

Chapter 1 introduced the substantial complexity of the concept of clinical depression. This chapter provides an introduction to the factors that have been shown through substantial research to increase the risk of experiencing depression. Given the remarkable variability in both the presentation of depression and the potential risk factors, my opinion is that the likelihood of a single model of depression with broad applicability, or a single intervention that has high levels of efficacy for all people who experience depression, is extremely low. Thus, while some models appear to have greater efficacy than others on average, and some models have greater acceptability to patients than competing interventions, the suggestion made in this book is that skilled clinicians need to know about major models of intervention and to balance those general models against the specific vulnerabilities and risk factors for the given patient to determine the specific treatment elements that have the highest likelihood of success.

Given the importance of psychological theory in the provision of care, Chapter 3 provides a brief review of major psychological theories for depression. In subsequent chapters, I argue that the cognitive behavioral framework best incorporates what is known about risk and resilience and suggest that it can form the basis of a treatment protocol. This said, cognitive behavioral theory has its limitations, and a more comprehensive and integrated model that takes into account the identification of risk factors and their treatment needs will be incorporated into an expanded CBT model. This model, almost by definition, needs to respond to the evidence from the biopsychosocial perspective on clinical depression.

CASE ILLUSTRATIONS OF RISK AND RESILIENCY

The following examples continue the two cases introduced in Chapter 1.[1] They build on the case descriptions by outlining Michael's and Miranda's various risk factors, with reference to the biopsychosocial model, as well as coping and resiliency factors.

The Case of Michael

Similar to many clients, Michael presents with a range of risk factors for major depression, and several aspects of his functioning can be related to the biopsychosocial model. Biological risk factors include reduced activity, poor eating patterns, sleep disturbance, and increased use of substances such as alcohol and caffeine. His history shows no evidence of a familial pattern of depression, but this issue was not adequately explored. Michael also exhibits some psychological risk factors for depression, such as self-recrimination and emotional and interpersonal avoidance. He has had an excessive focus on career success, possibly to the detriment of his relationships and other potential sources of gratification. He worries a great deal about his future but has avoided planning ahead. He presents as largely alone in the world as he is beginning to think about a transition to retirement.

It is also notable that Michael has several coping and resiliency factors that likely reduce his potential for depression. For example, although his pattern of

---

[1] All cases presented in this book are fictitious and represent illustrations drawn from my experience but not from any specific person.

alcohol and caffeine use are likely dysfunctional in the larger sphere of considerations, he uses them to manage his daily activities. He is gainfully employed and has a positive socioeconomic status. He is meeting the psychological needs of one of his core beliefs through his work, which is related to the need to be productive and "self-made." He has occasional contact with his two grown children, which he does enjoy, and would like to have the opportunity to develop these relationships further. He is in a stable relationship, although it is not particularly satisfying. Finally, he has access to medical assistance and pharmacotherapy to help to manage his symptomatology.

The Case of Miranda

Miranda's situation is not unusual for someone with depression: She clearly has some of the well-established risk factors for depression as well as several resiliency factors. Her case can be conceptualized from a biopsychosocial perspective, as all three domains are implicated. Within the biological realm, we know that Miranda's mother suffered from "nerves" and what was also probably an undiagnosed condition of depression. In this regard, it is possible that Miranda has some of the genetic risk factors for an increased stress response and depression herself. In addition, changes in appetite and sleep are two primary indicators that Miranda recognizes as symptoms of depression, which strongly implies that these physiological patterns are part of her typical response to stress. Finally, it appears that Miranda's two most recent episodes of depression were associated with the birth of her two children and were recognized as episodes of postpartum depression. The postpartum period for all people includes physiological changes in hormonal patterns, changes to dietary intake, and significant changes in sleep patterns associated with childcare.

Miranda also exhibits psychological characteristics of a person vulnerable to depression. She reported that she was a shy and somewhat anxious child, which suggests the possibility of low self-esteem. She appears to have a tendency toward self-blame. Her history also reflects a repeated theme of rumination and worry. While the case history provided in Chapter 1 focused on larger life events associated with these cognitive patterns, further experience working with Miranda revealed that she often anticipates potential problems in her day and revisits even relatively minor problems in the form of ruminative thinking. In addition, when Miranda is struggling with challenging life events, she tends to withdraw. This pattern was particularly clear after the relationship breakup when she was a young woman, but it recurs when she feels current stress. The pattern of withdrawal unfortunately has the consequence of providing her with more opportunity to ruminate and not manage the issues that are causing stress.

Miranda's life has relatively few social stressors, but they are certainly present. She likely learned some patterns during her years growing up with her mother, potentially coping through avoidance as well as learning not to rely on support from male people in her life because of her father's frequent absences. Although she had two long-term friends during her school years, the evidence is that she was not particularly socially active. Through lack of experience and practice, her social skills could be somewhat limited. The fact that she was rejected in an intimate relationship shortly after the completion of high school and was apparently unaware that her partner was being unfaithful could support the hypothesis of potential limits in her social awareness (although could also suggest a very deceptive partner). Either way, this event set up the possibility of concern about relationships and a potential fear of becoming close to others again. By her account, her current marital relationship is positive but has lost some of the romantic intensity of its earlier years. It should be noted that as a busy woman who works full-time and has two children, she reported few social connections with other women beyond work.

Taken as a whole, Miranda's depressive experiences encompass a range of biopsychosocial risk factors. It is notable, however, that she also has several resiliency factors to draw upon. She was able to complete her education and has been able to obtain and maintain satisfactory employment and a stable socioeconomic status. She has been able to develop an intimate partner relationship that is devoid of significant problems. She has twice delivered healthy children, and even though she worries about their health, on inquiry she recognizes that the disturbed sleep and coughs and colds that they experience are likely aspects of typical child development. She has coped between her depressive episodes. Asked to summarize her current life status, she recognized that it is "good."

3

Evolving Models of Clinical Depression

This chapter presents some of the development and history of treatments for clinical depression. The emphasis is on therapies that have been evaluated in research and can be said to be evidence based. However, a number of interventions that have been developed for people who struggle with depression focus on specific aspects of functioning, such as activity, diet, and sleep, and these more targeted interventions can also serve as effective tools to help a person recover optimal functioning. As such, both types of intervention models are presented here so clinicians can appreciate the range of intervention models and techniques that can be integrated into practice.

PSYCHOANALYSIS AND THE DEVELOPMENT OF INTERPERSONAL PSYCHOTHERAPY (IPT)

Sigmund Freud wrote the first psychological theory of depression (then called melancholia) in *Mourning and Melancholia* (Freud, 1917). He posited that while mourning or grief had many of the same features as melancholia, the major difference was that in mourning, an actual object (e.g., a person, loved object, or symbolic concept such as a position) was lost and grieved. In contrast, whereas melancholia also included loss, a person who developed melancholia had an excessive attachment to the lost object and had psychologically internalized aspects of it, which then led to negative feelings toward the self, self-denigration, and possibly the desire to injure or destroy oneself in the extreme. Freud also

https://doi.org/10.1037/0000398-004
Clinical Depression: An Individualized, Biopsychosocial Approach to Assessment and Treatment,
by K. S. Dobson

hypothesized that early experiences with loss could create unconscious connections to the experience, such that what may seem to be a relatively minor issue for one person could be a significant trigger to past loss for another and thus precipitate a depressive experience.

The psychoanalytic view held firmly for many decades and in part helped to explain the genesis of the first major subtyping of depression. This division occurred over time but was first seen in proposals to differentiate *endogenous* (literally, "caused from within"; presumably biologically based) forms of depression from what has been variously called *neurotic, exogenous,* or *reactive depression,* which is a response to psychosocial factors such as loss and the processes described by Freud. The endogenous–reactive distinction was viewed by some as the first major breakthrough in the understanding of the etiology of melancholia and was quickly associated with treatment recommendations consistent with this subtyping. The endogenous–reactive depression distinction was even incorporated into formal diagnostic manuals as recently as the third edition of the American Psychiatric Association's *Diagnostic and Statistical Manual of Mental Disorders* (American Psychiatric Association, 1980).

Freudian psychoanalysis has had lasting implications in the realm of diagnosis as well as significant long-term effects on the development of psychological models for intervention. It is notable that while Freud wrote specifically about melancholia as a disordered state, much of his other writing focused on broader personality themes. In a similar way, many theorists who followed Freud also deemphasized the importance of diagnostic formulations and instead wrote about broad constructs related to personality, neurosis, and even "human nature" (cf. Adler, 1927; Horney, 1937). For example, the psychoanalyst Karen Horney discussed the "neurotic personality" and presented the idea that neurotic behavior such as self-denigration and social withdrawal emerge from a dynamic interaction between innate personality dimensions related to inferiority and social experience such as interpersonal loss and rejection. In this regard, her theorizing built on Freud's seminal ideas but within a broader framework. From this perspective, the treatment of depression involved understanding the interaction between unconscious processes and social experience and the provision of conscious control over these interactional patterns.

Many psychoanalytic theorists who followed Freud deemphasized some instinctual or innate parts of Freud's theory and instead emphasized the critical nature of early interpersonal experience in the development of self and the ways in which social identity influences issues such as neurosis, which encompasses affects such as anxiety and depression. For example, Adler (1927) stated that "the affect of sadness occurs when one cannot console himself for a loss or deprivation. Sadness . . . is a compensation for a feeling of displeasure or weakness and amounts to an attempt to secure a better situation" (p. 212). Thus, this model recognizes an interaction between the vulnerable personality of the person who becomes sad and the circumstance of loss or deprivation itself.

Harry Stack Sullivan was a dominant figure within North American psychoanalysis; he significantly influenced theoretical models of personality in general and depression in particular. Sullivan (1953) proposed an interpersonal theory of psychoanalysis in which the self (or *ego*, using a term first employed by Freud) becomes defined by early interpersonal experiences but then is enlivened through the ways that this early experience creates formative dimensions of personality and is further reinforced through ongoing life experience. The interpersonal psychotherapy model of Sullivan and other ego analysts (Bowlby, 1960; Hartmann, 1958; E. Jacobson, 1964) emphasized the importance of the development of self as an entity separate from parents and other caregivers, but the theory reflected the idea that this developmental process contains the possibility of considerable disturbance. For example, children can be over-protected and not given the opportunity to develop a sense of competence and independence separate from the parents or caregivers. Conversely, childhood experiences that are demarcated by neglect or abuse can significantly affect the desire and ability to invest emotional attachment in others, leading to an adult who is unduly isolated and alone. As the interpersonal theory developed, this dynamic process between the needs of the child/adolescent/adult and the environment became increasingly clear (Winnicott, 1965), and thus generated the idea that the interpersonal self, or the self in relation to others, is the critical psychological process involved in either psychological health or states of dysfunction such as depression.

A major development in the application of interpersonal theory to depression occurred in the late 1970s as a consequence of a major psychotherapy trial conducted by the National Institute of Mental Health (NIMH) in the United States. The NIMH wanted to conduct a seminal study contrasting the efficacy of pharmacotherapy and psychotherapy in the treatment of depression and had determined that cognitive behavior therapy (CBT; described later in this chapter) would be one model of psychotherapy to test, but it wanted a comparator. As a result, a short-term model of interpersonal therapy (IPT) of depression was developed (Klerman et al., 1984) and then tested. The results of IPT in this trial were comparable to those of both CBT and pharmacotherapy (Elkin et al., 1989); this finding rapidly promoted short-term IPT as a validated intervention for depression (Weissman et al., 2000). Since that first study, IPT has developed from a model of individual psychotherapy to incorporate group methods (Wilfley et al., 2000) and studies with diverse groups such as older adults with depression, depressed persons receiving perinatal care, and patients in primary care settings.

The core elements of short-term IPT for depression are described in the original IPT manual (Klerman et al., 1984). The interventions ultimately selected for use rest on an assessment of the interpersonal issues faced by the patient, with appropriate interventions matched to those issues. Within the framework are four potential interpersonal themes or challenges that may be identified and associated with depression:

1. *Role transitions*: These refer to changes in one's roles or positions in life. They could include adolescent differentiation, young adulthood, parenthood, changes in careers, retirement, and other major shifts in roles.

2. *Role disputes*: These are conflicts in important relationships, particularly in those instances in which the parties involved have a difference of opinion about their respective roles and responsibilities. A common example is between intimate partners, but role disputes can also occur in child–parent relationships, in the workplace, or in other settings.

3. *Interpersonal deficits*: Limited social skills, poor social problem solving, and problematic interpersonal behavior are examples of interpersonal deficits that may be the target of intervention.

4. *Grief*: The IPT model holds that some instances of depression can be directly attributed to loss and the experience of grief. In the extreme, grief responses may follow the death of a loved one, but they may also be associated with lost relationships as a result of moving, lost abilities (e.g., the loss of a limb in a motor vehicle accident), or other critical losses related to the sense of social identity.

The model of short-term IPT follows a relatively standardized format. The typical length of individual IPT for a case of depression is about 16 weeks, and treatment is divided into an early or assessment phase, a middle phase, and a final or termination phase. Treatment begins with an assessment of the nature and severity of the client's depression. IPT therapists typically use the idea that depression is an experience that is unwillingly visited upon the client, and they encourage the client to accept a "limited sick role" in which they encourage the client to partially externalize their depressive experience. Treatment continues with assessment of people who are close to the client, the particular interpersonal theme(s) that the client may be experiencing, and an identification of which one is primary. At the end of this assessment the therapist offers the client a case formulation based on the IPT model, and, given consent, the therapist and client begin to work on repair of that theme.

The middle phase of IPT is the longest and involves a series of interventions mapped onto the interpersonal theme(s) that the therapist and client have determined are key to the case (Weissman et al., 2000). The specific interventions vary from case to case, depending on the case conceptualization and interpersonal theme(s) for that case, but they can include skills training, the development and use of appropriate interpersonal styles of interaction to address the client's issue, the development of social support to facilitate grief responses, discussion with others about new and developing role expectations, and the growth and use of social support. In general, sessions include some degree of psychoeducation about the interpersonal work, encouragement of adaptive social behavior, and the use of between-session assignments in which the client is encouraged to enact the desired interpersonal behavior change. Throughout this phase, the therapist continues to monitor the client's response to the interventions and to modify strategies or reorient therapy as necessary.

Finally, as the client begins to resolve some of the interpersonal issues that brought them to therapy, the therapist moves toward ending the treatment. This phase of therapy includes a review of the major strategies used in treatment, prediction and preparation for possible setback or relapse, and the encouragement to continue to actively engage the social environment.

BEHAVIORAL THEORY AND BEHAVIORAL ACTIVATION THERAPY

The first major psychological model to compete with the psychoanalytic model came from behavioral or reinforcement theory. In this model, the behavioral features of depression such as decreased activity, lethargy, and increased sleep were caused by insufficient positive reinforcement for activity in the environment (Ferster & Hammer, 1965). Reduction in reinforcement could result from the loss of reinforcers themselves (e.g., a loved one dies and no longer provides support and reinforcement), or the loss of reinforcer effectiveness (e.g., something that was once rewarding loses its value). Behavioral therapy for depression thus emphasized the need to recruit positive reinforcers for adaptive behavior through the development of new behaviors, new reinforcers, or the recognition of existing reinforcers.

Reinforcement therapy became the foundation for behavioral therapy of depression (Lewinsohn, 1974). Within this framework, response contingent positive reinforcement for behavior became the critical ingredient for treatment. It was imperative that the client increased behavior that could be positively reinforced, and so the scheduling of potentially positive events was integrated into behavioral therapy for depression. In some clients, the range of behaviors had to be increased, in order to "experiment" with novel behaviors, but for other clients the key ingredient appeared to be the reinstallation of previously positively reinforced behaviors. In some clients who lacked the requisite skills to obtain positive reinforcement in critical areas (e.g., social skills) skills training could be used in therapy (Lewinsohn et al., 1980). In the behavioral therapy of depression model, it was also recognized that some clients might have access to positive reinforcers, but not attend to them (Rehm, 1977), and so the idea of self-monitoring and increasing attention to positive reinforcers was added. One of the major aspects of most behavioral models of treatment for depression is the scheduling of positive activities. It is believed that this scheduling has the direct benefits of increased activity, the effects of positive reinforcement of positive activities, and a more adaptive emphasis on positive experience than may be seen in depression.

The behavioral model of depression (Lewinsohn, 1974) was written into a treatment manual entitled the *Coping With Depression Course* (CWD course; Clarke & Lewinsohn, 1989; Lewinsohn et al., 1984). The CWD course is a moderately well-structured program and was primarily intended as an educational program for use in a group format. The earlier versions of the CWD course were designed to be completed in sixteen 2-hour sessions scheduled over an 8-week period. Adapted versions include a shorter number of sessions, modular formats, and individual delivery. The course includes sessions related to identifying and scheduling pleasant activities, developing social skills, addressing negative thinking in depression, and using relaxation skills. Based on research in the 1980s, the CWD course has been modified (Lewinsohn et al., 1989) and applied to adults, adolescents, older adults, and Native Americans as well as in various international contexts. The CWD course has been described as "by far the best studied psychoeducational intervention for the treatment and prevention of depression" (Cuijpers et al., 2009, p. 522). It has a level of efficacy similar to other evidence-based therapies for depression, and several prevention studies have indicated it may reduce the likelihood of future depression.

In addition to the behavioral model of depression seen in the CWD course, other behavioral treatments have been developed and evaluated. Lejuez and colleagues (2001) developed a brief behavioral activation treatment for depression (BATD). This model focuses explicitly on the behavioral aspects of depression; it includes training in activity monitoring, the selection and enaction of activities designed to be antidepressant, and a contract with oneself and/or others to maintain behavioral plans. The model can be delivered in either individual or group format and usually involves weekly sessions over a 10-week period. Based on a 20-year review of the BATD program, Lejuez et al.(2011) developed a revised manual (BAT-R).

A model similar to the BATD and BAT-R can be seen in the work of N. S. Jacobson, Martell, and their associates (Jacobson et al., 2001; Martell et al., 2001, 2010). This approach grew from a component analysis of CBT (Jacobson et al., 1996) that suggested an approach based on behavioral principles and focused on providing overall structure in life, activity scheduling, identifying avoidance (and then working against avoidance), and enacting values-based behavior was effective in treating depression. The behavioral activation (BA) model of depression that emerged was originally delivered as an individual form of psychotherapy based on a client-specific model of the client's avoidant patterns and a strategy to overcome avoidance through activity scheduling, but it has also been delivered in a group format. A version of BA for adolescents has also been developed (Pass et al., 2015).

Although the specific behavioral models and therapies for depression described earlier have their unique aspects, they share several elements. Chief among these aspects is the need to monitor one's activity and then to purposefully plan and enact behaviors that are antidepressant. The choice and nature of these behaviors can be highly variable. Some may be chosen because they have a positive hedonic value, that is, they feel good (e.g., relaxation, bubble baths), whereas others may increase physical activity (e.g., walks, exercise), overcome avoidance (e.g., talking to a family member about a common stressor), or move the client in the direction of some value or goal (e.g., attending church, beginning night classes). From a theoretical perspective, it is not the nature of the behavior itself that matters but its function in the client's life and whether or not it is viewed as inconsistent with being depressed. Behavioral theorists also recognize that some clients may need help to implement their desired actions, and so skills training is often incorporated into the behavioral therapies, particularly with regard to common issues such as assertion or social interaction.

COGNITIVE THEORY AND COGNITIVE BEHAVIOR THERAPY

A third psychological model of depression that emerged in the late 1970s was the cognitive model (A. T. Beck, Rush, et al., 1979). This model emphasized the importance of the environment, the thoughts and appraisals a person who is depressed makes about their experiences, and the beliefs that underpinned these appraisals. This approach is primarily associated with the fundamental work of Aaron Beck and his associates in the United States—the approach Beck called "cognitive therapy"—and in particular a clinical trial that pitted cognitive therapy against pharmacotherapy in the treatment of outpatient clinical depression. This trial revealed approximately equal depression outcomes (Rush et al., 1977, 1978), which was exciting in its day. The publication of the treatment manual (A. T. Beck, Rush, et al., 1979) enabled clinicians to understand, replicate, and use this model broadly. The treatment was also used in the landmark NIMH-sponsored trial of CBT, IPT, and pharmacotherapy (Elkin et al., 1989), described earlier, which showed that CBT had roughly comparable effects to other treatments.

In part because of its relatively early development in the field, its success in research trials, and a clear and comprehensive treatment manual, cognitive therapy—and more generally CBT—has been extensively disseminated and evaluated. As Cuijpers et al. (2013) concluded, "There is no doubt that CBT is an effective treatment for adult depression" (p. 376), and in this sense it is unsurprising that CBT is now the essential intervention for depression globally (David et al., 2018). Reviews also note, however, that the effects are not as strong as they sometimes appear because of publication bias, and in some of the more extensive comparisons done between CBT and other therapies such as BA and IPT the differences are minimal to nonexistent.

An expanded CBT model has been developed over time (A T. Beck & Bredemeier, 2016), incorporating several risk factors related to depression such as genetic risk and negative early life experience. Its central components are the set of core beliefs that individuals develop and maintain and the ways that these beliefs interact with various life events and stressors to generate idiosyncratic and negative thinking in depression, which in turn yields negative affect and behavior. A 50-year review of the model (Hollon et al., 2021) indicated that while CBT for depression has limited claim to superiority over other well-developed treatments for depression in the short term and has comparable effects to the most recent pharmacotherapies for depression, it has a clear preventive benefit relative to continued antidepressant medications in the long term. Thus, CBT appears to be more beneficial for depression than are other therapies, based on current evidence.

In part because of its success, elements of CBT have been incorporated into other models of treatment. One clear example is the cognitive behavioral analysis system of psychotherapy (CBASP; McCullough, 2003), a model that integrates cognitive behavioral principles as well as techniques derived from interpersonal psychotherapy and applies them to individuals with chronic depression. CBASP uses a variety of interventions, including *situational analysis,* within which the momentary decisions that individuals make in their environment are reviewed to identify problematic ways of thinking about situations as well as problematic behavioral patterns. Further, the model includes an interpersonal discrimination exercise in which the client is provided education and training to recognize different interpersonal challenges and to respond optimally. As necessary, the CBASP program also includes behavioral skill training and in-session rehearsal of difficult interpersonal situations to maximize the likelihood that the client will have success in their day-to-day lives. As this brief description suggests, several elements of cognitive, behavioral, and interpersonal theories of psychotherapy are woven into the intervention model, but it is specifically targeted toward individuals who have perhaps not responded adequately to pharmacotherapy or other treatments for depression. Evaluations of the treatment model, including a meta-analysis (Negt et al., 2016), suggest that CBASP has a significant therapeutic advantage relative to both treatment as usual and interpersonal therapy and comparable efficacy to continued antidepressant medication. Given these results, this specific model of training appears to have merit for people with chronic depression.

Given the large amount of data from studies of CBT for depression, its comprehensive framework, and its efficacy in helping people who struggle with depression, this model forms the backbone of the interventions presented throughout this volume. However, this model alone is insufficient to manage the broad variability in the presentation of clinical depression. As such, interventions that derive from other perspectives are woven into the treatment recommendations found in the next section. These treatments could be described as a biopsychosocially informed version of CBT.

TREATMENTS FOR SPECIFIC ASPECTS OF DEPRESSION

As described earlier, it is now well established that at least three psychological treatments for people with major depression are well developed and evidence-based: interpersonal therapy, behavioral activation therapy, and cognitive behavior therapy. Each model emphasizes risk factors that contribute to the onset and maintenance of depression and then builds these risk factors into corresponding intervention strategies. It is important to note, however, that a variety of other treatment models have been developed for depression. The sections that follow present some of the treatments developed for specific aspects of depression or using a particular conceptual focus.

However, a couple of points are warranted. First, from my perspective, the three interventions I have discussed are the only comprehensive, evidence-based psychosocial approaches to depression in general. There certainly are other claims for antidepressant treatments. For example, various vitamins, supplements, natural food products (e.g., Omega-3 fatty acids) and other dietary approaches are claimed to prevent or treat depression, and evidence suggests that certain dietary patterns are associated with better mental health (e.g., Brookie et al., 2018; Jacka et al., 2010). It has been further suggested that multinutrients can serve as a treatment for depression (Kaplan & Rucklidge, 2021). At this time, however, although I fully subscribe to the idea of a healthy and balanced diet, I believe it is not clear that the evidence is strong enough to make a specific dietary recommendation with respect to depression.

The second point is that while the following models and interventions have supportive data, in my view, none constitutes a stand-alone treatment for depression in general. For example, while helping a person with depression overcome insomnia can have enormous benefit, especially if a primary symptom is related to sleep disturbance, we cannot assume that this intervention will have equal benefit for all cases. Thus, the following interventions need to be used either in concert with other treatments or when a client presents with specific problems.

CBT for Insomnia

Many individuals with clinical depression have sleep disturbance and, as discussed in Chapters 1 and 2, sleep disturbance itself is a symptom included in the diagnostic framework for clinical depression. Sleep disturbance is one of the paradoxical symptoms of depression, in that some people experience a decrease in sleep, whereas others feel tired and sleep more than usual. Although different individuals with depression have different symptom patterns, the most typical presentation is that clients who present with high levels of anxiety or are in transition from a state primarily involving anxiety have reduced sleep. This pattern can occur for some people when they go to bed and find that their minds are active, which interferes with sleep onset. Others may wake up in the middle of the night and begin to worry or ruminate about issues; for some, this pattern occurs in the early morning and prevents them from returning to sleep. These individuals often report fatigue and daytime tiredness and may nap during the daytime to compensate for loss of nighttime sleep, which unfortunately may have the consequence of disturbing the next night's sleep. In other clients, typically those who present with severe anhedonia (i.e., the inability to experience pleasure), the sleep pattern may involve increased fatigue, tiredness, and sleep in excess of what is normally required.

Some early researchers made a distinction between what they called "primary insomnia," or sleep disturbance that emerges in its own right, and insomnia that is typically a consequence of other mental and physical health problems (Nowell et al., 1997). Insomnia may in fact occur more frequently in the presence of anxiety disorders than in people with major depression (Ohayon, 1997), but it can be a sign or symptom of depression as well. Insomnia in the context of depression can be a highly distressing experience, and for some clients it contributes to a cycle of fatigue, inactivity, demoralization and self-recrimination, and sleep disturbance.

Interventions for insomnia have been well developed and evaluated for some time. Early efforts primarily emphasized what is now referred to as sleep hygiene (e.g., having regular bedtime rituals, ensuring the sleep environment is quiet and conducive to sleep, not ingesting caffeine or other stimulants in the later afternoon or evening), and there is little doubt that these interventions have a salutary effect on sleep. They are not recommended as a stand-alone treatment, however, as their effects are relatively modest compared to other developed interventions (Carney & Posner, 2016). The use of cognitive behavior therapy for insomnia (CBT-I) is highly recommended for clients who are depressed and experience significant sleep disturbance, and, for some clients, this intervention forms an essential aspect of the overall treatment plan. This application is described further in Chapter 7.

Exercise and Depression

In much the same way that sleep disturbance can form a critical precursor and vulnerability for depression in some individuals, inactivity and lethargy can be a critical and disturbing symptom for others. Just as in sleep, cycle motor activity levels are a paradoxical symptom of major depression, as some people become agitated and have excessive tremulousness or other behavioral signs of anxiety, whereas others have reduced activity. The pattern of reduced activity is more typically associated with increased levels of anhedonia and more severe depression, but when present, reduced activity may make it difficult for the person to engage in activities. These individuals might also engage in increased sleep.

Similar to the treatments for insomnia, intervention programs have been used for clients with low levels of activity and increased lethargy (Josefsson et al., 2014; Krogh et al., 2012). These studies vary in the type of exercise that is recommended, the amount of supervision provided, and the comparison conditions, so the literature is somewhat complicated. This said, a meta-analysis of the literature (Kvam et al., 2016) concluded that physical exercise, and in particular aerobic exercise (recommended at three times per week), has a moderate to large effect on depression compared to control conditions, although this effect was significantly attenuated at follow-up. Studies that directly compared aerobic exercise to antidepressant medication found that the overall comparison was not significant, suggesting that aerobic exercise has effects as large as medications. However, studies in which exercise was used as an adjunct to pharmacotherapy showed a moderate increase in the overall effectiveness of treatment. These results suggest that aerobic exercise has an important role either as a treatment alone or as an intervention that can be used in concert with other interventions.

It was noted earlier that behavioral activation strategies that attempt to increase antidepressant behavior can significantly reduce levels of depression. It also appears that exercise in its own right has benefits on mood, as well as physical fitness and possibly mortality (Murri et al., 2019). As seen in Chapter 6, incorporating aerobic exercise in the treatment plan is recommended for clients with depression who experience behavioral inactivity and who wish to engage in an exercise routine.

Mindfulness-Based CBT Approaches

A major innovation in the treatment of depression was the incorporation of mindfulness exercises in the acute treatment of clients, followed by development of a stand-alone intervention, mindfulness-based cognitive therapy (MBCT; Teasdale et al., 2000). It had been known for some time that rumination is often associated with depression, and rumination by individuals with depression often has a self-critical bent. Based on research with individuals who had recurrent depression, Teasdale (1988) developed a *differential activation model of depressive metacognition*, suggesting that, particularly for people with recurrent depression, not only are direct negative thoughts a risk factor for depression onset and maintenance but the inferences about these thoughts also predict whether or not someone will be susceptible to depression. The differential activation hypothesis suggests that these metacognitions explain recurrent depression (Teasdale et al., 2002).

Based on the differential activation hypothesis, Teasdale and colleagues (2000) adapted methods from Buddhist philosophy and practice, integrating the idea that one can be aware of negative experience and be fully attentive and mindful in the moment but not necessarily have a secondary response to this experience (e.g., the negative metacognitions associated with recurrent depression). They then adapted and integrated the practice of mindfulness into MBCT, an eight-session group-based intervention. The trials of MBCT indicated that the approach was significantly associated with reduced risk of relapse and recurrence, and the effects appeared to be particularly strong for participants with chronic depression, operationally defined as three or more previous episodes. MBCT was written into a treatment manual (Segal et al., 2013) and has an accompanying client workbook (Teasdale et al., 2014).

Since its development, MBCT has been used to prevent relapse in patients with depression and has been extended as a model for acute treatment of depression, specifically to address risk for depression in populations of older adults and for individuals with both mixed anxiety and depression (Strauss et al., 2014). A review of the benefits of MBCT suggested that although the model had been expanded, the strongest evidence for the approach remained as a relapse prophylaxis for depression (Segal & Walsh, 2016). Based on another meta-analysis, Y. Y. Wang et al. (2018) reported that across 11 randomized trials using MBCT in the treatment of acute depression, the short-term benefits were moderate and significant but the benefits disappeared by the end of follow-up analysis. In yet another recent meta-analysis that examined the effects of MBCT on depression in older adults, Reangsing and colleagues (2021) reported that the intervention was associated with moderate benefits on depression compared to control conditions; the effects were particularly strong for Asian participants, brief interventions, and interventions that included guided meditation exercises. On balance, it appears that MBCT and related mindfulness meditation interventions can be a valuable adjunct to other treatments for major depression, and they likely have significant benefit in lowering the risk of relapse for participants who were depressed but have recovered.

Process-Based CBT

A relatively recent innovation in the field of cognitive and behavioral therapies is known as process-based CBT (Hayes & Hofmann, 2018). This model is highly consistent with the approach taken in the current book, although it speaks to the broader field of CBT. In essence, what the authors of process-based CBT suggest is that evidence-based processes incorporate both models of risk and models of intervention that can be discerned and then applied broadly within the field of psychotherapy. Their work suggests that the range of models and interventions include behavioral, cognitive, emotion regulation, interpersonal, and cultural/value-oriented factors.

While process-based CBT, at least as formulated by Hayes and Hofmann (2018), takes a broad perspective on the field of CBT and psychotherapy, the current volume is focused on the clinical problem of depression. As such, not all of the interventions emphasized in a comprehensive process-based approach are relevant. Further, as noted earlier in this book, the emphasis here is to connect the recommended interventions as much as possible to these specific risk factors for depression. Thus, while the models presented in this chapter and those within the process-based CBT perspective are compatible, they are not identical.

STRENGTHS AND LIMITATIONS OF EMPIRICALLY SUPPORTED TREATMENTS

A relatively recent emphasis in the field of mental health has been the promotion of evidence-based therapies. Although the concept of requiring evidence to support clinical practice is not at all innovative in medicine in general, the idea that outcomes can be reliably and validly measured in the field of mental health, and that these outcomes should be the basis of clinical practice, has certainly been more contentious. This issue has been somewhat compounded by the fact that much of the research that examines the outcomes related to psychotherapy uses *diagnostically related groups* (basically, using the *Diagnostic and Statistical Manual of Mental Disorders* [*DSM*] or *International Classification of Diseases* [*ICD*] diagnostic criteria to define inclusion criteria for the groups who are provided treatment). In this regard, it has been suggested that connecting treatment methods to diagnosis is problematic and potentially reinforces a medical model in the field of mental health.

No doubt the criticisms associated with using diagnosis as a way to classify individuals and then provide treatment have merit. As noted in Chapter 1, clinical depression presents with many different symptom patterns. People with depression also vary in the chronicity of their condition, the severity, and other potential comorbid problems. As such, the idea that a single monolithic therapy is going to work for all people with depression is misguided at best. One potential development for the future is the application of case-dependent interventions, based on the particular signs and symptoms of a presenting client, and a sufficient evidence base to know the optimal interventions for different client presentations. Such a development is some years in the future.

Currently, many treatment studies suggest that our developed treatments have benefit, as reviewed in this chapter. We are therefore in a somewhat challenging circumstance in that we have treatments that "work," but since they are tied to a single diagnosis, they do not reflect the diversity of individuals with depression and therefore likely do not have the optimal outcomes that are possible. My argument is that while we should use the best approaches that we have, and in particular those with the optimal evidence supporting their efficacy, we need to expand our models to take into account the high degree of variability in the presentation of depression seen in the clinic. In essence, we need to take what is learned in nomothetic or group-based research, as is done in psychotherapy research, and integrate this knowledge with the idiographic or individualized application of what we have learned from psychotherapy research.

Summarizing the content of this chapter is not easy, as I have reviewed multiple perspectives on the treatment of depression. We are at a point in the field where we can state with confidence that some therapies for depression are effective, including interpersonal therapy, behavioral therapy, and cognitive behavior therapy. Further, we have a number of interventions and approaches that can be used to supplement or work in tandem with the evidence-based therapies, including CBT for insomnia, healthy eating, aerobic exercise, and mindfulness and meditative practices. At the same time, the large majority of the data that inform us about effective therapies comes from group research. As discussed in Chapter 1, however, depression can present itself in multiple different ways, even differently within the same client over time. As a consequence, while the evidence-based therapies are an excellent starting point to conceptualize depression and provide interventions, the nuances require that the therapist pay attention to each individual client's characteristics.

Much has been written about the importance of case conceptualization within psychotherapy (Kuyken et al., 2009; Persons, 2008; Zubernis & Snyder, 2016), and this perspective is also embraced here. It is always important to conduct an assessment of the client with whom you are working, to understand their unique needs and desires, to determine attainable targets of intervention, to select those techniques that have the highest likelihood of success, and to implement the selected interventions in a skillful manner, all while maximizing the collaboration between therapist and client. This set of activities requires a trained and skillful therapist, someone who has the flexibility to work with a range of presentations and client needs. I also note that as the literature on moderators and mediators of depression continues to grow, it remains important to stay up to date with recent developments in the field.

Chapter 4 addresses some of the issues involved in conducting an intake assessment and some major considerations when first interacting with a client who struggles with depression. Indeed, from this point forward, this volume is much less theoretical and much more practical. Generally, Part II of this book details considerations in the intake process, assessment, and case conceptualization. Following this discussion, the book shifts to interventions that are evidence based and/or conceptually sound.

CASE ILLUSTRATIONS OF TREATMENT MODELS IN CASE FORMULATION

The case examples of Michael and Miranda show how the various treatment models in this chapter can be used to understand an individual's experiences with depression.[1]

The Case of Michael

Michael's difficulties can be conceptualized in several different ways. One treatment model that could be applied is the biomedical approach, which would focus on his physiological symptoms and emphasize the importance of pharmacotherapy to counteract his sleep disturbance, appetite, and negative cognitions. A behavioral activation approach could be adopted, in which the focus would be on his activities, sleep habits, and behaviors and on increasing the range of pleasurable activities that Michael might experience. It also could help him approach rather than avoid difficult situations. The behavioral approach might also be indicated if further assessment indicates that Michael has some social skills deficits, which in part could explain why he has limited social contacts. A cognitive intervention might focus on Michael's excessive focus on career success and independence and on patterns such as his avoidance at work out of the fear that others may perceive him to be in some way failing or inadequate. Acceptance and commitment therapy could be used to examine the values that Michael exhibits and the extent to which his current activities reflect these values. Given that he apparently wishes to be in an intimate relationship, for example, the therapist could help him to explore whether his current patterns of interaction are helping to meet that goal. Finally, an interpersonal focus in this case could focus on interpersonal deficits and skills training that may be of benefit as well as the potential for role transition as Michael begins to imagine his shift from active employment to retirement.

Indeed, even a relatively straightforward case presentation like Michael's can be viewed from multiple perspectives. It is likely that any of the previously described models of therapy could be applied to Michael, and likely with roughly equal levels of success, although the outcome of any given therapy cannot be known in advance of its delivery. As argued in this volume, however, what may be ideal for Michael is an individually focused set of interventions that target his presenting problems and depressive symptomatology.

---

[1]All cases presented in this book are fictitious and represent illustrations drawn from my experience but not from any specific person.

The Case of Miranda

Miranda's experiences with her depressive episodes have been variously conceptualized. Her first experience with depression appears to have been precipitated by a negative relationship when she was 19 years old that led to a deep sense of personal confusion. On the one hand she was appropriately angry toward her partner for being unfaithful, but she also experienced deep embarrassment and shame that she had not anticipated or recognized his behavior. She recalled having some growing suspicions that all was not well in the relationship but did not speak up or take action as she doubted herself. Her patterns of rumination and self-recrimination were associated with her isolation and withdrawal. She was not seen by a health professional at that time and was not formally diagnosed with clinical depression, although it seems clear on review that she met diagnostic criteria for major depression for approximately 2 months. It was largely the pressure from her family, coupled with her own sense of a need to move on in her life, that led her eventually to become reengaged in the world, seek further training opportunities, and come out of her depressive shell.

Miranda's second and third episodes of depression were recognized and diagnosed relatively quickly. Part of this recognition was due to Miranda's prior experience and awareness of the signs and symptoms of depression as well as her ongoing care from health professionals throughout her pregnancy and after the birth of her daughters. Further, she was able to speak openly about issues such as sleep disturbance, which is a fairly common issue for young mothers and was recognized by her attending physician as potentially diagnostic of depression. Her family physician prescribed antidepressant medication quickly, which resulted in some relief of her symptoms. Her supportive counseling sessions after the birth of her second child also reinforced for Miranda the importance of self-care, in particular managing her diet and sleep.

While her major depressive episode resolved relatively quickly with intervention, her residual symptoms of worry, rumination, and withdrawal were never addressed in treatment; she also completed treatment with lingering and occasional sleep disturbance. Finally, relationship issues with her partner were never addressed in the treatment process. Although she was pleased with the remission from depression, Miranda wonders whether other issues might remain unexamined. Consequently, now that her daughters are in school, she has decided to resume therapy as she continues to feel unhappy and worried.

II

BEGINNING THERAPY AND TREATMENT PLANNING

4

The Intake Assessment

Developing a Case-Specific Treatment Model

Although it may sound somewhat counterintuitive, the best time to start conducting an intake assessment is before the client arrives at your office door. You should have any necessary materials available to conduct a proper and fulsome assessment as well as supplementary materials that you may need to refer to, depending on what you learn. This chapter covers some critical considerations necessary to prepare for and conduct an assessment with a client who presents with depression. The topics in this chapter help to provide a solid framework for beginning to work with a new client. Chapter 4 includes additional issues that arise early in the therapeutic interactions and is followed by additional chapters that present some critical evidence-based interventions that may be applied with a given client.

BEFORE THE CLIENT COMES IN

This book was written with the understanding that a variety of different health professionals might read it and that they may live in a different legal system than the one in which it was written (Canada). As such, some legal and ethical considerations presented in this chapter, and this volume more generally, may or may not apply to the setting in which you work. It is incumbent upon you to know your local standards and to determine which issues need to be respected and which may be ignored.

https://doi.org/10.1037/0000398-005
Clinical Depression: An Individualized, Biopsychosocial Approach to Assessment and Treatment,
by K. S. Dobson

Most regulated health professions maintain that a client's fully informed consent is necessary before any health service is provided. This process of informed consent applies both to the assessment of an individual and to the delivery of actual interventions. The best practice when working with any new client, therefore, is to have a short mental script in mind, to describe the process of informed consent, and to obtain it. Often, the first moments of the interaction involve the therapist welcoming the client, asking them how they would like to be referred to, providing their own preferred name for the client to use, and introducing the idea that the relationship is secure and confidential, up to the limits of the legal system in which the client is being seen.

For professionals in Canada (where I live), some of the legal limits of confidentiality include reports of credible child abuse or neglect, a court order to release documents based on some legal requirement, a need for the health professional to defend themselves against action from the client, and, of key relevance to clients with depression, an imminent risk of harm to the client or identifiable others. Put otherwise, if the client reveals that they are at imminent risk of self-injury or death by suicide, the health care professional has a legal requirement to take action to protect the client against themselves. This action can include working with the client to ensure that they get an assessment at a potential inpatient facility and might include informing the police so that the client can be taken to a facility for assessment. It is critical that you know the regulations that apply where you live and advise your clients of these legal limits before they even begin to discuss their problems, so that the client can choose what information to share with you.

A further consideration with respect to informed consent is the purpose of the relationship. The intake interview does not always end in a contract for therapy. Some cases are not well suited to treatment, some people are not at the interview of their own volition, and others you may choose not to see for your own reasons. As such, my recommendation is that you make a first agreement to undertake an assessment, after which both you and the client can determine whether or not to proceed to the treatment phase.

It is also notable that verbal consent to undertake an assessment is sufficient in some jurisdictions, whereas written informed consent is required in others. In jurisdictions in which an informed consent document is required, it is critical that you have this document available for completion with the client. It is also important that you determine whether the person is in a legal position to give consent. Competence to provide consent is generally assumed for adults, and some jurisdictions allow mature minors (i.e., people under the legal age of adulthood) to provide informed consent. However, in some extreme cases of depression the individual may not be able to provide informed consent, and in such cases you may need to identify an alternative person to provide consent. In the end, informed consent must come from someone who is competent and in a legal position to provide that consent.

Assuming that consent is asked for and obtained directly from the client or indirectly from another legally responsible person, the assessment can move along. In my practice, the next activity is typically to ask the client to complete intake questionnaires. As discussed later, many measures are available to assess depression and related constructs (Dozois et al., 2020; Nezu et al., 2000). As a clinician, you need to determine which tools best suit your practice and clientele, and you need to have these materials available and at hand.

Once you have obtained informed consent and have completed the assessment tools that your practice requires, it is worthwhile to review the assessment results with the client. My bias is always to include a standard depression measure in the assessment package, of the types that you intend to repeat if therapy goes ahead. Other secondary measures may be taken and repeated from time to time as the client's needs unfold. Should the assessment indicate a risk of self-injury or suicidal behavior, you will want to have a suicide assessment tool available to conduct a formal assessment of suicidal thoughts and impulses. You likely should also have available the form required in your jurisdiction for the release of information because you may want to request the client's permission to contact significant others if there is a suicidal crisis.

In summary, a prepared clinician comes to the first interview with a range of materials and possible interventions. Particularly when clients present with severe and chronic depression, issues of hopelessness may well arise. As such, you need to be ready to meet the client in a respectful but forthright manner, to ask critical questions, and to take decisive action if indicated. Assuming that all goes well, the initial appointment can typically proceed to an intake assessment interview.

MEASURING DEPRESSION AND CHANGE

As noted earlier, there are a large number of established questionnaires and other measures of depression (Antony & Barlow, 2020; K. S. Dobson & Scherrer, 2007; Hunsley & Mash, 2018; Nezu et al., 2000). These measures can be conceptualized as either self-report tools or measures based on interviews. Hundreds of self-report questionnaires exist—some are generic and ask about the broad construct of depression, whereas others focus on specific aspects of the symptomatology, and yet others have been developed or revised from other questionnaires to focus on specific age groups or populations.

Nezu et al. (2000) produced an excellent resource for any clinician to consider the wide range of depression instruments. This book lists not only 36 measures of depression but also 16 depression scales for specific populations (e.g., children, geriatric groups) and 42 constructs that are related to depression (e.g., measures of cognition, problem-solving skills, negative life events). Each measure is described briefly, and references are provided. A summary table is also provided, which lists translated versions of the scales and the languages. The major drawback with this resource is that it is dated and unfortunately has not been updated.

Dozois et al. (2020) reviewed a wide range of depression measures. The researchers noted that more than 280 measures of the severity of depression exist and highlight and summarize major assessment tools that have strong psychometric data, including 17 self-report scales. These scales range in length from 5 to 76 items and have formats that include yes/no; true/false; and 3-, 4-, and 5-point response formats. The estimated time for completion ranges from 2 to 25 minutes.

Given this enormous range of considerations, how does one select a measure for clinical use? My recommendation is both academic and pragmatic. For many years my own preference was the Beck Depression Inventory (BDI-II; A. T. Beck et al., 1988, 1996). In part, this preference was based on what was current and common when I learned my practice. In part, this preference was based on the facts that the scale was updated from its earlier version and has strong psychometric properties. Further, the scale provides a good range of responses, as each item is scored 0 to 3 and the potential range of total scores is 0 to 63. Approximate cutoffs have been established to indicate a transition from likely having a diagnosable major depression to being below the threshold for a likely diagnosis. The scale also includes items about a range of experiences that clients with depression may have, and so it is possible to focus on these specific items, when indicated, in intervention. For example, the BDI-II asks about self-denigration and has several items about the psychological experience of depression, so it can help to direct interventions in this direction. Finally, the BDI-II has two items related to hopelessness and suicidality (Item 2 and Item 9) that the therapist can monitor without needing to spend much time in the interview session. This quick monitoring allows the therapist to identify changes from session to session that can be explored further when indicated.

More recently, I have adopted the Patient Health Questionnaire-9 (PHQ-9; Kroenke et al., 2001; Kroenke & Spitzer, 2002) as my instrument of choice in therapy. The PHQ-9 (see Figure 4.1) has strong psychometric properties. Each item is scored from 0 to 3, resulting in an overall score ranging from 0 to 27, which allows the therapist to monitor progress in therapy. The items of the PHQ-9 are directly reflective of the diagnostic criteria in the *Diagnostic and Statistical Manual of Mental Health Disorders* (*DSM-5*; American Psychiatric Association, 2013), and an algorithm is provided to approximate a diagnosis of major depression. Although the scale is not a substitute for a formal diagnostic interview, the PHQ-9 can be used to ascertain if and when the client likely transitions from depressed to nondepressed status. Indeed, the sensitivity of PHQ-9 scores relative to a diagnosis is good, as is the scale's specificity to depression (A. J. Mitchell et al., 2016). The questionnaire includes an item related to suicidality, which can be monitored for change or further inquiry if indicated. Further, the scale can be administered and scored more quickly than longer alternatives. Of some importance, the scale is in the public domain and does not involve a user fee. Finally, the PHQ-9 has been translated successfully into multiple languages and so can be used broadly.

In addition to the BDI-II and PHQ-9, which are both for general assessment of depression, a variety of other tools exist. Some are useful for clients who present with concomitant anxiety and depression, as they include items in

FIGURE 4.1. The Patient Health Questionnaire-9

Over the last 2 weeks, how often have you been bothered by any of the following problems?

	Not at all	Several days	More than half the days	Nearly every day
1. Little interest or pleasure in doing things				
2. Feeling down, depressed, or hopeless				
3. Trouble falling or staying asleep, or sleeping too much				
4. Feeling tired or having little energy				
5. Poor appetite or overeating				
6. Feeling bad about yourself—or that you are a failure or have let yourself or your family down				
7. Trouble concentrating on things, such as reading the newspaper or watching television				
8. Moving or speaking so slowly that other people could have noticed? Or the opposite—being so fidgety or restless that you have been moving around a lot more than usual				
9. Thoughts that you would be better off dead or of hurting yourself in some way				

If you checked off any problems, how difficult have these problems made it for you to do your work, take care of things at home, or get along with other people?

Not difficult at all	Somewhat difficult	Very difficult	Extremely difficult
☐	☐	☐	☐

Note. Developed by Drs. Robert L. Spitzer, Janet B. W. Williams, Kurt Kroenke, and colleagues, with an educational grant from Pfizer Inc. No permission required to reproduce, translate, display, or distribute.

both domains (e.g., P. F. Lovibond & Lovibond, 1995; S. H. Lovibond & Lovibond, 1995; McNair et al., 1992). Should anxiety emerge as a clear comorbid problem, however, it is important to note that specific scales can be used to measure different dimensions of anxiety and different anxiety disorders (e.g., Ashbaugh et al., 2020; Campbell-Sills & Brown, 2020; Morissette et al., 2020). Further, if a clinician works in a clinic in which other clinical diagnoses or problems might present, it is recommended to have scales to measure these other issues as well (see Antony & Barlow, 2020). Finally, it is notable that depression may present somewhat differently in some populations. For example, the Geriatric Depression Scale (Yesavage et al., 1982) was developed with a focus on symptoms of depression that are particularly acute in geriatric samples, and it has been used to assess individuals with late-life depression (McKenzie & Harvath, 2016). Thus, while the focus in this book is on clinical depression in the general population, the savvy clinician will have a supply of appropriate measures for their specific contexts.

Interview-based measures also exist. A very commonly used scale is the Hamilton Rating Scale for Depression (HRSD; Hamilton, 1960, 1967). The HRSD has been a mainstay in psychiatric research and has the virtue of being a clinician-administered tool, so it minimizes the risk that clients might either underreport or overreport their symptoms. It is also a relatively long scale (23 items originally, although shorter forms exist) that provides a score with considerable range. The HRSD requires clinician training and takes about 10 to 15 minutes to administer, so it is not useful for ongoing clinical work; rather, it is recommended for intake assessments that require more rigor, or possibly for assessment in clinical trials, as it has become a kind of benchmark for newer trails. Revised and somewhat shorter versions of the HRSD have good psychometric properties (Kobak & Reynolds, 1999), and the HRSD correlates highly with self-report measures of depression. Problems with the reliability of interviewers and concerns about possible overemphasis on the somatic features of depression have led to a reduction in this scale's use (see Dozois et al., 2020, for a discussion).

There is also a formalized semistructured interview to assess and diagnose major depression. The Structured Clinical Interview for *DSM-5* (SCID-5; First et al., 2015) is a comprehensive system to create diagnoses for all *DSM-5* diagnostic categories, including the group of mood disorders (i.e., manic disorders, bipolar disorders, and the various subtypes of mood disturbance). The SCID-5 has an exhaustive Research Version, a streamlined Research Version that focuses on more common diagnoses, and a Clinician Version that emphasizes disorders most often seen in clinical practice. The SCID-5 must be administered by a trained clinician who knows the decision rules built into the *DSM* and the SCID-5 manual and can skillfully and efficiently move through the interview, as it can otherwise be very laborious. Completion of the entire Clinician Version of the SCID-5 takes between 30 and 120 minutes, depending on the positive indications the client provides that require further exploration. Unless a formal diagnosis or differential diagnosis is needed for insurance, agency, administrative, or legal purposes, it is not recommended to use the SCID-5 in regular clinical practice. That said, it is worthwhile to know the diagnostic criteria for major depressive disorder implicitly, as well as the most common subtypes of depressive disorder and the most common comorbid diagnoses, so that questions can be formulated during the intake interview to see if these diagnoses require consideration instead of or in addition to major depressive disorder.

SUICIDE ASSESSMENT

Suicidal thinking and actions are not uncommon aspects of the presentation of a person who is struggling with depression. Different health professionals may have different legal requirements when a client presents with suicidality. For example, physicians and psychiatrists may have the legal authority to involuntarily hospitalize a client and so have a duty of care to protect the client from themself. In contrast, a social worker may have a duty to help the client get to an assessment by a physician or psychiatrist, but nothing more. These types of duties exist only in countries and jurisdictions in which a mental health law requires such intervention; it is possible that no defined duty of care exists in places without such legislation. Clinicians who work with depression need to know their local legal framework and the duty of care they may be held to in the event of a client's injury or death.

Regardless of the legal duty of care, it is a tragedy if an individual gets to the point of despair and hopelessness that they see no option but their own death. The hopelessness model of suicide (Abramson et al., 2007) posits that the major psychological determinant of suicidal thinking and behavior is hopelessness, the perceived need for escape from an intractable problem and the absence of alternatives. Hopelessness has been studied extensively as a risk factor for suicidality and has been shown to be a strong predictor even up to 20 years into the future (G. K. Brown et al., 2000). Critical aspects of clinical work with clients who have suicidal thinking are understanding the problem(s) they face, their past efforts to remediate the problem(s), how they have come to adopt the belief in hopelessness, and the changes they perceive as essential to continue with their life.

Although hopelessness is a major psychological factor in the prediction of suicide, many other sociodemographic risk factors have also been studied. In one large international study of 21 countries (Borges et al., 2010), the 12-month prevalence estimates for suicidal ideation, plans, and attempts were reported as 2.0%, 0.6%, and 0.3% in developed countries and 2.1%, 0.7% and 0.4% in developing countries, respectively. These rates were not significantly different as a function of the nature of the country (developing or developed) and suggest rates of suicidal behaviors in the general population in the range of 0.3 to 0.4%. This low base rate makes suicide prediction very difficult, as events with low base rates often lead to their overprediction. In addition, events with low levels of occurrence (i.e., low base rates) are simply difficult to predict accurately. In the Borges et al. (2010) study, risk factors for increased suicidality were comparable across settings and included female gender, lower age, lower education and income, unmarried status, unemployment, parental psychopathology, adverse childhood experiences, and the presence of one of several mental disorders, including depression. Multiple other studies have examined risk factors (e.g., Nock et al., 2009; World Health Organization, 2014) as researchers attempt to integrate the research into a polysynthetic model of risk and resilience (see Joiner, 2005, for an excellent example).

In an effort to summarize what is known about risk, Turecki and Brent (2016) proposed that risk can be conceptualized at the population, individual, and environmental levels. Population risk factors include rapid social change, economic turmoil, and social isolation. Environmental factors include media reports (and possible contagion effects), access to methods for self-injury or death, and poor access to mental health care. Individual-level risk factors are complex and include distal or predisposing factors (e.g., family history, early adverse experiences), developmental or mediating factors (e.g., memory or problem-solving deficits; personality variables such as introversion, anxiety, and substance use), and proximal or precipitating factors (e.g., acute substance misuse, recent life events, hopelessness). Turecki and Brent proposed that suicide has "aetiological heterogeneity" (p. 1236) and, most important for the current purpose, concluded that the variability in risk factors at the individual level make it "difficult to provide an all-encompassing model of suicide risk or to suggest a clear treatment formula" (p. 1236).

An interesting study with a similar conclusion to that of Turecki and Brent (2016) attempted to discern the effect of psychosocial intervention on suicide rates by comparing the rates of death by suicide in trials that included standard care to the rates in trials with an additional active treatment (Crawford et al., 2007). Data from 18 clinical trials were obtained from a total of 3,918 treated participants. The authors reported that the rates of suicide were not significantly different between the two groups, with an overall suicide rate of 0.94% across both groups. This rate—less than 1%—was in samples that by definition had one of the major recognized risk factors for suicide, but as the authors noted, the relatively low rate of suicidal behavior makes it a very difficult phenomenon to study or to influence. In addition, suicidality often has a temporal aspect, in that the desire to die may become stronger for a period of time and then wane. It can be difficult to know precisely when a client is at the point at which they are at most risk to themselves.

Models of suicide risk have continued to evolve. One important model is the ideation to action model (Klonsky et al., 2016), which posits that although the risk factors for suicidal ideation may be similar to what is often cited (e.g., the presence of a mental disorder, depression, hopelessness, impulsivity, a history of self-injury), the risk factors for suicidal behavior include posttraumatic stress disorder, access to lethal methods, knowledge of the use of the lethal means, impulsivity, and a history of self-injury. Klonsky et al. recommended the use of evidence-based clinical assessment when a client presents with suicidal ideation, and they reviewed a series of published suicide measures, including both interview and self-report scales (see also Dexter-Mazza & Korslund, 2007). In particular, they suggested that the Scale for Suicidal Ideation (A. T. Beck, Rush, et al., 1979) and the Columbia-Suicide Severity Rating Scale (C-SSRS; Posner et al., 2008, 2011) have predictive validity. These measures are both interview-based. Self-report measures to consider include the Beck Hopelessness Scale (A. T. Beck et al., 1974) and the Adult Suicide Ideation Questionnaire (Reynolds, 1991), although Klonsky et al. (2016) also suggested that a single suicide item (Item 9 from the Beck Depression Inventory-II) has strong predictive value.

As a clinician, you may wonder how to assimilate all the information about suicide risk into a practical clinical skill. The best advice is to know the common risk factors for suicidal ideation and behavior and be ready to ask about them when hopelessness and/or suicidal ideation appear. I suggest you also differentiate between factors that are related to intent and those that are related to lethality. Exhibit 4.1 provides a sample of the types of questions that can be used in these two dimensions; I strongly urge you to first ask the questions related to intent. Once you ask these questions, pause and formulate an opinion about the strength of the client's intent for self-injury or suicide. You should also have some sense of what would need to change to reduce the perceived hopelessness of the client or to solve their problem(s). Having formulated this estimate of intent, ask the questions about lethality and again formulate an overall opinion about the imminent risk to the client. My suggestion to consider intent first is that therapists also become anxious, and it is quite possible that if you hear a strong expression of lethality from a client, you may overestimate their intent and take steps that are not indicated (and potentially harmful to your client's well-being or status among family, friends, or community).

EXHIBIT 4.1

Dimensions to Assess Related to Suicide Intent and Lethality

Intent

1. How strong is your desire to die right now?
2. How strong is your desire to live right now?
3. When you balance your desire to die and desire to live, which is stronger, or are they equal?
4. What factor(s) help to explain your desire to die (e.g., unsolved, hopeless problems)?
5. What factor(s) help to explain your desire to live, or might work against dying (e.g., family, stigma, insurance, fear of pain)?
6. How often do you think about dying? How long do these periods last?
7. When you think about dying, what is your response (positive, negative, or neutral)?
8. What would have to change to make life worth living?

Lethality

1. Do you have an intended method to die?
2. Do you have access to this method now?
3. Do you believe you have the ability to actually use this method?
4. Are you certain of the outcome if you use this method?
5. Have you made any plans for your death (e.g., returning borrowed items, apologizing for past wrongs, making a suicide plan, writing a suicide note, organizing your schedule not to be disturbed, not to be found)?
6. Have you previously attempted to injure or kill yourself?
7. Has anyone in your family died by suicide? Who?
8. Do you currently use alcohol or other substances that would affect your self-control?

This assessment has two primary goals. First and most urgently, you want to develop an overall estimate of the imminent risk to the client (low, medium, high) and to take the steps indicated where you live to protect the client from themselves. Once you ask the questions and formulate an opinion, you are professionally (and legally) responsible for the actions you either take or fail to take. As noted previously, your obligations depend on where you live and your professional role, and thus you need to know your local laws and regulations so that you can follow them. Also, you should know about local resources, agencies, and facilities that can be enlisted as supports. These supports can include 24-hour telephone emergency lines, engaging friends and family, emergency room assessments, and calling the police, as indicated.

Second, you should end the assessment with a better understanding of the client's view of themselves and their world and of why they believe that death is the "solution" to their problems. Ideally, you will have also gathered information about protective factors, things that you can help the client with to mitigate or reduce their intent and overall risk, so you can engage them therapeutically with regard to the problems in their lives. The development of a written safety plan that the client can refer to if their suicidality should increase is recommended (Stanley & Brown, 2012). The optimal long-term way to reduce suicidality is to help the client manage or resolve the issues that led them to that condition in the first instance. You should offer more than reassurance; meaningful engagement with the presenting problems is the preferred strategy.

Just a few last notes about suicide assessment. First, suicidality is not a static entity. Clients can become more or less committed to self-injury or death as therapy proceeds. Ideally, as their depression wanes and their life problems are solved, any sense of hopelessness will diminish, and risk will decrease. Be aware, however, that setbacks in treatment can lead to a sudden rise in risk, so be prepared to ask about suicidality in any session. If you work in a setting in which clients receive medication for depression as well as psychological intervention, it is possible that their energy level will improve before their life problems have been solved, and a period of increased risk may ensue. Second, while clients who harbor an intent to self-injury are much more likely to harm themselves than to harm others, in some cases a client may make a plan to injure or kill others as part of their suicide plan. It is important to retain a broad perspective with regard to possible risk so that you can protect yourself, others in the setting in which you work, and others in the client's life. Third, if you work in a profession and/or jurisdiction with professional and/or legal consequences for actions you take or do not take, be sure to formalize your assessment as much as you can and certainly keep a written record of the assessment and the opinions you have formed and the steps you took, completed as soon as possible after the client has left your office or the opportunity presents itself. If you work with a client who expresses hopelessness and/or the desire to die, be ready to reassess this topic regularly at the beginning of treatment, occasionally as the treatment evolves, and as indicated at any time. You should be prepared to stop whatever else you may be working on to do a suicide assessment. It is good practice to inquire in this area near the beginning of a session, rather than at what you think may be the session's end, in case a fulsome assessment and possible intervention is needed. Finally, be mindful that working with clients who talk about ending their lives can be stressful. Such discussions can create existential questions for you and can lead to clinician distress, particularly if a client engages in self-harm or suicidal action. Be sure to monitor your own wellness, and take steps to care for yourself and to provide optimal care to all clients.

THE INTAKE INTERVIEW

Many styles of clinical interviews exist (Hersen & Thomas, 2007), and there is no broad consensus on the optimal intake interview to use when working with clients who experience depression. A broad distinction between structured and unstructured interviews exists in the field, with the former more typically focused on the collection of standardized information (e.g., the SCID-5) but the latter more flexible and oriented toward interviews that can take different directions. Structured interviews typically provide a sense of comfort and direction to both the therapist and the client but run the risk of missing information that is not part of the interview. In contrast, unstructured interviews have the virtues of being flexible and responsive to the client's current concerns but run the risk of missing critical interview information because it is not emphasized by either the client or therapist.

My bias is that the intake interview should incorporate both structured and unstructured elements. Having completed the informed consent and whatever intake questionnaires are used, I typically make some kind of a statement such as "Now that we have the more formal parts of our first meeting completed, I want to hear from you in your own words what kinds of problems you have that have brought you here today." This type of statement signals to the client a shift in focus and a willingness to attend to their concerns. My intention is to have a 5- to 10-minute interaction in which the client names a set of problems or issues, to which I respond with a series of open-ended questions to clarify aspects of each problem. This interaction ends once the client indicates that they have listed all of their major initial concerns.

The Beginning Phase: Understanding the Client's Main Issues and Goals

In my experience, the unstructured part of the intake interview often begins with the client saying that a primary reason for coming to the appointment is that they are struggling with depression. This indication provides a perfect opportunity to explore the signs and symptoms that the client is currently experiencing. If a depression questionnaire such as the PHQ-9 has been administered before the interview, you can refer to it to identify symptoms that the client may have indicated. Ideally, a therapist knows the diagnostic criteria for major depressive disorder implicitly and can ask about possible symptoms, even if the client does not initially indicate which symptoms they are experiencing.

It is also important to assess the duration of the various depressive symptoms as well as any symptoms that are of most concern to the client. For example, a client may meet the diagnostic criteria for major depression but clearly signal that sleep disturbance is their primary concern. This type of information can be very useful during later discussion of the problems to focus on first in treatment. Further, as regards the assessment of symptomatology, it is critical to recall that major depression is often comorbid with other problems. Commonly co-occurring conditions include anxiety disorders, substance use disorders, eating disorders, posttraumatic stress disorder, and a variety of physical health disorders, including chronic pain, fibromyalgia, cancer, and physical injury. An effective therapist must be ready to assess these varied areas and in particular to determine whether the depressive disorder is primary or potentially secondary and subsequent to another mental or physical disorder.

If the client does not begin the unstructured interview by naming the problem of depression, my bias is to follow their lead and simply inquire about the concern(s) that they have named. For example, if the client suggests that they are having interpersonal problems with their partner, I might ask the name of the partner, the living situation, details about the problems, how often they occur, how severe the problems are (potentially assessing for risk and/or indication of domestic or partner violence), and how critical each problem is in the overall picture of the client's life. The therapist's role in this unstructured interview is to listen to the client, reflect the content and affect of what the client has said, and repeat back to the client in their own words what they have heard. Each topic likely should take no more than 2 or 3 minutes, at which point the inquiry can shift to other potential problems.

The intake interview continues until the client has named all the issues they want to initially present to the therapist. The client may selectively decide not to report issues they consider shameful or that might have legal consequences, and they be uncertain whether they have sufficient confidence in the therapeutic relationship to disclose. If important, these issues typically come back during future appointments, and an assessment can take place at that time. In some cases, the intake process can be relatively quick, as when a client has only one or two major presenting issues, whereas in other cases this process may take 10 minutes or more. The interviewer has the responsibility to move the dialogue along and not to get bogged down in any one area too quickly; by the end of this phase of the interview, the therapist and client generally share a broad picture. My preference for the conclusion of this portion of the interview is to make a statement such as "Well you've told me quite a bit about some of the issues you're facing, and I can certainly understand why you've come to see me. Just so I am clear, it seems as if your primary problems are . . ., and the main issue(s) you think would be helpful for us to address is/are. . . . Is that a fair summary?" If the client concurs with the summary, the intake interview moves along to the next phase. The client may want to provide clarification or nuance to the summary and may add other problems to the list in later sessions. A good supplemental question is "Is there anything that I have missed or that you would like to add?"

Some models of therapy suggest that a certain range of potential problems should always be probed. In her excellent book on case conceptualization in cognitive behavior therapy, Persons (2008) recommended the assessment of signs and symptoms of mental health problems, physical health, social and interpersonal problems, economic issues, and legal problems, among others. My position is that the clinician needs to anticipate that problems may occur in any area but not to specifically probe for problems in domains such as legal issues, for example, unless the client raises these areas themself.

The Middle Phase: Understanding the Client's History

Once the problems are named and some of the issues related to the severity and chronicity of the problems are understood, the interview typically shifts to understanding the client's history. My approach to this shift is to say something to the client such as "Now that I understand some of the problems you're facing, I would like to know a bit about your background. If it is OK with you, I would like to ask about your childhood and upbringing so I can better understand where some of these problems may have come from. Some of the questions I ask will be not relevant to you, but I ask these questions of everyone. Is it okay if we change directions just a little bit and let me ask you some specific questions?" I have yet to have a client demur, and so typically the interview shifts to a somewhat fast-paced, closed-ended set of questions. Again, the structure of this part of the interview can vary from client to client, but in general the questions follow the client's life span, with a brief set of probes if some potentially important issue emerges during the inquiry. Typical content can be seen in Exhibit 4.2; the interview more or less follows the life trajectory of the client. The focus is on gathering a lot of superficial information as efficiently as possible and tracking both the ups and the downs of the

---

EXHIBIT 4.2

Proposed Structure of the Middle Part of the Intake Interview

1. Date and location of birth
2. Client's number of siblings (if any) and birth order
3. Any prenatal developmental issues
4. Birthing problems
5. Early development (e.g., meeting developmental milestones, major illness)
6. Early social life, potential childhood adversity, parental or caregiver issues
7. Age of entry to school, adjustment to schooling (social and academic life)
8. Childhood changes (e.g., moving, changing schools)
9. Ending of grade school/potential postsecondary education
10. Adjustment to increased independence/early adulthood
11. Social life (including romantic and sexual relationships)
12. Completion of postsecondary education/entry into workforce
13. Potential romantic relationships/marriage/children (number/health, if present)
14. Major issues in adulthood (e.g., moves, illness, successes, losses)

---

client's general life patterns. It is particularly important to listen for life events that could make the client vulnerable to depression, such as parental or caregiver separation, social rejection, major illness, or perceived failure. Sometimes the client will say that during a particular time of life they experienced their first episode of depression, and so it is useful to make a mental note of this time for further inquiry.

The Final Phase: Contextualizing the Client's Problems Within Their History

A difficult but essential skill for an effective therapist is to listen to the client's history and begin to conceptualize the dynamic interplay between biological, psychological, and social factors that have culminated in their presenting problems. Often the client will have hypotheses about these issues, and these ideas are important to assess and understand. The therapist has to forfeit their own preconceived ideas about what might be the "worst" problem and attempt to view the issues from the client's perspective. Cultural, historical, and personal issues all influence the way the client sees their concerns, and to "join" with the client, the therapist needs to see the world as much as possible from behind their eyes. As such, it is critical to finish the intake assessment interview with two further steps. The first is to understand the presenting problem(s) in context. Once the history is completed, it is good practice to say something like "You have given me lots of good information about your past. I realize this is still pretty limited, and no doubt I will learn more about you as we continue to work together. I wonder, though, if we can go back and understand when your problems began. When would you say you first experienced depression?" This question may then precipitate an inquiry about the circumstances surrounding the first episode and lead to a preliminary understanding of the risk factors at play for this particular client. Having spent some time on this episode, it is worthwhile to ask how the episode ended (assuming it did) and whether or not any treatments were used. Strategies that were successful in the past often recommend themselves for reuse.

Depending on the age of the client and their history of depression, it may be necessary to repeat the process of inquiry about different episodes and how they began, their course, and their end. It is important during this inquiry to look for similarities among the different episodes, as the patterns may provide hints about the psychological makeup of the client and their responses to different psychosocial risk factors. Indeed, if a very clear theme emerges, it may be possible to generate a preliminary case conceptualization about the core beliefs the client holds and that interact with various life circumstances to eventuate in depressive episodes.

It is important while reviewing the client's history of depression to watch for variability. For example, it is not unusual to have a first episode of depression associated with a major life event, whereas recurrent depression often has less dramatic external factors involved and more of an internalized process, perhaps also including dysfunctional behavioral patterns such as avoidance or disturbed sleep patterns. It is essential to spend some time on the current episode of depression to understand its consistency and divergence with previous episodes of depression, major issues associated with the onset or maintenance of the depressive episode, and key problems that the client associates with the depression. As a therapist, continue to look for both short-term potential points of intervention and some patterns that may be incorporated into therapy in the long term.

Asking the Client About Their Self-Perception

One last exercise that I find helpful in beginning to develop a case conceptualization is to ask the client the three adjectives that they believe best describes them (see also D. Dobson & K. S. Dobson, 2017). This question is often introduced with a statement such as "I begin to see now a little bit about your background, and maybe even some of why you developed depression in the past. It certainly seems as if you are struggling with a number of current problems that could be helped by treatment. I have one last question to ask you, though, which is if I knew nothing about you, not even what you have told me today, how would you describe yourself? You can use any terms or adjectives you think that are appropriate; I am just interested in your own self view." I usually look for at least three terms but am happy to hear more if they come to the client's mind.

This question is asked with the goal of contrasting the client's self-perceptions against what the clinician has already learned through the first interview. Often, the terms that the client uses resonate with the history that they have provided and the beginning case conceptualization. In such cases, it is possible to build on this shared understanding with statements such as "Yes, that is kind of what I have been picking up about you. It seems that both your early experiences and your more recent depressions have left you holding certain views of yourself that make it difficult to change." Such statements show empathy and understanding and help to build a therapeutic alliance. Be attentive, however, if you hear self-descriptions that are at odds with your emerging understanding of the client. In such cases you may even express surprise and ask the client to explain where these other aspects of their sense of self come from. This information is part of the client's self-concept, and so it needs to be recognized and understood to develop a complete case conceptualization.

DEVELOPING A CASE CONCEPTUALIZATION

This chapter has already made reference several times to *case conceptualization*. Case conceptualization is, at its heart, the model that the clinician develops for the client. This model includes the manner in which their biopsychosocial history has led them to be vulnerable to depression or the other life problems they face, the way they have come to think about themselves and their relationship to the world, and the potential strategies that might be deployed to help them to a better future. The case conceptualization is something that both clinician and client share and that evolves as more information comes to light and as both parties develop what becomes an increasingly mutual understanding of the nature of the problems, their genesis and maintenance, and potential resolution.

The nature of the case conceptualization has been written about extensively, most often from a therapeutic orientation (J. S. Beck, 2021; Brand-de Wilde & Arntz, 2019; McWilliams, 1999; Persons, 2008). Theory-driven case conceptualization is a fundamental aspect of working with all clients, as the theory provides a conceptual framework to understand and treat the client's problems. As may be discerned in this volume, however, models have their strengths and their limitations. The adopted model directs the clinician's attention in certain directions and consequentially blinds them to others.

The case conceptualization of clients who present with depression is discussed in other chapters (in particular, Chapter 5), along with the implications of this framework for intervention. The process of case conceptualization begins with the first interaction with the client and continues through the final sessions. For example, observing the client's demeanor in how they greet you, how and where they sit, their openness or closeness in the first responses to your introduction, and the amount of detail they provide in their description of their problems are all sources of information that provide hints about the way they interact with new people in their environment. As a clinician, you will no doubt be paying attention to both the verbal and the nonverbal aspects of interactions with the client, as both sources of information can provide hints about the way the client views themselves and their approach to life. As you interact more with the client and gather content-related information, the case conceptualization may grow dramatically, but it is always important to recognize new information when you hear it so you can elaborate on your understanding and conceptual model of the client. In this regard, it is also critical to note that although it is useful to attend to material consistent with your developing case conceptualization, you especially need to note and inquire about things the client tells you or ways in which they behave that are not consistent with your developing model. These incongruent sources of information often compel a modification to the case conceptualization. It is also important to ask specifically about the client's strengths and resources. Clients who have faced depression often have used their best efforts to address this problem, and understanding their perception of the resources they have and how they can use them can be very instructive, especially when planning interventions.

DECIDING TO PROCEED WITH TREATMENT

A critical outcome of the intake interview is the decision to proceed with treatment or not. Most often, a client who has presented themself for assessment and who has willingly completed the questionnaires, informed consent process, and interview will be an amenable and appropriate person to engage in treatment. Unfortunately, in some instances the assessment leads the clinician to either a definitive or a probable conclusion that treatment should not proceed. This conclusion is a judgment call, one that is not easy to express to a client. Again, a planful clinician will have a list of other resources to which the client can be referred if the decision is not to proceed to treatment.

Some issues that may emerge during the assessment process that either alone or in combination might lead you to decide not to proceed include the following:

- A client is unwilling or unable to participate in therapy. It may be that their level of depression is so profound they cannot engage in sufficient action or dialogue to engage in the treatment process. In this type of case, it may be that inpatient treatment is required before psychotherapy begins.

- A client presents for assessment but is not engaged in the process. Such clients may be compelled to an initial appointment by family members or because of a requirement from a work setting, but they may not be invested in the process of change.

- A client's conceptual model of their own depression is not conducive to psychotherapy. For example, a client may have a strong belief in the biological model of depression and primarily believe that medications will help them to recover. Such clients can be referred for psychoactive medication.

- A client has responded adequately to a different treatment model in the past. For example, if you are primarily going to conduct interventions from a cognitive behavioral perspective but the client has previously had a very positive response to a different treatment model (e.g., emotion-focused therapy; Greenberg & Watson, 2006), it makes great conceptual sense to try to find a treatment option for the client that matches their previous success. In this circumstance, even if you might be successful in the treatment you provide, it is probably simply more efficient for them to return to a previously successful model of treatment.

- A client has significant interpersonal tension. It may be that the client has a value system or personal history the therapist finds morally unacceptable. For example, a client with a history that includes being convicted for pedophilia may be someone the therapist chooses not to work with. The therapist needs to be honest with themself and their client and to declare that this issue will get in the way of treatment. Conversely, it is possible the client perceives aspects of the way you talk or aspects of your values as unacceptable. You should ideally be receptive to this type of rejection and be ready to offer a list of alternative care providers or services to the client.

- Limited resources or other pragmatic considerations may work against the initiation of treatment. Clinical trials of psychotherapy for depression suggest that treatment often will last in the range of 16 to 20 sessions (Cuijpers et al., 2013, 2023). The specific length of treatment for a given case is in part dictated by the clinical response of a given client to treatment, and so resource considerations also need to be made. For example, if the client is paying directly for treatment in a private setting, the cost may be prohibitive. Treatment may be impractical if the client lives a long distance from the clinician's office, particularly if the client has a risk of suicidality. In these instances, you can work with the client to find more affordable and convenient options.

Assuming that the decision is made not to refer the client to other services but instead to begin treatment, my perspective is that it is best to undertake a modified consent process for treatment. This process ideally includes a description about the general approach to treatment, a preliminary estimate of the schedule and number of sessions that may be required, the cost implications of the treatment plan (if any), and the client's willingness to engage in the treatment process. As is discussed in Part III of this book, effective treatment of depression requires that the client not only attend treatment sessions and participate in discussions there but also translate the work of the session into action between appointments. Part of the informed consent for treatment necessitates that the client is aware of this obligation and they are at least tacitly willing to accept this responsibility. The client also needs to understand that part of an evidence-based approach to treatment is the need for recurrent measurement of the process of treatment as well as its outcomes. Thus, the client should recognize that they will be asked to complete various forms and questionnaires as the treatment proceeds.

Another part of the informed consent for treatment ideally includes the opportunity for the client to ask questions. Although you may not be able to provide all details of the treatment because the case conceptualization will develop and the client's response to different interventions cannot be fully predicted, you should do your best to give as complete information as possible. Ideally, the procedural details of the treatment are interspersed with supportive and encouraging statements. Although it is certainly not recommended to provide a guarantee to the client that treatment will be of benefit, you can engage the client with references to either the empirical literature on evidence-based treatments for depression or to your own experience with similar clients. It is useful to have materials available so that the interested client can read about effective treatment for depression and the forms that it may take (e.g., Academy of Cognitive and Behavioral Therapies, n.d.; Association for Behavioral and Cognitive Therapies, n.d.). Indeed, many organizations have created web-based information that can be provided to the client or printed for a client who does not have access to the internet.

Assuming that the client's presenting problems and depression are not too complicated or atypical, a sufficient intake assessment can often be undertaken in a single appointment. Some clinicians may purposely plan a longer initial appointment to ensure they can complete the process. It may be necessary to spread the intake across two appointments if a client has a particularly complicated presentation. The judgments are related to the nature of your work setting or practice, the issues the client presents with, and the opportunity to conduct a somewhat longer and more intensive intake process.

It is helpful to have the client leave the first appointment with an assignment (see J. S. Beck, 2021; D. Dobson & K. S. Dobson, 2017). This assignment helps the client to appreciate the idea that work goes on between appointments. It fosters a sense that the therapist wants to move ahead quickly, and it serves as a gauge of the client's willingness and ability to engage in the treatment process. The nature of the assignment varies somewhat from client to client, but some possible suggestions include the following:

- Ask the client to read information about the evidence base for the intended treatment, either on the internet or in printed form. If this assignment is given, begin the next session by asking what the client was able to read and what they took away from this reading. This discussion can often lead into a motivational interview, as described in Chapter 5.

- Request that the client think more about their current life problems. In some cases, a client has difficulty articulating the stressful events they're facing or elaborating on their problem list. In such cases, it can be helpful to provide a written list of these issues from the intake interview for the client to take home to elaborate. This assignment can lead to a further discussion about the client's problems in the subsequent session and help to orient the treatment to the major pressing problem(s).

- Ask that the client begin an activity log to record information about their typical daytime activities (see Chapter 7). Many clients who struggle with depression report that one of their problems is getting going; some say they have disturbances in their normal, nondepressed behavioral patterns. It takes a bit of time to explain this assignment to the client, so it is best used with clients whose problem lists are relatively straightforward and in cases in which it seems highly likely that changes in behavioral patterns will be part of the treatment plan.

- Ask the client to keep a record of their sleep patterns. Some clients who are depressed present with a strong sense of sleep disturbance, and it may be obvious from the first appointment that sleep will be part of the treatment plan. As with the activity log, it takes a bit of time to explain a sleep log to the client and to get them to record their sleep reliably. As such, assigning a sleep log at the end of an intake interview is relatively uncommon; it is typically used when it is clear that sleep is the dominant presenting problem.

Overall, what you do with the information gathered during the intake process and interview will vary dramatically from case to case, depending on the presentation of depression, the major problem(s) the client presents, the client's urgency to address their concerns, the initial case conceptualization, the immediately available resources for intervention, and other pragmatic considerations. Sometimes it is helpful not to do anything right away but rather to devote some time to reflect on what you have heard; you may then come back to the next appointment with an initial plan. Another important consideration in the planning of treatment is the interaction between the therapist and client itself. Given the importance of this relationship, this topic is the focus of Chapter 5.

CASE ILLUSTRATIONS OF THE INTAKE PROCESS

This continuation of the cases of Michael and Miranda focuses on the initial intake sessions and demonstrates the ways in which their therapists used the processes and guidelines outlined in this chapter.[1]

The Case of Michael

Michael's physician, Dr. Norton, had recognized his index case of depression and was able to prescribe an antidepressant medication to help with some presenting symptoms, and she recognized on a repeat visit that Michael's depression also included psychosocial aspects. Consequently, Dr. Norton referred Michael to a community clinic in the neighborhood. Michael somewhat reluctantly accepted the referral and attended what he considered to be a single consultation session approximately 3 weeks later.

On arrival at the clinic, Michael was seated in a moderately large waiting room with several other clients. He was given a demographic form to complete and after a short time was invited into a consultation office with Dr. Paula Mason, who he was told was a psychologist at the clinic. Dr. Mason took Michael into an interview room that had no personal materials and was used by different clinicians at different times. She and Michael sat down opposite each other, with a table in between. Dr. Mason began the appointment by explaining that the relationship was considered confidential according to the limits of the law, and she outlined the limits to confidentiality. She then asked Michael to say in his own words why he was at the appointment. In response, Michael indicated that he had been referred by his family physician for depression and that he was already on antidepressant medication. He indicated that he was feeling somewhat better than previously but still had some questions for himself, including ongoing problems with sleep, appetite, and weight; a sense of social isolation; and a vague wonderment about his future and retirement.

Following the discussion about presenting problems, Dr. Mason asked a series of questions about the various signs and symptoms of clinical depression. She focused on Michael's report of a sense of dread and low-level hopelessness and asked several questions about risk for suicide, which Michael denied. She then conducted a relatively brief history and congratulated Michael on his career success. At the end of this interview, which took about 45 minutes, she suggested that Michael would benefit from a course of

---

[1]All cases presented in this book are fictitious and represent illustrations drawn from my experience but not from any specific person.

interpersonal therapy (IPT), which she offered to provide. She briefly outlined that the focus would be on helping Michael to function better in his life, to focus on relationships, and to begin to think about his future transition to potential retirement. Dr. Mason suggested that the initial course of therapy would take approximately 12 sessions, although this estimation could be revisited as they went along. She also noted that as she was employed at the public health clinic, no fee for the treatment would be charged to Michael.

After consideration, Michael agreed to begin the process of therapy. Based on this decision, he was asked to sign two forms. The Consent for Treatment form indicated that Michael agreed to begin treatment for up to 12 sessions. It also noted the limits to confidentiality Dr. Mason had spoken about earlier in the appointment and the fact that no fee would be charged. Toward the bottom of the form was some legal information about storage of records, which Michael largely did not read before signing the document. Dr. Mason indicated that the second form, Release of Information, gave her and the clinic permission to communicate with Dr. Norton, first, that Michael had agreed to begin treatment and, second, about the progress made over the course of treatment.

The Case of Miranda

Miranda continued to experience occasional sleep disturbance after remission from her third episode of major depression. She noted a tendency toward poor eating practices, including an increased use of carbohydrates and a modestly increased use of alcohol. She was not losing weight as quickly as she had hoped but found it difficult to schedule time for exercise between her job and the two children, both of whom were in school. Her relationship with her husband Jules was positive but not terribly satisfying. They had some friends whom they saw occasionally, but between their own child-rearing demands, financial pressures, and her residual fatigue, they were not as engaged in social activities as might have been ideal. When alone, Miranda often found herself worrying about current issues and ruminating about her own depression and past experiences from time to time. She was aware that her occasional use of sleeping medications likely signaled an ongoing problem. While she perceived that she had improved since the third episode of depression, she had asked her family physician for a referral to a clinical psychologist because she was dissatisfied with her current state.

While she was waiting to see the psychologist at the first appointment, Miranda was given a printed copy of an informed consent document, two questionnaires about her symptoms (the GAD-7 and PHQ-9), and a brief set of questions about what she viewed as her primary concerns and her reason for coming for the initial assessment. At the appointed time, Dr. Josefina Morales welcomed Miranda into her office. The office was somewhat small, with a desk and chair in one corner, a small couch with a coffee table in front of it, and a matching side chair. The office decor was pleasant and neutral with several floral print pictures, a small grouping of diplomas and certificates, fresh flowers and tissues on the coffee table, and a few personal items on the desk. Dr. Morales directed Miranda to the couch and sat on the side chair with a notepad in hand. She began the session by ensuring that Miranda understood the issue of and the limits to confidentiality, as well as the financial arrangement that the appointments were to be paid by her husband's insurance.

Dr. Morales showed Miranda how she would score the two questionnaires and revealed that the score of 6 on the GAD-7 suggested a moderate but not significant level of anxiety, whereas the score of 13 on the PHQ-9 suggested that Miranda may be experiencing more depression than anxiety. They had a brief discussion about the symptoms that Miranda had reported, and Miranda generally agreed that the scores reflected her current functioning. Dr. Morales quickly noticed that the item on the PHQ-9 related to suicide was not elevated, which Miranda agreed was accurate.

The discussion turned to the list of problems that Miranda had identified on the information sheet. The problems focused on sleep and fatigue, appetite and weight, a low sense of motivation, concerns about the strength of the marital relationship, and a general sense of lack of purpose. Miranda was able to give a good summary of the history of her depressive episodes, including her treatments, and indicated a desire not to use medication in the future but rather to improve her coping strategies to manage periods when she felt low. She suggested that she and Jules were not currently planning to have more children and that given her age and history of perinatal depression she thought it was probably not well advised. When asked about the most pressing concern, Miranda suggested that it was probably the combination of fatigue and low sense of motivation, coupled with sleep disturbance. She thought that if she were able to become more active her appetite and weight would likely become less of an issue and that with increased activity, she would restore her sense of purpose. When queried, however, Miranda was not able to say what direction she might want her life to take, except in a vague sense to restore its previous level of functioning.

Having identified current problems and the client's major concern, Dr. Morales shifted the focus of the appointment and undertook an extensive history. At the end of the history, she asked Miranda for three adjectives that she thought described herself, to which Miranda responded, after some thought, "tired," "lonely," and "unmotivated." Dr. Morales reflected that these terms generally fit with her developing understanding of Miranda, although she was somewhat surprised that Miranda felt a strong enough sense of loneliness to put it amongst the three terms. In response, Miranda suggested that she was generally satisfied in her family and work life but wanted something more challenging and intense, as her life had become somewhat "boring." She also longed for more friendships and social connections beyond her family but reported that she lacked the time, energy, and opportunity to pursue them.

Based on this information, Dr. Morales proposed that she and Miranda begin work in the areas of energy, activity, and sleep but noted that they would no doubt also want to discuss issues related to motivation, life interests, and social relationships somewhat later. Miranda agreed that this would be a reasonable place to start, and Dr. Morales asked her to keep a record of her daily activities and a detailed sleep log. At the end of the appointment, Dr. Morales requested feedback about the interview. Miranda expressed some optimism about the treatment, regret that she had not come sooner, and a general positive feeling about Dr. Morales and her approach. In return, Dr. Morales expressed confidence in the treatment and said that she thought it would likely be helpful and that Miranda had the skills to benefit from it. On this basis, they agreed to schedule a follow-up appointment to begin treatment.

5

Optimizing Client Engagement in Treatment

As noted in Chapter 4, both the client and the therapist come to the initial appointment with some preconceived notions. You as the therapist bring general knowledge about depression, your theoretical training, and personal history with clients. You also bring along your disposition, general attitude toward life, and whatever current concerns or distractions may be active in your life. This background hopefully results in a therapist with the skills, training, experience, and personal demeanor to be helpful.

In a reciprocal manner, the client brings their background, personality, and knowledge about themselves into treatment. They have some level of self-understanding, and they certainly know what they have tried in the past to manage their depression. Some may have received treatment previously, and this experience will likely have either increased or decreased their desire for further treatment. For example, if they are seeing you because their past therapy experience did not work out, they may approach you and your treatment with skepticism. For that reason, it is important to inquire about past efforts at either self-management or formal treatment for depression in the intake process. You may find that some clients come to treatment with little to no information about what to expect; others may have received information from a family physician or other service provider or guidance from family members and friends. Some may have read about models of and treatments for depression on the internet, in a library, or in a book.

https://doi.org/10.1037/0000398-006

Clinical Depression: An Individualized, Biopsychosocial Approach to Assessment and Treatment, by K. S. Dobson

Various combinations of these experiences, from both the therapist and the client perspectives, can contribute to or detract from positive engagement and treatment. This chapter presents a number of the key considerations to optimize positive client engagement. I consider many of these factors to be modifiable, in that the therapist can monitor and adapt their own behavior. Many are things that the client will not necessarily be aware of, but you as a therapist need to be acutely attentive to them. Many of these issues are considered *nonspecific therapy effects* (Grencavage & Norcross, 1990; Huibers & Cuijpers, 2015; Oei & Shuttlewood, 1996; Wampold, 2001), as they are not connected to a particular theoretical model but are important contributors to outcome for all forms of treatment. Put otherwise, the context in which therapy skills are delivered is critical to the outcomes that are achieved. The factors discussed in this chapter are therefore essential but not sufficient for overall treatment success.

PSYCHOEDUCATION

As noted previously, clients come to therapy with their own models of understanding and formal and/or informal education about depression. Evidence suggests that matching treatment paradigms for the therapist and the client is part of a positive therapeutic alliance (Castonguay & Beutler, 2005; Karpiak & Norcross, 2022) and that a positive therapeutic alliance in turn predicts positive outcomes for clients who present with depression (Klein et al., 2003; Shirk et al., 2008). It is therefore important to assess the client's way of thinking about their depression at the beginning of treatment, educate the client about recent research and models of depression, inform the client about why specific methods or interventions are proposed as treatment moves along, and generally ensure that the client understands the rationale and strategy for treatment. In general, when a teachable moment arrives in therapy, it is useful to ask the client briefly about their understanding of the issue and then to support or improve the client's response if it is generally accurate or to correct it in an affirmative manner if not. Ideally, express confidence in your opinion but avoid being overwhelming or didactic from the client's perspective. If necessary (e.g., if the client expresses doubt about the information or guidance you provide), incorporate other resources, including materials from the internet, books and chapters, or other sources into the information. Gathering novel information about an issue could even serve as a between-session assignment if it is well suited to the stage of therapy and the client shows interest. Once the information is presented, however, it is highly advised to ask the client to restate their understanding of the issue to ensure that the information has been received and that you and the client are indeed on the same page.

Psychoeducation can often be built into treatment planning. In general, when introducing a new intervention, it is worthwhile to briefly articulate what the intervention is, what benefits it might provide, and some aspects of the mechanics or implementation of the intervention. It might even be helpful to name the intervention or give it a shorthand title, in particular if it is going to be commonly used in a given treatment, so that you and the client develop your own way of talking about the key interventions. Sometimes, the client might express a strong positive or negative reaction based on the description of an intervention and its implementation. If the response is positive, you and your client can work together to optimize its use and refine it in such a way that it has maximal benefit. Alternatively, if the response is negative, you need to stop and understand the reaction and then discern whether to proceed with the proposed idea, to modify it in some fashion, to have the client propose an alternative strategy that might achieve a similar end, or to fully back up and try something different. As a therapist, be mindful that not all clients are receptive to all forms of information or assistance.

INSTILLING HOPE AND POSITIVE EXPECTANCIES FOR CHANGE

An important role of the therapist in treatment for depression is to instill hope, to generally encourage the client to feel that their efforts will be rewarded with reduced depression and an improved quality of life. The nature of depression itself can involve negative experiences, decreased motivation, reduced activity, and helplessness and hopelessness, so it is critical to pay attention to the client's levels of hope and optimism and to address these issues directly if they are found wanting. Pliny the Elder, the Roman author, philosopher, and military leader, is quoted as saying "Hope is the pillar that holds up the world," and there is wisdom in this statement. Much of what is done in treatment is to build on the hope for a brighter tomorrow and to promote confidence that our efforts will yield a positive outcome.

Clients typically come to therapy with some sense of hope or optimism, but clients with depression perhaps less so than other clients. Given this issue, it is important to assess your client's general level of belief in change and their optimism about and confidence to engage each assignment used in treatment. Capitalize on change that is viewed in a positive and hopeful manner by the client but temper this perspective with a sense of realism. The work done in therapy should be presented in a positive manner, with a sense of assurance that you are willing to work with the client on their problems but not with a guarantee of success. One way to express this optimism is to collaborate with the client on solving what they view as their major issues. A sound general principle is "worst first"—that is, you and the client begin to address the major issue from their first-session problem list as the focus of treatment. Even within each session, I encourage you first to target the major issue, behavioral problem, or negative thought that the client presents. This "worst first" orientation communicates to the client that you have the skills to work on these issues and, assuming some degree of success, it is likely to achieve rapid and strong treatment response. Often, solving a larger problem can generalize to smaller important issues.

One caveat, and the encouragement to pursue the worst problem first, is to be realistic in your approach. For example, if a client's depression is in part driven by the loss of a major relationship (because of, say, infidelity) and the relationship appears to have no chance for reconciliation, it would not be strategic to foster the client's hope for recovery of the relationship. In such a case, it may be possible to join with the client about their desire for intimacy and the development of a caring relationship, but a persistent focus on a specific lost relationship is likely to be discouraging. In a similar manner, although you want to encourage the client in their efforts to work on problems, outlandish or excessive statements of support or cheerleading are likely to be perceived as insincere or artificial by clients in general and certainly by those who have depression as a presenting problem. In my experience, clients with depression suffer, and they know they are suffering, so overly hopeful or positive statements not only may be unhelpful but also may erode an otherwise positive and fruitful relationship.

MOTIVATIONAL INTERVIEWING

A therapeutic relationship issue that has received considerable attention is motivation. Intuitively, motivation refers to the desire and commitment to make changes, but it has been recognized for some time that this factor is sometimes elusive in behavior change. Early theorizing in the area of addictive behaviors made a distinction among individuals at the precontemplative, contemplative, preparation, action, and maintenance stages of change (Velicer et al., 1995). These stages of change helped to explain whether clients with addiction problems would begin the process of reduced use or abstinence of the substance(s) they used. This framework to understand behavior change attracted considerable theoretical and research attention (Hettema et al., 2005). W. R. Miller (1983) developed a model of motivational interviewing for people with alcohol problems, and the combination of a theoretical model of change and this style of motivational interviewing expanded into a formal model of change promotion that has since been expanded and used in a variety of health care areas that involve a commitment to behavior change (Frey & Hall, 2021; W. R. Miller & Rollnick, 2013; W. R. Miller & Rose, 2009; Wood, 2020).

In its current form, motivational interviewing (MI) rests on several assumptions and a set of core techniques. The assumptions are often summarized with the acronym OARS (openness, affirming, reflection, and summarizing), which refers to the idea that the clinician using MI will demonstrate several methods:

- Openness: The clinician will be open to understanding the client from their perspective, and as such they will use more open-ended questions in the interaction to enable the client to use their own way to express themselves.

- Affirming: Even while the clinician encourages behavior change, they will express understanding of how the client became as they are and will affirm the client's strengths and abilities to make change.

- Reflective listening: The engaged therapist will let the client know what they hear. The use of accurate empathy is a key principle in MI and includes the ability to demonstrate to the client an understanding of both the details of the issues they face and the associated affect.

- Summarizing: The effective therapist using MI will be able to summarize and say back to the client what they have heard in a manner that the client can agree to and can use as a steppingstone to consider change.

Predicated on the solid platform built by these four elements, the therapist using MI then engages the client in a wide range of possible exercises or techniques, focused on four primary elements of change. These elements include (a) engaging the client in a discussion about the advantages and challenges associated with change, (b) focusing the client on the desired changes and what these might actually look like in the client's life, (c) evoking the motivations for change from the client, and (d) planning the change(s) the client is prepared to make. As treatment proceeds, this process is recursive and may involve revisiting earlier steps in the behavioral change cycle. Many resources, including worksheets and materials, have been created to make this process easier for the busy clinician (Frey & Hall, 2021; Wood, 2020).

Although most MI research has been in areas such as substance use, gambling, and diet and exercise (Hettema et al., 2005), it is not surprising that motivational interviewing has applied to clients who experience depression, given the reduced motivation and behavioral inaction sometimes seen in depression (Naar & Flynn, 2015). In one trial in a primary care setting (Keeley et al., 2016), teams of clinicians were randomly assigned to deliver either "standard care" or "standard care plus MI." The authors reported better depression outcomes for participants in the standard care plus MI group than for participants in the standard care group. Patient Health Questionnaire-9 (PHQ-9; Kroenke et al., 2001) scores for clients in the enhanced group were significantly lower than those of clients in the control group at 36 weeks, with a moderate effect size (Cohen's $d = 0.41$). The outcomes in terms of remission, however, were not significantly different between groups. Thus, while some preliminary evidence supports the use of MI in treatment for depression, further study is warranted. It is also not exactly clear how Keeley et al. defined standard care or how the addition of MI methods would fare compared to an evidence-based treatment for depression.

Overall, it makes great sense to use MI methods to enhance care for all clients, particularly for clients who struggle with converting their intentions into action. As discussed in Chapter 3, behavioral activation (BA) is an evidence-based strategy for the treatment of depression that makes extensive use of designing and implementing behavioral change strategies. In this regard, you are encouraged to adopt the open, affirming, reflecting, and summarizing principles of MI. Indeed, it was specified in Chapter 4 that this stance can be taken even in the intake interview, particularly in the opening and closing phases of the intake process, to promote the client's sense that the therapist is empathic and attuned to their concerns. The same approach can be taken session by session. Even more, and as discussed throughout this book, an essential therapist skill is to translate discussions in the therapy session into some form of task or assignment between one session and the next. The goal is always to help the client to manage or better manage their life challenges. Reserve time in every session to seek application, to discuss with the client the advantages and risks or costs of the implied homework or behavioral change, to engage in a discussion about what the homework might be and how it might be implemented, and then to see what behavioral commitments the client is prepared to make. In this regard, MI is recommended as a strategy throughout the treatment of clients who have depression.

THE THERAPEUTIC RELATIONSHIP: WHAT WE KNOW ABOUT COMMON FACTORS

To me, one of the greatest diversions in the field of psychotherapy is the debate about the respective roles of common and specific factors. Common factors are the aspects of treatment that cut across treatment models, whereas specific factors are techniques presumably unique to a given model (or shared across models, in some cases). Although the genesis of this discussion is important (Castonguay & Beutler, 2005; Wampold, 2001) and makes historical sense in the context of some relative claims of efficacy for different models of therapy, the distinction is ultimately arbitrary and unhelpful. The therapeutic process rests on a therapeutic relationship, but the therapeutic relationship must translate into actions and techniques that are in service of the client's concerns. Both common and specific factors are needed in psychotherapy.

What has emerged from the research on common factors is a better understanding of the types of relationships that foster a positive relationship between therapist and client and that in turn promote benefit for the client (Norcross, 2011). Some of this literature can be dated to the pioneering work of Rogers (1957) and his focus on what he called "the necessary and sufficient" conditions for change in psychotherapy: positive regard from the therapist to the client, empathy, and genuineness. These attributes have been incorporated into a wide variety of models of psychotherapy. For example, the earliest book on cognitive therapy for depression (A. T. Beck, Rush, et al., 1979) devoted an entire chapter to the therapeutic relationship and mirrored many of the relationship attributes encouraged by Rogers.

An enormous body of literature has examined a variety of relationship factors in psychotherapy (Norcross & Lambert, 2018; Norcross & Wampold, 2019). Most of this literature is correlational rather than based on randomized trials, but clear and consistent patterns have emerged. Considerable research has suggested that the therapeutic alliance, collaboration, goal consensus, therapist empathy, collecting and delivering client feedback (i.e., monitoring in therapy), and cohesion in the context of group therapy all have consistently moderate to strong effects in psychotherapy (Norcross & Lambert, 2018). Other relationship factors that enjoy probable associations with therapy outcome include genuineness, emotional expression by the therapist, self-disclosure by the therapist, positive expectancies in therapy, treatment credibility, managing reactions of the therapist to the client, and repairing ruptures that may occur in the therapeutic relationship.

In this volume I have incorporated many common factors of psychotherapy into the description of the intake and treatment processes. I strongly encourage the development of a positive therapeutic alliance, goal consensus, accurate empathy, and the collection of outcome measures as strategies that should be incorporated into the standard care of every client with clinical depression. Further, these factors are recommended not only at the start of a relationship with a client but in every session. Thus, every session should begin with a review of any current issues the client may be facing and a willingness to further explore these issues, even temporarily, to maintain the cohesion and collaboration between therapist and client.

The literature has some limitations related to nonspecific or process variables in psychotherapy. It is not surprising that the focus in the literature is on therapists and what they bring to the psychotherapy relationship, as they have the greater responsibility in managing and directing the work. As a consequence, however, we know relatively little about client relationship factors and the ways in which they affect the therapeutic relationship, which is, after all, a bidirectional pathway. We also do not know as much as is ideal about whether the common factors that therapists are encouraged to bring into therapy can be trained or if they are more inherent in the individual as personality traits. For example, enhanced empathy is related to treatment outcome (Elliott et al., 2018), and evidence suggests that empathy can be trained (see Lam et al., 2011, for a review). Can other aspects of the therapeutic relationship or skills that promote a positive alliance also be trained? While technical aspects of treatment may be relatively easy to train in neophyte therapists, being comfortable in the therapist role and possessing true interpersonal competence may be less amenable to training and perhaps may be more of a reflection of life and clinical experience.

Collaborative Empiricism and Socratic Questioning

Two aspects of the therapeutic relationship in cognitive behavior therapy (CBT) warrant some discussion here, as they are commonly cited as key ingredients in treatment success. These issues are typically referred to as collaborative empiricism and Socratic questioning (J. S. Beck, 2021; Kazantzis et al., 2017). These two factors are also related to the larger literature on common or nonspecific treatment factors. Each is discussed here in turn.

Collaborative empiricism incorporates the combined elements of collaboration (goal consensus, a positive therapeutic alliance) and empiricism (the use of outcome monitoring, translating therapeutic discussion into actions that can be measured). At the level of an individual session, collaborative empiricism is the process of working with a client to develop measurable benchmarks of therapeutic progress and then using many of the skills related to motivational interviewing to encourage the client to take steps in the direction of these benchmarks. Collaborative empiricism focuses on making an effort rather than achieving a desired outcome. In fact, as therapy proceeds, both the therapist and the client who use collaborative empiricism together find out which strategies facilitate movement toward a shared goal and which fall short or may simply be ineffective.

Socratic questioning represents a metaphor. Socrates, the famous Athenian philosopher, is credited with founding Western philosophy. In his day, he had a school that employed what is commonly now referred to as the Socratic method—an interrogative style of inquiry through which contradictions can be exposed, lack of knowledge can be discerned, and new "truths" can emerge. The Socratic method is in some respects the antithesis of directive and didactic instruction. Within the field of CBT, Socratic questioning reflects an interrogative style in which the therapist takes the presumptive position that they do not know best but through inquiry can expose flaws in the client's logic or reasoning, can become aware of assumptions made by the client, and can work with the client to develop new ways to think about or consider problems in life. The Socratic method therefore can expose new and original ways to think about and possibly solve the presenting problems of the client with depression. In a therapeutic context, the Socratic method has been referred to as *guided discovery* (Kazantzis et al., 2017), which in some respects is the more helpful way to discuss this aspect of treatment, as it reflects the idea that the therapist does not know the endpoint of a given inquiry but can deploy inductive questioning to work with the client to understand their problems. Guided discovery is a critical aspect of case formulation in CBT, as it exposes the client's general way to construe the problems that they face, stumbling blocks that they may face, and strategies that may remediate these problems.

Both collaborative empiricism and Socratic questioning are key elements of the treatment of clients who struggle with depression. You are encouraged to reflect on your ability to use these relational tools and ways to develop them (Kazantzis et al., 2017). As recommended earlier in this text and demonstrated in the literature on therapeutic relationship factors, many elements of collaboration and empiricism are evidence-based elements of treatment. Research shows that increased use of Socratic questioning predicts session-to-session symptom change in CBT for depression (Braun et al., 2015); although the literature base is relatively limited, the available research supports Socratic questioning in the treatment of clients who are depressed (see also Vittorio et al., 2022).

Special Relationship Considerations for Clients With Depression

It is more or less axiomatic that individuals who experience clinical depression come to therapy feeling somewhat desperate. The chances are excellent that they have tried to cope with or remediate the problems they face and almost by definition have not been successful. They may have specific skill deficits that preclude them from solving their life problems. It may be that the issues they face are novel for them and pose challenges that are beyond their current coping capabilities. It is almost certain that they have tried their own informal strategies to resolve their depression or perhaps are coming for treatment because other efforts have failed. Given this likely scenario, certain issues in the therapeutic relationship with clients who are depressed may or may not be present in clients with other presenting problems.

One issue that may present with clients who experience depression is urgency. Because many of these clients have tried to resolve their depression previously, they may come seeking a relatively quick and dramatic reduction in their symptomatology. As discussed earlier in this volume, however, treatment often takes weeks or months for an individual who is clinically depressed. As the therapist, you should be realistic in the work you conduct and the likely outcomes and not overpromise success to any client, especially clients who are experiencing depression.

A second issue that can emerge when working with clients who are depressed relates to the nature of depression itself. Many clients with depression have low levels of motivation and social, occupational, or other forms of engagement. In fact, they might actively avoid challenging or difficult situations. One unstated but critical aspect of the treatment for depression is to help the client become reengaged in their environment and ideally to find purpose. You may find it somewhat challenging to work with a client who on the one hand says that they want to make changes but on the other hand finds it difficult to make these changes because of their depressed condition. An important attitude when working with clients is to be positive and encouraging but not to expect dramatic change in a short period.

Clients with any presenting problem will at times portray a pattern of helplessness in the face of their life obstacles, and as noted in Chapter 4 on intake assessment, clients who present with depression as a primary problem may also express hopelessness and despair. Some therapists find that working with these clients is itself frustrating and challenging. In this regard, it is important to monitor your own thoughts and reactions to your clients. If you find yourself adopting a helpless or hopeless attitude toward your client, check your own thoughts and realign therapy to ensure that you can provide positive support and effective interventions. Some therapists may find it unduly challenging to work with a large number of clients with depression at any point in time and may choose to limit their caseload for this reason. Therapists who find that their work with clients who struggle with depression is particularly challenging may benefit from extensive self-care or support or supervision from colleagues. Furthermore, part of the nature of depression is to have reduced affect and engagement and in some cases to become cynical or negativistic. It can be difficult for some therapists to maintain a positive and open demeanor in the face of this type of interpersonal presentation, and so it is likely a worthwhile consideration to decide whether you can effectively work with this type of clientele.

One aspect of avoidance that can appear in depression is early withdrawal from therapy. It is difficult to solve the problems that lead to depression, and clients who get some symptom relief may make the choice to leave treatment without fully addressing the risk factors that brought them to this state in the first place. For example, within the CBT framework, the interaction of core beliefs and life stressors is viewed as a critical part of the vulnerability equation. It is quite possible, however, that a client may learn some behavioral or coping strategies to manage the life stressors associated with their depression, but once the core beliefs or attitudes activated by these life events are exposed, the client may find the work too challenging or difficult. Although the decision to continue treatment, or potentially to leave treatment earlier than the therapist might think is optimal, is clearly the client's privilege, it can be challenging for therapists to see their clients leave the therapeutic process "too early."

Most clients do not present with a single problem. As noted earlier in this volume, depression is often comorbid with other issues, including anxiety, grief, physical health problems, injury, or drug and pharmaceutical issues. Further, clinical depression can present in many different variations. The effective therapist needs to be able to recognize different presentation patterns and to conceptualize the individual client before them, not based on general principles or theories but rather the specific collection of risk factors that lead the person to become depressed. Case conceptualization is a relatively advanced skill that can be challenging for some therapists. You may find it challenging in early years of clinical work to manage the range of issues that accompany depression; experience and access to resources and mentors can help you to develop the skill sets you need to work effectively with clients who present with depressive symptoms or major depression.

One last consideration when working with clients who are depressed is treatment failure. A review of the clinical trials (Cuijpers et al., 2013) suggests that about 10% of clients with depression drop out from therapy and the clients who remain have an approximate two-thirds success rate (although the success rate varies depending on the criteria; it is notable that most clients get some benefit from an evidence-based therapy for depression). As a clinician who works with depression, be ready to experience failure. Failure can emerge in the context of a specific homework assignment, a general problem that seems intractable, or changes in depression outcomes more globally. It is imperative when you work with all clients that you monitor your outcomes regularly, and in all indicated ways, so that you can respond quickly to whatever issues emerge. You also need to be able to discuss with your client ways in which the treatment is not having benefit and to join with them to redirect specific parts of treatment or the treatment plan more generally. Finally, you need to be able to have an honest discussion with clients about potential treatment failure; have a list of referral options available so that you can have this discussion if needed. One challenging aspect of working with clients who are depressed is that they may elect to stop coming for therapy, and you may or may not have the opportunity for a direct discussion with them about treatment options. Given the risk of hopelessness and suicidality associated with depression, it is good practice to have a concluding interaction and/or letter with your clients to clarify that the treatment relationship has ended.

In summary, although working with clients who present in the clinic with depression has many potential challenges, in practice most individuals who come for therapy are motivated to change, are willing to work with a trained clinician to mitigate or solve their life problems, are happy to learn and practice new skills, and appreciate the reduction in symptomatology they experience across the course of treatment. While the potential relationship problems that can emerge in working with clients are offered here as a kind of caution, something to monitor as you work with clients with depression, the positive interpersonal features of psychotherapy discussed in this chapter can promote a positive therapeutic relationship and increase the likelihood of clinical success. When built on the foundational bedrock of a sound therapeutic relationship, the varied interventions that are discussed in Part III of this book have a good prospect of clinical benefit.

CASE ILLUSTRATIONS OF ENGAGING CLIENTS IN THERAPY

A return to the cases of Michael and Miranda allows us explore the ways their therapists engaged them in the treatment process. In particular, we can see how Dr. Mason and Dr. Morales accounted for positive and mitigating factors and started to build the therapeutic relationship in the first session.[1]

The Case of Michael

Although Michael was initially somewhat reluctant to consider therapy, the referral from Dr. Norton, coupled with the facts that the intervention was covered under his health care and would be confidential, ultimately convinced him to agree to begin. He made a determination not to inform his partner Jon about the therapy program, at least at first, so that he could evaluate whether he wanted to continue and whether he wanted Jon's support or involvement. He also knew that he could easily attend the appointments with no one knowing, which was important to him. He left the intake interview with no homework but with a date for the first therapy session.

Several issues made the referral for treatment and the initial engagement in treatment somewhat less than ideal. For one, although Dr. Norton indicated that counseling might be supportive, she had already prescribed antidepressant medications and implicitly suggested that this approach may be all that would be required. In a sense, then, the psychological therapy was established as an ancillary or complementary part of the treatment program for Michael. The fact that the initial session was in a relatively sterile facility gave the impression that this work was not personalized and that Michael could attend or not, without much consequence either way. Third, although Dr. Mason

---

[1]All cases presented in this book are fictitious and represent illustrations drawn from my experience but not from any specific person.

approached the appointment in a positive manner, she did not end the session with a particular direction, supportive statements, or a strong impression of the likely outcomes of the work. Finally, Michael's approach to the treatment appeared to be ambivalent, as evidenced by his decision not to share this experience with his partner and the sense that he could withdraw relatively easily.

The Case of Miranda

Miranda entered therapy at her request and had the financial resources to see a private psychotherapist. She was well educated and in a stable relationship. While she regretted not coming sooner, the timing was such that she had more time and energy to commit to the process. She was fortunate to work with a therapist with whom she connected well. In short, she had many positive factors to facilitate her engagement in treatment. The inclusive manner of Dr. Morales' questions, her use of open-ended questions that allowed Miranda to express her own thoughts and feelings, and the selection of treatment goals that were important to Miranda also facilitated her increased engagement.

One major factor that potentially mitigated Mirada's engagement was that some of her treatment goals were vague and not yet clearly developed. Even her most clear goal, improved sleep, was not specific. In addition, her goals could have been prioritized more clearly. For example, while she expressed that she was lonely, she did not express an interpersonal goal. As such, Dr. Morales was less likely to work on this problem first, instead beginning with a more clear and focused problem. By doing so, some clear benefit and reduced depression severity might occur as the therapeutic relationship was developed. Good evidence suggests that early treatment gains predict a stronger therapeutic relationship in depression, so this was a good option for Dr. Morales.

6

An Organizational Model for the Treatment of Depression

aving read this far, you will likely appreciate that I am a strong advocate of evidence-based practice. You may also have noticed that most of the publications with my name attached are in the domain of cognitive behavioral theory and therapy (CBT; e.g., D. Dobson & K. S. Dobson, 2017; K. S. Dobson & Dozois, 2019; Kazantzis et al., 2017). You may have noticed reference to risk factors that are not necessarily tied to CBT models of treatment, a review of established treatments that are decidedly not CBT, and support for a number of evidence-based nonspecific treatment factors. As I have come to think about the field, we are at a point that although CBT still stands as the most established and viable specific psychosocial treatment for depression, the model needs to be expanded to be consistent with the most current and relevant research. In this chapter I review some critical features of CBT that are associated with positive outcomes and some adaptations and innovations that are needed to provide the optimal care for clients with depression. These discussions then lead into the subsequent chapters, which provide more explicit ideas about how to enact this organizational model.

CRITICAL FEATURES OF AND ADAPTATIONS FOR CBT FOR DEPRESSION

When CBT originated in the 1970s, much of what we now understand about risk factors was unknown, or perhaps was speculated but not yet substantiated. It was certainly recognized that individuals with depression often reduce

https://doi.org/10.1037/0000398-007
Clinical Depression: An Individualized, Biopsychosocial Approach to Assessment and Treatment, by K. S. Dobson

their engagement in their lives (Lejuez et al., 2011; Lewinsohn et al., 1980) and that activation and the use of more adaptive behavioral patterns could be beneficial for clients. It was further recognized that skill deficits may be present in depression, in particular social skills deficits, which may be remediated over the course of treatment (Lewinsohn et al., 1989).

A key understanding was that many people who are depressed engage in negative thinking, and an innovation of the CBT model was the idea that this thinking may be accurately negative in some circumstances but distorted in other instances. The concept of cognitive distortions led to a series of innovative treatment methods designed to help individuals with clinical depression to recognize that their thinking could be skewed or to some extent divergent from their reality and then to bring their thoughts and perceptions into alignment with their actual circumstances so that they could more effectively deal with or manage the issues they faced (Clark et al., 1999; Ingram et al., 1998).

Another major innovation within the CBT model for depression was the idea that clients with depression often hold attitudes and beliefs that make them vulnerable to these negative cognitive patterns and that identification and intervention with these foundational cognitive bases of depression were likely necessary to reduce the risk for future episodes (A. T. Beck, Rush, et al., 1979; Teasdale et al., 2000). Put otherwise, the identification and modification of negative core beliefs is not only a treatment strategy for the presenting episode of depression but may be a way to modify the risk profile or vulnerability for a future episode of depression.

As time has passed, the literature on risk and resiliency related to depression has developed. As noted in previous chapters, we can now state with confidence that some potent and fairly common risk factors for depression are not explicitly addressed in CBT. These issues include sleep disturbance, avoidance patterns, problem-solving deficits, and dysfunctional relationship patterns. The hypothesis is that to fully address the needs of a client with depression, a contemporary and competent therapist must be able to address not only the typical factors seen in depression and treated through CBT but also these more advanced and process-related issues. In this chapter, I review some of the key considerations in conducting clinical work with clients who are depressed to help you to orient yourself to this work. Having reviewed these considerations, the chapters in Part III delve into the practical aspects of designing and implementing effective interventions.

MAJOR PROCESS ISSUES IN THE TREATMENT OF DEPRESSION

In addition to the content of the problems the client presents in therapy, you may need to attend to a number of process issues. The following sections identify and discuss these issues and provide suggestions to optimize positive gain in therapy.

Balancing Reassurance and Reflection

As noted previously, the therapeutic relationship with clients who experience depression requires special consideration by the skilled therapist. In addition to the general help-seeking orientation that most clients bring to therapy, depression often carries with it a degree of helplessness or hopelessness not seen in clients with other presenting problems and diagnoses. Often, the most helpful general orientation with such clients is to express understanding for potential helplessness or hopelessness while expressing encouragement that the issues the client is facing can be successfully addressed. As a therapist, you will find it helpful to set a balance between optimism and enthusiasm on the one hand and empathy and realism on the other. Bear in mind that clients may overstate their depression or present issues as overly challenging, not because the issues cannot be addressed but as a consequence of their current thinking and affective states.

Some clients who are depressed come to therapy seeking emotional or practical support and express a degree of helplessness that may invite you to be overly engaged, to suggest solutions that may or may not be practical, or simply to make encouraging or supportive statements. I strongly encourage you to resist these impulses. In early interactions with the client, take a reflective stance so you can more fully understand the circumstances faced by the client as well as the ways in which they have responded to these circumstances before you offer statements that may be taken as unduly supportive. It is also critical in the first interactions with all clients, but in particular for people who are struggling with depression, to frame the issues as common and recurring life problems, not ones that you will permanently "fix" or "repair." From the outset of the interaction, it is useful to highlight to the client that the work you do together will help them to engage their life in a different way and hopefully will reduce the problems that they face. This type of dialogue will support you later in treatment when you suggest to the client that they need to take the ideas discussed in therapy and apply them in their lives between one therapy session and the next. One way to express this idea is to say that what is discussed in the therapy session is important but what takes place between sessions is actually more important. A given week has 168 hours, so a single hour is a minuscule part of the client's life.

Understandably, clients—regardless of their presenting problem—may at times become overwhelmed by their emotions. They may come into either the first or a later session preoccupied by a recent issue and find it difficult to think of much else. A client might dive right into this current issue and start to discuss it at length, if you provide the opportunity. Some therapists may feel that this response is supportive, but I again caution you not to focus directly on a given problem in any session without first conducting a standardized assessment of progress and a brief scan of the client's experiences since you last saw them. In the field of CBT, this work is often discussed using the metaphor of setting an agenda.

Agenda Setting

Although "agenda setting" is a relatively formal way to talk about structuring the session, the early phase of each session should provide a welcoming environment and a sense of organization and balance. It should also increase the likelihood that you will use your precious time together in an optimal manner. If you or your client does not like the term "agenda," you can raise the issue instead through questions such as "How will we spend our time today?" or "What are the important things that we need to focus on today?" These types of questions naturally lead to a broad survey of the recent work in therapy, current concerns of the client, skills or interventions that you want to introduce in this session, and the focus on broad outcomes. As the therapist, you need to keep a record and be mindful about the tasks the client has been trying to work in therapy and issues from previous sessions that you need to follow up on.

Within the prototypical "50-minute hour" that is common in Western therapies, the initial agenda-setting part of the session should take no more than 10 minutes. This beginning phase generally includes greeting the client and ensuring that they are comfortable. Having reviewed your notes from the previous session, you should already know whether the client had agreed to undertake any assignments, so take the initial few minutes to inquire about this work. If you asked the client to complete a questionnaire or mood rating, be sure to spend some time reviewing this information. You will have some idea about the progress of therapy overall and whether the current session is a good time to introduce a new intervention or skill in treatment. If so, it will likely be to your advantage to suggest that you have something new you would like to introduce in the treatment session. It is also collaborative to invite the client to discuss any current issue or concern they have, particularly if it might otherwise not get mentioned, and decide together the amount of time, if any, needed in the session to address that issue (e.g., relationship, collaboration, agenda, homework).

If the client is particularly despondent or in acute distress when they enter the therapy session, acknowledge this issue and find out what the current problem is. My suggestion is to identify the emotion and ask the client's permission to review other aspects of the treatment, including the questionnaire assessment or mood rating and engagement in any assignments, and then provide a general reorientation to the work that has been done in therapy. These kinds of reviews often help to ground the client in the therapy session, reduce their level of distress, and provide an opportunity to decide the relative importance of the current issue as opposed to others that you have been working on together. It is important, of course, to come back to the current concern of the client and to use the issue as an opportunity to understand more about the issues they face in their life, how they manage these issues and think about them, and how they generally respond when they are in a state of distress.

Although some therapists see agenda setting as a technical and perfunctory part of therapy, in fact it is much more. It communicates a desire to work together with the client in a collaborative fashion, it lets the client know that you are paying attention to the work they do both within and outside of the therapy session, it signals that you want to be effective and efficient with your time, and it helps to reduce the likelihood of surprises during the therapy hour. Many therapists have experienced a client with depression who goes through a therapy session and then, in the last few minutes, expresses their increasing hopelessness and desire to die or some major pending problem they face. This type of experience is distressing for both the therapist and the client, and it can often be prevented if the session begins with a formal review of symptoms that provides an opportunity for the client to talk about any major concerns or issues they are facing, after which you can structure your time together.

Having done a relatively brief check-in and having decided what topics are important in a given session, it is sometimes useful to be even more structured and assign provisional time limits for different topics. For example, the client may come into therapy with a current distressing situation and may be quite able to spend most or all of the session talking about this issue. If you engage in this type of discussion in your role as therapist, you may be communicating empathy and a desire to listen to the client. However, you are also implicitly endorsing the idea that a current concern can preempt any other work. You potentially lose the opportunity to build on interventions that you have already introduced in treatment. It is your responsibility as the therapist to ensure an appropriate balance between flexibility and structure so that you increase the likelihood treatment will move along in a positive direction. My experience is that often you can simply name the two or three topics for the session that emerged from the agenda setting and perhaps determine the order in which they will be discussed. With some clients, particularly clients who have difficulty organizing themselves or are distressed and want to focus on one issue, it may be necessary to be fairly structured, perhaps even to assign a rough time schedule to the session. Be mindful, however, that some clients do not appreciate this level of structure or may actively resist too much structure. Use your judgment as to what that appropriate level may be for the given client.

Typically, the 50-minute hour can accommodate about two or three topics. For each, ensure sufficient time is given to name the issue, identify the way in which the client is dealing with it, develop a treatment plan or suggested intervention for the particular issue, practice the intervention in session if indicated, and devise a way to carry this intervention forward between sessions as a homework assignment or other activity. Sometimes more short topics can be included, but be careful not to try to cover too much ground in a session. Clients often have limited memory for events in therapy (A. G. Harvey et al., 2016), so it is generally better to cover fewer topics more completely than to survey several topics in a relatively superficial manner.

Summarizing Key Takeaways and Developing Between-Session Assignments

As each topic in the session draws to a natural conclusion, it is often helpful to provide a mini summary of the issue and any ideas that emerge. For example, you may have asked a series of questions to understand the client better and to develop the case conceptualization. You might provide a concluding statement such as "This has been a very useful discussion for me, as it helps me to better understand. . . ." Often, an assignment will emerge from the discussion. If so, it may be helpful first to invite the client to say what they take away from the discussion and what assignment they think would be most useful. As with any skill, clients need to learn the process of therapy, and the first effort they make to provide a summary or to develop a personal task or assignment between sessions may be somewhat underdeveloped or unclear. If so, ask more questions about what the client understands to ensure you are both taking away the same understanding and, if there is an assignment, both of you know fairly clearly what it is and have good confidence that it can be attempted. If during the discussion of a particular topic you believe the client either does not fully understand or does not have the ability to undertake an assignment, you need to decide whether to continue in this direction or to defer the discussion about the assignment to a future session, when you may have the required time to fully develop the assignment for maximal benefit. Another option is to agree with the client that you will continue the discussion of a particular issue but truncate the discussion of a later topic in the session or not discuss it at all so that you can fully complete the topic you are currently considering.

As the session moves toward a conclusion, retain at least 5 to 10 minutes to wrap things up. It is often helpful to begin this final phase of a therapy session with a general statement such as "We have discussed several topics today, and it seems that our time is coming to an end. Maybe you could tell me what you think we focused on today and what you found the most useful." This type of statement signals the transition toward the end of the session and reminds the client of limited time to discuss any final issues. It also helps the therapist to better understand what the client has paid attention to and the major conclusion they have drawn. If the client responds with something close to your understanding, you can support them in what they say and perhaps add your own thoughts. In contrast, if the client has drawn a different conclusion than what you may have intended or if they only attended to one aspect of the session, this question allows the opportunity to broaden the discussion and ensure that the client attends to the full session. This type of open question can be helpful when developing the case formulation, as it may suggest that the client has focused on particular issues of high relevance to them but has paid less attention to ideas or methods that you may think are important but do not resonate with them.

Obtaining Client Feedback

As a final process issue, I strongly recommend that you obtain feedback from the client in every session. This process of feedback can be general, as in "How did you find our session today?" or it can focus on specific topics, as in, "Today we were talking about cognitive distortions quite a bit. Did you find that discussion helpful?" You can use the feedback question to ask about the session, as in the two previous examples, or you can use it to obtain specific feedback about your style as a therapist or the therapeutic relationship. My suggestion is that you seek feedback about the client's response to you in the first or second session so you can potentially adjust your behavior in a way that works better for them and so you can use this response in your developing case conceptualization about the way they relate to people such as yourself. I also strongly recommend that within the first four or five sessions you deliberately seek feedback about the therapeutic relationship. Questions such as "How do you think we are getting along together?" or "How do you find the process of coming to therapy and working with me?" are helpful prompts to encourage the client to discuss what they value about you and the treatment process as well as potential areas for refinement in the therapeutic relationship. Certainly, if you have had a therapeutic "rupture" with the client (e.g., a disagreement about a particular topic, a strong negative emotional reaction from the client about an issue you have discussed; Safran & Muran, 2000), take the time to debrief that interaction and find out if the client has any negative thoughts about you or the therapeutic relationship so they can be meaningfully addressed (Gardner et al., 2019). Soliciting feedback from the client serves an important communicative function in that it signals not only that you want to work collaboratively with the client but also that you are only human and are open to the idea that you can improve your own behavior to be as effective as possible. Some clients may be willing to self-denigrate but simultaneously view others as perfect, and in these cases the process of feedback seeking can open a fruitful discussion about the fact that no one is perfect and everyone can benefit from constructive evaluation.

MAJOR CONTENT ISSUES IN THE TREATMENT OF DEPRESSION

The preceding section of this chapter presented some issues related to processes that facilitate the treatment of clients who have depression. This section offers initial ideas about the content or foci of treatment for such clients. These ideas are significantly elaborated in the chapters that follow, but this section provides a good introduction to the orientation taken here and some of the common themes that emerge in the treatment of depression.

A repeated idea in this volume is that the treatment of depression should be problem focused. There are many risk factors for depression within the biopsychosocial framework, and the specific concerns for a given client will be unique to them and may even differ across time if they have recurrent episodes of depression. Chapters 4 and 5 discuss the importance of a very detailed problem assessment as part of the intake process as well as some typical concerns or issues that clients who are depressed may raise and that may become the focus of treatment. This information needs to be organized into a set of content concerns that may be the object of treatment, organized in terms of severity and order of importance. For example, if a client presents with significant sleep dysfunction and reports that their extreme fatigue makes it impossible for them to function in the daytime, it is critical to address sleep as one of the first orders of treatment. In contrast, a client who is primarily concerned about the loss of an important relationship and has excessive rumination about things they might or might not have done to preserve the relationship is more likely to benefit from an assessment and intervention related to their thought processes and beliefs about that specific relationship or relationships in general. Put otherwise, different clients require different problem solutions, which in turn require different combinations of interventions. At its essence, the multidetermined nature of depression makes the uniform application of any given theoretical model problematic.

My experience is that there often are predictable stages in the treatment of a client who struggles with depression. The initial stage focuses on behavioral change and activation. During this stage clients are often interested in regular and predictable daytime activities, beginning to address concrete problems in their lives, restoring the nature and quality of sleep, and establishing or reestablishing social connections. As discussed in Chapter 7, a wide range of behavioral interventions can be very effective in the early stages of treatment and can have significant reductions in depressive experience. Research suggests that the early phases of CBT in particular are associated with the largest reductions in depression scores (Tang & DeRubeis, 1999), and behavioral interventions typically dominate at this point in therapy.

Once the client has begun to reengage, treatment often focuses on patterns of interaction that have caused or maintained the depressive experience. At this point in therapy, skills deficits may become more obvious, and the therapist may need to provide more psychoeducation, in-session skills practice, and between-session assignments to solidify the practice of these skills. The specific skills will be dictated by the particular case and the clinically indicated interventions; they could include social skills, assertiveness, recognizing and modifying cognitive misinterpretations, interfering with the process of rumination, overcoming avoidance, or other appropriate psychosocial interventions. It is almost always the case that the earlier focus of intervention on behavioral issues has to be maintained even as the therapy shifts toward other cognitive and emotional patterns. In this stage of therapy, it is important to inquire about and encourage the earlier interventions, even as new areas come into focus and are added to the overall treatment program.

The combination of behavioral activation skills and successful attention to the psychosocial processes in the middle stage of therapy often yields a significant reduction in depression. At this stage of treatment, the client may have been coming for a period of weeks or months and ideally will have become reengaged in their life and skillful at the vulnerability factor or factors they brought into therapy. Within the context of CBT, the underlying vulnerability or risk factors can be addressed in this stage. Thus, although the therapist likely has identified beliefs and schemas as part of the case conceptualization and these identified beliefs and schemas figure into the earlier aspects of the treatment, these risk factors are not directly assessed, discussed, and potentially treated until this third stage of therapy. As the therapist, you need to bring a series of key skills to the treatment process to shift successfully to this focus in the latter stage of therapy, which is really about consolidating gains and the prevention of future episodes of depression. In my experience, this is the point in therapy at which interventions related to mindfulness and acceptance play a large role and can be successfully integrated into the overall treatment plan.

It is unlikely that an individual who presents with major depression will successfully and fully respond to a single intervention. More typically, some confluence of risk factors has led to the development of the client's depression, and it will take some combination of interventions to successfully help the client recover from the current episode of depression and, hopefully, prevent its recurrence. In Part III of this book, I present some common interventions used at the various stages of treating depression, with the intention that you will be able to understand and use these various skills appropriately based on the case assessments that you complete with individual clients.

CONSIDERATIONS FOR SELECTING INTERVENTIONS FOR DEPRESSION

A recurrent theme in this book is that there are multiple pathways into depression and a corresponding number of ways out. Conceptually, it makes sense that if a particular risk factor can be identified, then directly addressing that risk factor through one or more interventions should be the most effective and efficient strategy to help somebody with depression. At the current state of development of the field, however, no formula or algorithm can identify the interventions that will maximally modify particular risk factors. As an example, a client who struggles with sleep onset often will benefit from increasing regular exercise. From an intervention perspective, the suggestion is that the intervention with the highest impact should be offered first to a client, even if the intervention does not map precisely onto their risk factors. As discussed in Chapter 5, a general recommendation is to deal with the worst problem first, as long as the client accepts the rationale of a proposed intervention and is willing to use the method.

The previous paragraph of course begs the question as to which interventions are the most impactful. In Chapters 7 through 10, various ideas are presented: Each chapter presents major interventions first, followed by other potential but less commonly used strategies and techniques. It remains essential, however, for you and the client to develop and implement a system to monitor whether any given intervention is having the intended effects. While each intervention will suggest its own way to be monitored, you may need to be creative with the client to ensure that you can be as confident as possible that the intervention is being implemented as intended and that you have confidence that any positive outcomes are related to the intervention. Careful monitoring also allows you to know whether the intervention is successful and should be maintained, needs a bit longer to achieve its outcomes, is not having the intended effect, should be modified, or should be discontinued.

The combination of interventions that you recommend for a given client naturally depends on the case conceptualization you have developed (Kuyken et al., 2009; Persons, 2008; Zubernis & Snyder, 2016). One advantage current clinicians have, relative to past years, is that there are many effective techniques that can now be adopted. The challenge, especially for a relatively new therapist, is to flexibly and creatively use these interventions to their maximal effect. My recommendation, when first learning to treat clients who present with the focal problem of depression, is to work with and master some generally efficacious interventions so you develop expertise in the methods. Once you have more experience, and when the opportunity presents itself in therapy, you can try some more innovative ideas to see whether these methods also have benefit. As with your clients, you want to encourage consistent effort in yourself and to monitor outcomes carefully so you can discern if the way in which you have delivered the intervention is perhaps problematic or if the intervention is having the desired outcomes.

THE ROLE OF THE THERAPIST

This chapter has developed the idea that there are both common processes seen in the treatment of clients who struggle with depression and predictable stages of treatment associated with commonly used treatment techniques. As a therapist, it is your responsibility not only to deliver effective interventions in a timely manner but also to maintain an overall perspective of the case and the way it is proceeding. To accomplish these tasks most effectively, you are encouraged to evaluate the client's effort and success with specific interventions and the overall outcome of treatment. The outcome is best evaluated with a combination of standardized depression questionnaires or monitoring questions (usually weekly to begin, then on a less frequent basis if the case is progressing well) and checking in with the client on a regular basis about their perceptions of therapy—what is working well for them and what perhaps could be modified. Again, the recommendation is that check-ins should be done every session in the early phases of treatment but then can become less frequent as treatment moves along. Ideally, you and the client will both be comfortable enough to raise any concerns or questions about the progress of therapy or its outcomes at any time and to prompt a more thorough discussion. As the therapist, you are tasked with remaining open to signs of treatment problems and putting them on the table for discussion as soon as you recognize them.

CASE ILLUSTRATIONS OF TREATMENT PLANNING

As we continue to follow the cases of Michael and Miranda, we see how their therapists, Drs. Mason and Morales, focused on the clients' presenting problems and collaboratively developed tentative agendas and strategies for optimizing treatment in later sessions.[1]

The Case of Michael

At the time she began working with Michael, Dr. Mason was a relatively experienced psychologist at the community clinic where she worked. She had

---

[1]All cases presented in this book are fictitious and represent illustrations drawn from my experience but not from any specific person.

been trained in interpersonal therapy, which is an evidence-based treatment for depression that encourages therapists to look for one or more interpersonal patterns commonly seen in depression. Of her own interest, she had also taken some workshops on CBT and was somewhat familiar with thought records, cognitive restructuring, and core belief interventions. These latter approaches were supported by the clinic's director because they were evidence-based and relatively efficient in terms of client outcomes. Dr. Mason had responded well to this additional training and was making efforts in her practice to integrate her clinical skills for clients that needed this assistance.

Dr. Mason's impression of Michael was that he was doing reasonably well but had some clear interpersonal issues that were not being addressed and possibly some underlying beliefs that were problematic. Michael presented himself as a successful businessperson, and yet he struggled with some relatively focused issues for which he requested some assistance. Although Dr. Mason largely accepted this conceptualization, she was aware that Michael expressed worry and lack of closeness in his relationship with his partner Jon as well as a lack of clarity about his own future ambitions. In this regard, a focus on interpersonal deficits and possibly role transitions made sense to Dr. Mason. She was trained to ask questions about suicidality when Michael expressed even a modest degree of hopelessness. She further thought that it likely would be useful to administer a structured assessment tool to begin the second session. After Michael left the first session, Dr. Mason came to the impression that working on activity could be a good initial target for intervention and a way to engage Michael in treatment. She wondered how much of a focus on relationship issues would be needed: She did not think that Michael had a role dispute but rather thought that he was not engaged in the important relationships in his life, both at work and home. Michael's future and possible role transition to retirement was another important issue, possibly along with values clarification and future goal setting. Dr. Mason thought that these issues would likely arise somewhat later in treatment, however, and more as preventive strategies than as ways to address Michael's current case of depression.

The Case of Miranda

Dr. Morales saw Miranda for the second appointment, during which she began to formulate her understanding of the situation. She described the biopsychosocial model to Miranda and provided a general description of some risk and resiliency factors as well as typical treatment outcomes. Miranda expressed interest in the model, as she had previously read about perinatal depression. She was unaware of CBT and asked a number of questions about how it worked and how it might be applied in her case. Dr. Morales introduced the concept of collaborative empiricism, explaining how the two of them would operate as a "team" and would assess the effects of different strategies regularly. The symptom measures would be completed and discussed every few sessions. Each session would have a clear structure, including an agenda, which would always be set collaboratively.

Dr. Morales also noted that homework is an important component of therapy, as the therapy hour is only a small component of the client's week; to be effective, change must take place outside of therapy. Unlike some clients, Miranda was keen to take on some homework and immediately thought that she could be a role model for her daughters, who sometimes struggled to complete their work. She immediately apologized, however, as she had forgotten to keep her sleep and activity log. In response, Dr. Morales commented that she likely had not provided sufficient explanation and context for why these logs were important and noted that homework, even if partially completed, always provides information. They discussed several reasons why this homework had not worked, including incomplete goal setting, not fully understanding the rationale, and the busy week that Miranda had experienced.

Dr. Morales also discussed the importance of clear goal setting and prioritization, letting Miranda know that SMART goals (i.e., specific, measurable, achievable, relevant, and time limited) tend to work best. She provided several examples and asked Miranda to think of previous goals that she had set—one that had worked and one that had not. She opened a discussion of the various factors that either had gotten in the way or had been helpful. They spent the remainder of the session formulating goals, particularly related to sleep and daily activities. For example, the goal of "improved sleep" was clarified as "be in bed by 10 p.m., eliminate screens in the bedroom, and arise by 6:30 a.m." Dr. Morales stated that improved sleep would be an outcome of different behavior change strategies that would be gradually attempted following the collection of the sleep log information. They agreed to work on goals related to daily activities at the next session, following the completion of the daily activities log. Dr. Morales asked Miranda to make a list of 10 potential activities that were easily accessible, inexpensive, and interesting for the next session; they began this list together near the end of the session. Dr. Morales also provided a handout on sleep and CBT-I.

Dr. Morales provided a brief summary of the session, then asked for feedback and reviewed the homework. She told Miranda that she was welcome to call her by her first name, Josefina. Miranda appreciated the invitation to be more informal and expressed a positive reaction to the appointment. Dr. Morales also noted that Miranda appeared somewhat more animated than she had been in the first session.

Following the appointment, Dr. Morales worked on her hypothesized case formulation, including diagnostic and environmental considerations. She speculated on some of Miranda's core beliefs as she began to see signs of determination and self-efficacy as well as hope for the future. She predicted that being a full-time working mother of two young children would create both barriers and aids to her goal attainment. She was very busy and tended to put her family first, but she showed clear awareness of the impact of her actions on her children.

III

COMMON STRATEGIES FOR TREATING DEPRESSION

7

Behavioral Activation

Addressing Risk Factors for Depression

As noted earlier in this text, most clients come to psychotherapy with a set of problems they intend to attenuate or solve completely. Clients are often highly motivated to work on their problems and wish to see the benefit of treatment fairly quickly. In this regard, clients who are depressed are not different from other therapy clients. They typically know that they are depressed and not functioning at the level they wish, and often they have specific life stressors or difficulties that they want to address in therapy. Although they may be discouraged and possibly may feel somewhat helpless or hopeless, the fact that they have come for treatment is a clear signal of their desire to make changes. Most clients have tried strategies they had hoped would be successful and come seeking assistance because those efforts failed or at least were not fully successful. The most straightforward way to connect with many clients and to begin the process of treatment is therefore to identify their problem(s) and provide them with signals that you will help them work on their problems and that you have novel skills to use.

Part II of this book focused on developing a therapeutic relationship, orienting toward clients who experience depression, and determining an optimal intake process to establish some foundational ways to develop a working alliance with your clients. A positive demeanor and a sense that you are willing and ready to get engaged with the client are critical. In my experience, most clients present with what I consider to be "outcomes" of a depressive process, by which

https://doi.org/10.1037/0000398-008
Clinical Depression: An Individualized, Biopsychosocial Approach to Assessment and Treatment, by K. S. Dobson

I mean they know that they feel poorly and they know that they are functioning in some key areas of their life at a level below what they wish. Their short-term goals often correspond to these concerns, and they want to feel and cope "better." The idea of coping better can include overcoming avoidance or inaction or may involve learning new skills to apply to the problem list. These "behavioral" interventions are often effective methods to engage the client. They also are associated with significant reduction in depression when used well, and so they meet the client's goal of feeling better.

This chapter presents some commonly employed behavioral strategies for clients with depression. It is critical to note, however, that effective therapy does not involve simply assigning behavioral tasks to a client and assuming that they will comply and therefore feel better. As noted in the discussion about motivational interviewing in Chapter 4, it is important to ensure that any behavioral task or assignment is meaningful to the client and that they see benefit in making changes. At the very least, it is important to have a discussion with the client about the behavioral changes that they think will help them to deal with their depression and to connect the behavioral plan with that outcome.

In most cases, it is useful to spend some time to understand the client's values and to ensure that the action strategies are aligned with those values. A client who values spontaneity, for example, may struggle with setting firm action goals and plans. On the other hand, be mindful that even if a client has not had a history of planful action, they might respond very well if you work with them to develop a strategy that fits with their values and lifestyle. Perhaps they were raised in a family that had no established patterns and was somewhat chaotic. Each person is unique—approach the strategy you recommend with this idea in mind. See Chapter 10 for additional discussion of values and strategies to assess this important area.

The specific behavioral strategies discussed in this chapter include activity scheduling, behavioral activity, skills training, increasing physical exercise, improved diet, and effective sleep. These strategies are all associated with known risk factors for depression, and most clients will resonate with them because they can see, in a fairly straightforward way, that the interventions can potentially address their symptoms or problems. Relative to the more cognitive interventions discussed in Chapter 8, these strategies do not rely on abstract theory or reasoning. Instead, they address issues that are somewhat more discrete and practical. Many clients will get significant antidepressant benefit from these methods, if they are applied with skill and if the needs of the client match the interventions. In my experience, these strategies are often a good place to begin therapy, as they provide concrete grounding for the more abstract work that follows, provide a forum for you and the client to build a positive relationship, and to some extent provide a bit of a time buffer for you to learn about your client, develop your case conceptualization, and strategize about interventions that might be used somewhat later in the course of treatment.

PRINCIPLES AND THE PRACTICE OF ACTIVITY SCHEDULING

A commonly employed behavioral strategy in depression is activity scheduling. This strategy dates back to the earliest behavioral and cognitive behavior therapies for depression (A. T. Beck, Rush, et al., 1979; Lejuez et al., 2001; Lewinsohn, 1974; Lewinsohn & Clarke, 1984) and has been heavily incorporated into contemporary behavioral activation therapy (Martell et al., 2001, 2021). Activity scheduling is a potent intervention in depression and, in general, is something that should be developed in every session. Indeed, as every topic is discussed in therapy, you should keep your eye open for ways the client can take the discussion and convert it into a meaningful homework assignment.

A wide variety of questions can be used in the session to promote this discussion:

- "How do you think you could take these ideas we have been discussing and implement them at home?"

- "If you wanted to do something different this week, what would it be?"

- "It seems like we both agree that having more fun could be helpful for you. Would you like to give yourself a task or assignment to have more fun this week?"

- "What changes would you see in your life to know that you are making progress?"

- "It seems that you really value relationships but are not doing as much in this area as you would like. Would it be helpful to set some goals?"

Depending on the client's reactions to these prompts, discussion can take a variety of forms. The typical pattern is first to ask some motivational questions, in particular about why a given task or action might be of benefit and the ways in which it aligns with the client's goals and values. The goal is not to convince the client that they need to do a particular task; ideally, it is to see what activity they would value and wish to set for themselves. This discussion often relies on the use of Socratic questioning (see Chapter 6).

The general discussion about a behavioral task and why it could be of value is typically followed by a detailed discussion of the assignment and ways it might be structured. This discussion may be quick and easy if the task is fairly clear or if it has been discussed previously, but with some clients it may take a bit of time to fully develop, possibly occupying two or more sessions. Often, it is better to take your time to design a well-crafted task or assignment rather than quickly to do something formulaic but not fully adapted to the specific client.

Before you and the client agree to a particular assignment you generally want to follow these steps:

1. Ensure that both you and the client believe the assignment is important in treatment, with either a short-term or a long-term benefit.

2. Have the client state in their own words why this task is important to them.

3. Ideally, have the client design the homework assignment. It is acceptable to provide prompts or suggestions if necessary, but ensure that the client agrees with the importance and design of the final plan. As much as possible, avoid simply giving an assignment to the client.

4. Have the client describe the assignment in sufficient detail so you have confidence that they know what the task is and how to accomplish it.

5. Provide suggestions or instructions about how and when the assignment could be attempted if you have doubts about the client's ability to undertake it. If necessary, provide instructions for how to approach the task. If the task is an interpersonal interaction, possibly do a role play in the therapy office. If the instructions and training will take too long in the current session, you may decide to defer an assignment to a later session.

6. Consider the advantages and disadvantages of specifying a date and time to undertake the assignment, especially for clients who struggle with homework assignments. Consider starting the assignment in the therapy office or possibly doing it in session instead (e.g., making a difficult phone call).

7. Ask the client if there are any impediments or obstacles to the homework assignment. If there are, consider the advantages of problem solving these obstacles before you agree to the task. At this point, you may decide that the obstacles are sufficient to defer the assignment to a later appointment.

8. Advise the client that you will ask about their effort with the assignment in the coming session. Let them see or know that you are making a record of the intended assignment.

9. Assure the client that the focus will be on the effort and attempt rather than the potential outcomes of the assignment, since the latter cannot always be guaranteed.

In the next session, it is imperative to ask the client about the assignment. If they completed it, ask about both the process and the outcome, focusing on the effort and the way in which they undertook the assignment. If the assignment was well done and had the intended outcome, consider the merits of building on the assignment in an incremental fashion with similar tasks or missions during the current session. If the client attempted the assignment more or less as intended but the outcome was negative or not as expected, spend some time to debrief the situation. For example, the client may have made a plan to provide an assertive response to a request from somebody in their social arena, but this assertive response was greeted with unexpected hostility. An outcome of this type provides great information about the social circumstance that faces the client and can be very useful for discussion about what both you and the client have learned from the assignment. In some cases, if the outcome is highly different from what you and/or the client predict, you have new information to fold into the case conceptualization. It is also worth noting that some behavioral goals are fairly complex, and it may take some time and several failed efforts to approximate the desired outcome.

If the assignment was not attempted or was done in a halfhearted or incomplete manner, be sure to put it on the session agenda. When you get to that point in the session, try to understand what happened. If the problem was in the attempt, see if it makes sense to do some instruction or training and then reassign the assignment. Clients sometimes have negative thoughts or become discouraged during a task, so ask questions about the client's cognitions and emotions, as this information may provide clues about how to increase the likely success of a future attempt.

INCREASING ACTIVITY: THE ACTIVITY LOG

Many clients who experience depression come to therapy with dysregulated sleep–wake cycles, avoidance of issues that they could confront, or unproductive use of time. These behavioral patterns can be strengthened by rumination or self-denigration or by emotional patterns of helplessness and hopelessness. Often it is helpful for such clients to begin to reengage in their life through activity scheduling. This type of activation can help to increase energy, encourage more regular eating and sleep, and reduce unproductive time, which in turn helps clients to feel more productive and better about themselves.

Because so many behavioral dimensions could be targeted for change, it is often difficult to know where to begin. One relatively simple strategy to begin therapy is keeping an activity log. In its most simple form, an activity log is a table that includes the days of the week across the top and times of the day in the various rows. Exhibit 7.1 provides a very basic example of an activity log.

The hours of the activity log need to be customized to the individual client. The sample in Exhibit 7.1 begins daily at 8:00 a.m. and ends at 11:00 p.m., so the assumption is that these are the outer limits of the client's day. Another version could include all hours of the day, for example if the client is awake at night at various times. A client who does shift work may need a longer form. Yet another client might have their sleep–wake cycle shifted so that they regularly awaken in the early afternoon and then stay up until 4 a.m.

The sample activity log in Exhibit 7.1 is structured in hourly blocks. This format works well for clients who are reasonably active and have a major activity to write into each time block. This format could be discouraging for clients who are less active, however, as the form itself may highlight for them how little they do on a typical day. In such cases, it may make sense to have only a few blocks per day, such as "morning," "afternoon," and "evening," or other terms that fit for your client.

A typical strategy for the activity log is to include the major activity (or activities) that occur in each time block. My experience is that clients can reliably do this type of reporting for about a week, although often they go back at the end of a day to fill in the missing time blocks. One idea is to have them keep the log by their bed, desk, or other obvious place at home so they can complete the

EXHIBIT 7.1

Sample Activity Log

Time	Monday	Tuesday	Wednesday	Thursday	Friday	Saturday	Sunday
8:00–9:00							
9:00–10:00							
10:00–11:00							
11:00–12:00							
12:00–13:00							
13:00–14:00							
14:00–15:00							
15:00–16:00							
16:00–17:00							
17:00–18:00							
18:00–19:00							
19:00–20:00							
20:00–21:00							
21:00–22:00							

form at a regular time and it will be reasonably accurate. My sense is that the record on the activity log does not need to be "letter perfect," although the quality of the information will dictate how firm your conclusions may be.

A form such as the one shown in Exhibit 7.1 could be easily printed and given as a written assignment after the therapist and client agree on the days and time windows for the rows and columns. It could also be easily transmitted as a worksheet to be completed on a computer and then printed or sent electronically in advance of a client appointment. In theory, a client could keep an electronic agenda on their computer or smartphone instead of on a separate form. A client who keeps a written daily journal could use this format to record major activities throughout each day. Various smartphone apps also allow clients to record this information. The point is that the format is not fixed; it should be one that the client is comfortable with and is likely to use regularly and reliably.

Once the client agrees in principle to the idea of tracking their activity patterns, the immediate question becomes what the client should record. Useful information includes the diurnal cycle (i.e., typical time in bed and arising), how much alone time the client has, how many social contacts the client has, and who they are. A log should also reflect whether the client schedules regular meals, exercise, programs, or other activities. In short, an activity log provides a brief sketch of the week and its patterns. Be mindful that a single week may be quite representative of the client's lifestyle or it may be quite unique, so ask the client if it was chaotic or in some way not what the client considers as typical. It is usually worthwhile to repeat the exercise to see a stable baseline of physical activity.

A basic activity log may very quickly allow the therapist to suggest interventions. For example, a client who keeps fairly regular bedtime and waking times from Monday to Friday because of a job but then lets their schedule go on the weekend often suffers at the beginning of the week. If a client has a regular bedtime of 11 p.m. but then stays up until 2 a.m. on the weekend, I have given the simile that it is like traveling three time zones to the east for the weekend (e.g., Los Angeles to New York) and then coming home but expecting no jet lag on Monday! As another example, the therapist can sometimes see that the client has a pattern of going to school or work when they must but otherwise spending a lot of time in front of a screen. A 2021 survey reported a daily average of almost 7 hours of internet-connected activities for adults globally, with just slightly more than 7 hours for adults in the United States (Moody, 2022). When these activities are added to an estimated 3 to 4 hours of television per adult in North America, it becomes clear that the average adult has a lot of screen time. Because clients who are depressed are often more isolated and avoidant that other adults, they may spend most of their time interacting with screens.

A very early intervention related to the activity log was to examine more specifically the presence (or absence) of what were called mastery and pleasure events (A. T. Beck, Rush, et al., 1979). Mastery events were defined as activities in which the client felt a sense of accomplishment, success, or mastery, even if at a modest level. Pleasurable events, in contrast, were those in which the client felt a sense of enjoyment, pleasure, or hedonism. The logic of tracking these specific types of events was that both can be relatively uncommon among clients who struggle with depression and so first tracking these types of events and then possibly scheduling them once they were deemed to be deficient could be antidepressant.

The way you choose to track events on an activity log depends on the information you want to gather. For example, the client could put an "M" beside any event they determine to be masterful and a "P" beside any pleasurable event. Alternatively, the client might agree to rate every entry in their activity log to indicate how much mastery or pleasure it brings (e.g., a 1–7 rating scale or a 0–100% scale). Again, the value of this level of detail depends on the amount and quality of information you can reasonably obtain from a client. In my experience, it is usually sufficient to use the M and P labels to denote activities that might be usefully discussed in the following session. For example, if the client is to mark all pleasurable events with a P and they return to the next appointment with only one or two, this observation can lead easily into a discussion about the merits of increasing these experiences and how they might shift the client's depression. On the other hand, if the activity record is used to track not only the occurrence but also the level or degree of pleasure (e.g., on a percentage system), it may be possible to identify activities that had a very high or low rating and focus on them in the subsequent session to discern the process that led to such an extreme response.

Another advantage of a simple letter system for denoting events is that it can be easily modified. For example, I have had several clients whose problem lists suggested that a major issue was social isolation, and it was reasonable to expect that increasing social events would help their depression. We have used "S" first to track social events and then to schedule them. This type of recording can easily be modified to track "E" emotional, "S" stressful, "D" depressive, or any other types of events that are connected to the client's depression.

Yet another use of the activity log is to look for events that were not identified by the client within the category system you had developed but that, when you review the record, seem to be good candidates for discussion. Clients with depression sometimes fail to attend to positive events and underreport them, so if you think an activity may have been missed, you can inquire about it and find out why the client did not record it. Such an inquiry can provide good information about the way the client thinks about events, and you may also discover something about the way that the activities themselves or the client's construal of them has to change so that they can be seen more positively. A quick word of caution here, though—if the client perceives an activity on the log as not being pleasurable (as one example) but you as the therapist think it "should" have been pleasurable, "most people" might view it that way, or you would likely view it as pleasurable, it is highly inadvisable to try to convince the client to modify their perception. This type of interaction can create lack of collaboration and, at worst, can create friction or a disagreement and rupture in your alliance. You are better advised to ask one or two questions about why the client did not view the event in a more positive fashion, incorporate that understanding into your case conceptualization, and move on.

Imagine a scenario in which you and the client both agree that the activity log shows a current paucity of "S" social activities. Furthermore, you both agree that the client has expressed an interest in increasing these events as a possible strategy to reduce depression. The client advises you that they were more sociable before they were depressed; they believe that increasing these activities not only will get them out of their place more often but will decrease their screen time and maybe increase their activity to some degree. Before you simply assign the client increasing these activities, consider the following questions and issues:

- Does the activity fit with the client's overall therapeutic plan? If so, it may be worth pursuing. If it is tangential, it may have a relatively modest impact on the client's mood even if they have success. In the latter case, reconsider pursuing this activity except perhaps as an example of how activity scheduling can be used.

- Is the action clear to both you and the client? If the scene were recorded and independently viewed by you and the client, would you both recognize the activity when it happens? If in doubt, it may be worthwhile to be more specific. You might choose to set a date and time for the activity and plan precisely what the client will do. If you continue to have doubts, you might conduct a role play in the session so you have reasonable confidence that the client has the skills and ability to undertake the assignment.

- If you feel that the client does not have the complete ability to undertake the assignment, you might spend a few minutes to do some skills training. You could provide instruction, demonstrate some ways that the client could approach the situation, and discuss the assignment until you and the client both are confident that it can be done.

- The goal of any assignment is not to obtain a defined or predetermined outcome but to have the client make the attempt. Keep an eye open for possible impediments by asking the client directly if they can imagine anything that will prevent them from doing the assignment. If they have an obstacle in mind, see if you and the client can together create a strategy to work around it.

- Many clients who struggle with self-efficacy and depression give up or withdraw from a situation if they face a challenge. If you are working with a client who has these tendencies, it is worthwhile to acknowledge this fact, support the client in their efforts, and determine whether you and the client can develop some method that allows them to persist even in the face of external or internal challenges. For example, if a client has a homework assignment to take a 10-minute walk, they could use a self-instruction: All they have to do is take a short walk to see what effect it has on their mood. If they get the impulse to stop during the walk, they could use another prepared self-instruction to go for just one more minute, repeating this instruction as necessary to complete the task. As another example, some clients benefit from reporting their efforts between sessions. Thus, a client who has a specific assignment could be encouraged to send an email report to you as the therapist, acknowledging their effort. Be mindful, however, that building yourself in as a checkpoint has the peripheral implication that the client becomes more dependent upon you. It also means that you need to check your emails and respond to the client if this is part of the assignment.

- It is better to start small and have success than to pick a large behavioral change and have the client struggle or be unable to complete the assignment. Despite the natural inclination to try to "reach large" and solve problems quickly, using a more gradual process is often the preferred strategy. This principle is known as *graded task assignment* (A. T. Beck, Rush, et al., 1979; Martell et al., 2021), which involves early small successes and then intermediate steps on the path toward the ultimate goal. In some cases, you might develop a list of steps that help the client progress from where they are to where they wish to be, with the view that as they successfully undertake one step they can then move up the graduated list until, hopefully, they achieve the desired outcome. A more common strategy is to discuss with the client where they are now and where they want to be and then ask the deliberate question, "What do you think is a reasonable next step that helps you move in the direction of your goal?" This discussion can sometimes help you to recognize that the client sets goals that are too daunting and lead to disappointment. Sometimes you may discover that a client sets very small goals and that the larger ambition will take an unduly long period of time. Thus, you and the client can together work toward manageable but meaningful steps. A principle that I recommend is to follow the client's lead; if they think a particular activity is too challenging for them at present, scale the assignment back a little to optimize the likelihood that they will both make the effort and have success. On the other hand, if they feel they are ready and willing to undertake a large task, join them in the effort and see what happens. Either way, you are building your collaboration with the client and learning information about their strategies and abilities related to task assignments.

Summarizing all these issues, I like the acronym developed by the behavioral activation approach, ACTION (Martell et al., 2021). This acronym can remind you of the logical steps needed to propose and implement a potentially powerful behavioral action strategy. The acronym reflects six key behaviors:

- Assess the function of the client's behavior and the potential value of modifying the behavior.
- Choose an action that appears likely to have an antidepressant effect.
- Try. An attitude of "let's find out what happens" is critical to the success of action planning.
- Integrate the new behaviors into regular routines whenever possible.
- Observe what happens, both at the level of specific behaviors and in terms of overall levels of depression.
- Never give up. Try again if the first effort was not successful, and continue the action plans that have demonstrable benefit.

SOCIAL AND OTHER SKILLS

It is probably safe to say that everyone has strengths and limitations. Some people are more adept at physical tasks while others flourish in the social world. Few people are masterful in all domains. For individuals with clinical depression, not only is skill a potential factor in their difficulty solving their current problems, but the application of their skill may be hampered by their current ways of thinking and feeling. As noted in Chapter 2, many people who become depressed have experienced childhood adversity, sometimes in the form of disrupted parenting or other direct forms such as neglect or abuse. Families with disturbed patterns of parenting are less likely to impart critical social and life skills associated with success in society, and skill deficits may result.

One task for an effective therapist is to identify when clients struggle with social and other skills and when it is necessary to help them overcome these skill deficits. Skill deficits can arise in a wide range of areas, including study habits for students, financial planning and management, work and occupational habits, and social/interpersonal relationships. Less common skill-related issues may appear in home maintenance, time management, childcare, or even day-to-day activities such as gardening. Psychotherapists are not expected to be an expert in all of these domains, and the client may need to obtain external assistance in one or more areas if they lack the ability to manage the problems that they face. A client may need assistance to find local resources, including people or programs, to learn these skills, but they exist in most urban environments. For clients who live in rural or remote areas, it may be helpful for you as the therapist to recommend some web-based or written resources, but it may be relatively inefficient or even inappropriate for you to try to take on too many areas of expertise.

It is quite possible to incorporate psychological and social skill building into the treatment of depression. For example, if you encourage your client to do some activity scheduling in some area and discover that their skills are limited, it may be necessary to step back a bit and engage in skill building. One area in which skill deficits can manifest themselves in depression is social relationships (Segrin, 2000). Individuals who are depressed may think they do not have the right to their own opinions or may denigrate their thoughts and feelings and generally avoid interpersonal problems. These social patterns may be related to their current level of depression, but it is also possible that skill deficits explain why the client cannot successfully solve interpersonal problems. In either case, social skill deficits can result in limited social relationships, and lack of social contact and social support has been associated as a risk factor for depression (Santini et al., 2015; L. Wang et al., 2021).

A useful set of distinctions is made in the area of interpersonal assertiveness. On one end of the assertion spectrum is *passivity* or avoidance, in which the client with depression does not express their needs and wishes but instead allows others to dominate. The behavioral pattern of passivity is usually successful in the short term because it results in a nonconflictual relationship, but in the long term the client does not get their needs met. Indeed, after being passive for a long time, clients can become less aware of what their needs are or how to express them well. At the other end of the assertion spectrum is *aggression*, in which the individual pursues their own desires and thoughts without taking into account, or sometimes even to the detriment of, the feelings and concerns of the other person(s) involved. In my experience, clients who have a primary presenting problem of depression do not often express aggressive patterns, although they are often sensitive to these patterns in others and can very quickly adopt a passive response in return. The happy midpoint is *assertion*, which involves recognizing and expressing one's own needs and concerns while respecting the needs of others and negotiating a position in which both sets of needs and concerns can be respected and hopefully fulfilled. In reality, it is most adaptive to be able to be passive, assertive, or aggressive as the situation warrants and the specific pattern of interaction with a person unfolds. Strategic avoidance can be adaptive if the alternative is violent conflict, and sometimes being loud and aggressive is a useful way to get one's needs met, especially if the needs are not being respected. As with most skills, different situations will call for the appropriate use of various interpersonal skills and strategies.

Social skill deficits in clients with depression typically involve more passivity and avoidance than is optimal for mental health. In such cases, it can be quite useful to provide some psychoeducation about the assertion spectrum; to provide examples of passive, assertive, and aggressive behavioral patterns that are relevant to the client's life; and perhaps to engage in role plays in the therapy office so that the client can practice assertion, either related to specific planned interactions or in general. Social skills can also be well taught in group therapy, as the different members of the group can practice and role play different social interactions.

THE VALUE OF PHYSICAL EXERCISE

Although it is common wisdom that exercise is healthy and that some form of regular physical activity both reflects and promotes mental health, it is not unusual to find that clients who are depressed have either reduced or stopped regular exercise. The data clearly demonstrate, however, that physical exercise can have significant antidepressant effects (Choi et al., 2020; Josefsson et al., 2014). Further, the promotion of a regular exercise routine can yield a number of benefits, including increased metabolism, improved cardio and muscular fitness, better sleep, enhanced appetite and opportunity for nutrition, and improved longevity (Krogh et al., 2012). A meta-analysis of studies of exercise as a treatment for depression (Kvam et al., 2016) revealed a large effect size for physical exercise as compared to no exercise and a moderate effect size compared to usual care. Specific comparisons between exercise alone and other psychological treatments or antidepressant medication were generally not significant, but the overall recommendation from this analysis was that physical exercise should be considered as a viable adjunct to other evidence-based treatments for depression.

As with many interventions, not all forms of physical exercise are created equal. There is broad agreement that aerobic exercises, which increase the heart rate and respiration, are antidepressant; examples include walking, running, cycling, swimming, and cross-country skiing. As a result, most guidelines and recommendations focus on aerobic exercise to alleviate depression, although the Kvam et al. (2016) meta-analysis included some anaerobic exercises, such as resistance training, strength-based exercise, and weight training. It did not include studies that included yoga or tai chi or studies that provided only general guidance or encouragement to exercise.

Clinical recommendations based on the published literature generally concur on the importance of at least three weekly aerobic exercises, each of at least 30 minutes duration, to obtain an antidepressant effect (Baron et al., 2016; Nyström et al., 2015; Rethorst & Trivedi, 2013). The information about the recommended intensity of exercise is somewhat inconsistent, with some suggestions that less intense exercise may require three periods of 50 minutes of exercise. Intensity is also measured somewhat inconsistently across studies, with many studies using the simple method of heart rate but more sophisticated studies using VO2 max readings (i.e., maximum volume of oxygen consumed during exercise). With respect to heart rate, the general recommendation appears to be that heart rate should reach approximately 75% of an individual's maximum, although these maxima vary as a function of gender, age, and physical health. As such, a broad recommendation is that physical exercise programs should be undertaken on the advice of a family physician or exercise physiologist.

It also appears that self-administered exercise programs are more likely to end prematurely than those that are monitored (Nyström et al., 2015). It is therefore recommended that therapists and clients discuss how they want exercise to be monitored. A wide range of web-based and app-based exercise programs are available, many different self-help books include monitoring forms, and wearable items can monitor parameters such as steps and heart rate. If a client is working with an exercise physiologist or personal trainer, it is highly likely that some type of monitoring will be included in that work. It is important to understand what the client thinks would be the most convenient and helpful for them. In general, however, some type of external monitoring is strongly recommended, both so that the client can see their own progress and so they can report to whomever they are working with on these issues.

As a clinician who works with clients who are depressed, you may wonder how to incorporate exercise into the overall treatment program period. From my perspective, this work can be done relatively easily if the client is interested in this type of intervention. There are many motivational reasons to engage in exercise, as noted earlier; if the client has a history of regular exercise and associates exercise with feeling better about themselves, then the suggestion to initiate or restart exercise makes strong sense. It appears that the type of exercise chosen by the client does not make a major difference in its antidepressant effect, with the potential caveat that aerobic exercise is generally preferred. My suggestion, therefore, is simply to ask the client what type(s) of exercise they prefer and engage them in a motivational interview style of discussion about the perceived benefits of this exercise.

Assuming that you and the client come to an agreement about a particular exercise pattern, the discussion should turn to its implementation. As with other forms of activity scheduling, you should start at a level that is appropriate for your client and that takes into account their current activity level and overall physical health, their level of depression, and their expressed desire to increase exercise. A wide range of pragmatic considerations should also be involved in any assignment, including the need for equipment (e.g., a bicycle, weights, running apparel), the costs of the intended exercise (e.g., gym memberships), the convenience of the activity (e.g., is a viable walking or running area close to where the client lives?), and safety (e.g., does the client intend to walk or run alone in the evening?). The ideal intended exercise is one that is desired by the client, convenient, inexpensive and affordable, and safe. Another consideration is whether the activity is solitary or group based. Some clients prefer to exercise on their own schedule and/or alone, whereas others are motivated by social support and group encouragement. In the latter case, the optimal types of exercise could include organized sports such as baseball, soccer, pickleball, or whatever other activity is available and of interest. It is not necessary to choose one type of exercise; it is quite possible to cross-train with a combination of different types of aerobic exercise. In fact, for some clients, variety can help to maintain interest and participation.

A particular consideration relevant to exercise is that depression may occur in the context of other health problems. As noted in Chapter 1, many people who develop depression have a history of an anxiety problem or may have comorbid anxiety. In these cases, in particular if the client has either health anxiety or social anxiety, these considerations need to be taken into account when any exercise program is considered. If the client's depression is secondary to a physical condition, then that condition also should be taken into consideration. For example, if the client has a chronic pain problem and depression has developed subsequent to the pain and behavioral inactivity due to the pain, it would be imprudent to recommend or encourage any type of physical exercise that could exacerbate the issue associated with the chronic pain. In clients who have long-term depression and reduced or minimal physical exercise, increasing activity is itself sometimes associated with muscle fatigue and muscle pain. Depending on the type, frequency, and intensity of the exercise plan, you should discuss with the client the possibility of these reactions and how they can be mitigated. It may be that consultation with a medical practitioner or sports physiologist will be indicated to ensure that the exercise program is safe and likely to succeed.

Like activity scheduling, if you and the client decide to incorporate physical activity into the treatment plan for depression, it is essential that you inquire about the exercise program during every session. Some clients may start with a specific activity at a certain frequency and level of intensity and be satisfied simply to maintain this type of exercise. Others may find that as their depression lifts and their physical stamina improves, they wish to challenge themselves with more intense or different types of exercise. Yet others may become discouraged and find that the plan they had first adopted is too intense for their current level of fitness and that it needs to be scaled back. You need to plan time in each session to quickly inquire about the exercise routine and, if indicated, to make time to discuss any necessary or desired modifications. Even if the decision has been for the client to go to a gymnasium or sports center to work with a consultant or trainer, it is still worthwhile for you as the therapist to inquire from time to time about the physical activity and to express encouragement when indicated. Many clients get a sense of improved self-esteem, self-efficacy, and social support from physical activity, and to the extent that these issues are part of the treatment plan, they should be recognized and supported.

DIET AND DEPRESSION: THE IMPORTANCE OF HEALTHY EATING

Chapter 2 presented various models for risk and resilience in depression. One topic that was touched upon was diet. Consistent and compelling evidence suggests that a diet that includes more processed foods, sugars, and carbohydrates is associated with more health problems than diets without these characteristics and diets that include lower levels of processed foods are associated with better mental health overall (Brookie et al., 2018; Jacka et al., 2010; Lane et al., 2022). There are multiple arguments that certain dietary substances such as omega-3 fatty acids are antidepressant and suggestions that contemporary Western diets in particular are deficient in necessary oils, vitamins, and minerals required for optimal brain functioning (Kaplan & Rucklidge, 2021).

Unfortunately, few randomized clinical trials have attempted to discern a relationship between diet and depression outcomes. One notable exception was the SMILES trial in Australia, which compared a 12-week dietary intervention to a social support protocol of similar duration (basically a program that involved social contact and befriending) in the treatment of outpatient depression (Jacka et al., 2017). The dietary intervention included nutritional counseling, motivational interviewing, goal setting, and mindful eating, all of which were provided through one-on-one interactions with a clinical dietitian. The dietary emphasis was on increasing the intake of whole grains, vegetables, legumes, low-fat and unsweetened dairy products, nuts, fish, lean red meats, chicken, eggs, and olive oil as well as simultaneously reducing refined cereals, fried foods, processed materials, and sugary drinks. Alcohol consumption was permitted, but participants were encouraged to reduce the amount and to drink alcohol only during meals. The outcomes of this trial were that the group that received the dietary guidance shifted many of their eating patterns, whereas no such changes occurred in the social support group. Notably, although both groups had a reduced level of depression at the posttest, the depression scores in the dietary group were significantly lower at that timepoint than the scores of the participants in the social support comparison.

Although the Jacka et al. (2017) trial had some methodological limitations (e.g., less contact and higher dropout in the social support group than in the nutritional counseling group, somewhat small sample size), the overall pattern of information related to diet and depression suggests that certain food patterns are associated with better mental health in general and reduced depression in particular. In a large study with more than 10,000 participants in Spain, the Mediterranean dietary pattern (MDP) was associated with lower rates of depression (Sánchez-Villegas et al., 2009). The MDP is consistent with the Jacka et al. (2017) trial in that it encourages the consumption of vegetables, fruit, nuts, minimally or unprocessed cereals, legumes, olive oil, and fish (see also Muñoz et al., 2009). More generally, the MDP has attracted positive attention for its potential benefits on cardiovascular systems and lipid metabolism, anti-inflammatory patterns, and reduced obesity (Giugliano & Esposito, 2008; Morris & Bhatnagar, 2016).

Overall, it stands to reason that more healthy eating is likely to be associated with better overall wellness. People who are depressed are likely drawn more to foods that have a short-term boost associated with them, such as foods high in carbohydrates and sugars. Drinks that are high in caffeine (e.g., coffee, tea, sodas) may also be used by some clients as an antidepressant substance. In the same manner, some clients who are depressed and have concomitant anxiety may ingest more alcohol as a way to self-manage their tension, but in doing so they unfortunately may exacerbate their depression. Depression is also associated with eating disorders (Tan et al., 2023), and some research suggests that the association between anorexia nervosa and depression is related to the number of common risk factors (Calvo-Rivera et al., 2022). It is worth inquiring about diet with a client who struggles with depression. If there is no apparent cause for concern, it may be worthwhile to simply provide support for a balanced diet. On the other hand, a referral to a nutritional expert or dietitian may be indicated if the client appears to have more serious eating problems.

IMPROVING SLEEP PROBLEMS RELATED TO DEPRESSION

In Shakespeare's *Henry IV, Part 2* (Shakespeare, 1598/1950, 3.1.6), the king bemoans his sleep problems and recognizes the repose that sleep—"Nature's soft nurse" as he calls it—may provide. Many clients who struggle with depression have a similar and unfortunate relationship with sleep. Indeed, while sleep disturbance is one of the nine diagnostic criteria for depression (see Chapter 2), the evidence suggests that sleep disturbance often predates depression and is one of its principal risk factors, both in adolescents who are developing a first episode of depression (Goldstone et al., 2020; Lovato & Gradisar, 2014) and in individuals with recurrent depression (Lee et al., 2013). Sleep disturbance can take a variety of forms: In one study of 496 participants with depression (Nutt et al., 2008), 58% reported problems getting to sleep, while 59% and 61% reported problems waking in the night or early morning wakening, respectively (fully 97% of the sample reported at least one of these problems). Further, while 69% of the participants reported insomnia (i.e., reduced sleep), 10% reported hypersomnia (i.e., excessive sleep), and 21% reported both patterns.

We all sleep, and we all need sleep. That said, people vary in the amount of sleep they need every night and whether they feel better if sleep is in a single block or divided into a longer sleep and naps during the day. It also is clear that the need for sleep varies even within people and that it can change across the lifespan and under periods of stress. Resting, even if not sleeping, can also serve an avoidance function, in which the individual can protect their own space and time, although resting does not have the benefit of restful sleep. It is not uncommon to hear from clients with depression that they are often in bed and either worrying about events to come or ruminating about the past.

The physiology of sleep has been extensively studied, and it is clear that a complex set of hormonal, cognitive, emotional, and behavioral regulatory functions are associated with sleep. In general, circadian rhythms have a 24-hour cycle. Assuming a nighttime sleep, tiredness is typically the lowest in the morning hours and develops over the day, leading to fatigue in the evening hours and the desire for sleep. Tiredness is related to exposure to sunlight and variation in hormones that trigger fatigue and desire for sleep. As such, changes in exposure to sunlight associated with the seasons or more dramatic changes in exposure associated with shift work or travel across time zones can have dramatic effects on both the amount and the quality of sleep that a person can attain. It is also clear that a daytime nap interferes with the hormonal cycles for some people and can yield disturbed nighttime sleep as a result.

As discussed in Chapter 2, it is also known that many individuals who suffer from depression have increased rates of anxiety relative to the population at large, and it is well recognized that anxiety can lead to arousal, which itself can interfere with quality sleep (Carney & Posner, 2016). It is also worth noting that disorders other than depression and anxiety can affect sleep, including sleep apnea, restless leg syndrome, chronic pain, and other mental health problems such as bipolar disorder and posttraumatic stress disorder. When the pattern in a person's sleep problems is not clear, it may be worthwhile having a sleep specialist or sleep clinic conduct a thorough assessment and provide a more definitive diagnosis.

A number of interventions exist to help individuals who have insomnia, whether in the context of depression or not. The American Academy of Sleep Medicine has a well-developed website with considerable amounts of educational information for people who struggle with sleep difficulties (see https://sleepeducation.org/). They list a number of interventions for people with sleep problems to consider, including hormonal treatment (in particular melatonin), treatments to promote better oxygenation during sleep, light replacement therapy for people who may be struggling with diurnal variation or light deprivation, medications, and cognitive behavior therapy. Determining an optimal evidence-based intervention for a person with significant sleep problems is a matter of proper assessment and case formulation of the sleep problem. Even once the intervention is implemented, though, ongoing assessment may necessitate changes to the plan or its delivery. For clients who present with depression, two interventions are most commonly used: medications and cognitive behavior therapy for insomnia (CBT-I).

Sleep Medications

Sleep medications are among the most common interventions used with individuals who are depressed and have insomnia. In general, sleep medications are central nervous system depressants—that is, they reduce nervous system activity and allow the individual to become more tired and to sleep. In some cases, and in particular for clients with considerable comorbid anxiety, sleep medications can consist of anxiolytic medication to reduce the client's overall level of arousal and in so doing encourage the client to become tired and sleep more fully.

Sleep medications have several potential drawbacks. First, as they generally suppress the central nervous system, they can exacerbate other signs and symptoms of depression, such as fatigue, confusion, and reduced activity. Second, many clients develop a psychological and/or physiological dependence on sleep medication. This dependence can make it difficult to reduce or stop using these medications once the depression has lifted. Third, some sleep medications have rebound effects, such that reduction of the medication leads to sleep disturbance. Clients who feel better and have decided to reduce or stop sleep medication should be advised to expect some potential rebound effects. In general, the client's response to medication should be monitored; if they show these secondary responses, the medication should be reduced, stopped, or possibly changed. The prescription, monitoring, and modification of sleep medications should be done by someone with good knowledge about the variety of sleep medications and their indications, risks, and contraindications.

One other point about sleep medications in the context of depression is warranted. As noted previously, formal prescriptions for sleep are generally central nervous system (CNS) depressants. A number of nonmedicinal CNS depressants are widely available, however, and clients with depression sometimes start to use them on their own to manage their sleep. In Western societies, one of the most common such substances is alcohol. In particular, some clients want to sleep better and thus consume alcohol in the evening to make them feel more tired; they should be advised that this behavior can be unhealthy and may lead to increased sleep disturbance. Alcohol consumption should be monitored and possibly reduced. Other available substances in many societies include marijuana and its derivatives as well as opioid derivatives. If you are working with a client who expresses sleep problems, it is always worthwhile to ask if they are consuming alcohol or any other nonprescription substance, and if so, to ask about their pattern of use. Because nonprescription depressants can interact with prescribed sleep medications, these interaction effects should also be taken into account in any recommendations about either prescription or nonprescription substance use.

Cognitive Behavior Therapy for Insomnia

One notable development in the world of sleep treatments has been cognitive behavior therapy for insomnia, sometimes referred to as CBT-I (Carney & Posner, 2016). CBT-I has been evaluated in both open and randomized clinical trials, and the evidence suggests a moderate to strong effect on both subjective and objective outcomes (L. J. Mitchell et al., 2019; Trauer et al., 2015), in patients with primary insomnia and with comorbid conditions (Wu et al., 2015), and both in the short term and in periods up to one year (van der Zweerde et al., 2019) CBT-I is now generally considered as a first-line treatment for insomnia, and therapists who regularly treat depression should know some of the basic principles of CBT-I and should be ready to provide advice and intervention in this area.

CBT-I generally includes five groups of interventions, including relaxation, cognitive interventions, sleep hygiene, stimulus control, and sleep restriction. Which of these interventions, if any, will be of benefit depends on the way that the client presents with sleep difficulties, your assessment of which interventions will be the most helpful, and their actual implementation. In the sections that follow, each type of intervention is discussed in turn. A more complete description can be found elsewhere (e.g., Carney & Posner, 2016), as can useful forms for clients to work with (e.g., Carney & Manber, 2009). If you are a clinician who often works with clients who struggle with sleep, it may be beneficial to take advanced workshops or further training in this area.

Relaxation Techniques

Relaxation techniques for sleep are useful in a general way. These techniques are of most help for clients who struggle with anxiety and serve to generally reduce arousal and induce sleep. These techniques can include a wide variety of leisure and relaxation activities that are of interest to the client, such as warm showers, baths, mindful meditation, yoga, watching quiet movies, or listening to relaxing music. Another method to reduce arousal and increase relaxation is strategic avoidance of emotionally arousing situations, such as answering emails, speaking to individuals with whom you have problems, paying bills, or doing housework.

Some clients benefit from a focused and prolonged set of relaxation techniques, such as deep breathing exercises, progressive muscle relaxation, and mindfulness and acceptance techniques. Again, the client's preference should be considered when determining a relaxation technique to adopt and the extent to which formal training and practice in the relaxation technique is required in the therapy session. As noted earlier in this chapter, however, if you make the decision that you need to begin to undertake relaxation training with a particular client, it is critical that you maintain this focus, structure the practice or homework assignments so that the client has the maximum chance for success with the technique, and continue to monitor its use and outcome over the course of therapy.

Cognitive and Behavioral Interventions

Cognitive interventions are often helpful for clients who wrestle with sleep problems. It is not unusual for clients with depression to have negative thoughts, and lying alone in bed or even with a sleeping partner provides an excellent "opportunity" to engage in this type of thinking. Although the topic of rumination as a clinical focus is discussed later in this volume (see Chapter 8), rumination in the context of sleep is something that often needs to be addressed.

The specific technique or techniques that might be of use to a client will vary, so it can be helpful to experiment. A few strategies that may be effective to disrupt ruminative thinking follow.

- Leave the bedroom if rumination continues for too long. A general recommendation is that if you are thinking in a way that interferes with sleep for more than 15 minutes, you should get up, go to another room, and do some quiet activity until you are tired, at which point you can return to bed.

- Use distraction. Distraction can take a number of different forms, including counting backward by sevens, imagining all the items in a room that you lived in 20 years ago, listening to a quiet podcast, and putting on relaxing music at low volume.

- Gradually prepare for bed. Clients may be encouraged to focus on the tasks at hand, such as brushing their teeth or laying out clothes for the next day, rather than focusing on any particular distressing situations or events that may have occurred. This act of mental preparation for bed can help people to quiet their thoughts and be more ready for sleep when they actually get into bed.

- Recognize and deal with mental activity. Some clients who are depressed lie in bed and worry about a situation or ruminate about something that has occurred when instead they could do something constructive to manage the situation. For example, a client who has a difficult situation upcoming at work may think about things that they could do to reduce the distress. In such a case, it can be helpful for the client to have a notepad beside the bed or to use a recording device so that they can capture these thoughts and then perhaps put them aside and return to sleep. In a similar vein, some clients wake up in the night and think about activities that they need to do in the coming day. If they have a notepad beside the bed, they can quickly make a note to themselves and then let it go. Some clients find this strategy a useful way to return to sleep.

Some clients have beliefs about sleep that can become problematic. For example, they may believe that unless they get a certain amount of sleep, they will not be able to function the next day. They may have beliefs about the "unfairness" of their sleep problems and that insomnia "should not" happen to them. They may even have beliefs such as "If I can't sleep at night, I have to nap in the day to make it up," which justifies napping and inadvertently may exacerbate the nighttime sleep problem the next night. If you determine that a client may have beliefs that interact with their approach to sleep, it is important to assess these beliefs and the effect they have for the client. In some cases, psychoeducation may be of benefit; it may also be useful to encourage the client to experiment with different approaches to determine whether their beliefs are accurate or helpful.

Sleep Hygiene

"Sleep hygiene" is a general term for a wide variety of strategies that can be used to improve a client's approach to sleeping as well as the sleeping environment. Potentially useful strategies include

- Monitoring the intake of stimulants during the day and reducing them if necessary. In many societies, people drink one or another form of caffeine, which has a stimulating effect. Consuming caffeine in the morning can help people to become alert, and some evidence suggests that consumption of up to the equivalent of three cups of coffee per day is antidepressant (Choi et al., 2020), but overconsumption of caffeine can interfere with sleep. Afternoon or evening consumption of caffeine is generally discouraged, and if the total daily intake appears excessive, caffeine consumption should be targeted for reduction. Another common stimulant used in society is nicotine. Again, if nicotine use is high, in particular in the afternoon or evening, it should be considered for modification.

- Exercising regularly, even if the exercise is relatively light. As noted previously in this chapter, aerobic exercise is antidepressant in general, and good evidence indicates that individuals who engage in regular light exercise sleep better than people who do not (Choi et al., 2020; Josefsson et al., 2014). The type of exercise, its duration, and the intensity can all be matters for discussion. In general, however, exercise should not be undertaken directly before sleep, as the body needs time to return to a resting state before sleep is attempted.

- Altering dietary patterns. For example, eating a heavy meal or drinking a lot of fluid in the time leading up to bed may cause stomach distress or pressure on the bladder that interferes with sleep. It is generally recommended that meals and large amounts of liquids be stopped at least 2 or 3 hours before sleep is attempted, to give the body a period of time to digest the food and process liquids.

- Making the bedroom a relaxing environment, to the greatest extent possible. It should be of little surprise that the environment in which one attempts to sleep affects both the amount and the quality of sleep. Ideally, the space is dark and quiet, and many people prefer it to be somewhat cool. Further, the space ideally is one in which the client feels safe and secure and that they are not going to be disturbed. Developing this type of environment may be a challenge for some clients. People who live in large or multigenerational families, people who are forced by economics to share sleeping spaces, people who live in urban environments, and people who feel unsafe in bed or perhaps have been victimized while sleeping can all have significant challenges in meeting the ideals of a sleep environment. If your client reports any of these problems, it is likely worthwhile to spend some time to discuss strategies to improve the sleep environment, such as using ear plugs or a face mask, purchasing new window coverings, or rearranging sleeping arrangements and partners.

- Removing electronic devices from the bedroom. To the extent possible, televisions, smartphones, tablets, pagers, and other electronic devices should be removed from the sleeping area. It has been well established that the lights from televisions and smartphones interfere with the sleep cycle, and the noise and content of whatever is being communicated can lead to emotional responses that interfere with sleep (Chang et al., 2015; Silvani et al., 2022). Smartphones should be put on silent mode at night to minimize interruption. Some clients wake up in the middle of the night, look at the time, and begin to worry about the fact that they are not sleeping. Simply making the time less obvious may reduce the likelihood of this type of worry and sleep interruption. For example, clients who have a bedside alarm clock with a bright display should consider reducing the illumination of the display, turning the clock so that the time is not immediately visible upon awakening, or trying other strategies to reduce the likelihood that the clock interferes with sleep.

Stimulus Control

In the context of sleep disorders, *stimulus control* refers to the idea that beds should be associated with sleep and intimate encounters, but little else. To the extent that this type of association can be developed, the bed should become a place of refuge and quiet rather than worry and rumination, anxiety, or distress. Strategies for sleep hygiene and managing the sleep environment will go some distance to help the client associate the bed with sleep. Other potential strategies include the following:

- Use the bed only for sleep and intimate encounters. Do not use the bed for making phone calls, playing games, watching television, or other potentially stimulating activities. In general, try to use the bedroom only when needed for sleep or to obtain items found only in the bedroom. Again, this recommendation can be challenging for people who live in small environments or in locations at which the bedroom is perhaps one of the few safe and personal refuge points, but clients who overuse the bedroom learn not to associate the bed and bedroom with sleep.

- Avoid daytime naps. Napping interferes with the normal diurnal cycle and the ability to sleep when nighttime comes. If an individual is so tired that they feel they must sleep during the day, it is advisable to control the length of the nap. For example, set the alarm for 30 minutes and get up when the alarm goes off. If somebody else is available to help, and assuming that the relationship is not problematic, that person might monitor the client's sleep and wake them after a defined period, such as 30 minutes.

- Set a limit on the time that they can stay in bed before they exit. This strategy is especially useful if the client wakes in the middle of the night or the early morning. A common idea is to use a 10- or 15-minute limit—if the client awakens and is unable to return to sleep within that time period, they should get out of bed, move to another area, and engage in some light activity. For example, they might read or listen to relaxing music until they feel fatigued and are ready to return to bed to sleep. Clients are strongly discouraged from getting up from bed to turn on any device such as the television or smartphone. They are advised not to read emails or other potentially stimulating materials and instead should maintain a quiet disposition as much as possible. If the client goes back to bed and cannot sleep for another 10 or 15 minutes, they should repeat this process throughout the evening or night until they can return to bed to sleep.

- Set a regular time to get out of bed every morning, and use it every day of the week. This strategy is one of the most powerful stimulus control interventions. For example, if the client has to be at school or work at 9:00 a.m. most days and they need 1.5 hours to get ready and get to where they need to be, they should set their alarm for 7:30 a.m. every day, including the weekend. The rationale for this recommendation is that changing the wake-up time can dramatically shift the sleep cycle and significantly interfere with sleep, particularly at the end of the weekend. It is not surprising that, in the Western world, many people with sleep problems have the worst problems on Mondays and Tuesdays, as they have effectively undermined their sleep cycle by changing their wake-up time during the weekend. Because some clients resist the idea of a regular wake-up time, one strategy is to encourage them to experiment for several weeks to see the effects on their sleep cycle. Many clients find that their overall sleep has higher quality and is more fulfilling with a regular wake-up time, and after several weeks it may be possible to make minor modifications to the weekend schedule in a way that does not interfere with the weekly sleep cycle.

Sleep Restriction

The final intervention discussed here is sleep restriction. Although it is last in position, sleep restriction is a highly effective technique for many clients who struggle with insomnia. An important aspect of working with clients with insomnia is knowing when and how to use sleep restriction. Sleep restriction is predicated on the idea that more efficient sleep is generally associated with higher quality sleep and a healthier relationship between the client and sleep in general.

Sleep efficiency refers to the percentage of time that the client is asleep (i.e., not dozing or lying in bed trying to sleep) while in bed. To determine sleep efficiency, the client can use a sleep log to estimate two key data points, time in bed and time asleep. For example, if the client went to bed at 11:00 p.m., the calculation begins at this time, even if they did not sleep. If the client finally left the bed at 7:30 a.m. the next morning, the time spent in bed is 8.5 hours. The second data point is the amount of time that the client actually slept while in bed. To calculate this data point, time spent in bed not sleeping is subtracted from the total amount of time spent in bed. For example, if the client woke three times (for any reason; bathroom visits and lying in bed ruminating are treated the same for this purpose) and over the course of these three times was awake for 2 hours, then the amount of time sleeping that night would be estimated as 8.5 minus 2, or 6.5 hours. Sleep efficiency is then calculated as the ratio of time asleep divided by the total amount of time in bed, multiplied by 100. In the example, the calculation would be (6.5/8.5) * 100, or approximately 76.5%.

Exhibit 7.2 shows a set of questions that may be integrated into a sleep log. The format in which this information is collected is not critical, as long as the information is captured in a reliable fashion. Most clients like to have the sleep log on their bedside table so that they can complete the log quickly in the morning before they actually get out of bed. As with most diaries or logs, the closer in time to the actual event that the record can be made, the more likely it is that the record will be accurate.

EXHIBIT 7.2

Elements of a Sleep Log or Sleep Diary

1. Write the date and day of the week.

2. Record what time you went to bed with the intention to sleep.

3. Record how long it took to get to sleep.

4. Record the number of times you woke during the night. What were the reasons, if known (e.g., bathroom needs, outside sound)?

5. What was the estimated total amount of time you were awake in the night?

6. Record what time you woke up in the morning and did not fall asleep again.

7. Record the time you actually got out of bed.

8. Rate the quality of sleep (this rating can be done using a rating scale from "bad" to "excellent," a rating number such as 1 to 7, or a percentage, as long as the anchors are set and understood by the client and therapist).

9. Record anything unusual about this night's sleep or a needed comment.

Note. Data from Carney and Posner (2016). Record forms can be found in many sources and in a variety of available apps and web-based platforms.

People vary in both the total amount of time they sleep in a given night and their sleep efficiency. It is therefore helpful to ask the client how rested they feel and, over time, to correlate their sleep efficiency with their perceived quality of sleep. Generally, people report satisfying sleep at around 90% sleep efficiency, and this generally becomes the goal for sleep restriction intervention. If a client has 90% sleep efficiency, then by definition they are largely using the bed for sleep.

The issue then becomes how to improve sleep efficiency if it is below 90%. It should be obvious that having the client spend more time in bed is not going to lead to this outcome, and although some clients believe that they should go to bed earlier or lie in bed in the morning to doze and catch up on their sleep, this strategy is likely to reduce sleep efficiency, not improve it.

An effective method is *sleep restriction*. The client may keep a sleep log or sleep diary for a week or two, until a relatively stable estimate of sleep efficiency is determined. The client may also simply estimate the average amount of sleep that they obtain. For example, the previously described client was sleeping approximately 6.5 hours of sleep at night and had a sleep efficiency of 76.5%. Let's assume for the sake of this example that the client is a university student who normally needs to get to campus by 9:00 each morning. Let's further assume that they require 2 hours after they wake up and get out of bed to get organized and get to their first class. The client would be instructed to set their clock at 7:00 a.m. and get out of bed shortly after the alarm goes off every day of the week during this retraining period. However, to obtain 6.5 hours of sleep, the client theoretically needs to go to bed at 12:30 a.m. Therefore, during the period of sleep restriction, the client might be instructed to go to bed at 12:30 and get up at 7:00 a.m. daily while their sleep efficiency would continue to be monitored. If the client can maintain this sleep cycle, their efficiency is likely to rise fairly rapidly to 90% or more.

Assuming that the client's sleep efficiency increases, it is likely that they will report some daytime fatigue. This is normal and expected; in fact, it is a sign that the program is being successful. Once an efficiency of 90% or more is attained, it becomes possible to shift the time to go to bed earlier (e.g., in half hour blocks), as long as sleep efficiency remains high. Over time, the optimal times to enter the bed and to get up in the morning can be determined for each client, with the goal of maintaining a high level of sleep efficiency as well as improved quality of sleep. If clients can maintain the discipline to follow this regimen, successful sleep regulation can be attained in as little as a few weeks. Of course, deviations from the program will yield setbacks, often in the form of decreased sleep efficiency and decreased quality of sleep.

Sleep restriction can be a highly effective technique, presuming that the client is successfully prepared for the intervention, is given good instructions and support during the process, and is motivated not to undermine the program through deviation. Because most clients report increased daytime fatigue during sleep restriction therapy, it is often useful to engage other insomnia-related interventions in conjunction with sleep restriction to optimize the likelihood that the client successfully undertakes the required changes. Some of the techniques described previously, such as relaxation strategies, cognitive interventions, and sleep hygiene are recommended to help the client manage their daytime fatigue. If the therapy is successful, the client can enjoy the benefits of improved sleep efficiency and quality after a few weeks and can begin to experiment with changes in their sleep patterns. For example, they could purposely take a daytime nap on a weekend day and see the effect of this napping on their nighttime sleep. Based on these experiments and evaluations, the client can then determine their optimal sleep pattern.

Combining and Adjusting Sleep Interventions

In summary, a combination of strategies can be used to help clients who struggle with insomnia as a part of their depressive experience. As the therapist, it is ideal if you know these interventions and can evaluate the client's sleep patterns, their ways of relating to the bed and bedroom, their beliefs and thoughts about the importance of sleep, and the general way in which sleep fits into their daily routine. As noted earlier, people vary a fair bit in terms of their need for sleep and the way that they integrate sleep into their lifestyle. Sleep patterns change both across the lifespan and in response to short-term variables (e.g., travel across time zones, the use of substances, acute illnesses), and although it is helpful for clients to create some pattern and predictability to their sleep, it is important also to tolerate some flexibility and change. As with most elements of daily life, this process becomes a matter of discussion, negotiation, and experimentation.

THE VALUE OF PERSISTENCE

Malcolm Gladwell wrote "practice isn't the thing you do once you're good. It's the thing you do that makes you good" (Gladwell, 2008, p. 37). His "10,000-hour rule" was that to achieve true excellence in any skill, you need to practice it correctly for around 10,000 hours. Although this number and the reference for it have been debated, the clear notion is that people are exceedingly unlikely to adopt a new idea or skill and suddenly become its master. Anyone who has coached children or youth in sports, has helped others to learn a new skill-based activity, or has themselves tried to learn a new complex task will quickly appreciate that behavior change is not easy, even when someone is motivated to learn and has few limitations.

I believe that all clients typically do the best they can with the knowledge, skills, and opportunities they have. In some cases, people who develop depression have not had opportunities to learn or practice behaviors that could prevent them from becoming depressed, or perhaps they have not learned adequate coping strategies to use when they start to experience depressive symptoms. In other cases, the experience of depression itself leads the client to engage behavioral strategies, such as avoidance, that unwittingly exacerbate the problem of depression. Your job as therapist is to help to conceptualize the behavioral technique that might help the clients to reduce their depressive symptoms in the short term and hopefully prevent them in the long term. Behavioral strategies are often a foundational aspect of the treatment of depression, and these strategies also often lead to techniques in cognitive restructuring, which are discussed in Chapter 8.

CASE ILLUSTRATIONS OF BEHAVIORAL ILLUSTRATIONS

Next, we revisit the cases of Michael and Miranda to show how their therapists, Drs. Mason and Morales, implemented various behavioral activation techniques to focus on the clients' most immediate and actionable issues early in treatment.[1]

The Case of Michael

When he attended the first treatment appointment, Michael discovered that Dr. Mason had a therapy room in the clinic. Dr. Mason explained that the intake room where he was first seen was used before clients were accepted into treatment and that most of the therapists had a dedicated private office.

Consistent with her plan, Dr. Mason began the appointment by administering the Patient Health Questionnaire-9 (Kroenke et al., 2001). She was somewhat surprised to see that it was relatively elevated, with a score of 20.

---

[1]All cases presented in this book are fictitious and represent illustrations drawn from my experience but not from any specific person.

She reflected to Michael that this score indicated a moderate to high level of depression, which Michael endorsed. Dr. Mason then inquired about Michael's desire to continue with treatment, and he expressed moderate enthusiasm. Dr. Mason then briefly described the major issues that she had identified, including his disengagement in his relationship and his current questions about his own functioning at work. She framed these as interpersonal concerns and suggested that it would be helpful for Michael to think more about both his current and desired roles in life. She also noted that if he were on the verge of making a major life decision and transition to retirement, then this issue also should be considered in therapy, as it presented both a risk for future depression and an opportunity to set more positive patterns for the future.

Michael largely agreed with the presentation by Dr. Mason. He indicated that he had never been in treatment with a psychologist before and that he was unsure of what to expect. He was somewhat anxious about privacy and potentially being seen by someone he knew in the waiting room. In return, Dr. Mason said that treatment was a process they worked out together and that he could express his concern at any time he felt that he either did not understand or did not agree with the approach.

Having come to this agreement, Dr. Mason suggested that one way for Michael to begin the treatment process was to focus on some of his more concrete and specific concerns. She noted that he was relatively inactive, which often contributed to reduced mood. She also made the important connection that increased physical activity is often associated with better sleep as well as improved cognitive functioning. Based on this rationale, she and Michael discussed ways to incorporate a moderate degree of regular physical exercise into his routines. Michael indicated that he had a treadmill that his partner often used, but he had difficulties with running due to his limp. He noted that he had enjoyed swimming in the past and that there was a local pool near where he lived. Together, they agreed that he would go to the facility to enquire about the rates and hours. He initially said that he would go three times over the next week, but Dr. Mason suggested that he scale back his expectations. She was mindful that such an increase in activity would be quite a lot, and as they did not yet even have information about the facility, this plan might be impractical. She informed him that she had had many clients set similar goals and end up discouraged, so they agreed that he would simply gather information for now.

Dr. Mason took the opportunity that Michael had presented and asked about his partner Jon and their relationship. In response, Michael indicated that he felt lonely and that he would be happy to reengage with his partner, if he were interested. Dr. Mason asked Michael to think about his current level of interaction, relative to that which he would prefer, and said that this was something they could discuss at the next appointment.

The Case of Miranda

Following the conceptualization, planning, and goal setting, Miranda and Dr. Morales—Miranda now referred to her by her first name, Josefina—chose to begin with behavioral activation. Miranda came for the next session, pleased that she had completed the logs. However, she noted that she had had a difficult time coming up with activities that she might be interested in. As they reviewed the logs, they agreed that Miranda's days primarily consisted of getting the family ready for the day, driving the girls to school, going to work, picking the girls up from after-school care, completing chores around the house, and preparing dinner. Miranda commented that the log was very informative as it reaffirmed her thoughts that her husband was not very involved in family life and that she truly did not have much time to engage in activities for herself. She reported that weekdays felt very repetitive and boring, and she sometimes felt that she was just "going through the motions" of life without any pleasure. She also noticed how isolated she was, with all the routine tasks that she was required to do.

The sleep log indicated that her bedtime tended to be variable, as she often spent an hour or so by herself after everyone else went to bed. Unfortunately, she was drawn to social media and mindless scrolling through other people's beautiful pictures, which clearly triggered some resentment and negative thoughts about herself. Josefina asked her about these thoughts and commented that they were opinions rather than facts but did not elaborate further. While she was tempted to provide further information about cognitions, she was aware that was not the main focus of the session. She let Miranda know that having these thoughts and feelings prior to going to bed might interfere with sleep, and they agreed that Miranda would limit the use of her phone and other devices after 7 p.m., leave the phone outside the bedroom, and use an alarm clock for a wake-up reminder. They discussed why this strategy might be successful.

After noting that Miranda had a great deal of responsibility in her daily life, they brainstormed some potential interesting activities to complete the list. Josefina commented that although scrolling social media sites before bed was not helpful, it did provide some information regarding her interests. She tended to look at travel photos, home decorating, and current fiction bestsellers. With this feedback, Miranda was able to come up with some ideas, such as joining a book club, redecorating some parts of the home, and planning a summer vacation for the family. She immediately noted that she did not have the time, energy, or money to do most of these activities, and Josefina suggested some ways to break the overall ideas down into smaller, more manageable steps.

The next two sessions were spent working on Miranda's sleep patterns and daily activities. She took the steps to enquire about and join a women's book club available at her local library. While Miranda had limited time to read and felt too tired in the evenings, she and Josefina came up with the idea that she could listen to audiobooks while she was driving. She also began parking her car a bit farther away from work and began walking first for 20 and then for 30 minutes each workday. Her sleep gradually became more routinized and structured, which led to less fatigue and a bit more energy.

8

Cognitive Restructuring in the Treatment of Depression

Earlier in this volume I noted that cognitive behavioral theory and therapy have become dominant forces within the conceptualization and treatment of depression. This evolution is no doubt partly due to the success of cognitive therapy for depression in outcome trials (Cuijpers et al., 2023). The early and well-developed treatment manual (A.T. Beck, Rush, et al., 1979) also spurred the dissemination and use of cognitive theory and therapy. Further, and in large part because of these two factors, many researchers around the world have studied cognitive aspects of depression, either those that underpin therapeutic initiatives or cognitive features in their own right (Clark et al., 1999; R. A. Engel & DeRubeis, 1993; LeMoult & Gotlib, 2019; Phillips et al., 2010; Rock et al., 2014).

The defining feature of the cognitive model of depression is its focus on thought patterns. It is perhaps axiomatic that how we think affects how we feel and behave. Thus, if we confront a situation and interpret it in one direction we might respond positively, but someone else who has a negative interpretation may feel bad and act accordingly. A major innovation of the cognitive model of depression is the recognition that while some negative cognition in depression may be realistic and reflect challenging circumstances, other aspects of cognition may be biased or distorted in a fashion that is consistent with the individual's current depressed state or their core beliefs and values (A. T. Beck, Rush, et al., 1979). The identification of the model as a *diathesis–stress framework* (A. T. Beck & Bredemeier, 2016) underscores that although life stressors are important in

https://doi.org/10.1037/0000398-009
Clinical Depression: An Individualized, Biopsychosocial Approach to Assessment and Treatment, by K. S. Dobson

the development of depression, individuals also bring their unique diatheses, or vulnerabilities, in the form of biological substrates and core beliefs that influence the interpretations of and responses to these stressful events.

This chapter presents some prototypical ways in which individuals who experience depression might interpret different situations. I suggest that three broad classes of negative cognition are seen in depression, and three corresponding types of cognitive interventions can be used when working with the cognitions of clients who suffer from depression (see also D. Dobson & K. S. Dobson, 2017). Two of these classes of cognition could be described as at a surface level, in that they involve the spontaneous interpretations of specific situations, experiences, or events. The third class of cognition, however, involves elaboration of these more immediate reactions and adds a somewhat deeper level of processing. Within the cognitive behavior therapy (CBT) literature, the first two classes of cognition are often referred to as automatic thoughts, as they involve the immediate processing of circumstances, whereas the last class involves broad inferences, beliefs, or meanings that are attached to these immediate experiences.

Given this conceptualization, the three categories of cognition include automatic thoughts that are potentially distorted, automatic thoughts that are drawn from inferences about the situation or circumstances, and thoughts that incorporate the meaning of direct experiences or automatic thoughts. Within this framework, the first class of interventions that I describe includes those that use the client's own words and experiences as evidence to counter their maladaptive cognitions. I use the term "evidence-based interventions" because they use fairly direct tests of the client's cognitions, through either historical information or evidence gathered in the therapy process. The second class of interventions I call "alternative-based interventions," as they involve the development and consideration of alternative thoughts to the clients' negative thoughts. The third class of interventions are "meaning-based interventions," as they involve consideration, review, and possible modification of core beliefs or schemas. In this chapter, I focus on the interventions that are focused at the level of automatic thoughts—the evidence-based and alternative-based categories (meaning-based interventions are discussed in Chapter 10). These interventions are sometimes considered aspects of cognitive restructuring since the focus is on the content of surface thoughts and experiences.

It is worth restating that these categories of interventions focus primarily on the content of what people are thinking, which is to say the language that the client uses to describe their experience. The interventions that target these types of cognitions therefore also focus on the content of the client's cognition, for example to encourage the client to view the situation more accurately and in a less biased fashion or at least to think of alternative and more adaptive ways to think about and respond to the situation. This process of intervention is distinct from interventions that focus on the process of thinking. Much has been written, for example, about the fact that people with clinical depression tend to have repetitive negative cognition, even in the context of relatively minor prompts or stimuli. Both the content of ruminative thoughts and the thought processes themselves are important to consider when treating rumination. As such, the process of repetitive negative thinking can sometimes be targeted for intervention without a focus on what the client is actually saying to themselves. The latter part of this chapter includes a number of interventions that can be used to disrupt ruminative thinking in depression.

MONITORING COGNITION IN DEPRESSION

Before a therapist can discern which thoughts to target for intervention, it is critical to develop a sound and efficient way to capture and organize these thoughts. Everyone has literally thousands of perceptions, reactions, and thoughts every hour, and it would be impossible to attempt to understand and conceptualize all of them. Because cognition is, by its nature, invisible to others, a clinician can know only what the client is able to articulate and discuss. Thus, any discussion of cognition in the clinical setting relies on the client's awareness of their own cognitive processes, their ability and willingness to share these perceptions and thoughts with you, your acumen to attend to and pick up on the most salient experience that is relevant to treatment, and your clinical ability to choose and use a matching intervention effectively. Fortunately, several strategies can be used in this work; some of the key methods are discussed next.

Open and Genuine Inquiry via Socratic Dialogues

An essential ingredient of understanding the client's thoughts is the ability to inquire in an open and genuine manner. Socratic questioning and dialogue are key features of effective CBT, and I argue they are essential ingredients of all effective psychotherapy. Listening to the client without judgment and trying to understand their experience fully are not easy skills. A metaphor that I think is helpful is that your job as therapist is to see the world as your client does and to imagine how you could have the same experiences as the client, given their circumstances, if you adopted their beliefs and values. To the extent that you can achieve these goals, I believe you will be able to understand even the most disturbed emotional and behavioral patterns. From another perspective, I am suggesting that you need strong empathy for your client; as much as you are able, you need to understand their thoughts and impressions that eventuate in their depressive experience.

   The primary strategy to develop an understanding of the client is inquiry. In general, it is not useful to ask the question "Why?"—as in "Why did you get so upset in this situation?"—because this line of questioning runs the risk of creating defensiveness in the client and having them feel judged by you. Indeed, "why" questions are often viewed as accusatory. Rather, questions can more effectively take the form of "How do you understand your level of distress in this situation?" or "What was it about the situation that led to your distress?"

These latter forms of questions will typically elicit much of the same information, but they do so in a way that respects the client's knowledge and expertise
and reduces the risk of negative reactions. As a bit of a side comment, I have
noticed that some clients will repetitively use the "Why?" question with themselves. I have suggested to them that even if we don't know the full reason why
something occurred, we often have our own ideas and conjectures. I have
encouraged these clients to try to shift the discussion to an exploration of what
their ideas are, and then we have been able to explore together which ideas
have more or less substance.

Socratic dialogue sometimes reveals that the client has limitations in their
ability to access and express their internal experience. Sometimes people are
socialized in a way that does not focus on psychological experiences, and their
language has a relative paucity of words to describe what they are thinking and
feeling. As one quick example, I have worked with clients who described themselves as "upset" and used this adjective across a number of different situations.
I looked for opportunities to try to clarify a more precise term for their emotional (and/or physical) experience, and I advised the clients that the word
"upset" is not as clear to me as a more descriptive and complete adjective. In
some cases, I gave the client a list of words for emotions (e.g., English Study
Online, n.d.) and encouraged them to broaden their vocabulary as much as
possible. Sometimes adding a qualifying word (e.g., "I was really anxious") can
help you as the therapist to determine which emotional responses are the
strongest and therefore need more attention. In other cases, we've expanded
the discussion to talk about the physiological signs or symptoms the client had
experienced and labeled with terms such as "upset."

Sometimes, a client says that they have no particular thoughts, that their
emotional experience or behavior is the only thing of which they are aware. My
sense is that often these clients need some psychoeducation about the cognitive
model so they can understand that some form of self-statement or automatic
thought necessarily precedes their other reactions (although see Zajonc, 1980,
for an alternative viewpoint). Some clients benefit from additional reading,
examples from the therapist, extensive Socratic dialogue, or extended practice
with the thought record, described in the next section.

Formulating a Transactional Framework via Thought Records

Another strategy to help the client to give you more information that can be
used in therapy is to provide them with the framework you are using to understand their experience. For example, it is possible to draw a conceptual diagram
of the biopsychosocial approach to depression and show them that although
multiple factors are involved in the genesis and maintenance of depression,
moment-to-moment experience is largely determined by how we think about
and interpret events around us. Within this transactional model, you can
explain that everyone has beliefs and values that they "carry around" within
themselves. These fundamental parts of our identity are formed from the

culture we live in, the early childhood experiences we had, the educational system we experienced, the music and popular culture we took part in, experiences with our friends and family, and the many ways in which we think about ourselves on a day-to-day basis. Once these beliefs are established, they directly influence what we pay attention to, shape the ways in which we interpret our experiences, direct the content of our memory, and influence the meanings that we attach to experience. Even more, our beliefs about ourselves and the world directly influence the types of situations we are willing to put ourselves into, and in this regard these beliefs become a self-reinforcing system.

As suggested, our core beliefs and values shape the situations that we enter. We often go into situations with expectations about what may happen, and then, not surprisingly, we look for confirmatory evidence about our predictions. Even when unexpected events occur, our beliefs influence the ways in which we attend to different aspects of the situation and the meanings and interpretations we draw. Thus, the interactions among our core beliefs and the attributes of different experiences ultimately direct the stream of automatic thoughts that we have, and in turn those automatic thoughts directly influence the emotions we experience and the behavioral responses we select in different situations.

Many clients with whom I have worked have found it helpful to see this process drawn out via a thought record. Often, when I first hear a reasonably good example of this process from a client, I take a piece of paper or a whiteboard to draw this image and use their example to show how their automatic thoughts have emerged (i.e., the interaction between beliefs and the event) as well as the consequences of having these automatic thoughts. This elucidation of the cognitive process is an educational experience for most clients. It helps to direct them to pay attention to their thinking, and it helps me to assess how adept they are at this process and to understand the factors involved with their increased distress.

As the client begins to monitor and report their thoughts and reactions to different situations, it becomes possible to formalize this process. Often, the process includes some psychoeducation about how our automatic thoughts can be linked to our emotional and behavioral responses and potentially some discussion about this process, should the client have questions or a different understanding of the origins of their emotions and actions. Some clients understand better when they are given reading material (e.g., Burns, 1980).

The formalization of this process may include a thought record. Thought records are a systematized way to record the impressions, observations, and thoughts related to a particular event; they are a record of automatic thoughts. As noted earlier, everyone has many thoughts every minute, let alone every day, so the critical issue becomes what the client attends to and records. Typically, clients are instructed to pay attention to strong negative emotions and then to use those emotions as a prompt to deconstruct the situational elements and thoughts that led to those emotional responses. In working with clients who have significant levels of depression, the emotional focus is often on sadness or depression, although any emotional response can be the target of a thought record. My own bias when first starting this work is to identify with the client the most likely distressing emotional reactions they will have, help them to develop a way of talking about and reporting this experience on the thought record, and then encourage them to focus on this emotional response. I encourage the client to write down other strong emotions that occur during the homework as well so that we can discuss them later to more fully understand the client's emotional experiences. With some clients, the emotions associated with depression, such as sadness and helplessness, may become somewhat less potent as therapy moves along. Further, other emotional responses such as anxiety about the future or anger toward others may start to emerge as more dominant themes. The thought record should be approached in a flexible manner so that these new experiences can also be captured.

Thought records come in different forms can be completed in different ways. In some respects, the actual format for recording this information is less important than the fact that the client is attending to their thoughts and recording them in a systematic fashion that they can bring into therapy. Exhibit 8.1 presents a version of the "classic" thought record (A.T. Beck, Rush, et al., 1979). It begins with a denotation of the date and time that the event occurred. It includes a brief description of the situation, the emotional responses, and their intensities.

Interestingly, when this form was first developed, the columns were arranged in the order of emotional response, situation, and thoughts. This format was used because the emotions were often the precipitants for the client to recognize that an event had occurred that warranted recording, and they essentially related the situation and thoughts back to the emotions. From my perspective, that model is less than ideal for two reasons. First, it does not present the model that is being trained in its proper sequence: The proper sequence should be that first an event occurs, then the event is interpreted, followed by an emotional response. As such, my bias is to order the columns in this manner, even though the work with the client might first focus on the emotional reactions and then go back to try to understand the aspects of the situation and the thoughts that led

EXHIBIT 8.1

Classic Thought Record

Date/time	Situation	Emotional responses (type and severity)	Automatic thoughts
Saturday 9:30 a.m.	Home alone; no particular plans for the day	Lonely (70%) Sad (40%) Frustrated (55%)	No one cares about me. I could die today, and no one would know. Why can't I organize my life to do something meaningful?

Note. This form is to be filled out by the client between sessions to monitor significant thoughts and reactions that can later be explored with the therapist. This exhibit demonstrates one sample response that a client might provide. Other rows can be added as needed by the client.

to the outcome. Second, as noted by others (Persons, 2008; Persons et al., 2019), the original format does not include a column for behavioral response. As noted earlier in this book, the behavioral patterns of people who are depressed (and anxious) often involve avoidance or escape, and it is sometimes the case that even if the client does not have a strong emotional reaction to a situation, they have a strong behavioral response. Given this pattern, I always encourage the client to attend to both the emotional and the behavioral reactions they have once they have a strong interpretation of the situation. Exhibit 8.2 depicts the format I typically encourage the client to use to capture their automatic thoughts.

It is worthwhile noting that the same information can be captured in many different ways. Certainly, a preprinted form is likely the easiest. This said, a spreadsheet could be used instead, as could a free-form diary rotation. A number of web and app-based systems can be used to record automatic thoughts. Again, it matters less how this data is collected than that it is systematically collected and brought into therapy. The client can bring a form with them if that method works, or in some cases they can collect information in an electronic form and send it to the therapy office in advance of session. It is worth noting that for most clients, the process of accurately collecting the thought record involves some practice. It is critical to encourage the effort to collect these thought records even if the first few instances are somewhat impoverished or incomplete. In fact, if you find that it takes considerable work to get a complete thought record, you

---

EXHIBIT 8.2

Modified Thought Record

Date/time	Situation	Automatic thoughts	Emotional responses (type and severity)	Behavioral reactions
Saturday 9:30 a.m.	Home alone; no particular plans for the day	No one cares about me. I could die today and no one would know. Why can't I organize my life to do something meaningful?	Lonely (70%) Sad (40%) Frustrated (55%)	Gave up on idea of maybe going shopping. Turned on television and did nothing.

Note. This form is to be filled out by the client between sessions to monitor significant thoughts and reactions that can later be explored with the therapist. The first row provides an example response to guide the client, who then fills out the remaining rows.

have likely also discovered that the client does not reflect on their experience much and may need more assistance with this task in the future. If so, you can use this information either to simplify the thought record for that client or to expect that this part of therapy will be more effortful and slower than it might be otherwise.

When you have a thought record in front of you, the question becomes how to approach it with the client. An attitude of inquisitiveness and exploration is likely going to be the most productive, and the use of Socratic questioning can be very helpful to explore the ways in which the client has constructed their reactions to different situations. My tendency in this work is to ask the client which situation on the thought record was the most distressing to them, and I typically focus on that situation first. Indeed, even within a situation, I try to identify the most distressing thought and focus on it to understand its genesis and consequences as much as possible. My rationale for this focus on the worst problem first is twofold. First, this approach signals to the client that you are willing to address even their most disturbing situation and emotions, and so it expresses a kind of optimism about your ability to help them. Second, understanding and significantly improving a strong negative reaction will be the most efficient way to help the client feel better.

STRATEGIES TO MODIFY NEGATIVE THINKING

Imagine that you are the therapist who has been given the thought record presented in Exhibit 8.2. How would you respond? My suggestion is that you first ask the client for more information about the situation. How was it that, at this particular time on this Saturday, this set of thoughts and emotional responses came into the client's awareness? Was there some particular stimulus or trigger event? It is worthwhile to get enough information about the situation that you can to some extent imagine yourself in the same space as the client and in the same type of setting or condition. You might then ask the client about the thoughts, using Socratic questioning to try to understand how the thoughts linked to the emotional and behavioral responses. The first few times I do this work with a client, if we have a written record, I may take out a writing implement and draw a line between different automatic thoughts and their emotional and/or behavioral responses. Sometimes in this process we discover that some automatic thoughts are not particularly connected to any response, and we have a discussion about whether other emotional reactions or behavioral patterns have not been captured on the form. In other cases, certain responses do not appear to have a preceding thought, and a discussion ensues about from where these reactions emerged. My implicit goal is to understand the client's thoughts in the situation well enough that, by the conclusion of this process, I could imagine having the same type of emotional and/or behavioral reactions as they have.

In the process of discovery, it often becomes apparent that the client may have interpreted a situation in a more negative fashion than is warranted, or perhaps they have engaged a habitual depressive behavioral response to a triggering situation. In some cases, it may appear that the distress is not caused by the original automatic thought but rather is related to the secondary meaning attached to the original automatic thought. It may become clear that the distressing thought is actually a question (e.g., the "why" question), and a further discussion may be required to fully understand what the client is thinking about the event.

In my view, therapeutic responses to negative automatic thoughts generally fall into one of three broad classes of interventions that depend on the nature of the automatic thoughts (see also D. Dobson & K.S. Dobson, 2017): *evidence-based interventions, alternative-based interventions,* and *meaning-based interventions.* Evidence-based interventions are particularly relevant for negative automatic thoughts that involve a clear misperception or distortion of a triggering event. Much has been written about cognitive distortions in the field of depression, and therapists often look for distortions believing that they can be corrected fairly easily. Indeed, these distortions are often good places to begin. However, even clients with significant levels of depression may have negative thoughts that are not distorted; the problem may be in the ways in which the client responds to the situation. In these latter cases, considering alternative ways to look at the situation and engaging in alternative-based interventions is usually productive. A primary automatic thought may be related to the situation, and a second level of thinking may be a direct response to that automatic thought (see also J. S. Beck, 2021). Finally, for the most distressing automatic thoughts, a meaning or interpretation is almost always given at the secondary level to the original automatic thought. These meanings typically are derived in part from the events but also from the client's core beliefs or values. As such, meaning-based interventions often move into the domain of core belief work (see Chapter 10).

Most clinicians have likely seen lists of cognitive distortions—many different versions of these lists are available on the internet and in various publications (e.g., J. S. Beck, 2021; D. Dobson & K.S. Dobson, 2017; Leahy et al., 2012; Padesky & Greenberger, 2021). In some publications, these patterns of automatic thought are referred to as thinking errors (e.g., Sokol & Fox, 2019) to denote that although they may not necessarily be distortions, they are problematic and in this sense an error. Table 8.1 provides a list of

TABLE 8.1. Cognitive Distortions or Thinking Errors, Arranged by Optimal Type of Intervention Mode

Evidence-based targets	Meaning-based targets	Evidence- and alternative-based targets
All-or-nothing thinking	Jumping to conclusions	Magnification/minimization
Overgeneralization	Emotional reasoning	Labeling
Discounting the positives	"Should" statements	Blaming self or others
Mind-reading		
Fortune-telling		

common cognitive distortions/thinking errors, organized by optimal intervention type.

Evidence-Based Strategies to Modify Negative Thinking

Evidence-based strategies work best with negative thoughts that represent cognitive distortions or misperceptions, as presented in Table 8.1. For example, all-or-nothing thinking represents an extreme cognition. The client may use words like "everything," "nothing," "always," "never," or "100%" that suggest the perception that things are black or white, positive or negative, but with little to nothing in the moderate range. A classic example would be a statement such as "I always fail."

All-or-nothing cognitions almost cry out to be tested against the lived experience of the client. Although it is theoretically possible that bad things "always happen," it is unlikely. Helping the client recognize that their experience is not as negative as they may first perceive can be beneficial. To engage in this type of intervention, it is important for you as the therapist to listen for counterexamples and to be confident that extreme statements can be contrasted with actual experience. Then, when an automatic thought recurs, you can propose to the client that it might be useful to examine whether the automatic thought is accurate. If the client concurs, you can work together to identify counterfactual pieces of evidence from their own experience, things you have heard in therapy, or homework assignments that you and the client generate to find out if their automatic thoughts are veridical or not. This process has sometimes been likened to a court proceeding in which the client is encouraged to be more like an objective judge—to weigh the evidence for and against their original negative thought objectively and to determine whether the thought has merit. This approach has also been termed "trial-based cognitive therapy" (de Oliveira, 2016).

Similar evidence-based techniques can be fairly easily generated for the cognitive distortions of overgeneralization and discounting the positives. In both instances, the client is not attending to the full range of experience; as such, purposefully reviewing with the client their automatic thought, the evidence that supports or is consistent with it, and the evidence that is contradictory or at least not fully supportive is often a worthwhile use of time. In mind-reading (i.e., situations in which a client thinks they can know the intentions or thoughts of others without asking) and fortune-telling (i.e., situations in which a client thinks they can foretell what will happen in the future, often in the context of interpersonal relationships), the common thread is that the client is making inferences or judgments that lack evidence. In these cases, the client can be encouraged to recognize their tendency to make conclusions even if they do not know what the other person is thinking or what the future may hold, as appropriate, and then can be encouraged to seek out information that would help to make an informed decision.

Although the evidence-based interventions can be used as stand-alone interventions, it is often recommended to take these interventions one step further and combine them with alternative-based interventions.

Alternative-Based Strategies to Modify Negative Thinking

Some negative thoughts do not lend themselves easily to evidence-based interventions. For example, emotional reasoning is a cognitive distortion in which the client uses their current emotions as a way to interpret an event around them. In such an instance, it may be possible to look at the event more objectively and to imagine what a nondepressed person might think in that situation, but the key aspect of the intervention is likely going to be to ask the client to entertain an alternative idea. For example, imagine that a client who is struggling with depression decides to go to a movie. During the movie, they recognize that their mood has not improved, they come to the conclusion that the movie must be disappointing or poorly done, and they leave midway through the movie. Although in theory you could help the client to dissect the movie in greater detail and come to a more dispassionate assessment of the merits and limitations of the film, helping the client recognize that their emotional reasoning led to a self-fulfilling prophecy (i.e., leaving) is likely to be much more useful. It may also be helpful to generate alternative thoughts that the client could have had and to imagine what the outcomes would have been. For example, rather than leaving the movie, they might have said to themselves, "I am not particularly enjoying this movie, but at least I am doing something positive by getting out of my apartment and into the world" or "I have not enjoyed this movie up until this point, but I am going to give it the benefit of the doubt and see if it gets better." These alternative thoughts could provide the client with an incentive to continue to engage in activities that are inconsistent with depression and that give the client enhanced exposure to different experiences.

Another example of cognitive distortions that lend themselves to alternative-based interventions are "should" statements. "Should" statements can be directed either toward oneself, in the form of personal directives, or toward others in terms of expectations or demands. Often, "shoulds" are intimately tied to core beliefs or values that the client holds, and they become activated when the client or others around them fail to meet the expectations or values that are implicitly connected. For example, a client with depression may go out of their way to make a social connection but find that the other person fails to reciprocate some type of invitation. The client may feel hurt and express the idea that the other person "should have" extended a return social invitation. It likely would serve some value for you as the therapist to clarify exactly what happened (mostly to confirm that the "should" is idiosyncratic and perhaps unreasonable), but in terms of an intervention, it is likely that looking at different ways to interpret the situation is going to yield the best clinical outcome. It might be possible to generate an alternative such as

"My belief is that you should always reciprocate a social invitation, but other people may not have the same idea or value," "Just because I think people should return social invitations, that does not mean everyone has the same value," or "If I would like more social contact with this person, I could make a second invitation."

Combining Evidence- and Alternative-Based Strategies

Although the preceding discussions imply that evidence-based and alternative-based interventions are distinct, in many cases both will be useful. Imagine you are the client, and the therapist used an evidence-based strategy to point out that your black-or-white thinking was inaccurate and that there are shades of grey between the polar opposites you had first imagined. If the therapist stopped at this point, you might infer that they think you are foolish, illogical, or simply wrong. It is therefore important for you as the therapist to empathically state your understanding of the reasons the client might see things more negatively than is warranted, help them to generate a balanced and realistic view of what is going on around them, and then encourage them to generate a moderate interpretation consistent with the evidence. In some cases, it may be appropriate to generate an alternative, evidence-based thought. For example, if the original negative thought was "I always fail" and the evidence review suggests otherwise, the client might be encouraged to adopt a more realistic statement such as "I sometimes fail, but I'm doing the best I can." In this way, evidence-based interventions can be melded with alternative-based interventions.

In the discussion of evidence-based interventions, I noted that after the evidence reviews are completed, it is often useful to try to derive a new way of thinking about the situation consistent with the full evidence. In the discussion of alternative-based interventions, I also suggested that it is often worthwhile to fully describe the situation first to ensure the alternatives that the client or therapist generate are credible in the context of the particular situation. A number of cognitive distortions ultimately require both evidence-based and alternative-based interventions. As one example, labeling is a cognitive distortion that involves the client's perception of some attribute or behavior in someone else, an interpretation, and an associated label. For example, the client who experiences the failure of someone to return a social invitation may call the other person "rude." This type of perception often involves attending selectively to the negative attributes of the other person and then applying the "rude" label. An ideal intervention is likely going to be one in which the full range of behaviors of the other person is first reviewed to ensure the client is not selectively attending to certain behaviors, discounting positive features of the other person, or missing information that is inconsistent with their ultimate conclusion. Socratic questioning can often be used in this phase of intervention to fully explore the situation and the client's thoughts to see if they are consistent with each other. It is then important to understand how the client views the label itself (in this case, "rude"), to determine if the other person's behavior has actually met this threshold, and to consider some other accurate but more positive way to interpret the situation. Questions at this phase could include "What makes a person 'rude'?", "What is 'rudeness'?", "Is being rude situational, or does it reflect the other person's personality?", or "Is there some other way you can explain the other person's behavior?" These questions encourage the client to consider their definition of the label, to see if the situation merits the label, and to encourage other—hopefully more positive—ways to consider the situation. Thus, the intervention may need to rely on a combination of both evidence-based and alternative-based interventions to yield the best possible outcome. Indeed, many cognitive distortions incorporate both a primary perceptual aspect (the evidence) and an interpretation (the meaning) that need to be reviewed for optimal benefit (see also J. S. Beck, 2021; D. Dobson & K.S. Dobson, 2017).

THE PROBLEM OF RUMINATION

Rumination is a type of cognitive process that is not unique to depression (Bravo et al., 2020), but it reflects a type of cognition commonly seen in clients with depression. Rumination has been defined as "a stable, enduring, and habitual trait like a tendency to engage in repetitive self-focus in response to depressed mood" (Watkins, 2016, p. 24; see also Nolen-Hoeksema et al., 2008; Nolen-Hoeksema & Watkins, 2011). It has been argued that this pattern of thinking is often learned in childhood and may be modeled by parents, but regardless of its origin it reflects a repetitive pattern of attempting to mentally solve life's problems.

According to Watkins (2016), rumination is most likely to emerge in one of two instances. First, rumination may occur when a person sets an unreasonable or unattainable life goal and so recurrently comes back to the issue of how to solve or attain the goal. Second, rumination may emerge when a person dwells on issues or problems that have already occurred or are ongoing and the client either fails to have the requisite skills to solve the problem or simply repetitively asks themselves questions such as "Why did this happen?" or "What does this event mean about me?" Thus, it is possible that rumination may lead to positive change in the sense that the individual may realize they need to learn new skills, lower expectations, or derive new understandings about past experiences. Rumination-focused interventions, in contrast, address unhelpful and depression-related rumination (Watkins, 2008) that can sometimes also serve an avoidance function.

Clinicians are fortunate that a lot of attention has been paid to the issue of rumination and a treatment model is specifically targeted toward clients who engage in ruminative thinking (Watkins, 2016). Rumination-focused cognitive behavior therapy (RFCBT) is targeted toward clients who engage in unproductive repetitive thinking, and while RFCBT can stand as a treatment in its own right, aspects of rumination-focused intervention can also be integrated into the care of clients with depression, when indicated. Some of the major ways in which this work can be done are described here; for a more complete understanding of this approach, refer to Watkins (2016).

If the client engages in ruminative thinking, the pattern will often emerge early in the course of treatment. Often, the process is that a goal is named, the repetitive pattern of thinking emerges, and the client becomes disengaged from action. Indeed, a functional analysis of the role of rumination often shows its outcome is that the client becomes stuck in their thoughts, becomes emotionally distraught (either more anxious, if the problem is in the future, or more depressed, if the event is historical), and chooses not to take action. If the therapist inquires about alternative ways to conceptualize the problem or potential coping strategies, the client remains stuck in a pattern of repetitive and unproductive thinking and may even negate any suggestions offered by the therapist. In some cases, the client may demonstrate limited problem-solving ability or skills deficits related to ongoing stressors that seem to be unsuccessfully managed.

Given that the rumination can take different forms and may have different outcomes, it is critical to start the process of rumination-focused interventions by engaging in considerable assessment to understand the role of rumination for a given client. Assessment may include Socratic questioning of specific rumination experiences, the use of a thought record to examine when rumination begins and what its effects are, or a formal functional analysis of the antecedents and consequences of rumination. It is often helpful in this process to normalize rumination as a common phenomenon whenever a person is faced with an ongoing stressor but to also recognize that it can maintain or exacerbate depressed mood.

Once rumination has been assessed and the client understands that the process is not helpful for them, a number of potential interventions can be used, including but not limited to skills training, increased activity to minimize avoidance, and goals clarification. It is also possible to intervene more directly with ruminative thinking, such as by having the client develop an increased awareness of rumination and an alternative coping behavior when rumination is noticed. For example, the client might be encouraged to take a short walk whenever they notice that they have begun to ruminate, if this would be appropriate. It may also be possible to develop therapeutic experiments in which the client formally develops a range of alternative responses to rumination and then tests the various responses to determine the best outcome. Once this result is known, the client is encouraged to be more flexible in the response to rumination and ideally to employ the optimal strategy most often. Another potential intervention is to have the client purposefully engage in rumination at a scheduled time so that they can practice adaptive responses to rumination when it begins. This purposeful engagement in rumination has an incidental benefit—it teaches the client that rumination is a cognitive process that is, at least to some extent, under their control.

This type of exposure intervention can be done based on trigger events (either imagined or in real life), the repetitive thoughts themselves, or the emotional patterns that typically elicit rumination. A final recommended strategy is compassion training (Gilbert, 2009, 2010). Although the strategy of being more kind toward oneself and less critical emerged from a tradition other than psychotherapy, compassion training has a definite role for people with self-critical ruminative thinking, and interventions based on compassion-focused therapy (Gilbert, 2010) may be indicated if a client engages in severe and punishing rumination.

As noted previously, RFCBT can be delivered as a stand-alone treatment, and it has been evaluated in both individual and group formats. In a randomized trial of participants with residual depression assigned either to treatment as usual or treatment as usual plus up to 12 sessions of individual RFCBT, the group that received RFCBT showed significantly lower levels of residual symptoms and higher remission rates, with these results mediated by change in rumination scores (Watkins et al., 2011). Similar benefits appear in others studies as well, suggesting that rumination-focused intervention has considerable merit for clients who struggle with repetitive and unwanted thinking (see Watkins, 2022; Watkins & Roberts, 2020, for reviews).

CHANGE YOUR THOUGHTS, CHANGE YOUR WORLD

Mentation has been listed as a defining characteristic of the species *Homo sapiens*. The human ability to imagine a future that has not yet occurred and to reflect on both our personal past and the history of the world in general is a remarkable asset when deployed in a positive manner. Our thoughts can also drag us down, inject demoralization into our lives, and lead to passivity and helplessness. This is not news, however, as many years ago Norman Vincent Peale wrote, "Change your thoughts and you change your world" (cf. Peale, 1952). What is different now, however, is that a large number of strategies have been developed to help individuals who have negative thinking connected to a wide variety of conditions, including depression.

In this chapter, I have described a wide range of potential interventions. As a clinician, I often hear that people feel overwhelmed by the range of possible strategies. My encouragement to you as a therapist is to listen to your client, ask questions and try to understand the world from their perspective as well as you can, and then attempt to match the intervention to the problematic thought processes you hear. This process is not perfect by any stretch of the imagination, and so it is important to assess the client to determine which interventions seem to have benefit and which do not. Augment, practice, and encourage those interventions that seem to work, but shift away from those that perhaps do not. Finally, as with any skill, encourage the client to continue to practice the cognitive interventions whenever and wherever they can.

CASE ILLUSTRATIONS OF COGNITIVE RESTRUCTURING

The case examples of Michael and Miranda show how their therapists, Dr. Mason and Dr. Morales (who Miranda calls by her first name, Josefina), implemented the cognitive restructuring strategies reviewed in this chapter.[1]

The Case of Michael

Although Dr. Mason did not intend to engage in formal cognitive restructuring, Michael indicated several important shifts in his thoughts over the next few appointments. For example, he went to the swimming pool to learn about its operating hours and services and ended up staying and swimming. He felt better afterwards, so he went a second time during the week. He noted that on the two days he swam, he slept somewhat better. He also felt good that he had started this activity and began to have ideas about other types of activities he might pursue. As an example, he saw an advertisement for deep-water running at the pool, which he had never considered. Dr. Mason and Michael discussed potential activities. Swimming was an activity that Michael had previously enjoyed as a young adult, and so it made good sense to start this activity again. Michael spontaneously offered to swim twice more in the coming week. In contrast, although he was not ready to pursue deep-water running in the short term because it was a new activity and he was concerned that he was unfit, he was willing to consider it in the future. Dr. Mason also helped Michael to see that his shift in thought, to be more positive and open to experience, itself had a positive effect on Michael's mood.

The other major issue that affected Michael's thinking was that his partner, Jon, had noticed his exercise and had made a positive comment. He offered that they might do some regular evening walks when the weather was good. Michael was both surprised and pleased by this response and was unsure how to build on this positive indication. Dr. Mason spent some time using Socratic questioning to understand the thoughts that led Michael to be surprised, and then they discussed how one's predictions do not always match experience. Dr. Mason was able to build on this idea and to suggest that Michael might benefit from looking for circumstances that did not match his prior predictions and new ways to experience and think about his world. Together, they discussed how Michael approached his intimate relationship and came up with some ideas for Michael to build on this early success with Jon.

To capitalize on Michael's positive response to intervention and his new ways of thinking about his relationship, Dr. Mason inquired about whether Michael saw any room for changes in his interpersonal relationships at work. Michael discussed his recent pattern of increased silence and withdrawal at work, and together he and Dr. Mason came to the conclusion that this interpersonal style

---

[1]All cases presented in this book are fictitious and represent illustrations drawn from my experience but not from any specific person.

was likely less than optimal. They discussed alternative ways that he could function at work, including increased contact with some key personnel. Although initially this change in interpersonal style was somewhat challenging for Michael, he reported over the next few weeks that he was feeling more comfortable again at work and that with the combination of his increased activity, improved sleep, and a somewhat improved relationship at home he was feeling overall improvement. A repeated Patient Health Questionnaire-9 (PHQ-9; Kroenke et al., 2001) in Session 6 revealed a score of 12, which, compared with his previous score of 20 in Session 2, suggested that his depression level had indeed reduced since the outset of treatment.

The Case of Miranda

Josefina had gradually noted some of Miranda's cognitions during the sessions and sometimes commented on their negativity. She had provided some general information during the description of CBT in earlier sessions, and during Session 4 she provided psychoeducation regarding cognitive distortions and their potential impact on mood and actions. She offered a number of examples that were particularly relevant to Miranda. For example, Miranda tended to blame herself for the breakup with Thomas, her first significant romantic partner more than 20 years ago; she still had thoughts such as "I was less desirable than the other women" and "I was a naïve fool not to have seen it coming." She had recently received a raise in her pay at work and had thoughts such as "It must be a general raise that everyone received, as I didn't do anything to deserve it." At her first book club meeting, she worried that "I don't have much to offer in these discussions and others will think I'm stupid." Josefina gently went through each example, asking how much she believed each thought and the consequent feelings. Miranda reported feelings of shame, guilt, anxiety, and sadness. Through the questioning, Miranda began to see that Josefina did not always agree with her thoughts and that they were not 100% accurate. Prior to this discussion, she had understood the concept of negative thoughts in a somewhat theoretical manner but had not really applied it to examples from her own life. Josefina used questions in therapy such as "What would you tell a friend in this situation?" to encourage Miranda to be more flexible in her thinking.

Josefina brought out a blank thought record, and the two of them went through a detailed example using the situation from the book club. Josefina asked Miranda to keep a thought record for homework, completing one to two examples per day. In addition, she asked Miranda to continue to do homework related to sleep routines, daily walking, and listening to audiobooks. At the end of the session, Miranda told Josefina that she had emailed one of her old school friends and they had arranged to go for lunch. She was somewhat sheepish, as this step was not part of her "official" homework; Josefina told her that this step likely indicated that Miranda's confidence was growing and her mood improving, with the latter confirmed by the PHQ-9 results.

Miranda completed her thought records for the next session, although she had difficulty coming up with alternative thoughts. Josefina told her that many clients have this struggle because the thoughts are automatic and highly believable. Together, they worked through the records, identifying distortions and potential alternatives. While the alternatives were not as credible to Miranda as the automatic ones were, she was able to see that they might have some merit. For example, being quiet during a book club meeting might not be interpreted by others as "stupidity," but maybe it could be seen as shyness because she was new to the group or even quiet disagreement with the group's discussion. She realized that several other people had been fairly quiet; she had not had negative thoughts about them but was simply somewhat inquisitive about why they had not spoken much. Josefina supported this type of wondering, as it revealed that Miranda had not jumped to any conclusions about others' silence, just as others might not have formed negative opinions about her.

Problem-Solving Therapy Applied to Depression

Some readers may find it unusual that a chapter on problem solving is placed at this particular point in this volume. Often, other books present a fairly direct progression from assessment and intervention at the level of automatic thoughts to the assessment and intervention at the deeper level of core beliefs or schemas. My perception, as discussed more fully at the beginning of Chapter 10, is that often in the treatment of clients with depression we do not proceed directly to the level of the core belief work. In such cases, a useful framework for the overall approach to the work is to consider the initial presenting problems of the client, the way that these problems have been approached in therapy and hopefully reduced or minimized, and the residual problems. Thus, while you as the therapist may have used an implicit problem-solving framework, this point in treatment is often an opportune time to discuss the problem-solving framework with the client. My experience is that if you have had some successes in treatment up to this point, the client is often ready and willing to step back from their day-to-day experience with depression and reflect broadly on their previous strategies to manage depression, as opposed to those that have been developed over the course of treatment. In this regard, using a problem-solving framework is often helpful for them to see how their prior problems have been managed and to conceptualize ways in which remaining problems can be addressed.

The other reason to place this chapter at this point in the book is that problem-solving strategies most often involve behavioral and/or automatic

https://doi.org/10.1037/0000398-010

Clinical Depression: An Individualized, Biopsychosocial Approach to Assessment and Treatment, by K. S. Dobson

thought types of interventions, which are discussed in greater detail in Chapters 8 and 10. Problem solving can include discussing new ways to approach sleep dysfunction, activity levels, ways of thinking about and responding to events, and potentially skills training if relevant to the solution of a given problem. Although it is possible that the client's core beliefs are part of the problem as well, this is less commonly seen in treatment, and as such I have deferred that discussion until Chapter 10.

"Problem solving" is a broad term for a set of interventions that assist the client to manage and potentially rectify their life problems. Problem solving can be effectively used in the treatment of clients with depression, and it serves well as a general life skill. *Problem-solving therapy* (PST) has existed for some time (Nezu et al., 1989, 2013) and was first developed in the context of social problem-solving issues that clients might have. PST was applied to clinical depression early in its development (Nezu et al., 1989; Nezu & Perri, 1989) with positive results. Meta-analyses of PST for depression confirm that the approach represents an evidence-based treatment for depression in its own right (Bell & D'Zurilla, 2009; Cuijpers et al., 2018; Kirkham et al., 2016).

THE PROBLEM-SOLVING FRAMEWORK

The PST approach recognizes that some clients have skill deficits in the area of managing problems, that negative thoughts can interfere with existing problem-solving skills, and that people's natural ability to solve life problems may be compromised when they are under stress. Given these considerations, it is not uncommon that a multipronged response is necessary to ensure the client who struggles with problem solving has the requisite skills and that they can apply them appropriately. In this regard, PST has been viewed as both a skills-based program and a reflection of a more general problem orientation.

The orientation aspect of PST refers to a general set of beliefs or assumptions about the value and importance of problem solving as well as the client's more specific sense of personal competence in problem solving as a strategy. Clients who are more optimistic about dealing with problematic situations and who believe that their own skills and competence will permit them to apply problem-solving strategies are notably more likely to engage in these activities. It is therefore important that when you determine problem-solving strategies are appropriate for a given client, you also assess these two elements of the problem orientation (much as is done in motivational interviewing, discussed in Chapter 5). Should the client express doubts about the value of problem solving or their own personal problem-solving efficacy, it is worthwhile to assess these cognitions further and to try to encourage the client to experiment with problem solving rather than simply accept that there is little they can do.

The definition of a "problem" within the PST framework is broad. While many people think about problems as external to the individual (e.g., something in the social environment that causes distress), other issues can also be framed as problems. For example, emotional responses can be framed as problems and targets for change. For a client with negative emotions, the goal could be to reduce the intensity, frequency, or duration of the feelings involved. In another case, the problem may be a perceived insufficiency of positive emotions. Behavioral responses of the client, including avoidance or withdrawal, can also become targets for problem solving, as can problematic ways of thinking or interpreting situations. Indeed, the concept of a problem is highly flexible. It is worth noting that a problem can be identified by either the client or the therapist, as long as both agree to work on the issue in a collaborative fashion.

PROBLEM-SOLVING STEPS

Most problem-solving models use a sequential framework to consider the appropriate steps. Different versions of the problem-solving cycle exist, with some including four steps whereas others include as many as eight. A common framework applied in the context of depression appears in Figure 9.1 (Nezu et al., 2013). The five steps include problem definition, the generation of alternative potential solutions to the problem, the selection of the best apparent choice among these potential solutions, implementation of the proposed solution, and evaluation of the outcome. If the problem-solving strategy has been successful, it is possible that the therapist and client can exit the problem-solving cycle. However, in some instances it may be necessary to reconsider the problem in light of a failed strategy and begin the problem-solving cycle again or, if the problem is not fully resolved, to reconsider its nature and develop and implement supplemental or different problem-solving strategies.

FIGURE 9.1. A General Problem-Solving Framework

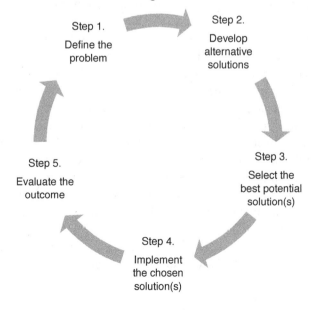

Step 1.
Define the problem

Step 2.
Develop alternative solutions

Step 3.
Select the best potential solution(s)

Step 4.
Implement the chosen solution(s)

Step 5.
Evaluate the outcome

Step 1: Define the Problem

The first step of problem solving is to clearly and operationally define the "problem," ideally in such a deliberate manner that it can be reliably assessed and monitored over time.

Step 2: Develop Alternative Solutions

After the problem is defined and operationalized, the second step of problem solving is to generate a wide range of potential solutions to the problem. Many individuals have a tendency to identify a first and likely strategy and then to begin to consider how to implement it. The PST framework, however, encourages clients to avoid the tendency to rush to the first possible solution and instead to "think outside of the box" to generate a variety of possibilities.

Several principles are often discussed at this point of problem solving. One is the variety principle, which suggests that the more different types of solutions that can be generated, the more likely that one (or more) is going to be successful. Another principle is that the more alternative potential strategies that can be identified, the more likely one is to be successful. A third principle is to suspend judgment. Rather than evaluating each alternative as it is generated, the idea is to produce as many possible ideas from a range of different perspectives first and then go back to each and evaluate its merits in turn. Indeed, one therapeutic strategy can be to suggest options that are clearly fanciful and inappropriate to the client, just to encourage the idea of adopting diverse ways to think about the problem.

Step 3: Select the Best Potential Solution(s)

The third aspect of PST is to take the list of alternative solutions, evaluate each one systematically, and select one or more that seem the most practical and helpful. Considerations can include the likelihood that the solution can be implemented at all, the costs associated with the solution (including time, money, energy, or other considerations), and the likelihood that the solution can yield the desired outcomes if successfully implemented. Sometimes this discussion makes it clear that more fundamental skills training is necessary to help the client implement a desired solution, and treatment might step back somewhat from solution implementation to skills training before the strategy is fully considered. For example, the client may have a chronic interpersonal problem in their work setting, which might be addressed through a strong assertive interaction by the client. If an assessment indicates that the client does not know how to be assertive, it is well worth the time to do some assertiveness training before the decision is made to try to implement that strategy.

It is important to note that clients who struggle with negative thinking or depressed affect may be relatively quick to rule out potential solutions, so it is commensurately important for you as the therapist to ensure that every potential strategy gets a fair consideration before determining whether it is viable. The ultimate aim of the third step of problem solving is to select the solution(s) that have the highest likelihood of success. Again, be mindful that more than one alternative may be available; if so, it may be possible to choose one potential solution and implement it while holding other alternatives in reserve should they become necessary. On the other hand, I caution against exploring and testing too many alternative solutions, as this process can be time-consuming and ultimately discouraging. My opinion is that three or four options is likely a good number to demonstrate flexibility but to also retain a focus on high-probability solutions.

Step 4: Implement the Chosen Solution(s)

The fourth stage of PST is to implement the chosen method(s) that might mitigate or solve the problem. As described in Chapter 7 regarding general activity scheduling, this stage is optimally done in a collaborative manner with the client, who should be invited to exercise significant control over the way in which they implement the strategy. It is often worthwhile to spend some time using motivational interviewing strategies to ensure that the client can state the reason the solution is important to them and how the chosen strategy might help them in their therapeutic work. Should the client struggle in this communication, you can certainly provide some prompts or encouragement, but my recommendation is that you have a strong endorsement of the problem-solving strategy from the client before you accept it is in place. Even further, if you have questions in your mind about the client's ability to undertake the assignment, it is often worth the time to specify issues such as when the client will undertake the strategy, what it will look like in practice, and how you and the client will know a reasonable effort was made.

Again, it is important to note that the principal outcome of PST is the effort to reduce the problem. It cannot always be guaranteed that any particular strategy will be successful, and so the attitude of "Let's try it and see" has to be kept in mind for both the therapist and client. Of course, the goal is to choose a strategy that has the highest chance of success, and it would be generally unwise to deliberately have the client implement strategies that have a low probability to achieve the desired outcome. Even with this caution, however, it may sometimes be worthwhile to have the client implement the strategy they think will be successful, even if you are somewhat less optimistic, so you both can learn what are effective and ineffective implementations for the client's particular circumstances. In a very real sense, even a complete "failure" provides new information about what the client can do and what happens in their social environment when they make the effort. Even unsuccessful strategies provide information and can lead to a revision or reconsideration of alternative problem-solving methods.

Step 5: Outcome Evaluation

Consistent with a recurrent theme throughout this volume, any homework assignments need evaluation. A critical stage of PST is to assess the effort that is made as well as its outcome on the problem. For many problems, an immediate solution may not be available, and it may be necessary to monitor a problem-solving strategy over a period of weeks to ensure the strategy is implemented consistently and to evaluate the problem-oriented changes that occur. If the strategy takes some time to be fully realized, it is critical for therapists to monitor this activity every session so the strategy and its outcomes are not forgotten.

In many instances, even with an optimal and effective strategy, problems may linger: They may be partially resolved, or they may recur. For example, if a client engages coping strategies that solve an interpersonal problem in the first instance but the other person relapses into problematic behaviors, the situation may require ongoing intervention. A critical phase of PST is therefore to determine whether the problem is unresolved, partially resolved, or fully resolved and then, if necessary, to reengage the problem-solving cycle to address any remaining issues. It is also important to recognize that not all of life's problems can be effectively dealt with by problem solving, and sometimes unsuccessful outcomes can lead to a larger discussion about the problems that are and are not ultimately solvable at the individual level.

COMMON ASPECTS OF PROBLEM SOLVING

PST has a number of virtues. It is a positive, problem-oriented strategy that can be used to tackle life's problems. It is explicitly action oriented and encourages the client to move from a passive position into one of competent action. Through the sequential stages of the problem-solving model, the client's problem orientation, their ability to think outside of the box and come up with novel strategies to cope with problems, their social skills and other competencies, their cognitive interpretations and potential distortions, their level of motivation, and their ability to stick to an action plan once determined are all assessed and become potential areas for intervention. Further, the problem-solving model is not constrained by any a priori assumptions about the types of intervention needed to solve a given problem for a given client. As such, the model is highly consistent with the idiographic case formulation approach that is foundational to the current volume. As stated in other places (e.g., Nezu et al., 2019), the PST approach has been applied with success to a wide variety of clinical problems, again a reflection of its transdiagnostic utility and broad applicability.

Although PST often uses concrete strategies to solve problems (e.g., skills training, motivational interviewing), in a certain way problem solving itself can be considered a type of metaskill. Therapists have developed various problem-solving worksheets and formats (Nezu et al., 2013), and problem solving can be discussed with a client in a general manner, as opposed to dealing with a particular situation. In my experience, an optimal way to integrate problem-solving strategies into therapy is to find a particular problem early in the course of treatment and to use the problem-solving framework implicitly. Particularly if the strategy has been successful, if the client is not too distressed, and if the client has the ability to reflect on their own experience, it may be an opportune point in therapy to introduce the generic problem-solving model. Having had a successful experience with this approach already will help the client see the utility of the model, and, depending on their response to the generic approach of problem solving, you and the client can work together to look for other opportunities to engage the problem-solving process.

Problem-solving therapy has been recast as *emotion-centered problem-solving therapy* (EC-PST; Nezu et al., 2019; Nezu & Nezu, 2018), "based on a biopsycho-social, diathesis–stress model of psychopathology" (Nezu et al., 2019, pp.172). It is predicated on the idea that negative affect is a key issue in the lives of people who face problems, both in the sense that the problems themselves lead to emotional distress and with the recognition that negative affect itself can perpetuate challenges to effective problem solving. One particular inno-vation is the stop, slow down, think, and act (SSTA) approach. Rather than responding to problem situations in a previously used but emotionally laden fashion, the SSTA approach encourages the client to stop (the emotional pat-tern), slow down (and engage the problem-solving cycle), think (creatively and productively about strategies that might solve the problem), and act (imple-ment the strategy and evaluate its outcomes). Within the EC-PST approach, issues such as helplessness and hopelessness are directly addressed, with the view that a positive problem orientation will encourage hopefulness and the desire at least to attempt problem solution. In most other respects, however, the EC-PST approach is highly consistent with earlier work on problem-solving treatments.

One feature of PST for clients is not often discussed but is very valuable in the treatment of depression, from my perspective. While many psychosocial approaches to depression consider the problem as largely generated from within the client, the PST approach explicitly recognizes both external and internal factors in the genesis and maintenance of depression. This approach is therefore an explicit diathesis–stress model, and it recognizes that people who end up having problems such as depression may indeed live in a prob-lematic world. As discussed in Chapter 3, people who experience adverse childhood experiences, live with relative deprivation, are subject to victim-ization, are socially isolated, or live in punishing and aversive environments are at increased risk of experiencing depression relative to people without such risk factors. In this regard, the problem-solving framework can be a highly effective way to support clients and to address the real-life problems that they may face. This stance is highly collaborative and acknowledges that we all live somewhere, even if that somewhere is potentially hostile and depressogenic.

CASE ILLUSTRATIONS OF PROBLEM-SOLVING THERAPY

The cases of Michael and Miranda show how their therapists, Dr. Mason and Dr. Morales (who Miranda calls by her first name, Josefina), used the problem-solving framework identified in this chapter.[1]

The Case of Michael

Dr. Mason was not formally trained in PST and did not explicitly incorporate this approach into her work with Michael. At the same time, some of her ways of identifying issues, setting objectives, talking with Michael about ways to achieve these objectives, and then following up to see whether Michael had used these ideas certainly paralleled aspects of problem-solving strategy. As an example, Michael's relationships at work had become somewhat distant and avoidant before he was in treatment. Once he and Dr. Mason had identified and named this "problem" in treatment, however, they both began to identify ways in which Michael could modify his interpersonal relationships to become more engaged and interactive. He began to see that he tended to withdraw when he was worried about his functioning and when his mood was low. He worried that others would see his perceived weaknesses and think less of him. In the past, he had seen depression as a personal failing.

The process implicitly involved identifying a number of alternative things that Michael might do, including taking some interpersonal risks, evaluating these various alternatives, and selecting the most likely plan of action. For example, Michael was encouraged to speak to others more at work, even at times when he might feel somewhat shy. Michael also recognized that he had not been accepting any invitations to social functions, and so he purposely asked to be involved in birthday celebrations and attended a holiday event. On the other hand, when a coworker was involved in a motor vehicle accident, Michael considered visiting the person in hospital, but they were fairly quickly discharged. He decided against a visit at their home, as he thought this too "intimate." Michael was able to try to reimagine the type of person he wanted to be at work and to successfully implement some of the ideas that were discussed. Dr. Mason continued to monitor whether Michael was using the strategies and their outcomes, which is an important part of formal PST.

The Case of Miranda

Miranda came into the session very upset and frustrated. She reported that she had made some demands of her husband, Jules, to be more involved in their home and family life. He reacted negatively, stating that he worked very hard, made more money than she did, and was already involved. She disagreed and

---

[1]All cases presented in this book are fictitious and represent illustrations drawn from my experience but not from any specific person.

pointed out that he did far less than she did. They had an argument and did not resolve the problem at all; in fact, Jules slept in the spare bedroom that night. Because of the situation, Miranda felt overburdened and tired, and she had not completed her therapy homework. She had slept poorly because she was ruminating about the situation, and she felt guilty. She also started having some thoughts about the breakup that she had with first serious romantic partner, Thomas, more than 20 years ago, and she wondered whether Jules would leave her if she were "too demanding" of him. She had not monitored her thoughts and did not initially notice the pattern of catastrophic thinking, but she quickly picked it up when Josefina pointed it out.

Following a discussion and gentle challenge of Miranda's predictions, Josefina introduced the concept of problem solving and described the steps involved. She went through a neutral example in which many people might use this strategy, such as needing a new vehicle. She noted that it is more common to use problem solving with nonemotionally tinged topics than with personal or relationship issues. The problem was defined as "limited time for myself due to full-time work and responsibilities with the children, home, and family." Some of the solutions generated included hiring a cleaning service, lowering her standards, looking for a carpool for the girls, asking a relative to help with driving, having a family meeting, making specific requests of her husband in a nondemanding way, and asking her daughters to help tidy up and set the table. Miranda needed some encouragement and support to generate ideas beyond the involvement of her husband. Each idea was discussed, and after some were eliminated (e.g., hiring a cleaning service was too costly), she was asked to consider the remaining potential solutions as a part of her homework. She was also asked to track her thoughts, including her thoughts about the problem solutions, using the thought record.

Miranda returned to the following session feeling less upset and frustrated than she had been in the previous session. She had spoken to Jules in a calm way, and they had a joint discussion about all the options. They were able to agree on several choices, and he agreed to take on driving the girls to school twice a week. He informed her that he sometimes hesitated to offer to do tasks around the house, as she had tended to criticize what he had done in the past and sometimes redid things. He told her that he saw her as having very high standards, so he fell into a pattern of leaving her alone to complete tasks. While she initially was somewhat defensive, she was able to listen to his opinion and put "possible high standards" on the agenda for the session. She had also completed a thought record on this situation, which Josefina commended her for doing.

Josefina reviewed the steps of problem solving, particularly how to assess the outcomes, refine the solutions chosen if necessary, and circle back to the original problem if needed. The two of them specified exactly what the chosen solutions were and agreed to review them during the next session.

10

Modifying Core Beliefs and Schemas Associated With Depression

Although theories of cognitive development tend to emphasize abstract aspects of cognition, perhaps one of the most important series of changes that occur in childhood is the development of the sense of self. As early as age 4 most children can manipulate objects in the world and have begun to learn that they can influence things around them. By age 8, children have typically formed schemas and organizational frameworks about the world (e.g., colors, shapes, common objects) and have developed the concept of object permanence (Piaget, 1928). At the stage of what Piaget called formal operational thinking, which occurs at roughly age 11, children can think logically, recall autobiographical events from their own life, develop and test hypotheses, and begin to imagine events that have never occurred. By this age children also have a sense of self and experience the world through the filter of this developing identity. Further, children begin to have clear preferences and to choose activities based on this developing sense of self. This process of self-determination helps to make these emerging attributes more stable (Piaget & Inhelder, 1962). As has also been noted, our beliefs about ourselves and the world affect our behavioral rules and assumptions as well as the coping strategies we imagine can be effective in our personal worlds.

The idea that the sense of self emerges in childhood is certainly not novel (see also Erikson, 1959; Gergen, 1971), nor is the idea that the self largely emerges as a reflection of the social experiences of the developing child. This sense of self has also been referred to as "personality" (Eysenck, 1953), although multiple frameworks exist to conceptualize this broad construct. In his

https://doi.org/10.1037/0000398-011
Clinical Depression: An Individualized, Biopsychosocial Approach to Assessment and Treatment, by K. S. Dobson

description of the healthy personality, Erikson (1959) placed a premium on the relational aspects of self and suggested that psychological health comprises factors such as basic trust in others (vs. distrust), autonomy (vs. shame and doubt), initiative (vs. guilt), industry (vs. inferiority), and identity (vs. identity confusion). Erikson further argued that in adulthood a healthy personality is reflected by attributes such as intimacy, generativity, and integrity.

I invite you to consider what this and other books have suggested about the psychological nature of depression. Individuals who experience clinical depression are often characterized as not having basic trust in themselves and others, doubtful and possibly anxious, often avoidant or inactive, and potentially unsure of their direction. If a person has suffered from abuse or rejection, they may harbor ideas of unlovability or social unacceptability. Many of the strategies discussed in this volume are geared toward increasing energy, motivation, effort, and activity while combating self-denigration and negative cognition. In combination, these interventions are conceptualized to implicitly create the corrective experiences that will develop a more positive sense of self and a willingness to engage the world.

MODELS OF CORE BELIEFS AND SCHEMAS

As hinted earlier, multiple models conceptualize the attributes of the sense of self. These models include the ideas of personality traits, values, roles, beliefs, and schemas. These models have in common the ideas that the sense of self has a semipermeability to it, that a consistency helps to define the way a person views themselves, and that this consistency can be expected in most people by late adolescence or early adulthood. This sense of self is a function of biological predispositions and the culture in which one is raised, both positive and negative early life experiences, potential trauma, parental modeling, socialization, the outcomes of early experiments in trying to influence the world and others, and more. Even the clothes that are worn, the music and media with which one identifies, and one's personal demeanor help to reveal who we are as developing selves and with whom we wish to relate (or not!). Historically, identities have often been connected to a particular geographical location and space, but in a world in which communications approximate the instantaneous, the sense of belongingness to a social group based on where one physically resides has become increasingly fragile. In summary, much has been made about schema theory and therapy in the psychological literature (Horowitz, 1991; Kovacs & Beck, 1978; Segal, 1988; Young, 1994). Even so, confusion about the concept of the schema itself remains (James et al., 2009). The next sections provide some discussion about alternative views of the schema concept and ways in which these views are related to the field of depression.

The Cognitive Triad and Sociotropy–Autonomy Models

In his early writing about depression, A. T. Beck and colleagues referred to core beliefs about the self, world, and future as the *cognitive triad* (cf. A. T. Beck,

Rush, et al., 1979); they identified prototypical negative beliefs in each domain, including the self as damaged, worthless, or unlovable; the world as harsh and punishing; and the future as dark and foreboding. Other authors have also made reference to core beliefs, fundamental beliefs, and irrational beliefs, often with the same idea of stable ways of thinking about and organizing autobiographical experiences, interpreting current events, and predicting the future. In this book I choose to use the language of "beliefs," although my conceptualization is broad and potentially includes values, personality traits, and schemas.

In addition to discussions about the optimal way to conceptualize and discuss the structure of the sense of self (e.g., beliefs vs. schemas), there have been multiple efforts to encapsulate the main content themes that should be captured within these models. The cognitive triad was an early such effort in the area of depression, and efforts were made to measure the triad, its stability over time, and its susceptibility to change in therapy (Anderson & Skidmore, 1995; Beckham et al., 1986). A fairly early effort to identify key belief domains related to depression was the distinction between sociotropy and autonomy (A. T. Beck et al., 1983). Conceptually, people who are high on the personality dimension of sociotropy have greater need for interpersonal affiliation and dependency and are susceptible to feelings of sadness or depression if their interpersonal relationships are disturbed, damaged, or broken. In contrast, people who are high on autonomy need independence and recognition of their achievements. People who are high on autonomy are susceptible to depression if they perceive themselves to fail or if they do not get the recognition they believe is warranted.

The Sociotropy–Autonomy Scale (SAS; A. T. Beck et al., 1983) was developed as a 60-item scale to measure vulnerability for depression. The SAS was subjected to considerable study, and while the sociotropy scale tended to yield coherent results and to correlate in an expected manner with depression and other conceptually similar measures (Bieling et al., 2000; Cappeliez, 1993; Robins et al., 1989), the autonomy scale had less consistent results and less strong correlations with hypothetically related constructs (Bieling et al., 2000; Clark et al., 1997; Clark & Oates, 1995; Moore & Blackburn, 1994). Factor analyses revealed that both dimensions likely had subfactors built into them (Bieling et al., 2000). Finally, prospective research examining the interactions among sociotropy, autonomy, and their corresponding life events had mixed results (Iacoviello et al., 2009). Thus, while the constructs have intuitive merit, their utility at a clinical level, particularly for the dimension of autonomy, has been limited.

Schema Therapy Model

In addition to dimensional models of personality factors that could be related specifically to depression are general schema models related to psychopathology and treatment. Two models are discussed here, as both have relevance to the conceptualization and treatment of depression. The first of these approaches is most often called *schema therapy* (J. E. Young, 1994; J. E. Young et al., 2003).

This model was developed by a psychologist who trained with Dr. Aaron Beck in CBT but then expanded the model of schemas, integrated aspects of attachment theory and psychoanalysis into the model, and developed treatment paradigms for the resultant model of what were termed *early maladaptive schemas* (EMS). Although the numbers and precise dimensions of personality schemas vary somewhat in different sources (e.g., Oei & Baranoff, 2007; Yalcin et al., 2020), five broad domains are generally cited, all of which have subdomains, yielding a total of 18 specific EMSs (J. E. Young et al., 2003; see Exhibit 10.1). The EMS dimensions of disconnection/rejection and impaired autonomy and/or performance correspond fairly well to the concepts of sociotropy and autonomy, respectively. However, in contrast to the sociotropy/autonomy bidimensional approach, the schema therapy model provides precision through its various EMS subtypes.

J. E. Young and colleagues (2003) posited that schemas typically develop early in life as a result of early life experiences. They proposed not only that EMSs have a content dimension but that they can be represented through various modes of expression. They suggested the child mode, the dysfunctional coping mode, the dysfunctional parent mode, and the healthy parent

---

EXHIBIT 10.1

Early Maladaptive Schema Domains From Schema Theory

1. **Disconnection/rejection**
   i) Abandonment/instability
   ii) Mistrust/abuse
   iii) Emotional deprivation
   iv) Defectiveness/shame
   v) Social isolation/alienation
2. **Impaired autonomy and/or performance**
   i) Dependence/incompetence
   ii) Vulnerability to harm or illness
   iii) Enmeshment/undeveloped self
   iv) Failure
3. **Impaired limits**
   i) Entitlement/grandiosity
   ii) Insufficient self-control and/or self-discipline
4. **Other-directedness**
   i) Subjugation
   ii) Self-sacrifice
   iii) Approval-seeking/recognition-seeking
5. **Overvigilance/inhibition**
   i) Negativity/pessimism
   ii) Emotional inhibition
   iii) Unrelenting standards/hypercriticalness
   iv) Punitiveness

Note. Adapted from *Schema Therapy: A Practitioner's Guide* (pp. 14–17), by J. E. Young, J. S. Klosko, and M. E. Weishaar, 2003, Guilford Press. Copyright 2002 by J. E. Young. Adapted with permission.

mode. A person's way of presenting themselves to the world and, in particular, their interaction patterns with other people reflect their specific mode of expression. Although many of the modes are dysfunctional, the model also recognizes that people can have a healthy adult mode, which includes attributes such as being problem oriented, taking action, nurturing self and others, being responsible, and forming healthy relationships, among others.

According to J. E. Young et al. (2003), schema therapy involves the assessment of the schemas that a client may have adopted as well as the modes of expression of their EMSs. This assessment can be done in the therapy session and can include one or more questionnaires developed to assess EMSs (see Schema Therapy Institute, n.d.). The Young Schema Questionnaire (YSQ) comes in both a long and a short form and has been studied primarily through factor analysis (Glaser et al., 2002; Schmidt et al., 1995; Stopa et al., 2001). Somewhat surprisingly given the complexity of the schema model, the YSQ appears to have support as a therapeutic assessment tool, although some have warned that its use in some clinical settings should be done with caution and only in concert with clinical interview to confirm the results of the questionnaire (Oei & Baranoff, 2007).

Emotional Schema Therapy

Emotional schema therapy is based on a schema model that focuses on the importance of emotions in psychopathology, in particular, how a person develops beliefs about emotions and ways to respond to them. Leahy (2015) took the eminently reasonable stance that all people have emotions and that although some (hopefully many) are positive, people inevitably experience disappointments, tensions, and worries in life. Furthermore, Leahy argued that emotional responses almost certainly have evolutionary and adaptive value. As one relevant example, grief and sadness are often healthy emotional responses to loss, as they arise as a result of emotional and psychological investment in the person or object that was lost. However, some beliefs about emotions may be problematic. Examples of dysfunctional beliefs about emotions are that they are "out of control," shameful, nonsensical, or even bizarre; these beliefs reflect higher order cognitions and secondary appraisals. Moreover, if a person attempts to suppress, ignore, hide, or otherwise eradicate emotional experiences (e.g., through substance use), then these behaviors may strengthen the negative appraisals related to emotions in the first instance.

Emotional schema therapy was developed to help normalize all emotional experiences, understand the genesis of emotional response, and express and validate a broad range of emotions. The approach uses validation as a key method through which the therapist attempts to undermine negative beliefs about emotionality and to engage the client in a range of emotional practices through experiential exercise, homework, and practice. The specific forms of practice are naturally linked to the emotion that is the target of intervention. For example, in a large study of psychotherapy clients that used the Leahy Emotional Schema Scale (Leahy, 2002), the strongest emotional schemas related to depression were high levels of risk aversion (avoidance), negative beliefs about emotion, and low scores on psychological flexibility (Leahy et al., 2012). These results are highly concordant with the view that clients who are depressed benefit when they do not engage in the avoidance of difficult circumstances and experiences and that they benefit from the direct discussion of the role of emotion and the adaptive value of emotions such as sadness and the need for enhanced flexibility and willingness not to engage in experiential avoidance. Leahy (2001) introduced the *portfolio theory of depression*—the idea that depression is related to a life investment strategy dominated by perceptions of low general self-efficacy, risk aversion, low predictability and control, increased regret, and a tendency to avoid or postpone action. Negative emotional schemas, when present, offer excellent targets for clinical intervention (see Leahy, 2015).

Alternative Models and Frameworks

Before moving on to the clinical assessment of beliefs and potential intervention in psychotherapy, I would be remiss not to mention that while I consider the preceding belief/schema models to be the most relevant to depression, other schema models and therapies based on personality traits certainly exist (cf. Rasmussen, 2005; Riso et al., 2007). Arntz and colleagues (Arntz & Jacob, 2012; Arntz & van Genderen, 2009; Arntz et al., 2021) have a well-developed schema model that in some respects resembles the work of J. E. Young et al. (2003). Although this model was originally designed to address borderline personality disorder, its most recent incarnation (Renner et al., 2013) is considerably expanded, and aspects of it certainly relate to depression.

Finally, as argued more fully later in this chapter, an alterative framework to the assessment of beliefs and schemas relates to values. As with beliefs, values reflect a person's culture, developmental history, and unique ways of appreciating and interacting with the world. Values are conceptualized as relatively stable in adults and as dispositions that interact with events around us, as is the case for personality traits, beliefs, and schemas. Values can be positive, such as being supportive of others, or negative, such as valuing self-aggrandizement above all else. The one distinguishing aspect of values is that they often have a moral or ethical tone to them; they encourage "proper" or socially appropriate conduct. In this regard, the clarification of a client's values can have significant benefit, as it may help them to orient or reorient their future activities to be more consistent with their values than perhaps their recent experience was. More on this theme later in this chapter.

THE ASSESSMENT OF BELIEFS IN THERAPY

Prior to any intervention with a client's beliefs, it is important to assess them and to consider them from both a developmental and a cultural perspective. This assessment work includes the client's major historical experiences as well as their linguistic, cultural, religious, and spiritual background. This assessment information becomes part of the case conceptualization process, and it is worthwhile to be somewhat slow and purposeful in this work, rather than moving too quickly to intervention.

"Worst First" Assessment

As suggested in Chapter 5, it is often advantageous with clients who are depressed to target relatively simple or straightforward problems for early intervention. This approach provides some immediate support and relief to the client and often encourages the client to make further efforts. It helps to strengthen the therapy relationship and to have both the therapist and the client feel positively toward each other. It provides time for the therapist to continue to collect information about the client, including their skills in various problem domains, their psychological mindedness and ability to attend to their own cognitions and inner experience, and the ways in which they regulate and manage their own emotions, and ultimately it provides an opportunity to assess and conceptualize their core beliefs.

It has been my experience in therapy that it is often possible to discern the client's belief system through the ways they interact with the various problems and interventions that transpire during the course of treatment. Sometimes, if I have sufficient evidence, I propose to the client what I see as their belief(s). For example, if a client struggles with assertion, I may make the observation that they often put the needs or opinions of others ahead of their own. If they concur, I may take the further step to inquire whether they see themselves as less deserving than others. This type of interaction can be quite easily integrated into dialogue and provides a fairly direct way to assess the relevant beliefs of the client.

I have also experienced clients who spontaneously reveal core beliefs in observations of themselves. These clients are usually psychologically minded and able to track their cognitive patterns. Depending on the stage of therapy, the other interventions taking place at the time, and practical considerations such as the point in the therapy session when the observation is made, these comments may easily lend themselves to discussion, inquiry, and potentially further assessment. As the therapist, it is important for you to be mindful of these observations by the client and either tuck them away for a future session or spend a bit of time discussing the client's beliefs as they are presented.

Questionnaires

Another strategy to identify core beliefs is the use of questionnaires. As discussed earlier in this chapter, various questionnaires have been developed to assess core beliefs relevant to depression, including measures of the cognitive triad, sociotropy and autonomy, J. E. Young et al.'s (2003) schema model, and Leahy's (2015) emotional schema model. I have deployed all of these questionnaires at one time or another with clients. I have used them to confirm a strong suspicion about a particular core belief domain, and I have used them as psychoeducational tools to talk to the client about the measure, their unique score, and the relevance of the tool for their own life. I have also used more complicated multidimensional schema questionnaires, particularly in cases with a clear interaction among multiple schemas or beliefs and in cases in which I struggled with the optimal case conceptualization.

These measures are certainly worth exploration. They can be obtained relatively easily through a web-based search engine, and scoring protocols have been developed for both long and short forms of the questionnaires. When using these scales, it is important to be aware of potential copyright considerations. The scoring and interpretation of these measures is also fairly complex, particularly with the multidimensional scales. Further, to my knowledge, no computerized program is available to score these questionnaires, so a cost–benefit consideration needs to be made in terms of the time the questionnaire will require relative to the clinical information it will yield.

Inferential Questions

A common strategy to identify core beliefs is to ask the client about the inferences or meanings that they draw in different circumstances. For example, a thought record might identify a distressing automatic thought, which you as the therapist might recognize as recurrent and potentially related to a core belief. Rather than challenging the automatic thought, you may elect to ask the client what meaning they attached to the situation or what inference they would draw if the automatic thought were valid. This type of inferential question typically elicits a meaning beyond just the specific situation, and it can be used effectively to identify relatively quickly a core belief that the client holds. The *downward arrow strategy* (J. S. Beck, 2021; Burns, 1999; D. Dobson & K. S. Dobson, 2017; Sokol & Fox, 2019) uses this process of inferential chaining. It begins with a discrete automatic thought in a particular situation and then proceeds through a series of inferential questions to identify the underlying core belief. Common questions used by the therapist in this technique are "What does this situation mean to you?", "Do you have any ideas about why this situation is so distressing?", and "What is it about the situation that bothers you?" (cf. J. S. Beck, 2021; D. Dobson & K. S. Dobson, 2017; Sokol & Fox, 2019).

A great feature of inferential questions and the downward arrow strategy is that they can be used in conjunction with other methods. For example, it is relatively easy to make a connection between the use of the thought record and this type of inferential questioning. Inferential questions can also be used in real-life situations, as represented on the thought record, and hypothetical situations that may not yet have occurred. One method I have employed quite often is to use a file record as the first instance for a set of inferential questions and then to modify the situation in imagination to see whether the same types of inferences are made. This type of compare-and-contrast methodology can sometimes help to identify the meanings that the client uniquely associates with distress. Inferential questions can also be used with behavioral responses:

You can ask the client what it would mean to them if a particular action was or was not taken. The compare-and-contrast strategy can then be used to find out the meanings the client might attribute to different types of actions that they or the people around them might take.

Historical Reconstruction

Another strategy to identify core beliefs is historical reconstruction. When you begin to ask questions about the client's beliefs, it is not uncommon for the client to explain where the belief came from. They may relate early developmental experiences, common wisdom at the time they were growing up, or things they learned from songs and cultural events. Again, if the phase of therapy seems appropriate and there is adequate time in the therapy session, historical comments can sometimes be explored to determine the genesis of a core belief. Similarly, it may be that the client makes a comment such as "This situation reminds me of. . . ." Because autobiographical memories are often a key part of core beliefs, this type of reference to something from the client's past can provide an opening for historical questioning.

Priming

Yet another strategy to try to activate and assess beliefs is priming. Priming is a general term for any strategy that might potentiate or increase the likelihood of the use of a belief. This strategy is more likely to be useful if you as the therapist have a fairly good idea of the belief so you can design the priming strategy to yield a result. For example, imagine you are working with a client who likely holds the belief that emotions are intolerable or that they will have some strong, irremediable response if they experience a strong emotion. For this client, you could purposely conduct an emotional prime in the session to see if these beliefs can be activated and to address the cognitions and emotions that the prime evokes. A well-developed mood induction procedure designed to evoke depression (Kenealy, 1986; Velten, 1968) could easily be adapted for the therapy office. Another version of priming could be the assignment of homework that is likely to interact with the client's beliefs. For example, you might encourage a perfectionistic client to purposely do less than their ideal on some homework assignment. This type of priming helps both you and the client to learn when their belief gets activated and how they respond when this type of activation occurs. Ideally, this type of homework assignment would be set up collaboratively with the client, and both you and they would be alert to the types of reactions that might occur.

One final note about activation procedures is that they can yield very informative information if the prime occurs but the belief does not get activated. This type of information can help you modify your case conceptualization or shift the prime. If a priming strategy is used repeatedly, it can help to document that a belief is becoming less potent over time and is less easily activated.

Psychoeducation

A final strategy that recommends itself for belief assessment is psychoeducation. Sometimes a review of the treatment model helps the client link their current problems to their history and long-term beliefs. Various materials can be given to clients so they can read about core beliefs and how they function (cf. Burns, 1999; McKay & Fanning, 1991; Parent, 2006; J. E. Young & Klosko, 1993). Depending on the specifics of the client, you may offer biographies, anonymized stories from your former clients, or selected revelations about yourself to help the client to see that everyone has core beliefs that shape how we live our lives. These stories can help demonstrate that although beliefs are understandable in historical context, they are not immutable and can be changed if desired and if the proper supports are in place.

THE ETHICS OF BELIEF CHANGE IN PSYCHOTHERAPY

One of the less discussed issues in the field of psychotherapy is when not to undertake personality or belief change with the client (for exceptions, see J. S. Beck, 2021; D. Dobson & K. S. Dobson, 2017). In my experience, many clients who struggle with depression when they first come for treatment obtain significant benefit from the wide variety of interventions focused on physiological functioning, behavioral activation, emotional processing, and automatic thought work. Often the assessment of core beliefs and the process of understanding some of the psychological roots of the client's depression are highly informative to them and help to provide a framework to answer the "why?" question that many clients have. I have had many clients, however, who get to the point in therapy at which they are feeling better and their core beliefs have been exposed and then make the conscious choice not to proceed with core belief change. Some situations in which this decision makes sense and can be supported follow.

- Some clients with depression have focal problems such as sleep or primary life issues that they need to solve, and when these issues are managed in therapy they have no need for further intervention at the level of core beliefs.

- Some clients feel significantly better after problem-solving and other interventions, and even if they are aware that they still hold core beliefs that may be less than fully functional, they decide to stop therapy. In these cases, my recommendation is to discuss with the client a potential remaining vulnerability and, to the extent you can in your practice setting, encourage them to return for therapy if they experience early signs of relapse. Ultimately, however, the decision to continue or to end treatment always resides with the client.

- In some instances, belief modification will almost necessarily also implicate the client's values. Their moral system, their cultural identity, or their religious practices may be challenged. My perspective in these situations is to help the client understand the relationships among their values and current problematic issues, explore with them the changes, if any, they are willing to contemplate, and respect their decisions in this regard. As therapists, we need to be mindful that we have our own beliefs and values, and it is important not to impose them on others.

- In some situations, the client has a clear negative belief that reflects their history and affects their current functioning, but the belief itself is highly distressing. Indeed, changing core beliefs can be highly destabilizing and may be associated with increased distress for a time and perhaps unclear identity (J. E. Young et al., 2003). I believe it is helpful for the therapist to expose the advantages and challenges associated with belief change and to respect the client's decision to proceed or not.

- Sometimes the therapist recognizes the potential benefits of belief change for the client but fails to fully appreciate the implications of change for the broad social environment. As one example, a client who lives in an abusive relationship may benefit from changing the beliefs that allow them to live in this circumstance. It is possible, however, that the partner will not accept these changes, and there are risks to the integrity of the family unit, particularly if children are involved. Again, my perspective is that the client should be as fully informed as possible to make a decision and the therapist should support them in whatever decision they make.

- For practical reasons, belief change may not be indicated. The client may have limited resources, limited insurance coverage, or insufficient time and energy in their life to engage in broad belief change. This work is not easy, and it often takes time, and so it is worthwhile to pause and consider if this step is justified.

- Finally, if the therapist–client relationship is problematic, belief change may not effectively or easily take place. This type of intervention is challenging and often increases client distress. It likely should be entertained only if you and the client have a good working relationship. In contrast, if problems have arisen in the therapist–client relationship, it may be better to defer this decision, avoid belief change work, or possibly refer the client to another therapist for this phase of treatment.

INTERVENTION STRATEGIES WHEN WORKING WITH BELIEFS RELATED TO DEPRESSION

As is true for so much else in the field of psychotherapy, multiple intervention strategies are available for clients when belief change is indicated. Many sources can be reviewed with respect to this work (e.g., Arntz & Jacob, 2012; Arntz & van Genderen, 2009; J. S. Beck, 2021; D. Dobson & K. S. Dobson, 2017; Leahy, 2015; Riso et al., 2007; J. E. Young et al., 2003); presented here is a distillation of the main idea to contemplate when working with a client who recently has been or who continues to be depressed.

Identify Dysfunctional Beliefs and Offer Alternatives

Many strategies are available to promote change in dysfunctional beliefs. Typically, these strategies begin with identifying and naming a dysfunctional belief or pattern, which then becomes the object of intervention. It is important in doing this work to provide a label or description for the belief work pattern and to make clear that this label is a general label for the client and that labeling is really another form of cognitive distortion. Identify the psychological pattern you wish to modify, as this change becomes an achievable goal. As a quick example, you might identify the belief that the client is helpless to deal with some life problem but not that the client is helpless in general.

Having identified the dysfunctional pattern, it is often worthwhile to spend some time with the client to imagine what an alternative might be for them. As one example, if the client has a history of abusive relationships and has determined that they are "unlovable," a variety of alternative possibilities can be imagined. The polar opposite belief might be "lovable," but this contrast may be viewed as too distant from the original negative belief to be credible. It may be useful to introduce the idea of degrees of belief or the idea of movement toward an alternative, rather than perceiving two dichotomous states. Another possibility might be to set "being loved," or "loving myself first" as the desired and point, rather than "lovability." These ideas are certainly more attainable than the more extreme alternative of "being a lovable person," although "being loved" is not within the client's control, and so this alternative belief may not be an ideal therapeutic alternative to move toward.

Explore Advantages and Disadvantages of Core Beliefs and Alternatives

After identification of the existing core belief as well as a potential alternative, a relatively straightforward intervention technique is to consider the advantages and disadvantages of each. This work can often be done on a piece of paper or whiteboard with two columns, one for the old and one for the new core beliefs. Each column can then be divided into two sections reflecting the advantages and disadvantages. You can also divide the advantages and disadvantages into short-term and long-term issues. For example, it may be that new and more adaptive beliefs have short-term disadvantages (e.g., energy, effort, stress) but long-term advantages (e.g., less stress, lower risk of depression). It is often helpful to recognize the temporal aspect of both old and new beliefs.

There is often a tendency when discussing advantages and disadvantages to denigrate the old (and likely negative) core belief and to overpromote the alternative. When doing this work, it is important to be fair to both beliefs and to recognize that even the most negative and dysfunctional core belief probably developed at a time when it "made sense" or was adaptive. For example, a child who is physically abused by a caregiver might develop the core belief that they are flawed and unlovable; this perspective may make perfect sense for a relatively helpless youth—indeed, the caregiver may be literally communicating this idea to them. In this sense, in its historical context the development of this negative belief was an advantage, as it helped the child to make sense of the experiences they were going through. The problem emerges, however, when they take this core belief and bring it forward in their life to a point at which they could exert agency but don't, because of this preexisting core belief. In the same manner, it is important to acknowledge that even an attractive and possibly attainable alternative core belief likely has some disadvantages. For example, changing the core belief itself is going to be disruptive and may create some instability for a time. Adopting a new core belief may require significant changes to the client's lifestyle. In some extreme cases, a modified core belief may require the repudiation of social contacts or may lead to physical threat. It's important in doing this work to acknowledge these potential disadvantages and, if indicated, to problem solve ways to deal with them, assuming the client wishes to move forward.

Positive Data Log

Another relatively easy intervention related to core belief is the positive data log (J. S. Beck, 2021; D. Dobson & K. S. Dobson, 2017). This technique involves monitoring evidence that the client is already moving in the direction of the positive belief or they have life experiences they have been minimizing or disregarding that would be inconsistent with the negative core belief and more consistent with the positive belief being considered. This strategy works well for clients who are functioning reasonably well but may be selectively attending to experiences.

Clarify Values

Imagining a new sense of self or a new set of beliefs to adopt can be challenging for somebody who has experience with depression, particularly if that depressive experience has been either longstanding or recurrent. One method that often helps clients engage in this process is to help them clarify their values. Values are similar in some respect to beliefs, in that they are often longterm ways of construing experience and are often based on early childhood and developmental experiences. They also often have a cultural and temporal nature, as they are affected by the social environment in which a person is raised and lives. In contrast to beliefs, however, values provide a sense of direction and purpose. Thus, whereas a belief may simply reflect the way things are, values push or pull in different directions, and our consistency or inconsistency with our values is often fundamental to our self-evaluation.

Values clarification can be used in treatment to encourage a client to discuss the values they hold close and want to promote rather than encourage them to think about a new sense of self. Many different forms of values-clarification exercises have been developed (Hayes et al., 2011; T. Lundgren & Larsson, 2018; Witteman et al., 2021; Zettle, 2016), and many different web-based forms can be used to conduct values clarification, but the essence is to look at different domains of experience and either generate one's own set of values or determine the extent to which the values on the worksheet are consistent with one's own. One method is the *bull's-eye technique* (Lundgren & Larsson, 2018; Lundgren et al., 2012), in which the client lists values in various domains of their life and then self-evaluates the extent to which their current actions and lifestyle are consistent with these values—close to the bull's-eye—or perhaps are somewhat distant and in need of modification. Often, the outcome of values-clarification work is the identification of a relatively small number of values that the client wishes to promote, followed by a discussion of how they might live their life in a way consistent with the values. Acceptance and commitment therapy (Hayes et al., 2011) is extensively involved in the discussion of values and then commitment to a life that is consistent with these values.

Another technique that can build on values clarification is *time projection* (D. Dobson & K. S. Dobson, 2017). In this technique, the therapist invites the client to imagine themselves at a future time, possibly a few years in the future or even theoretically at the end of their life. The time chosen likely should depend on the client's age and circumstances as well as their willingness and ability to do future projection. The therapist asks the client to think about the type of person they want to be at that future timepoint and the ways in which their values would be reflected in the work they do, the relationships they have, the place they live, and their general approach to life. This discussion of a possible future self can then readily be turned into a set of plans and immediate steps that the client could take to live their life in a value-based manner. This discussion could be framed as the development of a personal mission statement and strategic plan, if this idea resonates with the client. A modification of the time projection technique is to have the client think forward to after they have died. In this variation, the therapist invites the client to consider how they would like to be remembered, perhaps at their funeral. If it seems indicated, the client might write their own eulogy. Clinical judgment needs to be used when working with clients with depression, of course, as you certainly do not want to promote the idea of preparing for death.

As noted previously, clarification of the client's values is necessarily embedded in their culture and personal history. Within the Western tradition, people often focus on values in the personal and interpersonal arenas, typically with a focus on the beliefs, thoughts, emotions, and behaviors that are valued. For many people, the discussion of values also moves into the spiritual realm, and as a therapist you should be ready for these discussions if and when they occur. In North American Indigenous cultures, for example, the medicine wheel makes reference to the physical, emotional, mental, and spiritual aspects of life as equally important and essential. For many clients, the discussion of values evokes consideration of good and evil or desired and undesired states to move toward or away from, respectively. The discussion about values may lead some clients to seek spiritual or religious practices and/or communities. Particularly in pluralistic and multicultural societies such as the one in which I live, a healthy degree of humility and a commensurate curiosity about other cultural, spiritual, and religious perspectives is likely a positive therapeutic stance to take (Dobson, 2022).

Ask Clients About Belief Change Requirements

When clients are considering belief change, I often find it helpful to ask them directly what experience they would need, or what evidence they would have to gather from their environment, that would compel them to shift their belief in the direction of the preferred new alternative. Another way to frame this question is to ask the client how they would know, based on their own lived experience, that they have adopted and incorporated the new belief into their way of looking at themselves and the world. These questions may elicit a discussion about potential ways the client currently discounts positive information and, more importantly, may encourage the client to think about the concrete attitudinal and lifestyle changes they need to make to be fully compelled to believe that their belief system has changed. After they have had this discussion in the therapy office, it becomes possible to design homework assignments in which the client purposefully does things that are consistent with their new and more positive core belief to obtain the necessary evidence to promote change. This work can also be done in imagination: The therapist can ask the client to imagine how they might respond to various changes and then assign homework to use the responses that appear to have the greatest potential for success. Again, in doing this work it is critical to recognize that certain risks may be taken, and so it is important to ensure the client thinks through and plans for any potential negative responses from others as they begin to make changes.

Using Real-Life Experiences

One advantage of the client beginning to make concrete behavioral changes in their life is that they begin to gather direct experiential evidence that can either promote further change or, in some cases, lead to the discovery of limitations. For example, a client may decide they wish to behave more assertively in their relationships. As a first step, they might advise people around them that they have recognized that they have not taken care of themselves in the past and they are going to make some changes in this regard by being more assertive. By making such a public statement, it becomes possible to know who among the client's contacts will support them in their efforts to change and who might not support them or might actively resist these changes. In making these kinds of declarations, the client can discover where their social support lies and potentially can identify individuals who perpetuate their negative beliefs about themselves.

Confrontation

Another technique that has been promoted for belief change is confrontation (D. Dobson & K. S. Dobson, 2017; J. E. Young et al., 2003). Confrontation can take a number of forms, depending on the therapeutic strategy and goals. A relatively minor form of confrontation is for the therapist to point out some limitations of the client's current way of thinking and behaving and perhaps some interpersonal concerns or issues with the therapist themself. Ideally, this form of confrontation is done in the context of an overall positive therapeutic relationship, one that is strong enough to tolerate some tension.

One form of confrontation can take place if the client learns that individuals in their social environment are not allies but instead perpetuate their negative beliefs about themselves and others. In this situation, the client might be encouraged to confront the people and to let them know they want a different relationship. As suggested previously, because interpersonal confrontation can be challenging, as the therapist you should ensure that the client is fully prepared for this type of intervention and has the skills and commitment to resist negative feedback that might be directed at them. Should the client have a negative response to confrontation, it is important that you take responsibility for what you have attempted. You should have a good rationale for your intervention and should be able to explain it. Even if the confrontation is taken in the spirit that was intended and does not lead to a negative reaction, it is often worthwhile to debrief the intervention and show how the client's nonreactive response shows good flexibility of thinking and/or development in therapy.

Confrontation can also be historical. For example, a client may discover through historical analysis that the way they were treated as a child was foundational for the development of negative core beliefs and their caregivers did not fully act in their best interests. In such a case, it may be possible to use an imaginal confrontation between the client as a youth and their caregiver, with the client standing up for themselves and experiencing an alternative to the original negative interaction. Yet another form of confrontation could be to have the client write a letter or create some type of document, directed toward a parent or other negative force from the past, in which the client expresses their negative response and confronts the other person about their behavior. The letter or document need never be sent, of course, but it can be a precursor to other forms of confrontation. For example, a client may get a sense of purpose from writing a letter or document and may then choose to send it to the transgressor. It may even be possible to make an appointment with the parent or other transgressor and to confront them directly. The nature of and extent to which this form of confrontation is used will obviously be affected by the client's circumstances, and it can range from relatively mild forms of confrontation to direct and emotionally charged interpersonal challenges.

ACCEPTANCE-BASED STRATEGIES FOR WORKING WITH BELIEFS

The process of psychotherapy generally involves the identification of maladaptive processes and then the selective use of evidence-based strategies to help the client overcome these processes (Hayes & Hofmann, 2018). This emphasis on change has certainly been the tradition in the field of depression, regardless of the theoretical model (A. T. Beck, Rush, et al., 1979; Beutler et al., 2000; Weissman, 2001; Weissman et al., 2018; Wells & Fisher, 2006; Yapko, 1997). This orientation makes perfect sense to me; in the many clients I have seen who experience depression, it has been rare that someone has said that they learned to appreciate the experience. Much more typically, depression is experienced as onerous and unremitting, a significant deviation from one's usual or desired state.

Given the more typical focus on intervention and change, it is somewhat paradoxical that an intervention based on acceptance has developed in the field of depression. This work grew, however, from the realization that depression had a high rate of recurrence, even among clients successfully treated with an evidence-based therapy such as cognitive behavior therapy (Segal et al., 1996, 2006; Teasdale, 1988). The argument was that these clients likely had a sensitization to negative experience and that if or when they experienced recurrent sad mood they had a cognitive reactivity to this experience, which eventuated in even more distress and a possible recurrence. In a sense, it was argued that these clients retained a belief in the unacceptability of negative affect, and this belief yielded processes such as avoidance of negative affect, excessive focus and rumination on negative experience when it occurred, and negative beliefs about unwanted emotional experience (Teasdale et al., 1995).

Mindfulness-Based Cognitive Therapy

Predicated on the idea of differential activation of depression in people with prior experience and cognitive sensitization, it may be that teaching clients a different way to relate to negative affect could reduce their susceptibility to recurrent depression. The early developers of what is now referred to as *mindfulness-based cognitive therapy* (MBCT; Segal et al., 2013; Teasdale et al., 2014; Williams et al., 2007) turned to Eastern traditions of mindfulness and meditation and adapted work that was being done in medicine (Kabat-Zinn, 1990, 1994) to assist clients to experience negative affect without negative or depressive meaning attached to it. MBCT was developed as a group-based modularized intervention in which clients were systematically encouraged to fully experience their bodies through experiential exercises and homework practice. Exercises included the body scan, mindful activities, and purposeful attention to emotional states. Early trials of MBCT revealed that it had a preventive value in depression, and later trials suggested that this effect was particularly present for clients with three or more prior episodes of depression (Kuyken et al., 2016; Segal & Walsh, 2016). Studies now show that clients who practice the exercises have better response than clients who don't use these exercises, but other research suggests that MBCT is not more effective than further sessions of CBT for the prevention of relapse or recurrence (Farb et al., 2018).

An important question related to the use of MBCT and mindfulness in general is its optimal place in the process of therapy. When this technique was first developed, the suggestion was that it could be used following other active treatment, in particular as a prevention strategy for relapse or recurrence. It has since been used with success as a primary treatment method, and extensive studies have looked at the applicability of mindfulness interventions for a range of disorders. My sense is that the methodology is optimally used once the client has some relief from their original degree of depression and when they are at a point in therapy at which they will consider exposure to negative experience and learning how to live with the negative experiences that naturally come along with living a full life. This shift in focus from a "doing" mode to a "being" mode is a delicate one, and it appears to be a critical feature of the shift to acceptance (Segal et al., 2013).

Other Acceptance-Based Interventions

It is possible to incorporate acceptance-oriented interventions into the latter stages of work with clients with depression without the need for formal mindfulness-based practices or MBCT. It is important in making this shift to recognize formally with the client that you are not becoming complacent about negative experience or "giving up" in the effort to promote change. Acceptance is not the same as resignation. Rather, this shift is predicated on the idea that stress, anxiety, and depression are normal parts of everyday life, and learning to live with these experiences is important in its own right. To promote a positive attitude toward the full range of emotionality, potential interventions include the following:

- Encourage the client to taper appointments and to have more time between appointments to experience a range of situations. This type of self-practice can enable the client to use more self-regulation, to develop more tolerance of different situations, and to recognize that negative experiences often pass without formal intervention.

- Suggest that the client use self-sessions between appointments. They can formally set an agenda, decide on appropriate intervention strategies, and apply these strategies to themselves. Again, the goal is for the client to learn that they themselves can manage problems as they emerge in their daily life or choose simply to note problems without taking formal action.

- Encourage the client to adopt practices that may not change their negative beliefs but can promote resilience and self-efficacy. The range of possible activities can be anything the client accepts, including personal development, hobbies, social engagement, and seeking spiritual guidance. The development of these strengths can help the client to offset any negative experiences that may occur in the future.

- Remind the client that they have developed interventions and skills to address negative thinking and behavior consistent with depression. This general approach, also called metacognitive therapy (Wells, 2009), encourages clients to step back from their immediate thoughts and experience and look at the bigger picture. This approach is consistent with the ideas that thoughts do not define reality, just because you feel something does not make it true, and there are multiple potential perspectives on different situations and experiences. Encouraging the client to consider these alternatives gives them freedom to pursue different ways to respond to life's events. Strong evidence suggests that metacognitive therapy can have significant benefit for several psychological conditions, including depression (Normann & Morina, 2018), although further research is warranted.

CASE ILLUSTRATIONS OF MODIFYING DYSFUNCTIONAL BELIEFS AND SCHEMAS

In the cases of Michael and Miranda, we can see how their therapists, Dr. Mason and Dr. Morales (who Miranda calls by her first name, Josefina), implemented strategies to help them replace their core dysfunctional beliefs and schemas with more adaptive alternatives.[1]

The Case of Michael

One interpersonal theme that Michael had identified early in treatment was that of the self-made man. As Dr. Mason began to understand Michael better, it became clearer to her that this identity led him to take a distant position in his relationships. For example, in the work environment he clearly positioned himself as "the boss," which to his mind meant that he could not express weakness, confusion, or any vulnerability. In his relationship with his partner Jon, he had taken on the role of being distant rather than open and communicative, and he did not want to show him any perceived failings. These beliefs led him to be very focused on privacy, and he worried that others would think less of him if they knew about his depression.

A surprise that Michael encountered over the course of therapy was that as he became more engaged at work, he recognized that others were doing well without him and the business continued to thrive, notwithstanding his own current depression and level of functioning. He was particularly impressed with the manager of the company, and after a discussion with Dr. Mason, he took the risk to express this opinion. He was very surprised and pleased that this colleague, Marco, was touched by this encounter. He discussed the incident with Dr. Mason, who supported the idea that if Michael were able to

---

[1]All cases presented in this book are fictitious and represent illustrations drawn from my experience but not from any specific person.

reach out to others he might be surprised more frequently. Together, they agreed that he would take the risk to let his partner know more fully about his depression and therapy and to thank him for being with him through his challenges. This discussion with Jon, when reported back to Dr. Mason, reinforced that he was highly supportive of Michael, and they both agreed that they had unfortunately grown more distant in recent years. Jon congratulated Michael for going for therapy and asked him to continue letting him know how it was going.

One consequence of Michael's improved functioning and shifting relationships was that his depression became significantly reduced. In Session 8, his Patient Health Questionnaire-9 (Kroenke et al., 2001) score was 7, which had decreased from his previous scores of 20 in Session 2 and 12 in Session 6, and he reported to Dr. Mason that he felt significantly better than he did when he first saw her. He also reported that he had been thinking a lot about himself as a person and what he wanted to do with the rest of his life. As part of the treatment program, Dr. Mason and Michael shifted their discussions to consider the implications for the future and potential retirement. Dr. Mason framed these experiences as a type of loss, in that Michael had for many years positioned himself as a strong and independent businessperson, but also an opportunity to redefine his identity and potentially take on new roles. Michael expressed ambivalence about this process, but over the course of several weeks he brought up the idea of selling his business, reinvigorating his relationships, and possibly pursuing other interests. He took the opportunity to speak more regularly with his two children, and he talked to them about his ideas for the future. He wondered if they might be interested in planning a family vacation. He was surprised to discover that they were highly supportive of his taking the burden of his business off of his shoulders and either becoming a part-time employee of the company or selling the business altogether.

Part of the discussion that Michael and Dr. Mason had related to this possible role transition related to the values that he held. It became clear that Michael was strongly propelled by beliefs about the importance of honest work, effort, and integrity in relationships. Together, he and Dr. Mason discussed ways in which these values could be enjoyed in retirement, and while they came to no firm conclusion, Michael expressed a sense of hope and optimism that this line of thinking could be very helpful for him.

The Case of Miranda

Following a number of sessions working on cognitive restructuring, Josefina began to notice clear patterns in Miranda's thoughts. She had already speculated about some of Miranda's core beliefs, and those beliefs were confirmed. Miranda had clearly learned that "thoughts are not facts" and was able to challenge her thoughts, both in the session and to some degree outside the session. She was able to do this challenging when she completed the thought records and was attempting to do it in the moment. Some of her core beliefs appeared to be "I am undesirable to most people," "I am uninteresting," and "To be accepted, I must do things to a very high standard." She also had several positive beliefs, including "I am hardworking and capable," "I am a good mother," and "The future is bright."

Josefina and Miranda had a discussion about these beliefs. Miranda already felt that the first two (being undesirable and uninteresting) were somewhat lessened. The one regarding standards had been challenged by her husband, and she agreed that this belief led to some difficulties for both her and her husband. She further thought that she may be serving as a poor role model for her children. They had made some compromises regarding household and family tasks, and she was working hard not to be critical. For example, Miranda was pleased that she had not commented when her husband had been 5 minutes late picking up the girls from an activity. She realized that she accepted many other people who had lower or different standards than her own.

While Josefina was tempted to propose further therapy focused on core beliefs, she also noted that Miranda had responded very well to the treatment that had taken place and that her beliefs were already "softening." At this time, she chose not to suggest it, as she decided that it might not be necessary.

IV

ENDING TREATMENT AND OTHER CONSIDERATIONS

11

Ending Therapy and Relapse Prevention

In the ideal world, a client presents for therapy when their own attempts to solve a set of problems has proven unsuccessful; in the case of a client with depression, the symptoms either are not improving or perhaps are becoming more significant. Depending on the place that you practice, your profession (e.g., psychiatrist, psychologist, social worker), and local rules and regulations about access to treatment, the client has either referred themselves to you or was referred by a family physician or other health care provider. You conduct a thorough intake assessment, select the set of interventions that are appropriate to the client's needs, work with the client to implement these strategies and evaluate their outcome, and over time help the client to successfully resolve the problems that they initially presented for treatment with. In the process, their scores on a depression assessment instrument have reduced, and if they met criteria for major depression at the beginning of treatment, this diagnosis no longer applies. You and the client have worked together in a collaborative fashion, and you appreciate the effort that the client has made while they value your expertise and have a positive relationship with you. You mutually recognize that the client may have continuing problems and issues in their life from time to time, but they have the skills generally to manage. You advise the client that if they need your assistance in the future, all they need to do is make contact, and a short return to therapy can be negotiated. On these bases, you mutually agree to end the therapy relationship.

Of course, this ideal situation sometimes happens in the world of psychotherapy. Perhaps more often, however, treatment comes to a conclusion with

https://doi.org/10.1037/0000398-012
Clinical Depression: An Individualized, Biopsychosocial Approach to Assessment and Treatment, by K. S. Dobson

one or more ideals not realized. It may transpire that the case conceptualization you develop and present to the client does not match their expectation for therapy, and treatment ends early. It may be that the client gets some benefit from treatment and learns some new ways to mitigate their depressive experience, but when long-term issues in either the client's belief system or their life experiences emerge as higher order priorities, the client becomes less committed and ends treatment early. It may be that practical considerations interfere with the process of therapy, such as limited financial resources, restrictions on insurance coverage, system-level policies that dictate how many appointments a client may have, or simply the amount of time and energy it takes for the client to continue treatment.

Psychotherapy research suggests that approximately two thirds of clients who present with a diagnosable case of major depression receive benefit, lose the diagnosis of major depression, and achieve remission or recovery (Cuijpers et al., 2014). The distinction between these two terms is that "remission" refers to the loss of the diagnosis, whereas "recovery" suggests that the client stays in a nondepressed state for at least a period of months. However, a two-thirds success rate still yields one third of clients who either end therapy early or do not satisfactorily resolve their presenting problem. Furthermore, clients who remit are at increased risk of a subsequent episode of depression, as compared to clients who fully recover (Bockting et al., 2009; Krijnen-de Bruin et al., 2022).

Given that many individuals with clinical depression have more than one episode, and further given that providing care until the client is recovered reduces the risk of relapse or recurrence, it makes good sense for the benefit of both the client and the health care system more broadly to provide extended care for people with depression. Unfortunately, for the reasons cited previously, many clients fail to receive treatment that achieves remission, and many may not fully attain recovery even if their status has improved.

Further, as treatment evolves, the targets of intervention tend to shift. In my experience, most clients first come for treatment because they are experiencing emotional and behavioral symptoms of depression. Typically, they report feeling unhappy, and they indicate that they cannot achieve what they want out of life or solve the problems that they face. Often, a precipitating event or situation prompts the client to seek assistance, and they want to resolve that event or situation in the early stages of treatment, if possible. As the process of therapy unfolds, other problems get added to the initial list, such as coping strategies that are less than effective, ways of thinking about and solving problems, core beliefs, values, social and environmental problems, and other topics. These issues are folded into the case conceptualization and become potential targets for intervention.

Often when treating clients with depression, you as the therapist begin to see patterns, whereas the client might not, or at least the client might not fully appreciate the biopsychosocial processes that have eventuated in their current experience. For example, you may recognize that a client who experiences a recent bereavement and who lost a parent to death early in life has triggered memories of the earlier experience, even if the client has not made that connection. You may recognize that the client unfortunately did not learn the skills in their earlier life to deal with problematic situations or people who require assertive responses, and you may see the benefit of skills training to help the client resolve the current issue and reduce the risk of relapse. You may recognize that the client has learned a pattern of emotional avoidance, and you may believe that a program of mindfulness would help them to be less reactive to emotional distress when it occurs. You may see silent beliefs or assumptions that the client has not recognized as a pattern in their life but may make them vulnerable to negative thinking and maladaptive behavior. Depending on your particular theoretical model, you may have ways of discussing or thinking about these issues that you can share with the client to educate them and help them to see the wisdom of intervention, possibly more than they had first requested. Every case is unique, and one of the repeated themes in this volume is that an idiographic case conceptualization must drive the range of interventions that are appropriate for a client. As you learn more about the client, you will no doubt see further opportunities for intervention.

CRITERIA FOR ENDING TREATMENT

Given these considerations, you may be wondering how you can ever determine to end treatment. I believe three general criteria can be used in combination to make this determination: outcome assessment, client satisfaction, and practical considerations.

Outcome Assessment

The first criterion for determining a potential end to treatment is outcome assessment. As noted earlier in this volume, I strongly encourage the use of one or more validated psychometric tools to document change in treatment, for the sake of both the therapist and the client. For example, if you have used the Patient Health Questionnaire-9 (PHQ-9; Kroenke et al., 2001) as a measure of overall depression, you can go back into the files and plot the changes in PHQ-9 scores. This plot can be shared with the client, and together you can make a determination about the success of treatment. It is not unusual to discover an early, relatively sharp decline in depressive symptoms, followed by a middle phase of treatment in which scores gradually decrease but may show a sudden increase from session to session, and then a later stage of therapy with relatively lower depression scores. This pattern reflects the benefit of addressing an acute problem in the early phases of treatment. The middle phase of treatment, in which the client shows somewhat more variable depression scores, often reflects the development of skills and interventions, with some successes and some failures. In the final phase of therapy, the client is often no longer depressed, and the long-term themes that created vulnerability can be addressed to reduce the risk of relapse and recurrence.

Even if you do not use a standardized depression tool, you may have developed a particular rating system for a client's distress. For example, you may have been asking the client to rate their weekly mood on a rating scale from 0 to 100%. If so, you could review the session notes and plot the intensity of these ratings across time to look for a pattern. If you used a problem intensity rating scale, the same thing can be done with these ratings to see whether the presenting problem or problems have been resolved. Ideally, your choice of assessment device and method was matched to the client's presenting problems and needs, and you should have evidence to help determine whether the client's problems have been resolved. If so, the data can be used to make the argument that the end of treatment is warranted; if not, the data can be used to encourage further intervention.

Client Satisfaction

A second broad area to consider when thinking about ending treatment is client satisfaction. Even if depression scores have not greatly improved or if the client has continuing problems in their life, it is quite possible that they feel that the process of therapy has given them some new understanding about the genesis and maintenance of their issues or skills that they can apply themselves in the future. I have had some clients who benefited greatly from the opportunity to share their experience and to obtain a sense of validation for their struggles. In these cases, even if the therapist is confident that further gains can be made in therapy, the client may feel a sense of satisfaction and be willing to undertake further change on their own. My strong suggestion is to support the client as much as possible in their decision, to help them to recognize both what they have learned and what perhaps has not yet been addressed in treatment, and to return to therapy as quickly as possible if the need arises. More formal strategies about how to end the treatment relationship in this type of case are described later in this chapter.

Practical Considerations

The third type of circumstances in which end of treatment is indicated are practical. For example, the system in which you work may limit the number of appointments that a client can have in a particular period. Session or funding limitations in private insurance may dictate that the client can receive only a certain number of therapy appointments. If the client is paying directly for services, they may have a very real limit on their personal resources. In some instances, a looming situation may have served as the precipitant for the client to seek out an intervention, and even if the client did not fully address the problem, its passing may significantly reduce their desire to continue treatment. Even issues such as a change in employment, time restrictions within the day, new interpersonal responsibilities due to childbirth or moves within the family, or any of hundreds of other practical issues may interfere with treatment. Each situation requires a unique response, and to the extent that you can help the client resolve the practical issues that might interfere with treatment, this is to their benefit. On the other hand, sometimes it is important to recognize that practical considerations cannot be overcome and that moving to a satisfactory end of treatment should be pursued.

RESIDUAL SYMPTOMS AND REMAINING PROBLEMS

A thorny problem associated with ending treatment is that the client may continue to have some focal problems and/or residual symptoms. For example, although their depression score may have reduced overall, they may from time to time have sleepless nights. Or perhaps the client's sense of self-esteem and personal coping have improved but they continue to have to deal with a challenging family member and have self-doubts about responding effectively.

Residual symptoms are frequent in the treatment of depression. Using the data from a study of 108 patients who were successfully treated to remission with pharmacotherapy (Nierenberg et al., 1999), Israel (2010) computed that only 17.6% of the participants had no residual symptoms and that fully 57% had two or more remaining symptoms. As noted previously, because residual symptoms are risk factors for relapse or recurrence, it makes sense to continue to work with a client with a focus on remediation of specific symptoms, to the extent that this option is feasible. It may make sense to agree to work with the client for a specific and short number of sessions with a primary focus on the residual symptoms or any remaining specific problems. At the end of those sessions, you and the client can revisit the problem and make the decision to continue treatment or not.

On the other hand, sometimes long-term symptoms, habits, or behaviors will not quickly resolve but the client needs to end treatment, even as they may struggle with some residual symptoms or problems. In this case, it is worthwhile to have the client review the range of skills and interventions that they have learned over the course of therapy, to encourage them to continue to apply these skills as necessary, and to monitor the severity of the residual problems. Ideally, the client has information about how to monitor their overall level of symptoms and depression; they can also be encouraged to return to therapy should the problems become more severe, start to interfere with other aspects of the client's life, or take on a more general depressive form.

In contrast to monitoring residual symptoms and trying to minimize or suppress them, an alternative strategy is to encourage the client to accept ongoing distress and symptomatology that may ebb and flow over time. Interventions associated with acceptance and commitment therapy or mindfulness-based cognitive therapy for depression may be quite appropriate. Particularly for symptoms that predated the development of the index episode of depression (i.e., the episode that was just treated) and that continue to manifest themselves even if the client has generally improved, the optimal skill for the client may be to learn to adapt to having those symptoms present from time to time. In this regard, it has been noted that the primary prodromal symptom of depression is sleep disturbance and its accompanying fatigue (Fava et al., 1990); sleep disturbance has also been noted as a primary symptom that predicts recurrence of depression (Dombrovski et al., 2008). Clients who have residual sleep disturbance but can either develop effective strategies to manage this issue or learn to adapt to life with disturbed sleep likely have a better long-term course than individuals who developed secondary distress to their ongoing sleep problems.

Major depression is often a problem secondary to an anxiety disorder (see Chapter 1), and the developmental pattern of major depression often begins with a nervous or anxious youth who develops an anxiety problem in adolescence or early adulthood and later develops a depressive disorder. This pattern is certainly not universal—some people have other patterns of onset—but for clients who have this more typical anxious precursor to depression, it is quite possible that their anxiety symptoms become more manifest and significant as the depression lifts. Such cases may not have residual symptoms of depression as such, but signs and symptoms of anxiety may remain as a residual phenomenon. It is worthwhile to review with the client the nature and extent of these symptoms, their relationship to risk for relapse, the skills that the client has learned during therapy to address these symptoms, and ongoing surveillance and intervention methods that may be indicated. As an example, many clients who have elevated self-doubt see this symptom increase in severity during a depressive episode, but as the depression lifts, they may continue to question their personal self-efficacy and ability to manage difficult situations. If your conceptualization is that this residual symptom is a vulnerability factor for relapse or recurrence, it makes excellent sense to continue to address this problem in therapy even as the client is not depressed. In other cases, while a secondary problem of depression may have been satisfactorily treated and resolved, another primary problem may continue (e.g., chronic pain) that requires ongoing treatment in its own right.

For some clients with depression, it makes sense to end treatment even though the client has remaining life problems. Sometimes these issues are long-term, such as limited education, low socioeconomic standing, poverty, or living in substandard housing. Another frequent issue is a hostile interpersonal world, possibly with family members who have disagreements or a long-term relationship that is abusive. Personal therapy can certainly address some of these issues, and as the therapist you can help the clients to make decisions about some of these longstanding life issues. In contrast, some problems are likely to persist well beyond the end of treatment and in some cases may take years to resolve or manage effectively. Some situations may require affiliated social service and health care professionals, so even if you have made the decision to end your treatment with a given client, it is ideal if you are attuned to local services and can help the client to make a connection to address the unresolved issues. Indeed, if you recognize ongoing issues such as housing problems, it makes good sense for you to engage these outside services even as you continue treatment, with a view that some of these services may continue after the end of formal care.

Managing Concurrent Pharmacotherapy and Psychotherapy

Another issue that may emerge as you move toward the end of therapy is the management of any concurrent treatments. In many parts of the world, it is relatively easy to obtain antidepressant medication but significantly more difficult to obtain a referral for an evidence-based psychosocial intervention. Given this disproportionate access to certain types of treatment, it is not at all uncommon in my experience to see clients who have already begun a course in pharmacotherapy even as the referral for other treatment was in progress. In some cases, and in particular for people with severe or chronic patterns of depression, it may make sense to continue both types of treatments simultaneously. Some evidence suggests that antidepressant medications tend to have a more rapid rate of response than psychosocial interventions, and they may help to energize a client to make the psychosocial interventions more effective. My experience is that if a client is already on medications when they start to receive a psychological intervention, it is generally advised to continue the medication through cooperative consultation with the prescribing physician. If the client begins to feel significantly better, it may be possible to discuss ending the pharmacotherapy, even as the client continues in another treatment. In fact, it is well recognized that clients who end pharmacotherapy for depression often experience a rebound effect (B. H. Harvey & Slabbert, 2014; Henssler et al., 2019), particularly if the withdrawal is fairly sudden. Having the opportunity to be in psychological therapy during this period often provides a source of reassurance to the client as well as an opportunity to monitor any increase in symptomatology.

One benefit of having a client end a course of pharmacotherapy while continuing psychological intervention relates to the way that they understand their depression. In my experience, it is unfortunately a reality that some physicians maintain a biomedical model of depression and tend to minimize or discount psychosocial risk and maintenance factors. Clients who are being treated by such physicians sometimes directly, but also sometimes in a more subtle manner, hear the message that medications are the preferred evidence-based treatment and that their depression is "biological" in nature. As I have argued throughout this volume, evidence generally supports a more comprehensive biopsychosocial model of depression, and there is good reason to believe that evidence-based psychosocial therapies can have equal or in some cases superior outcomes to pharmacotherapy. In some cases, it is quite revelatory to clients to see no return to depression even though they have ended their course of pharmacotherapy but have continued with psychosocial intervention. It is distinctly worthwhile to discuss with the client the attribution they make for their treatment outcomes and to consider what has effectively helped them or helped to maintain their lack of depression. Ideally, from a biopsychosocial perspective, the client should be encouraged to make the attribution that their whole self has benefited from both the medications and the psychosocial intervention and that both have a role to play in maintaining their future good health.

If the client has been engaged in a concomitant therapy, it often makes sense to continue that treatment after you finish your work with the client. For example, if the client had a chronic course of depression for which pharmacotherapy was prescribed, it may make sense to continue that course of treatment after psychosocial intervention finishes. In other cases, prior signs or symptoms of anxiety or residual anxiety symptoms may warrant an ongoing anxiolytic prescription. These decisions should be left to a discussion between the client and the prescribing physician, but your assessment of current symptomatology, ongoing issues, and risk for relapse and recurrence can certainly help to inform that discussion. As such, it is recommended that, to the extent possible, you obtain the client's consent and directly speak to the prescribing physician (assuming you are not the prescribing physician) about the potential benefits and risks of ongoing pharmacotherapy.

Some clients may be engaged in other forms of psychological intervention. I can think of clients who initially came for individual treatment but had relationship issues that were fundamentally part of the problems, and couples therapy or family therapy was indicated. It may make sense to refer these clients to the other form of treatment and to stop individual treatment for a time, or it may make sense to have parallel approaches address different aspects of the client's problem list. I have even seen a pattern in which a client begins individual treatment, has a series of couples therapy sessions, and then returns to individual treatment. You and the client together should make these decisions based on your mutual case conceptualization, available resources, and your understanding of the strategies most likely to help the client resolve their presenting problems. I know of no formal decision tree for such recommendations or set of practice guidelines; these decisions largely remain a matter of best clinical judgment and negotiation.

POTENTIAL STRATEGIES TO END TREATMENT

The following discussion rests on the assumption that you have been working with a client for a time. Initially, you conducted a thorough assessment of the client's symptoms and presenting problems, which led to an effective case conceptualization. You were able to engage in psychoeducation, develop a sound working relationship, and deploy appropriate interventions with the client, which helped them to develop new skills and understanding of their problems and ultimately led to significant symptom reduction and resolution of the presenting problems. In this context, the following sections present some things to consider as you move toward the end of treatment.

Overtrain Clients

Before the end of treatment, consider the process of overtraining. Overtraining involves challenging the client to seek situations that are actually more difficult than those they might normally encounter, in order that they can practice their new skills. For example, if they have a distressed relationship with one of their parents and it has been lingering for some time, a possible assignment is to interact with that parent to establish a new way of relating that is associated with less risk of depression. As another example, if a client is taking a low dose of antidepressant medication concomitant with your treatment, before the end of therapy they could conduct a trial of withdrawal from the medication to see if it is needed for their long-term well-being.

Review and Consolidate

Hopefully, you have included quite a bit of psychoeducation and information sharing with the client during the sessions in which you have worked together. The client may have learned some of the names of the techniques (e.g., evidence gathering, working against avoidance, thought monitoring, healthy diet), and you and the client may have developed some novel and idiosyncratic techniques that have been antidepressant for them. As you move toward the end of treatment, it is useful for both you and the client to review the treatment. You will have progress notes to read through, and the client may have forms they have used or notes that they have taken. Based on this review, you and the client can develop a list of successful interventions that the client can take away at the end of treatment. Some clients benefit from developing a therapy folder that includes various forms they used and handouts that they received over the course of treatment. Some clients with whom I have worked kept a therapy diary in which they recorded their homework assignments, thoughts, and impressions about what was beneficial or not. One client I saw was foresighted enough that when a given strategy was particularly successful, they made a note to themselves. At the end of treatment, we had a readily compiled short list of effective strategies that they could review and think about implementing in the future. Essentially, my suggestion is that you gather whatever materials you have used over the course of treatment, review what was beneficial (or not), and create a personalized set of ideas for the client if they need them in the future.

Create Bigger Gaps Between the Final Few Sessions

A suggestion seen in other treatment books (J. S. Beck, 2021; D. Dobson & K. S. Dobson, 2017) is to space out the last few sessions. This strategy allows the client more time between one appointment and the next to gather life experience and practice with the interventions that have been successful. It is particularly useful for clients who may be somewhat anxious about ending therapy because it maintains contact even as the intensity of the contact is reduced. It can also be useful for clients who have a limited number of therapy sessions due to insurance programs or copayment schemes—they can keep the therapy moving along in a way that respects potential financial concerns. This strategy is also recommended if you as the therapist have some questions or doubts about the client's ability to manage after the end of treatment. Spacing out the last few sessions gives you more opportunity to assess their ability to maintain progress and whether further intervention may be indicated.

Continuation Therapy

A suggested approach to increasing long-term gain is to shift from regular therapy appointments to continuation therapy. The idea is to have less frequent but regular appointments as part of the process of fading out therapy. Based on an earlier recommendation, Jarrett and colleagues (1998) conducted a trial in which clients who had recovered from major depression were randomly assigned to eight monthly follow-up appointments during a continuation phase of care or were given no follow-up appointments. The results clearly revealed the value of continuation care, as the rates of remission and recovery were significantly higher in the continuation group (Jarrett et al., 2001; see also Vittengl et al., 2009). Interestingly, a later analysis of the data indicated that the participants who had more risk indicators benefited more from continuation care (i.e., had better outcomes), suggesting that continuation treatment may be most indicated for participants with residual symptoms and ongoing challenges (Vittengl et al., 2010).

Schedule a Follow-Up Assessment

With clients who have a particularly high probability of relapse, another potentially useful strategy is to make a follow-up appointment for assessment. For example, you and the client could agree that although treatment is ending, you will see each other for a 6-month follow-up appointment, at which time you can assess their level of symptomatology, any current issues or problems they are facing, the tools they continue to use from your current treatment, and whether return to therapy may be indicated. Research has been done with the use of planned booster sessions to see whether even a small number of scheduled appointments can lead to better long-term success. While some early research suggested this strategy is not useful (Baker & Wilson, 1985), more recent research suggests that booster sessions can be useful to maintain treatment gains and reduce risk of relapse (Hollon et al., 2002). In any event, if a client is struggling with a fairly discrete and short-term problem some time after the end of treatment, it makes excellent sense for them to return for a few sessions to address the current problem and perhaps review some of the more useful skills that they had learned in the course of treatment.

Predict Relapse or Recurrence

When working with clients who have had recurrent depression, who have significant residual symptoms, or who face ongoing life stressors, it can be helpful to predict that they will likely experience a relapse or recurrence. While a negative prediction may seem somewhat contradictory in a therapeutic relationship, it can be reassuring to the client to know that you as a professional see them as at risk. This discussion can then lead into a review of the importance of ongoing home assessment of symptomatology. For example, you can remind the client about assessment measurements such as the PHQ-9, and if the depression assessment tool that you have been using is not copyrighted, you might provide them with a copy to take home and use as a self-assessment tool. Early screening and recognition of increased symptomatology by the client can potentially lead to a quick return to treatment, which in turn should theoretically be associated with relatively rapid response to treatment and success if a further round of intervention is needed.

ACCEPTANCE-BASED APPROACHES TO RELAPSE PREVENTION

Chapter 10 included discussion of acceptance-based interventions as an important part of the overall plan to end treatment. As noted there, mindfulness-based cognitive therapy (MBCT; Segal et al., 2013; Teasdale et al., 2014) was developed as a strategy to reduce the risk of relapse in clients who had successfully recovered from depression. The model explicitly recognizes that cognitive disturbance and emotional distress are normal and predictable parts of the human experience but also that some clients who had been depressed are particularly attentive and reactive to new emotional problems. As such, MBCT trains clients to know their body more fully than might have been the case otherwise and to learn to accept a range of experiences, including some distress. Research evidence has revealed that this approach reduces the risk of relapse in depression, in particular for clients with a higher number of recurrent episodes (Kuyken et al., 2016; Segal & Walsh, 2016).

Given the value of mindfulness-based strategies for relapse prevention in clients with depression, it makes excellent sense to consider with the client whether any such intervention should be integrated into their care. With some clients, it is quite easy to recommend that they use meditation, yoga, or other reflective practices as part of their overall self-care strategy. Urban centers often have many facilities and programs available for a client to use, if they have the interest. Some clinical settings have adopted formal MBCT training and make it available to appropriate clients as part of the transition to the end of treatment. Where these programs may not be readily available (e.g., in more rural settings), the use of self-help materials is recommended. As an alternative, if you are trained and the client has interest, it may be possible to integrate a focus on mindfulness into treatment. Because no accepted algorithm is currently available to assist with making the transition from a symptom-focused intervention that aims to reduce depression to one that shifts to an acceptance-based practice with a focus on depression prevention, this work requires some ingenuity and collaboration between you and your clients.

One question that remains in the field of depression care is how best to transition from change-oriented interventions to acceptance-oriented interventions as therapy moves toward completion. As noted throughout this volume, most clients come for depression treatment because they are dissatisfied with either their current functioning or circumstances in their life. Typically, they are seeking strategies to change the problems that they have brought into therapy. For clients who are at an initial stage of treatment, or for those who are in particular distress, the idea that acceptance strategies can be an effective way to respond to depression is likely to be rebuffed. My experience is that clients need some relief from their presenting problems and symptomatology to be willing to entertain and integrate acceptance-oriented interventions into practice. Certainly, a therapeutic rupture may occur if the client senses that the therapist is recommending that they should accept an intolerable situation or "put up with" the problems that brought them into treatment. As such, the shift in focus from change to acceptance needs to be handled in a clear and thoughtful manner, with careful attention to the client's response to this shift. As suggested throughout this volume, your case conceptualization of the issues that brought the client into therapy, the client's response to previous interventions that were offered and used, the way in which the client conceptualizes their own problems and symptomatology, and the resources available to you in the process of therapy all figure into the final decisions you make about how to manage this transition.

ENDING VERSUS "TERMINATION": THE CLIENT'S PERSPECTIVE

Of note, the word "termination" has not been used in this chapter to this point. In fact, even though this concept has a long tradition (e.g., K. S. Dobson & Haubert, 2008; O'Donohue & Cucciare, 2008), I recommend that we discontinue using this term in the field of psychotherapy in general and in particular in work with clients who experience depression. My reasons for this recommendation are mostly pragmatic. I recognize that the word "termination" literally and simply refers to the end of something, but in many societies it has taken on a somewhat pejorative connotation. For example, "involuntary termination" is often the phrase used when a person is released from a position, either with or without cause. "Termination" also has an unfortunate association with the violent film *The Terminator* (Cameron, 1984) and is often seen as a permanent, irrevocable ending. I also argue that the word "termination" is more often interpreted as something that is done to another person rather than with their active participation and agreement.

Another aspect implicit in the word "termination" that I think is less than ideal is that it does not fully takes into account the client's perspective. Thus, while you may be compelled by clinic rules or professional standards to close the file for a client, and you may see your work with the client as concluded, their life goes on, and they may well see you as "their therapist" even after they have completed active treatment. I am mindful that the concept of termination originated largely in a therapeutic model in which the therapist and client "worked through" their relationship and that ending that relationship in a mature manner was considered an important part of the therapeutic process (Holmes, 2014; Reich, 1950). In contrast, I argue that because contemporary models of psychotherapy often include a collaborative element, the idea of finishing the relationship is less relevant. Even more, with a clinical problem such as depression, which has high rates of remission and relapse, the entire concept of ending therapy may be unhelpful. As noted earlier in this chapter, clients who have recently recovered from an index episode of major depression often benefit from referral for additional interventions such as MBCT, continuation sessions, or booster sessions. The fact that all these strategies have evidence to support them, in terms of both increasing the rates of remission and recovery and reducing the risk of relapse and remission, begs the question of when a client should be considered actually "finished" in the course of treatment.

WHEN YOUR BEST EFFORT DOESN'T WORK: REFERRING FOR OTHER CARE

Even the most empathic, well-trained, and well-intentioned therapist will from time to time encounter a client with whom they either cannot or choose not to work. In some instances, personality or relationship issues may interfere with the development of a working alliance. In other cases, the client's level of depression and passivity may be such that they cannot fully engage in psychological intervention unless and/or until some kind of other interventions such as medications are in place. In some cases, the client's presenting problems pose a moral or philosophical dilemma for the therapist, such that not starting therapy would be indicated. Furthermore, not all clients will respond when an evidence-based therapy is initiated. Broadly speaking, approximately 10% of clients with depression who start psychotherapy drop out of treatment before it has been given a reasonable opportunity to succeed. Of the clients who stay in therapy, it is estimated that about two thirds will attain a marked improvement or possibly recover from their index episode of depression (Cuijpers et al., 2013, 2023). Unfortunately, these statistics suggest that about 40% of the clients who begin an evidence-based therapy either drop out or do not respond.

In earlier chapters, I recommended that you measure treatment outcome on a regular basis. If you are doing so, you and the client will become aware if they are not responding to treatment. At a certain point, it becomes incumbent on you as the therapist to consider the ethics of continuing to work with a client who does not seem to be benefiting from your services. Even more challenging, a client with depression who is not responding to treatment may begin to experience demoralization or possibly hopelessness. As hopelessness and suicidal thinking are often a part of the construct of depression, it is important for therapists to be cognizant of this possibility and to assess a client's hopelessness in therapy, should it arise. As the therapist, you have the responsibility to be attentive to your client's needs and to ascertain whether you are able to help them.

Responsibility to the client is a clear issue related to treatment nonresponse in depression, but therapists also have responsibilities to themselves and their families. An important way in which therapists protect themselves is through the provision of appropriate and evidence-based practice, suited to the client and case conceptualization that you develop. Another important aspect of self-protection is documentation. Certainly, in the country where I live (Canada) and in many others, it is critical that the therapist maintain a current and detailed case record that might become the object of a lawsuit and reviewed in a court of law. This record should include documentation of the client's efforts in therapy, the interventions that have and have not been successful, the results of any outcome measurement, and your impressions and observations of the client and process of therapy. If you have given a good-faith effort to help the client but have not experienced notable success after a reasonable period (I suggest approximately 8 weeks), you may need to make the determination that the client's needs may be better served by an alternative treatment model and/or therapist. Typically, when treatment is initiated I make a prediction with the client about possible outcomes in the work that I do, and I suggest that we conduct a semiformal review of treatment progress approximately 8 to 10 weeks into the program of treatment. This message signals that a positive response is not guaranteed, that outcomes will be monitored, and that treatment will be amended if necessary. It is then critical that the review takes place at the 8- to 10-week mark and that necessary changes are made.

It is never easy to admit that one's best efforts are insufficient. Health care professionals are socialized to be compassionate and empathic, and our clients typically expect this type of relationship. Even more, clients typically come to therapy expecting a positive outcome, even if they have themselves failed in their efforts to resolve their own current life problems. Warning signals for treatment failure need to be honestly appraised. Such signals include depression scores that do not change, presenting problems that continue, client passivity or avoidance, missed appointments, open disagreement about the therapeutic conceptualization or treatment plan, increased client helplessness and hopelessness, a client who adopts other interventions while in treatment with you, and your own growing discouragement about the client's progress. In general, you can assume that if you have noted these issues, the client has made the same assessment. It is important to raise your observations and concerns with the client, discuss them together, do some problem solving to make appropriate adjustments to therapy, or agree to end treatment and make a referral.

CLIENT ABANDONMENT

Client abandonment has been recognized in some courts as professional malpractice. Abandonment occurs when a therapist stops seeing a client despite knowing that the client continues to be in distress and potentially in need of care and without making an appropriate referral. Professional guidelines in Canada suggest that three alternative and appropriate therapists or services should be provided to the client to avoid a possible claim of abandonment (Evans & Dobson, 2021). The therapist has no obligation to check with these professionals or services or to see if they are available, as this responsibility lies with the client. As noted, when working with clients with depression, it is important that you as the therapist keep in contact with other health care professionals the client may be seeing (e.g., their family physician) and that you retain a list of alternative resources for instances in which your care is rejected by the client or seems not to be helpful. Finally, it is worth noting that abandonment can be inferred if the therapist needs to step away from practice because of ill health or retirement. In law, the implied concept is a fiduciary relationship between the therapist and client—once a fiduciary relationship has been established, it also needs to be ended in a professional manner (Evans & Dobson, 2021).

MOST DEPRESSION TREATMENTS END POSITIVELY

Rather than end this chapter on a negative note, I want to reinforce that the majority of clients with depression who seek an evidence-based treatment will benefit. As noted earlier, about 90% of clients who start an evidence-based therapy complete some course of treatment, with a success rate of approximately two thirds for clients who stay in therapy. Further, a percentage of the clients who do not fully benefit will learn certain skills or techniques that they can take away and use when required. Given these rates of positive outcomes, depression is one of the areas of psychosocial practice that should receive enhanced funding and attention from governments, insurance programs, and the public at large. Treatment can often end in a positive manner, with a satisfied client and a therapist who feels that they have made a positive change in the client's life. I have had clients say that their life was "saved" in therapy, and while I take such comments with a grain of salt (mostly because I view treatment as a collaborative process and one in which both partners get credit for its outcomes), it is gratifying to think that treatment has made such a remarkable and positive impact for a fellow human.

CASE ILLUSTRATIONS OF ENDING THERAPY

The cases of Michael and Miranda show how their therapists, Dr. Mason and Dr. Morales (who Miranda calls by her first name, Josefina), ended treatment using strategies outlined in this chapter.[1]

The Case of Michael

As the 12th appointment approached, Dr. Mason reminded Michael that the treatment had initially been scheduled for 12 sessions. Michael expressed his thanks to Dr. Mason. He noted that he was continuing to engage in regular swimming and evening walking, sometimes with his partner, Jon. He noted that his sleep and eating habits had improved and that over the course of the past several weeks he had lost some weight, about which he was quite pleased.

As is typical in formal interpersonal therapy, Dr. Mason offered to share her conceptualization of his case. She expressed the idea that Michael's sense of self as an independent and strong person had been part of his downfall. Indeed, when he started to experience some symptoms of depression, his inability to identify with these symptoms gave him little room, except to become more distant from others and secretive about himself, even as he began to engage in increased self-denigration and criticism. While he did not formally have a role dispute or argument with others, his sense of his role and responsibilities was not consistent with his perceived weakness, which led to increased stress and strain in his various relationships. The other issue that Dr. Mason identified was that his identity as a "self-made man" had the unfortunate consequence of limiting his ability to imagine alternative futures. When they began the discussion of a possible transition to retirement, he had difficulty seeing how he could fulfill his sense of his identity. The discussion about values and alternative ways to meet these values, even with role transitions, was very helpful for Michael and opened up the possibility of a different future.

One issue that Dr. Mason and Michael discussed in the 11th appointment was whether they should continue treatment. Michael's PHQ-9 score on this session was 6, which is indicative of minimal to mild depression and indicated significant improvement from his initial score of 20 in Session 2. He was feeling better about himself and believed that he could continue without formal treatment. He noted that he was continuing to take the antidepressant medications that had been prescribed by his family physician, Dr. Norton. He wondered if that treatment was necessary, and Dr. Mason agreed to write a report about the treatment program and his progress and to send it to Dr. Norton in advance of Michael's next medical appointment.

In the 12th and final session, Dr. Mason indicated that she felt that Michael had made considerable progress. She noted in particular his improved understanding of his own sense of self and interpersonal relationships; his willingness

---

[1]All cases presented in this book are fictitious and represent illustrations drawn from my experience but not from any specific person.

to be more open with others; the changes he had made in his physical activities and physiological functioning; and the improved relationships he had with people at work, Jon, and his children. Michael added that he thought that his relationships with his children would improve further, based on recent plans to get together and their enthusiasm for him to make other changes in his life. They ended treatment as scheduled, although Dr. Mason recommended that Michael return to treatment should the need arise. They identified some signs that he could watch for, such as avoidance, low activity levels, and sleep disturbance.

When Michael visited Dr. Norton a few weeks later, he expressed gratitude for the referral for treatment. He reported his PHQ scores to her and offered the opinion that he was no longer depressed, even though he had some residual symptoms. Based on this understanding, Dr. Norton recommended that Michael remain on his antidepressant medication for at least several more months, at which time they could review and decide whether continuing medication was indicated.

The Case of Miranda

After completing 12 sessions, Miranda had clearly improved. Both her GAD-7 and PHQ-9 were in the normal range. Her sleep was improved, which she attributed to the strategies that she worked on for homework. While she occasionally slipped into old habits, she was pleased, and the payoff of feeling less fatigued made it easier for her to continue. Her appetite was normal; she enjoyed cooking and was involving her daughters in meal planning. She commented that most of her goals had been met. She was becoming more comfortable with the women in her book club and planned to continue attending at the local library. While she still had few close friends, she was realistic that addressing this issue would take time. The lunch with her old friend had gone well, and they had agreed to get together again. She continued to incorporate short walks into her day. She was feeling more confident at work, which was related to cognitive change as well as positive feedback that she had received.

Although Josefina had raised the issue of ending therapy in Session 10, Miranda felt that she was ready a few weeks later, in Session 13. She was sad, as she found the sessions to be meaningful and helpful, and she said that she would miss Josefina. Josefina provided feedback regarding Miranda's progress, reiterated some strategies that had been particularly helpful, and attributed the change to her hard work. They discussed future goals for Miranda to continue to work on, and Josefina predicted that issues would continue to arise in the future. She commented that she had enjoyed working with her and that although the current therapy was complete, she could reinitiate treatment in future should problems arise. She also recommended that Miranda work on her own to continue to develop confidence in her coping strategies, reminding her that clients sometimes attribute change to their therapist rather than themselves, so engaging in their own cognitive behavior therapy can be helpful. She encouraged Miranda to continue to evaluate her goals and to set aside time each week for thought records. Miranda was relieved to hear that Josefina could see her again, if needed and recommended.

Josefina informed Miranda that risks for relapse for depression are high, particularly for a person who has had multiple episodes. She suggested that Miranda consider attending a MBCT group that was offered at no cost at a local mental health clinic. She noted that this intervention is particularly helpful for people who have had three or more episodes. Miranda accepted the referral and indicated that she would follow through, partly as she had had such a positive experience with individual treatment.

Following the last session, Josefina wrote a summary note and provided a copy for Miranda. She closed the file and sent a brief note to her family physician regarding her progress and outcomes. She then sent the referral for the MBCT group.

12

Other Considerations in the Treatment of Depression

M uch of the emphasis in this book to this point has been on the ideographic assessment of each client who presents with clinical depression, the assessment of their unique risk and resilience factors, and the application of evidence-based interventions that correspond to the clinical presentation of each client. Almost by definition, this type of clinical practice requires a clinician with a broad and advanced understanding of the clinical presentation of depression, given the incredible complexities that this presenting problem can include. The two clinical cases of Michael and Miranda that accompany the various chapters of this book are real-life presentations of the ways in which individual differences can be incorporated into treatment even while respecting the general principle of using scientifically validated interventions.

This chapter includes a number of issues that either have been discussed in the clinical literature related to the treatment of depression or that should be part of the integration of service delivery. These issues include comorbid problems presented with depression, the potential integration of individualized and other treatment modalities, and developments of delivery methods for the treatment of depression.

COMORBID PROBLEMS IN DEPRESSION

This book has largely discussed the phenomenon of major depression as a unique clinical syndrome. In practice, however, depression often appears in the context of other presenting problems. As discussed in Chapter 1 of this volume,

https://doi.org/10.1037/0000398-013
Clinical Depression: An Individualized, Biopsychosocial Approach to Assessment and Treatment, by K. S. Dobson

it is not uncommon to see one or more anxiety disorders in clients who present with depression as their primary problem. Often, the anxiety problems predate the depressive episode, and many clients who have recovered from depression are left with issues related to anxiety, such as apprehension and worry, hypervigilance, increased stress response, and sleep disturbance. Anxiety and depression have several features in common, and the development of the *unified protocol* (Barlow et al., 2010) to address issues related to these commonly concurrent problems speaks directly to the importance of considering anxiety when treating depression.

In brief, the unified protocol is a transdiagnostic model developed from the understanding that emotional disorders often have common elements, including emotional distress, increased physiological reactivity, negative cognitions related to emotional processes, behavioral patterns such as avoidance, and potentially negative beliefs that underpin some of these experiences. Key features of the unified protocol are emotional awareness, exposure to emotions and/or emotional experience, and addressing negative cognitive patterns. Many of these features are consistent with this volume and its focus on depression, even though the unified protocol was largely developed by theorists and clinicians whose background was in the area of anxiety (Barlow et al., 2016; Farchione et al., 2012; Mansell et al., 2009). From an evidence-based perspective, and to the best of my knowledge, although studies have addressed the comparative efficacy of the unified protocol for other specific anxiety-related treatment protocols (Barlow et al., 2017), no direct randomized study has compared the efficacy of the unified protocol for emotional disorders to the efficacy of a depression-specific intervention. Although I have no evidence to support the following statement, my own suspicion is that while the unified protocol has strong outcomes for anxiety symptoms and results in significant reductions in depression scores (Sauer-Zavala et al., 2020), a more focused approach is likely to yield a better outcome. A randomized controlled study could provide evidence that could affect future treatment protocols for individuals presenting with depression and symptoms of other emotional disorders.

Clinically, my own sense is that if a client presents with significantly elevated depression and anxiety, it is best to begin treatment with a focus on the depressive symptomatology. This work can include behavioral activation; direct intervention related to eating, exercise, and sleep; and an initial effort to identify negative emotional and cognitive patterns. Even as the focus on depressive elements continues, it is likely that signs of emotional distress and anxiety will also emerge, which can be folded into the overall clinical case conceptualization. Further, as the depression lifts it is highly likely that anxiety will remain, and in such cases a shift in focus from the depressive elements to those related to anxiety can take place. Thus, in a complex presentation of anxiety and depression, both aspects can be assessed and treated, but the clinician needs to make clear decisions about the focus of intervention so that the appropriate outcomes can be measured.

Depression can often present as a secondary problem to other clinical syndromes and issues. For example, clients with chronic pain often develop depression as a secondary problem. Clients who use substances, in particular substances that have a depressant effect on the central nervous system (e.g., alcohol, sedatives, barbiturates, major tranquilizers), can also present with symptoms of depression or even a fully developed syndrome (McHugh & Weiss, 2019). A large percentage of individuals with psychotic disorders develop depression as a consequence of the lack of control and the psychosocial disturbance associated with the psychosis (Addington et al., 1998; Fenton, 2000). In all these situations, although the depressive aspects can certainly be monitored and interventions can be targeted toward specific elements of the depressive syndrome, best practice suggests that the premorbid disorder should be the primary focus of intervention. For example, in the case of somebody who is significantly abusing alcohol but also presents with depression, the focus should be first on the reduction or cessation of alcohol consumption, with continued assessment of the impact of these changes on depression and other potential responses. Once alcohol consumption is at a stable and reduced level, it becomes possible to reassess the client's presentation of depression, to develop a case-specific profile of risks and resiliency factors, and to design idiographic and evidence-based interventions for the client's depressive symptoms.

Clinical trials of depression have been criticized because they often require the participants to have a primary presenting problem of depression, few comorbid diagnoses, no significant substance use problem, and in some cases minimal or no suicidal ideation. It has been rightly suggested that such clinical trials provide evidence for the efficacy of treatment in relatively rarefied conditions, which do not often replicate in clinical practices (Lilienfeld et al., 2013). Effectiveness trials for interventions often include broad criteria for the inclusion of clients; perhaps as a result, they tend to have somewhat lower outcomes than efficacy trials do (Cuijpers et al., 2023). As the field evolves, more real-world studies of clinical outcomes for interventions will likely be conducted so that the impact of comorbid presentations can be assessed.

INCLUDING SIGNIFICANT OTHERS IN THE TREATMENT PLAN

It has been noted several times throughout this volume that a major risk factor for depression is social isolation and, in turn, that behaviors often associated with being depressed are social withdrawal and avoidance. In contrast, one of the most protective factors is social engagement (Choi et al., 2020). Given these fundamental pieces of information, it should come as no surprise that depression often affects individuals in intimate relationships (Beach et al., 1990; Sheffield, 2003; Whisman & Bruce, 1999; Whisman et al., 2021). In a review, Goldfarb and Trudel (2019) noted that marital distress is associated with high levels of concomitant depression and that marital distress highly predicts future depression and relapse after recovery from a prior index episode. A notable aspect of this review is that while the authors reviewed potential moderators and mediators of the relationship between marital distress and depression, only two variables emerged as robust predictors. One was communication style, in that couples with more negative patterns of communication and prior marital distress had higher levels of depression than distressed couples without this mediator. The other variable that appeared to be a fairly robust moderator for later depression was neuroticism, although this variable is probably not unique to the context of couple relationships.

A clear implication of the relationship between marital distress and depression is that it is critical to inquire if a client is in an intimate relationship and, if so, to assess the quality of that relationship. There are a number of well validated measures of marital distress and satisfaction (Heyman et al., 1994; Ward et al., 2009), and although each measure is built on a particular model of relationships, they tend to have common features. These features include shared understanding, communication quality, the distribution of duties and responsibilities, mutual respect, common or joint activities, attitudes toward finances and goods, and having children (Brkljačić et al., 2019).

One logical question that should be considered when a client presents with significant depression and is in a distressed intimate relationship is whether to treat the client individually or to engage in couples therapy (Chambless et al., 2012). In general, couples therapy is indicated when couple distress has predated the depression and appears to be a predictor of the client's depressed state; the client themself conceptualizes their depression as linked to their intimate relationship; both parties agree to participate in couples therapy as part of the treatment regimen; and no negative indicators such as significant relationship disputes, intransigent patterns of disagreement or violence, or ongoing infidelity severely reduce or prevent a positive relationship outcome. It is critical in making the decision to proceed with individual treatment or couples therapy to identify the client (e.g., the individual who is depressed or the intimate relationship itself) and the person or people who should provide informed consent. If the goal is clearly to try to treat an individual's depression through couples intervention, this outcome should be clear to all parties before any intervention is offered.

If you as the therapist come to the opinion that the client would benefit from couples therapy to treat their depression, consider whether you can provide this treatment program. In many jurisdictions, couples therapy is seen as a distinct specialty, and referral to an appropriate therapist may be indicated. It is generally not recommended that a therapist see an individual client, then conduct couples therapy, and then return to individual treatment, as it may become confusing as to who the client actually is. Further, it is possible that issues may emerge in either the individual or the couples sessions that should not be discussed in the other format, and so keeping information clear can become a problem. In such cases, it is likely better for you as the therapist to continue individual treatment and refer the couple for intervention from a specialist. To my knowledge, no well-established or validated algorithm is available to make the decision about the treatment model that might be better indicated, so this matter becomes one of case conceptualization, client agreement, and perhaps some trial and error.

The treatment of depression in couples therapy often involves a number of specific elements (Beach et al., 1990). These elements include a general commitment by both partners to sustain and enhance the relationship, the development of a positive perspective on treatment, engagement in joint positive activities, recognition and modification of problematic communication, open discussion of relationship problems and ways to manage or cope with these issues, issues related to problem solving for common life difficulties, physical intimacy, and troubleshooting specific relationship challenges (Campo, 2018; Whisman & Beach, 2012). Couples therapy often has the benefit of reducing depression when one member of the couple is depressed. As such, while couples therapy may be less focused than individual treatment for depression, this modality may be highly relevant in certain cases.

DELIVERY MODELS FOR DEPRESSION TREATMENT

This volume has focused on the issues that are critical to assess and intervene with in clients who struggle with depression. This discussion has included ideas based on diverse theoretical models and has emphasized an idiographic assessment and treatment plan. It also needs to be recognized that treatments can be delivered in different formats. This section briefly presents comparisons of individual and group therapy and of in-person and distance treatments.

Individual Versus Group Treatment

As noted several times throughout this volume, depression is often associated with social withdrawal, isolation, and avoidance. Earlier in this volume, it was also noted that some clients who develop depression struggle with social skills, whereas others have negative interpersonal beliefs that directly contribute to their depression. As a quick example, a person who suffered abuse or neglect as a child might develop a belief about being unlovable and uncared for. This person might learn to avoid intimate relationships as a result of this belief and not benefit from the protective value of intimacy. They may not have learned a range of social skills nor had the opportunity to practice the skills that they know. When they are faced with challenges as an adult, their coping individual resources may be inadequate, and they may become vulnerable to depression. Individuals with this type of history may benefit from group therapy, as the delivery model itself provides the opportunity to watch and learn from others as well as to practice new and perhaps challenging social skills in a safe environment.

Another rationale for the provision of group therapy is that many clients who develop depression go through a developmental process of being shy and anxious, potentially developing a social anxiety or other anxiety disorder, and eventually suffering from clinical depression. In such instances, social anxiety and depression are often highly comorbid, and the client experiences aspects of both conditions. For these clients, group therapy is often indicated as a treatment of choice because it offers a safe and therapeutic environment in which to develop and practice social interactions. Group therapy can also help clients to change their cognitions about social relationships and hopefully to develop adaptive and positive beliefs about social interaction.

A pragmatic consideration in the delivery of group therapy is that it is possible to deliver group interventions to many clients at the same time. However, group interventions may deliver aspects of psychoeducation and skills development in a relatively standardized fashion that does not meet the needs of each individual client, and so the treatment may not be appropriate for all clients.

The relative efficacy of individual versus group therapy has been studied, and the results are not entirely clear. A meta-analysis that compared nine trials comparing group therapy to individual psychotherapy for depression indicated no significant difference in the effect size between the two treatment categories (McDermut et al., 2001). These results were consistent with another meta-analysis of a variety of clinical conditions (McRoberts et al., 1998), in which the authors argued that the clinical outcomes of individual and group therapy are not significantly different and that group therapy is more cost-effective than individual treatment. Although the general pattern is that outcomes associated with group therapy are similar to those for individual therapy, a later meta-analysis (Cuijpers et al., 2008) reported that the available evidence suggested that individual therapy was more effective for depression in the short term. Unfortunately, the limited number of studies, the quality of the extant research, and the relatively small comparative difference were such that the authors cautioned that further research is necessary to draw firm conclusions. Finally, in a recent review of meta-analyses, Jank and Pieh (2016) suggested that while individual and group treatment have similar clinical outcomes, dropout rates are somewhat higher in group therapy.

A variety of treatment models have been manualized for group practice, including behavioral treatment, problem-solving therapy, cognitive behavior therapy, mindfulness-based cognitive therapy, and interpersonal therapy. Some reports indicate that group treatment can be integrated into routine clinical practice with relative ease (Thimm & Antonsen, 2014). Although a number of logistical issues are associated with group treatments (e.g., screening and assignment, ensuring an adequate number of clients to make a viable group, the need for common meeting times and locations, privacy concerns, special considerations and practice guidelines that attend to group therapy in general; American Group Psychotherapy Association, 2007; Yalom & Leszcz, 2020), group therapy certainly does recommend itself as an efficacious approach for the treatment of depression.

One question that has been asked with respect to group therapy for depression is whether there are specific clinical indicators or predictors of better or worse outcome. In a study of group cognitive therapy for depression, Kavanagh and Wilson (1989) reported that personal self-efficacy regarding control of negative cognitions was associated with stronger treatment response than lower levels of self-efficacy. In another treatment study, Hoberman et al. (1988) reported that low pretreatment levels of depression, better social functioning, perceived mastery over events (a concept similar to self-efficacy), and early and positive perceptions of group cohesion predicted more positive outcomes. In a study of pretreatment with adolescents with depression, Clarke and colleagues (1992) reported that better outcomes were associated with lower levels of intake depression, lower levels of intake anxiety, higher enjoyment and use of pleasant activities, and higher levels of positive cognition. It does not appear that more recent reviews of predictors of group therapy for depression have been conducted. The results of such a review could certainly be of benefit, however, for practitioners who want to optimize the outcomes of group psychotherapy for depression.

In-Person Versus Distance Treatment

An enormous benefit associated with the development of treatment manuals in psychological therapies is that some manuals can be effectively converted into self-help, guided, web-based, and app-based formats. Indeed, a whole industry is connected to the delivery of evidence-based treatments for depression in a variety of distance formats. Some intervention models have been developed as stand-alone treatments, whereas others are conceptualized as complementary to work that clients might do with a live therapist.

Given the wide range of distance delivery methods in the field of depression treatment, it is difficult to provide global statements about their relative efficacy or preferred options. Table 12.1 provides a summary of various ways in which treatments for depression have been extended into distance formats. These interventions are based on a variety of theoretical orientations, although the majority are derived from either behavioral or cognitive behavioral models. Further, these interventions have been in existence for almost 4 decades. The earliest self-help materials for depression were based on behavioral therapy (Lewinsohn et al., 1978) and cognitive therapy for depression (Burns, 1980), but they have been supplemented with a variety of other approaches, including schema therapy (J. E. Young & Klosko, 1993), mindfulness (M. Williams et al., 2007), and others. There are also integrative self-help manuals for depression that target a variety of risk factors (Jongsma, 2004; Paterson, 2002) or focus on relapse prevention (Bieling & Antony, 2003).

Distance delivery of psychosocial treatments has obvious potential advantages. First, and most directly, these treatments can provide access to millions of clients who might otherwise not be able to access face-to-face psychosocial intervention because of distance, hours of access to clinicians, and/or the direct costs of services. In large countries such as Canada, where I live, it would literally be impossible to provide access to everyone who would benefit from treatment for depression. Second, the relative cost of distance therapy is lower than

TABLE 12.1. Definitions of the Distance Formats for the Treatment of Depression

Format	Definition
Self-help	Self-help materials can be given to a client in either printed or digital format, and they can be used either as an adjunct to other treatment or as a stand-alone intervention.
Guided	Guided materials are designed purposefully to be used in concert with live therapist intervention. This format often involves digital materials, as they can be more easily shared than printed documents, but both types of materials may be used.
Remote	Remote therapy involves trained therapists who are in a physical setting separate from the client. A variety of treatment models may be used, and the therapist interventions may be supplemented with digital materials.
Web-based	These treatment programs exist on a web server. This technology requires users to have a login (typically secure) and may involve stand-alone treatment.
App-based	These treatment programs have been purposely designed to work on a smartphone. Some web-based programs are available in this format, and some apps are either stand-alone treatments or provide supplementary materials for therapist intervention.
Virtual reality	Virtual reality involves a client obtaining intervention through visual technology, either in person or in remote settings. It is not often used in the treatment of depression.

the cost for live treatment. Once a distance model of intervention has been developed, it can be easily replicated in either print or electronic format, and so the cost per unit of service is commensurately lower. Third, once a treatment has been formalized in either written or electronic format, the content does not vary (although it may be updated with new editions). In this regard, the fidelity of the treatment is uniform, and clients may be assured that they obtain access to the optimal presentation of the program. In contrast, it is quite possible that live clinicians modify, vary, or drift from a treatment protocol (Waller, 2009) and perhaps may not offer standardized treatment.

Notwithstanding the advantages, distance delivery also comes with a few challenges and caveats. A major challenge is that because the treatments are standardized, they are not adapted or flexible for the unique needs of a particular client. For example, a client who is living in extremely challenging circumstances likely will benefit more from a problem-solving strategy than from one focused on cognitive distortions and modification of negative thinking, but the program that they attend may not have this flexibility built into it. A second issue is that self-directed treatments are associated with a relatively high dropout rate (Donkin et al., 2011; Eysenbach, 2005), certainly higher than for in-person therapy. A meta-analysis of digital interventions for depression (Moshe et al., 2021) found that the presence of a live therapist, even if only occasional and over digital technology (e.g., telephone, internet), significantly improved completion of digital interventions and was associated with better treatment outcome. A third issue associated with self-directed treatments is that while they make use of research evidence from clinical treatment trials, many digital interventions are not directly evaluated. In saying this, I recognize that many of the programs are evaluated, but one of the issues in digital technology is that there is often a profit motive to develop and deliver programs as quickly as possible, which sometimes leads to a push to rapid deployment rather than formalized treatment development and evaluation.

A pressing question that emerged in the context of the global COVID-19 pandemic was how to deploy and deliver evidence-based psychosocial treatment at a distance. Indeed, if the pandemic has any silver linings, one may be the boom in deployment of distance delivery and technology. These deliveries matched extremely well with a thorough meta-analysis of digital interventions for the treatment of depression (Moshe et al., 2021). In that analysis, 83 studies that included random assignment of participants with depression to a digital intervention or to either an active comparison or a control condition were reviewed, and the efficacy of digital interventions was examined. A major conclusion was that although digital interventions collectively were associated with a moderate effect size of 0.52 in clinical outcomes, the individual results showed large variability. This positive pattern of results held, however, regardless of whether studies included participants based on elevated depression severity scores or formal diagnosis. Second, although only a small number of well-done trials permitted a direct comparison, the studies that examined the difference between digital interventions and individual face-to-face therapy found no significant difference in clinical outcome. Finally, an interesting result was that internet-based interventions had a somewhat greater efficacy than stand-alone smartphone apps or treatments that included a combined internet and app-based delivery.

A major result of the Moshe et al. (2021) meta-analysis was that any form of digital intervention was associated with higher dropout than any clinician-delivered intervention. The overall completion rate for unguided digital interventions was 53.67%, indicating that almost half the participants dropped out before receiving the entire treatment. In contrast, 76.31% of the participants completed the interventions that included some form of therapeutic guidance. Not surprisingly, when treatment completion was included as a factor in the computation of treatment success, treatments that included a live therapist and therapeutic guidance had significantly better outcomes.

A variety of other variables were also examined as potential moderators of outcome. Moshe et al. (2021) observed that clients who began treatment with higher depression symptom severity benefited more from treatment than individuals with lower initial severity did. In contrast, comparisons between clients based on somatic symptoms, gender, and age suggested similar clinical outcomes, although the number of available comparisons for some of these contrasts was small. Finally, studies that were conducted in university settings and had relatively high internal validity (i.e., referred to as "efficacy" studies in the article) had significantly better outcomes than studies that were conducted in clinical settings (referred to as "effectiveness" studies). This pattern of results is not unusual in clinical trials and likely reflects the variability in participant characteristics and perhaps lower adherence to treatment in the effectiveness trials than in the efficacy trials.

Taken as a whole, the research strongly suggests that distance and digital delivery of treatments for depression are viable and that they are associated with a moderate effect size and not, on average, significantly different from face-to-face treatment. A major qualification to this statement, however, is that digital interventions must be augmented by at least some level of guidance to reduce the problem of attrition—without some form of human contact, the treatment dropout rate is higher and the outcomes are significantly worse. The available literature does not indicate the appropriate level of human contact to augment digital therapy, and so this question must remain for future research. This said, large trials of internet-based therapy supplemented with therapist contact for depression have been conducted (Hadjistavropoulos et al., 2016) using regular twice-weekly brief therapist phone consultation. A study that compared standardized to elective phone support suggested that the optional approach led to about half as many contacts as standardized support and significantly lower program completion rates (56.5% versus 82.4%; Hadjistavropoulos et al., 2017). It appears that regular monitoring and reporting are important in this model of delivery, and such a result is not that surprising for a disorder in which avoidance, self-denigration, and pessimism are common aspects.

Overall, it appears that digital and distance forms of treatment for depression are likely to continue to develop. In particular, the enormous human need for effective treatments for depression will drive the development and dissemination of distance-based technologies. As this area evolves, I hope that several considerations remain front of mind. First, although the access to internet and distance technology is good to excellent in the developed world, much of the developing world continues to rely on unstable technology, shared access to computers and the internet, and significant concerns about privacy. These issues are all significant barriers to the global use of internet and distance-based therapies and will continue to need to be monitored over time. Second, as noted previously, the development and availability of distance technologies in and of themselves is likely not going to solve the problem of depression globally. The problem of attrition is significant with stand-alone technological delivery, and some form of human assessment, monitoring, and guidance appears to be a requirement for optimal rates of completion and program outcomes. How this integration of human and technological services may be optimized needs further study and guideline development.

A final concern for me is that of program adaptability and flexibility. As has been argued throughout this volume, individuals who struggle with depression have different combinations of risk and resilience factors and likely respond best to interventions that match their unique characteristics. If this assertion is correct, then the optimal distance-based technology is one in which treatment modules can be selectively applied to individuals based on the idiographic assessment of their unique needs. It is likely that some form of computational model will eventually be necessary to determine which modules to select or that a human with training in the treatment of depression will have to make this determination and then follow up with repeated monitoring. My suspicion is that a combination of human and distance-based delivery of treatment, whether in the form of internet-based programs or specialized apps, is likely to be discovered as the optimal combination for personalized and yet widely disseminated depression care.

INTEGRATING PSYCHOSOCIAL TREATMENTS AND SOMATIC INTERVENTIONS FOR DEPRESSION

The arguments in this volume are based on the biopsychosocial model, which encourages consideration and exploration of a variety of perspectives on the issue of depression. At the same time, relatively little has been said about biomedical perspective, and you could indeed be critical that this volume does not emphasize the biology of depression as much as is warranted. The emphasis seen in this volume is obviously related to the fact that I am a psychologist with primary expertise in the areas of psychosocial models and interventions. I am also mindful that many excellent articles and books deal with the biological aspects of the mood disorders, including major depression (cf. Nemeroff et al., 2022; Schatzberg & DeBattista, 2019). There are indeed hundreds of studies of the neurochemistry of depression, endocrinology, immunological systems, anatomy, brain imaging, and both genetics and epigenetics. Relatedly, a host of somatic interventions have been developed and used with clients who struggle with depression, including antidepressant medications, electroconvulsive therapy, transcranial magnetic stimulation (TMS), vagal nerve stimulation, deep brain stimulation, and the use of exploratory medications such as ketamine and psychedelics. Even within the domain of antidepressant medications a large number of treatment options has been developed, including monoamine oxidase inhibitors (MAOIs), tricyclic antidepressants (TCAs), selective serotonin reuptake inhibitors (SSRIs), serotonin–norepinephrine reuptake inhibitors (SNRIs), dopamine reuptake blockers, serotonergic receptor antagonists, and noradrenergic antagonists.

One of the hopes of the field of biological psychiatry is that, with enough study and a large enough range of treatment options, it may be possible to map certain biomarkers of depression onto corresponding treatment paradigms. The pharmaceutical industry is highly invested in this process, as there is the hope that certain drug regimens may be identified as the preferred treatment response to particular biological phenotypes. This approach has sometimes been referred to as "precision psychiatry" (Williams & Hack, 2022), which is related to the broad theme of "precision" or "personalized medicine" (National Research Council, 2011). Personalized medicine is highly analogous to the model embedded within the current volume. The argument is that if we can understand biopsychosocial risk factors for a given individual and their depression, it may be possible to target those risk factors with indicated treatments. A major difference, of course, between the paradigm behind precision medicine in psychiatry and the current model is the wide framework that includes biological, psychological, and social factors.

In the country where I live, Canada, socialized medicine is available, and the ideal model is that every citizen would have access to a primary care physician when the need arises (I note that this ideal has not been achieved, as many people do not have a primary care physician). For individuals in crisis or for people who do not have a primary care physician, a wide range of walk-in clinics and emergency services are available to attain care. In practice, the first health care professional that a person with depression usually sees is a physician. Physicians often carry a biomedical slant in their conceptualization of patient problems, and they literally carry a prescription pad, which is often the first recourse that they use when they recognize that someone is struggling with clinical depression. Often, an antidepressant scrip is the only intervention that is offered, as there are wait lists for mental health services, an inadequate supply of trained mental health practitioners, potentially the need for copayment or insurance involvement, and simply the difficulty of negotiating the relatively obscure mental health system. From the client's perspective, because they will typically have confidence that an antidepressant medication is an evidence-based treatment, they may be less likely to follow a psychosocial alternative, even if it is evidence-based. As such, psychosocial involvement typically occurs after the client has had two or more unsuccessful courses of antidepressant medication and either the physician or the client emphasizes the need for an alternative or supplementary model of care.

The model of care seen in Canada is found in many other advanced countries, and the use of antidepressant medication has become ubiquitous. For example, Brody and Gu (2020) reported that from 2015 to 2018, 13.2% of all adults in the United States aged 18 and over had used antidepressant medications in the previous 30 days. This rate of use of antidepressant medications is significantly higher than the base rates for clinical depression, and this pattern is not unique to the United States. For example, a detailed report in *EuroNews* (Yanatma, 2022), based on data from the Organization for Economic Cooperation and Development, revealed that the average daily consumption of antidepressant medication across Europe had increased almost 2.5 times from 2000 to 2020. In fact, the rate of increase was between 4.5 and 5.8 times in the countries of Slovakia, Estonia, and Czechia, the countries with the three highest rates of increase.

For a psychosocial clinician, an important takeaway message is that it is highly likely that, if you work with clients with depression, a good proportion will have had a course of antidepressant medication or will be taking such medication when you see them. My own perspective is that the choice of treatment should be that of the client, and I have certainly worked with many clients who are simultaneously taking medication and seeking psychotherapy. In these cases, I ask for the prescribing physician's name, especially if that person is also the client's primary care physician, and I ask for the client's informed consent to communicate with the physician. My goals in doing so are usually twofold. One goal is to advise the physician that their client is seeing a secondary health care professional and to be mindful that any changes they make to treatment programs may affect that work. The secondary goal is, in effect, to caution the physician that any clinical changes they see in their client should not automatically be attributed to any medications they are taking but may be the result of a combination of forces.

If I am seeing a client for a psychosocial intervention and the client has an existing prescription, not only do I ensure good communication among the treating health professionals, but my bias is to talk to the client to ascertain their understanding of the medication and what it is for and to ensure that they know that the medication may have both clinical effects and side effects. If the client reports indications of a side effect or problem to me, I strongly encourage them to speak to the prescribing physician and see if there is cause for concern and if the prescription can be maintained. To the extent possible, I encourage the client not to deviate from the prescription and to remember to take the medication on a regular basis. We continue to apply the psychosocial interventions that are indicated and continue to monitor treatment outcomes. My hope is that, even though the medication is not varied, the client's efforts in behavioral activation, problem solving, cognitive work, or whatever other interventions have been applied will yield significant reductions in depression, and the client will be able to attribute the reduced level of depression to the psychosocial changes. Predicated on such a success, clients often have an increased sense of autonomy and self-reliance, and they may have more agency if novel problems arise in their lives. In this case, and assuming that the overall level of depression has eventually reduced and stabilized, it may be possible, if they choose, for the client and their prescribing physician to discuss whether to continue with medication.

A relatively common assumption in the field of mental health is that if one treatment has benefit, then the combination of two evidence-based treatments will yield a greater outcome. Unfortunately, this assumption does not appear to be true with respect to the combination of pharmacotherapy and psychosocial intervention for depression. In the largest meta-analysis conducted to date, Cuijpers et al. (2023) reported that cognitive behavior therapy (CBT) and pharmacotherapy for depression were not statistically different in their clinical outcomes over the short term but CBT showed significantly better outcomes in the 6 to 12 months following the end of treatment. Further, although the combination of CBT and drug therapy for depression was not significantly better than CBT alone, the combination outperformed the use of drug therapy as a standalone treatment for depression. This pattern of results, which has been recognized for some time now (cf. Hollon et al., 2005), clearly implicates CBT as the stronger long-term treatment modality as compared to pharmacotherapy and provides a powerful rationale for the use of CBT as the first line of treatment for clients with clinical depression. On the other hand, for clients already engaged in a trial of antidepressant medication, these results suggest that the addition of CBT is likely to enhance treatment outcomes. Unfortunately, these data do not speak to the comparative or adjunctive use of other modalities of psychosocial intervention. Given that the Cuijpers et al. (2023) meta-analysis suggests that the effectiveness of CBT is comparable to that of pharmacological interventions, it seems likely that the adjunctive use of other evidence-based psychosocial treatments for depression will augment whatever benefit comes from the use of antidepressant medication.

THERAPY IN THE REAL WORLD

Much of this volume has been written as if a client were interacting with a single service provider and that treatment decisions can be made more or less with impunity from others or from practical considerations. Of course, the "real world" rarely works this way, and there are often significant considerations in the design, selection, and execution of treatment programs for depression. This chapter presents issues related to comorbidity, interpersonal considerations in the design of treatment, the use of others in delivering therapy, and the use of combinations of treatment modalities. Additionally, no treatment for depression is delivered in a cultural or social void—effective treatment needs to consider the client's social environment, the other people in the client's life who might need to be considered and/or consulted, and the broad sociocultural context. These special considerations require you as the clinician to think about depression in a broader and more complex fashion than you might otherwise. It is important to be aware of likely comorbid conditions that either precede or accompany depression and to consider alternative ways to deliver evidence-based care, including group therapy, couples therapy, and the use of digital technologies. Finally, although you are not expected to become expert in the wide range of biological interventions for depression, you should at least have a working knowledge of these interventions to be able to help your client conceptualize which treatments they prefer and potentially to navigate the mighty waters of health care systems.

V

FUTURE DIRECTIONS IN UNDERSTANDING AND TREATING DEPRESSION

13

The Next Steps in Evidence-Based Psychotherapy for Depression

As noted in the Introduction to this book, the word "depression" is deceptively simple. It refers to a mood state, a physical condition, and a mental disorder. As a disorder, it is defined by a variety of signs and symptoms that can vary dramatically in presence or absence, severity, and chronicity. Some people never experience depression in their lives, whereas others have a single episode, and yet others can have recurrent episodes of depression. Some episodes of depression emerge on the heels of a clear precipitant, whereas others seem to originate without a particular cause.

In this book, I have adopted the term "depression" as a shorthand proxy for the concept of clinical depression, or what is technically diagnosed as major depressive disorder in the current *Diagnostic and Statistical Manual of Mental Disorders* (5th ed., text rev.; *DSM-5-TR*; American Psychiatric Association, 2022) and as depressive disorder in the *International Statistical Classification of Diseases and Related Health Problems* (11th ed.; *ICD-11*; World Health Organization, 2019). I have referred to the risk factors for depression as if they uniformly increase the likelihood that someone will experience clinical depression and have discussed interventions for depression as if they are relatively equivalent in their ability to diminish depressive symptoms. While these conventions make this book more straightforward and simple, they are likely inaccurate.

In fact, the relative risk of various risk factors for depression is not fully understood at this time. We do not know, for example, whether genetics are a significantly greater risk for depression than adverse childhood experiences are. In fact, most researchers in the field (myself included) tend to explore a set of

https://doi.org/10.1037/0000398-014
Clinical Depression: An Individualized, Biopsychosocial Approach to Assessment and Treatment, by K. S. Dobson

factors that are of interest to themselves and tend not to build comprehensive or comparative risk models. Even further, although some studies have attempted to build integrative models of depression (e.g., Backs-Dermott et al., 2010), these models are based on average or aggregate data and do not necessarily speak to the risk profile for any unique person.

An analogous criticism to the one I have just made about risk factors can be applied to the literature on depression treatments. Most studies of the treatment of depression use major depressive disorder as the primary inclusion factor (although many treatment studies select participants based on a depression severity score) and apply a particular treatment model to the participants as if everyone would respond to the treatment model in a uniform manner. As argued throughout this volume, however, each person who suffers from depression likely has a unique symptom profile and set of risk indicators and thus is likely to respond optimally to a personalized set of interventions. As our treatment studies investigate the average response of the average study participant, it is probable that our studies underestimate the potential true efficacy of psychosocial interventions for depression.

Based on the conceptual criticisms that I have offered, in this volume I have strongly advocated for a biopsychosocial model for clinical depression in which the broad range of risk and relative risk factors are incorporated into the assessment of any given person who presents with depression. I have further advocated that the assessment of clients with depression must include their unique symptom presentation as well as the most appropriate case conceptualization based on the assessment of risk and resiliency. Consistent with these arguments, I have argued that clients should be offered interventions that match their unique presentation, based on an idiographic case conceptualization and the best possible evidence supporting the treatments most likely to reduce the experience of depression.

INCORPORATING NEW INFORMATION INTO FUTURE MODEL DEVELOPMENT

I made the comment in the Introduction that this volume was more than 4 decades in the making. My intent was to reflect on the fact that I have worked in the field for many years and to note that the field of depression theory and research has grown immensely. We have reached a point at which a large number of known risk and resiliency factors related to clinical depression are known, and we have a large arsenal of interventions that have been studied, both in the more rarefied world of efficacy trials and in the real world of effectiveness studies.

As discussed in Chapter 2, a large majority of the research on risk and resilience in depression is predicated on correlational and longitudinal studies. True experiments in the field of depression are relatively uncommon, as is true for most forms of psychopathology. Indeed, the nature of psychopathology research makes most true experiments unethical by definition, as it would be entirely inappropriate to assign participants randomly to receive or not receive known or suspected risk factors for depression. Given this limitation in our knowledge about vulnerability factors for depression, the field is largely reliant on analogue research, accidents of nature, and large cohort studies that look at the relationships among risk factors at either one point or across time. To the extent that these various study methodologies yield converging data patterns, our models of depression have and will continue to become stronger, and our ability to generate matching interventions will grow (cf. Dozois & Dobson, 2023). I also note that this perspective is largely consistent with process-based CBT (Hayes & Hofmann, 2018)—the effort of process-based CBT is to identify evidence-based core processes that cut across diagnoses and the interventions that relate directly to vulnerability factors in psychopathology. A major distinction between the current volume focused on depression and process-based CBT, however, is that I believe that different forms of psychopathology may well have unique risk factors and vulnerabilities that need to be recognized and addressed in both theory and therapy. A second distinction is that whereas process-based CBT is wedded to a particular theoretical model for intervention, my current thinking is that a more inclusive approach to treatment models is necessary to move the field forward.

In contrast to the relatively weak scientific methods for studying risk and resilience, the field of psychotherapy research is replete with well-done randomized clinical trials. We can now declare with confidence that a number of evidence-based treatments "work" for the average person who struggles with depression, including behavioral activation therapy, cognitive behavior therapy, interpersonal psychotherapy, problem-solving therapy, CBT for insomnia, mindfulness-based cognitive therapy, acceptance and commitment therapy, and more. Much of this literature has focused on the care of individuals who are already experiencing depression, however, and while some studies examine preventive strategies for depression (Chen et al., 2022; Hoare et al., 2021; Hu et al., 2020) and others look at prevention of relapse (Beshai et al., 2011; Bockting et al., 2010, 2015; Robberegt et al., 2022), these latter two areas receive an unfortunately smaller proportion of attention. This said, however, it appears that many of the risk and resiliency factors that play a role in the onset of depression are also relevant for relapse and recurrence, so there is good reason to believe that the same interventions will have benefit in both regards. In particular, I suggest that the abilities to develop strong social connections and to use these connections at times of adversity are highly recommended as skills that both prevent the onset of depression and reduce the likelihood of relapse or recurrence (Cruwys et al., 2013; Weziak-Bialowolska et al., 2022).

MOVING TO EVIDENCE-BASED AND EVIDENCE-INFORMED PRACTICE GUIDELINES

One of the recurring themes in this book is the importance of evidence-based practice. In its most simple and direct form, evidence-based practice builds on studies about risk and resiliency factors as well as clinical trials to identify the targets of intervention and treatment methodologies with the highest probability of success in terms of resolving the presenting problems of the client. At the same time, as is well known by clinicians, general models and validated treatments do not fit every client, and in the delivery of a well-validated treatment it is often necessary to modify the way things are presented and the specific techniques to use at any time as well as to manage issues in the therapy relationship. As such, treatment must be individualized in a way that meets the client's needs and can be integrated into their way of living.

A second critical aspect of evidence-based practice is directly related to the idiosyncratic nature of psychotherapy. As noted in Chapter 4 on intake assessment, it is critical when helping clients with depression to identify the presenting problems. These problems will include the signs and symptoms of depression and may also include a variety of life circumstances, stylistic coping strategies, dysfunctional thought patterns, predisposing values and beliefs, and more.

It is simply not possible to know if your treatment is efficacious with an individual client unless you measure outcomes. These outcomes can include the symptoms of depression, which can be measured relatively easily by any of a large number of depression severity tools. I have recommended the Patient Health Questionnaire-9 (Kroenke et al., 2001), as it is a brief, well-validated, open-domain, and highly translated measure that maps onto *DSM-5-TR* and *ICD-11* criteria, but a number of other measures also map onto the construct of depression. My strong bias is that as a clinician you should adopt one of these tools, get to know it well, and use it regularly with your clients to measure outcome. The other class of outcomes can be highly variable in treatment for depression. You might be interested in measuring sleep cycles, activity levels, or a wide variety of other targets of intervention. Some outcomes will be dictated by the nature of the interventions themselves, as in the case of measuring sleep for clients with insomnia, but others may be more amorphous. It is worth noting that the Goal Attainment Scale (GAS; Kiresuk et al., 1994) is a general tool that can be used in psychotherapy to measure outcomes. The GAS is highly recommended as a tool to collect patient-oriented outcome ratings, and it can be used in a highly individualized and personally relevant manner (Clair et al., 2022).

To put this idea in its simplest form, it is impossible to have evidence-based practice without collecting evidence. In this regard, I submit that it is not adequate to use general principles, broad knowledge, or even evidence-based interventions from clinical trials to do evidence-based practice. Rather, clinicians need to identify relevant goals for every client, to collaborate with the client on some meaningful metric of these goals, and to measure these outcomes over time. I would add briefly that by "measure" I do not necessarily mean assigning a number to the client's experience. It is quite easy and appropriate in some cases to use qualitative interview methods and the client's own language of experience to know whether outcomes are being achieved. The important point is that it is only through the collection of evidence/experience that you and the client know that their presenting problems are being addressed and hopefully resolved. The collection of some type of outcome information is pivotal, should it be discerned that the treatment is not leading to the desired outcomes and that a change of direction is necessary.

Throughout this volume I have used the term "evidence-based" as if its meaning is clearly understood. In fact, there is considerable debate about the amount and type of information necessary for assessment tools or interventions to be considered evidence-based (Barkham et al., 2010; Christon et al., 2015). Typically, at least two independent investigations should provide relevant data and yield consistent results, but even within such a definition questions arise as to the sample of participants, the specific interventions, the fidelity and internal validity of the study, the sample size, the generalizability of the research, and the criterion that was used to declare a positive result. As noted repeatedly, considerable amounts of psychological research have been difficult to replicate (Wiggins & Christopherson, 2019), and the costs and effort to conduct high-quality psychopathology and psychotherapy research is significant, which further reduces the likelihood of repeated methods. Given this concern, a less-demanding idea has also been advanced: "evidence-informed" theory and practice. Evidence-informed notions are based on models or research results that likely generalize to the question being examined, but they are often advanced in the absence of direct research. Several times in this volume I have made reference to ideas that are, from my perspective, likely correct, but I have not provided a direct study or citation. I submit that it is important that we are all clear about when the evidence permits a strong claim, versus when we make inferences based on principles and practices that are either logical or are likely correct based on past research. In either respect, it is critical that we measure our outcomes and use our client-specific evidence to both shape and modify interventions that we offer.

One other important concept in the field of evidence-based and evidence-informed practice is the relatively recent emphasis in the field on implementation science (Damschroder et al., 2009; Weiner et al., 2023). "Implementation science" is a broad term for a rapidly emerging field in which evidence from one conceptual model or area of practice is taken and implemented in a new context. By "new context," I mean a variety of possible forms of generalization. For example, a treatment for depression that was developed in a predominantly White middle-class sample in Germany and was found to have benefit could be culturally adapted and studied in a comparable sample of participants in Poland. As another example, a screening and intervention program for perinatal depression developed in North America could be adapted and implemented in rural China. The core principles of implementation science are that the putative effective ingredients are identified, some form of scientifically acceptable data are collected in an original context, appropriate modifications to the tool or practice under study are made in a new context (e.g., language, idioms, cultural practices), a replication study of some form is conducted, and the results from the replication are compared to the original to determine whether the practice in the new culture conforms generally to the original. Already there are a number of frameworks for the conduct of implementation science and a variety of acknowledged factors that need to be considered before a disseminated practice is considered to be evidence-based or, at least, evidence-informed. Within the field of depression, we now see many replications of studies and trials in various laboratories around the world (e.g., Wagenaar et al., 2020), and it has become relatively easier to see the aspects of theory and practice that can be considered successfully disseminated through implementation science.

IMPLICATIONS FOR TRAINING AND DISSEMINATION

Of course, it is one thing to conduct a study and show positive results for a theory or intervention within a relatively small sample of participants and a relatively controlled methodology but an entirely different thing to broadly disseminate any particular strategy, treatment, or therapy, no matter how well intentioned, developed, and validated. For example, many studies leave little doubt that CBT for depression "works" in a global sense and that its outcomes are equal to pharmacotherapy in the short term across the range of depression severity, with relatively fewer side effects and dropouts from care, and that it is more effective than pharmacotherapy in the long term (Cuijpers et al., 2023; Fournier et al., 2022). Contrast this evidence, however, with the advice found in the American Psychiatric Association's (2010) *Practice Guideline for the Treatment of Patients With Major Depressive Disorder*, which states in regard to the choice of an initial treatment modality that

> antidepressant medications can be used as an initial treatment modality by patients with mild, moderate, or severe major depressive disorder. Clinical features that may suggest that medications are the preferred treatment modality include a history of prior positive response to antidepressant medications, the presence of moderate to severe symptoms, significant sleep or appetite disturbances, agitation, patient preference, and anticipation of the need for maintenance therapy. (p. 30)

Although the guideline refers to other interventions, they are notably placed after the discussion of antidepressant medication and are given much less attention. For example, while various pharmacotherapies and somatic interventions are given 15 pages within the guideline document, psychotherapy of all types is provided a scant two pages.

I do not mean to suggest that the effective dissemination of treatments for depression or other problems has not occurred. When the research evidence is sufficient, clinicians, educators, and researchers pay attention to what is happening in other parts of the world, and effective interventions are spread. In this regard, CBT for depression has been integrated into a wide number of training programs around the world and is a government-funded intervention in some countries (although with certain rules and regulations to limit government liability; see Terjesen & Doyle, 2022). For example, nationally funded programs for CBT for depression can be found in countries as far apart as Australia, England, and Germany. It is also notable that some countries are beginning to provide funding for other models of evidence-based treatment, such as seen in the National Institute for Health and Care Excellence (NICE, 2022) guidelines from the United Kingdom.

A critical challenge for the delivery of optimal care for depression is training. A variety of issues emerge in this context. Perhaps the fundamental issue is what should be trained. As argued in this volume, a wide variety of strategies can be used to effectively help clients deal with the problem of depression, and by implication all of these strategies should be trained for use in clinical practices. Many of the approaches discussed in this volume have training programs and curricula, and all have various books and therapist manuals that describe how to deliver them. In theory, any practitioner could pick up and adopt any or all of the interventions described here. Immediately, however, the broad usage of treatments raises the potential question of treatment fidelity (McGlinchey & Dobson, 2003). Fidelity includes adherence to a particular treatment or intervention as well as the competence to use that treatment at the right time and with the right client. Overall, I argue that we do not know as much as ideal with respect to how to train clinicians to use evidence-based therapies with optimal fidelity. Further, as is implicit through this volume, it may be that the optimal care for a given client is a combination of treatments, and there truly are very few efforts to develop algorithms for combining effective psychosocial interventions. A further issue related to training is the question of who should be responsible for this work. A considerable amount of training for psychosocial interventions occurs in professional programs, often affiliated with or embedded within university settings. The dissemination of treatments through the universities is somewhat haphazard, however, as different university programs may elect to focus on one particular model or another, and the fact that university faculty often are tenured for a long time can sometimes lead to reduced innovation and adoption of new techniques. University-based education also is primarily focused on the development of new professionals, not on continuing education and professional development of existing clinicians. As such, professional organizations have a large duty to ensure that continuing education is valued or ideally required, that evidence-based practice is available through continuing education, and that the quality of this education is high.

Another consideration in the dissemination of evidence-based treatments for depression is determining the target for training. Many of the interventions that are highlighted throughout this volume could be implemented by individuals with relatively little advanced education or training in the field of mental health. For example, behavioral activation programs that include mild to moderate levels of aerobic exercise can have significant benefits for clients who struggle with depression, and such programs could be effectively delivered by people outside of the health care system. On the other hand, some of the more advanced models of care, such as working on values or core beliefs, likely require a highly educated and trained clinician to minimize the risk of inappropriate or possibly damaging intervention. In many parts of the world, access to training is largely controlled within professions, but this mechanism is neither ideal nor effective for dissemination. In fact, many professions are more likely to restrict training than to promote the widest possible use of therapy procedures. In some jurisdictions, governments are effectively circumventing professional standards by creating new categories of service providers, such as psychotherapists or counselors. Whether this strategy is an efficient alternative to promote evidence-based care, however, is also the topic of some discussion (Cook et al., 2017).

The optimal model of care for clients with depression likely requires clinicians with sets of complementary skills and competencies. Ideally, the first point of contact for someone with depression will be a well-trained expert who can diagnose major depression, its subtypes, and possible comorbid diagnoses. This expert should know about and be able to use validated assessment tools to measure the severity of depression. They should also have the skill to conduct a comprehensive intake interview and generate an initial case conceptualization. Part of the case conceptualization needs to include consideration of the wide range of risk factors discussed in this volume and consideration of the corresponding potential interventions. After a treatment plan is determined, however, aspects of the client's treatment can be administered by other clinicians. For example, exercise programs could be administered by physical therapists, treatment of insomnia could be administered by a sleep specialist, social skills training could be offered by a group therapist, and antidepressant medications could be prescribed by a medical practitioner (or nurse practitioner in some jurisdictions). To the extent that various health professionals are involved for a given client, however, it becomes necessary for the members of the treatment team to communicate with each other, to assess the benefits and limitations of each aspect of the overall treatment plan, to modify the collected set of interventions as appropriate, and to determine when the treatment program can be ended. Ideally, a case manager or other individual is assigned the task of ensuring this level of communication and treatment integration.

A CALL FOR THE INTEGRATION OF PRACTICE-BASED EVIDENCE AND EVIDENCE-BASED PRACTICE

This volume includes a wide discussion about how to optimally conceptualize and treat clinical depression. I have discussed how to consider the biopsychosocial model of depression and its various elements, how to assess risk and resiliency factors in depression, how to work sensitively and appropriately with clients who experience depression, and how to apply a wide range of potential interventions. Throughout, I have consistently emphasized the use of existing research evidence and evidence-informed practice if no specific, germane study is available to guide assessment or treatment. A clear theme is the need to integrate evidence into practice when feasible but to temper this integration through an idiographic assessment of the client's needs and desires for treatment, what might be acceptable within a given moment and therapeutic time, and ultimately what is strategically going to help the client recover in the most efficient and effective way possible. A corollary notion is the need to gather evidence (from self-report scales and questionnaires, therapy logs, or client statements) about the efficacy and effectiveness of the work that you do with your clients. This notion has been referred to as "practice-based evidence" (cf. Barkham et al., 2010; Thompson et al., 2000; Watson et al., 2013) and includes feedback from clinical applications based in a specific context and with a particular set of clients, which then shapes the ways in which clients are integrated into the practice, assessed, and provided care. For example, it may be that certain interventions are preferred within a particular cultural and language group, whereas other interventions are viewed less favorably. This type of evidence should be incorporated into the treatments that are offered and received. Even more, and to the extent possible, treatments should not only be driven by the evidence at the level of a practice but directly divided by the input and feedback from individual clients. Ultimately, the goal of service provision should be to meet the needs of the clients who are being served. Given the challenges and potential despair associated with the problem of clinical depression, we can all do no less.

REFERENCES

Abela, J. R. Z., Brozina, K., & Haigh, E. P. (2002). An examination of the response styles theory of depression in third- and seventh-grade children: A short-term longitudinal study. *Journal of Abnormal Child Psychology*, *30*(5), 515–527. https://doi.org/10.1023/A:1019873015594

Abela, J. R. Z., Hankin, B. L., Haigh, E. A. P., Adams, P., Vinokuroff, T., & Trayhern, L. (2005). Interpersonal vulnerability to depression in high-risk children: The role of insecure attachment and reassurance seeking. *Journal of Clinical Child and Adolescent Psychology*, *34*(1), 182–192. https://doi.org/10.1207/s15374424jccp3401_17

Abramson, L. Y., Alloy, L. B., Hogan, M. E., Whitehouse, W. G., Gibb, B. E., Hankin, B. L., & Cornette, M. M. (2007). The hopelessness theory of suicidality. In T. Joiner & M. D. Rudd (Eds.), *Suicide science* (pp. 17–32). Kluwer Academic Publishers. https://doi.org/10.1007/0-306-47233-3_3

Academy of Cognitive and Behavioral Therapies. (n.d.). *Why cognitive behavioral therapy?* https://www.academyofct.org/page/WhyCBT

Addington, D., Addington, J., & Patten, S. (1998). Depression in people with first-episode schizophrenia. *The British Journal of Psychiatry*, *172*(Suppl. 33), 90–92. https://doi.org/10.1192/S0007125000297729

Adler, A. (1927). *Understanding human nature*. Greenberg.

Alloy, L. B., Abramson, L. Y., Whitehouse, W. G., Hogan, M. E., Panzarella, C., & Rose, D. T. (2006). Prospective incidence of first onsets and recurrences of depression in individuals at high and low cognitive risk for depression. *Journal of Abnormal Psychology*, *115*(1), 145–156. https://doi.org/10.1037/0021-843X.115.1.145

Alloy, L. B., & Riskind, J. H. (2006). *Cognitive vulnerability to emotional disorders*. https://doi.org/10.4324/9781410615787

American Group Psychotherapy Association. (2007). *Practice guidelines for group psychotherapy*.

American Psychiatric Association. (1968). *Diagnostic and statistical manual of mental disorders* (2nd ed.).

American Psychiatric Association. (1980). *Diagnostic and statistical manual of mental disorders* (3rd ed.).

American Psychiatric Association. (2010). *Practice guideline for the treatment of patients with major depressive disorder* (3rd ed.). https://psychiatryonline.org/pb/assets/raw/sitewide/practice_guidelines/guidelines/mdd.pdf

American Psychiatric Association. (2013). *Diagnostic and statistical manual of mental disorders* (5th ed.). https://doi.org/10.1176/appi.books.9780890425596

American Psychiatric Association. (2022). *Diagnostic and statistical manual of mental disorders* (5th ed., text rev.). https://doi.org/10.1176/appi.books.9780890425787

Anderson, K. W., & Skidmore, J. R. (1995). Empirical analysis of factors in depressive cognition: The cognitive triad inventory. *Journal of Clinical Psychology, 51*(5), 603–609. https://doi.org/10.1002/1097-4679(199509)51:5%3C603::aid-jclp2270510504%3E3.0.co;2-z

Andrade, L., Caraveo-anduaga, J. J., Berglund, P., Bijl, R. V., De Graaf, R., Vollebergh, W., Dragomirecka, E., Kohn, R., Keller, M., Kessler, R. C., Kawakami, N., Kiliç, C., Offord, D., Bedirhan Ustun, T., & Wittchen, H. U. (2003). The epidemiology of major depressive episodes: Results from the International Consortium of Psychiatric Epidemiology (ICPE) Surveys. *International Journal of Methods in Psychiatric Research, 12*(1), 3–21. https://doi.org/10.1002/mpr.138

Antony, M., & Barlow, D. (2020). *Handbook of assessment and treatment planning for psychological disorders* (3rd ed.). Guilford Press.

Arntz, A., & Jacob, G. (2012). *Schema therapy in practice.* Wiley.

Arntz, A., Rijkeboer, M., Chan, E., Fassbinder, E., Karaosmanoglu, A., Lee, C. W., & Panzeri, M. (2021). Towards a reformulated theory underlying schema therapy: Position paper of an international workgroup. *Cognitive Therapy and Research, 45*(6), 1007–1020. https://doi.org/10.1007/s10608-021-10209-5

Arntz, A., & van Genderen, H. (2009). *Schema therapy for borderline personality.* Wiley.

Arroll, B., Chin, W. Y., Martis, W., Goodyear-Smith, F., Mount, V., Kingsford, D., Humm, S., Blashki, G., & MacGillivray, S. (2016). Antidepressants for treatment of depression in primary care: A systematic review and meta-analysis. *Journal of Primary Health Care, 8*(4), 325–334. https://doi.org/10.1071/HC16008

Ashbaugh, A. R., McCabe, R. E., & Antony, M. M. (2020). Social anxiety disorder. In M. M. Antony & D. H. Barlow (Eds.), *Handbook of assessment and treatment planning for psychological disorders* (3rd ed., pp. 180–212). Guilford Press.

Askari, M., Daneshzad, E., Darooghegi Mofrad, M., Bellissimo, N., Suitor, K., & Azadbakht, L. (2022). Vegetarian diet and the risk of depression, anxiety, and stress symptoms: A systematic review and meta-analysis of observational studies. *Critical Reviews in Food Science and Nutrition, 62*(1), 261–271. https://doi.org/10.1080/10408398.2020.1814991

Association for Behavioral and Cognitive Therapies. (n.d.). *What to expect from CBT.* https://www.abct.org/get-help/what-to-expect-from-cognitive-behavioral-therapies/

Backs-Dermott, B. J., Dobson, K. S., & Jones, S. L. (2010). An evaluation of an integrated model of relapse in depression. *Journal of Affective Disorders, 124*(1–2), 60–67. https://doi.org/10.1016/j.jad.2009.11.015

Baker, A. L., & Wilson, P. H. (1985). Cognitive-behavior therapy for depression: The effects of booster sessions on relapse. *Behavior Therapy, 16*(4), 335–344. https://doi.org/10.1016/S0005-7894(85)80001-0

Barker, E. D., Copeland, W., Maughan, B., Jaffee, S. R., & Uher, R. (2012). Relative impact of maternal depression and associated risk factors on offspring psychopathology. *The British Journal of Psychiatry, 200*(2), 124–129. https://doi.org/10.1192/bjp.bp.111.092346

Barkham, M., Hardy, G. E., & Mellor-Clark, J. (2010). Improving practice and enhancing evidence. In M. Barkham, G. E. Hardy, & J. Mellor-Clark (Eds.), *Developing and delivering practice-based evidence* (pp. 327–353). John Wiley & Sons, Ltd. https://doi.org/10.1002/9780470687994.ch13

Barlow, D. H., Allen, L. B., & Choate, M. L. (2016). Toward a unified treatment for emotional disorders—Republished article. *Behavior Therapy, 47*(6), 838–853. https://doi.org/10.1016/j.beth.2016.11.005

Barlow, D. H., Farchione, T. J., Bullis, J. R., Gallagher, M. W., Murray-Latin, H., Sauer-Zavala, S., Bentley, K. H., Thompson-Hollands, J., Conklin, L. R., Boswell, J. F., Ametaj, A., Carl, J. R., Boettcher, H. T., & Cassiello-Robbins, C. (2017). The Unified Protocol for transdiagnostic treatment of emotional disorders compared with diagnosis-specific protocols for anxiety disorders: A randomized clinical trial. *JAMA Psychiatry, 74*(9), 875–884. https://doi.org/10.1001/jamapsychiatry.2017.2164

Barlow, D. H., Farchione, T. J., Fairholme, C. P., Ellard, K. K., Boisseau, C. L., Allen, L. B., & May, J. T. E. (2010). *Unified protocol for transdiagnostic treatment of emotional disorders: Therapist guide.* Oxford University Press.

Baron, D. A., Lasarow, S., & Baron, S. H. (2016). Exercise for the treatment of depression. In L. C. W. Lam & M. Riba (Eds.), *Physical exercise interventions for mental health* (pp. 26–40). Cambridge University Press. https://doi.org/10.1017/CBO9781316157565.004

Beach, S. R. H., Sandeen, E. E., & O'Leary, K. D. (1990). *Depression in marriage.* Guilford Press.

Beck, A. T., & Bredemeier, K. (2016). A unified model of depression: Integrating clinical, cognitive, biological, and evolutionary perspectives. *Clinical Psychological Science, 4*(4), 596–619. https://doi.org/10.1177/2167702616628523

Beck, A. T., Epstein, N., Harrison, R. P., & Emery, G. (1983). *Development of the Sociotropy–Autonomy Scale: A measure of personality factors in psychopathology.* University of Pennsylvania.

Beck, A. T., Kovacs, M., & Weissman, A. (1979). Assessment of suicidal intention: The Scale for Suicide Ideation. *Journal of Consulting and Clinical Psychology, 47*(2), 343–352. https://doi.org/10.1037/0022-006X.47.2.343

Beck, A. T., Rush, A. J., Shaw, B. F., & Emery, G. (1979). *The cognitive therapy of depression.* Guilford Press.

Beck, A. T., Steer, R. A., & Brown, G. K. (1996). *Beck Depression Inventory manual* (2nd ed.). Psychological Corporation.

Beck, A. T., Steer, R. A., & Carbin, M. G. (1988). Psychometric properties of the Beck Depression Inventory: Twenty-five years of evaluation. *Clinical Psychology Review, 8*(1), 77–100. https://doi.org/10.1016/0272-7358(88)90050-5

Beck, A. T., Weissman, A., Lester, D., & Trexler, L. (1974). The measurement of pessimism: The hopelessness scale. *Journal of Consulting and Clinical Psychology, 42*(6), 861–865. https://doi.org/10.1037/h0037562

Beck, J. S. (2021). *Cognitive behavior therapy: Basics and beyond* (3rd ed.). Guilford Press.

Beckham, E. E., Leber, W. R., Watkins, J. T., Boyer, J. L., & Cook, J. B. (1986). Development of an instrument to measure Beck's cognitive triad: The Cognitive Triad Inventory. *Journal of Consulting and Clinical Psychology, 54*(4), 566–567. https://doi.org/10.1037/0022-006X.54.4.566

Bell, A. C., & D'Zurilla, T. J. (2009). Problem-solving therapy for depression: A meta-analysis. *Clinical Psychology Review, 29*(4), 348–353. https://doi.org/10.1016/j.cpr.2009.02.003

Beshai, S., Dobson, K. S., Bockting, C. L. H., & Quigley, L. (2011). Relapse and recurrence prevention in depression: Current research and future prospects. *Clinical Psychology Review, 31*(8), 1349–1360. https://doi.org/10.1016/j.cpr.2011.09.003

Beutler, L. E., Clarkin, J. F., & Bongar, B. (2000). *Guidelines for the systematic treatment of the depressed patient.* Oxford University Press. https://doi.org/10.1093/acprof:oso/9780195105308.001.0001

Bieling, P. J., & Antony, M. M. (2003). *Ending the depression cycle: A step-by-step guide for preventing relapse.* New Harbinger Publications, Inc.

Bieling, P. J., Beck, A. T., & Brown, G. K. (2000). The Sociotropy–Autonomy Scale: Structure and implications. *Cognitive Therapy and Research, 24*(6), 763–780. https://doi.org/10.1023/A:1005599714224

Bloch-Elkouby, S., Gorman, B., Lloveras, L., Wilkerson, T., Schuck, A., Barzilay, S., Calati, R., Schnur, D., & Galynker, I. (2020). How do distal and proximal risk factors combine to predict suicidal ideation and behaviors? A prospective study of the narrative crisis model of suicide. *Journal of Affective Disorders, 277* (September), 914–926. https://doi.org/10.1016/j.jad.2020.08.088

Bockting, C. L., Hollon, S. D., Jarrett, R. B., Kuyken, W., & Dobson, K. (2015). A lifetime approach to major depressive disorder: The contributions of psychological interventions in preventing relapse and recurrence. *Clinical Psychology Review, 41*, 16–26. https://doi.org/10.1016/j.cpr.2015.02.003

Bockting, C. L. H., Spinhoven, P., & Huibers, M. (2010). Cognitive behavior therapy and relapse prevention for depression. In C. S. Richards & M. G. Perri (Eds.), *Relapse prevention for depression* (pp. 53–76). American Psychological Association. https://doi.org/10.1037/12082-002

Bockting, C. L. H., Spinhoven, P., Wouters, L. F., Koeter, M. W. J., Schene, A. H., & the DELTA Study Group. (2009). Long-term effects of preventive cognitive therapy in recurrent depression: A 5.5-year follow-up study. *The Journal of Clinical Psychiatry, 70*(12), 1621–1628. https://doi.org/10.4088/JCP.08m04784blu

Bohman, H., Låftman, S. B., Päären, A., & Jonsson, U. (2017). Parental separation in childhood as a risk factor for depression in adulthood: A community-based study of adolescents screened for depression and followed up after 15 years. *BMC Psychiatry, 17*(1), Article 117. https://doi.org/10.1186/s12888-017-1252-z

Borges, G., Nock, M. K., Haro Abad, J. M., Hwang, I., Sampson, N. A., Alonso, J., Andrade, L. H., Angermeyer, M. C., Beautrais, A., Bromet, E., Bruffaerts, R., de Girolamo, G., Florescu, S., Gureje, O., Hu, C., Karam, E. G., Kovess-Masfety, V., Lee, S., Levinson, D., . . . Kessler, R. C. (2010). Twelve-month prevalence of and risk factors for suicide attempts in the World Health Organization World Mental Health Surveys. *The Journal of Clinical Psychiatry, 71*(12), 1617–1628. https://doi.org/10.4088/JCP.08m04967blu

Borrell-Carrió, F., Suchman, A. L., & Epstein, R. M. (2004). The biopsychosocial model 25 years later: Principles, practice, and scientific inquiry. *Annals of Family Medicine, 2*(6), 576–582. https://doi.org/10.1370/afm.245

Bouteyre, E., Maurel, M., & Bernaud, J. L. (2007). Daily hassles and depressive symptoms among first year psychology students in France: The role of coping and social support. *Stress and Health, 23*(2), 93–99. https://doi.org/10.1002/smi.1125

Bowlby, J. (1960). Grief and mourning in infancy and early childhood. *The Psycho-analytic Study of the Child, 15*(1), 9–52. https://doi.org/10.1080/00797308.1960.11822566

Brand-de Wilde, O., & Arntz, A. (2019). Schema therapy. In K. S. Dobson & D. J. A. Dozois (Eds.), *Handbook of cognitive-behavioral therapies* (4th ed., pp. 249–270). Guilford Press.

Braun, J. D., Strunk, D. R., Sasso, K. E., & Cooper, A. A. (2015). Therapist use of Socratic questioning predicts session-to-session symptom change in cognitive therapy for depression. *Behaviour Research and Therapy, 70*, 32–37. https://doi.org/10.1016/j.brat.2015.05.004

Bravo, A. J., Kelley, M. L., Mason, R., Ehlke, S., Vinci, C., & Redman, J. C. (2020). Rumination as a mediator of the associations between moral injury and mental health problems in combat-wounded veterans. *Traumatology, 26*(1), 52–60. https://doi.org/10.1037/trm0000198

Brkljačić, T., Glavak Tkalić, R., Lučić, L., Sučić, I., & Kaliterna Lipovčan, L. (2019). A brief scale to measure marital/relationship satisfaction by domains: Metrics, correlates, gender and marriage/relationship status differences. *Drustvena Istrazivanja (Zagreb), 28*(4), 647–668. https://doi.org/10.5559/di.28.4.05

Brody, D. J., & Gu, Q. (2020). Antidepressant use among adults: United States, 2015–2018. *NCHS Data Brief, 377*(377), 1–8. http://www.ncbi.nlm.nih.gov/pubmed/33054926

Brookie, K. L., Best, G. I., & Conner, T. S. (2018). Intake of raw fruits and vegetables is associated with better mental health than intake of processed fruits and vegetables. *Frontiers in Psychology, 9*, Article 487. https://doi.org/10.3389/fpsyg.2018.00487

Brown, G. K., Beck, A. T., Steer, R. A., & Grisham, J. R. (2000). Risk factors for suicide in psychiatric outpatients: A 20-year prospective study. *Journal of Consulting and Clinical Psychology, 68*(3), 371–377). https://doi.org/10.1037/0022-006X.68.3.371

Brown, G. W., Craig, T. K., & Harris, T. O. (2008). Parental maltreatment and proximal risk factors using the Childhood Experience of Care & Abuse (CECA) instrument: A life-course study of adult chronic depression—5. *Journal of Affective Disorders, 110*(3), 222–233. https://doi.org/10.1016/j.jad.2008.01.016

Brown, G. W., & Harris, T. (Eds.). (1978). *Social origins of depression: A study of psychiatric disorder in women.* Routledge. https://doi.org/10.4324/9780203714911

Brown, G. W., & Harris, T. O. (Eds.). (1989). *Life events and illness.* Guilford Press.

Burns, D. D. (1980). *Feeling good: The new mood therapy.* Avon Books.

Burns, D. D. (1999). *The feeling good handbook.* Penguin.

Burton, R. (1621). *The anatomy of melancholy: What it is, with all of the kinds, causes, symptoms, prognostics, and several cures of it.* https://www.gutenberg.org/files/10800/10800-h/10800-h.htm

Cacioppo, J. T., Hughes, M. E., Waite, L. J., Hawkley, L. C., & Thisted, R. A. (2006). Loneliness as a specific risk factor for depressive symptoms: Cross-sectional and longitudinal analyses. *Psychology and Aging, 21*(1), 140–151. https://doi.org/10.1037/0882-7974.21.1.140

Calvo-Rivera, M. P., Navarrete-Páez, M. I., Bodoano, I., & Gutiérrez-Rojas, L. (2022). Comorbidity between anorexia nervosa and depressive disorder: A narrative review. *Psychiatry Investigation, 19*(3), 155–163. https://doi.org/10.30773/pi.2021.0188

Cameron, J. (Director). (1984). *The terminator* [Film]. Orion Pictures.

Campbell-Sills, L., & Brown, T. A. (2020). Generalized anxiety disorder. In M. M. Antony & D. H. Barlow (Eds.), *Handbook of assessment and treatment planning for psychological disorders* (3rd ed., pp. 213–252). Guilford Press.

Campo, C. (2018). Systemic couple therapy as a tool to approach depressive disorders. In R. Pereira & J. Linares (Eds.), *Clinical interventions in systemic couple and family therapy* (pp. 31–44). https://doi.org/10.1007/978-3-319-78521-9_3

Cannon, B., Mulroy, R., Otto, M. W., Rosenbaum, J. F., Fava, M., & Nierenberg, A. A. (1999). Dysfunctional attitudes and poor problem solving skills predict hopelessness in major depression. *Journal of Affective Disorders, 55*(1), 45–49. https://doi.org/10.1016/S0165-0327(98)00123-2

Cappeliez, P. (1993). The relationship between Beck's concepts of sociotropy and autonomy and the NEO-Personality Inventory. *British Journal of Clinical Psychology, 32*(1), 78–80. https://doi.org/10.1111/j.2044-8260.1993.tb01030.x

Carney, C. E., Edinger, J. D., Meyer, B., Lindman, L., & Istre, T. (2006). Symptom-focused rumination and sleep disturbance. *Behavioral Sleep Medicine, 4*(4), 228–241. https://doi.org/10.1207/s15402010bsm0404_3

Carney, C. E., & Manber, R. (2009). *Quiet your mind and get to sleep.* New Harbinger Publications.

Carney, C. E., & Posner, D. (2016). *Cognitive behavior therapy for insomnia in those with depression: A guide for clinicians.* Routledge/Taylor & Francis Group.

Carvalho, J. P., & Hopko, D. R. (2011). Behavioral theory of depression: Reinforcement as a mediating variable between avoidance and depression. *Journal of Behavior Therapy and Experimental Psychiatry, 42*(2), 154–162. https://doi.org/10.1016/j.jbtep.2010.10.001

Castonguay, L. G., & Beutler, L. E. (Eds.). (2005). *Principles of therapeutic change that work.* Oxford University Press. https://doi.org/10.1093/med:psych/9780195156843.001.0001

Chambless, D. L., Miklowitz, D. J., & Shoham, V. (2012). Beyond the patient: Couple and family therapy for individual problems. *Journal of Clinical Psychology, 68*(5), 487–489. https://doi.org/10.1002/jclp.21858

Chang, A.-M., Aeschbach D., Duffy J. F., & Czeisler C. A. (2015). Evening use of light-emitting eReaders negatively affects sleep, circadian timing, and next-morning alertness. *Proceedings of the National Academy of Sciences, 112*(4), 1232–1237. https://doi.org/10.1073/pnas.1418490112

Chapman, D. P., Whitfield, C. L., Felitti, V. J., Dube, S. R., Edwards, V. J., & Anda, R. F. (2004). Adverse childhood experiences and the risk of depressive disorders in adulthood. *Journal of Affective Disorders, 82*(2), 217–225. https://doi.org/10.1016/j.jad.2003.12.013

Chen, C., Beaunoyer, E., Guitton, M. J., & Wang, J. (2022). Physical activity as a clinical tool against depression: Opportunities and challenges. *Journal of Integrative Neuroscience, 21*(5), 132. https://doi.org/10.31083/j.jin2105132

Choi, K. W., Stein, M. B., Nishimi, K. M., Ge, T., Coleman, J. R. I., Chen, C.-Y., Ratanatharathorn, A., Zheutlin, A. B., Dunn, E. C., Breen, G., Koenen, K. C., Smoller, J. W., the 23andMe Research Team, & the Major Depressive Disorder Working Group of the Psychiatric Genomics Consortium. (2020). An exposure-wide and Mendelian randomization approach to identifying modifiable factors for the prevention of depression. *The American Journal of Psychiatry, 177*(10), 944–954. https://doi.org/10.1176/appi.ajp.2020.19111158

Christon, L. M., McLeod, B. D., & Jensen-Doss, A. (2015). Evidence-based assessment meets evidence-based treatment: An approach to science-informed case conceptualization. *Cognitive and Behavioral Practice, 22*(1), 36–48. https://doi.org/10.1016/j.cbpra.2013.12.004

Clair, C. A., Sandberg, S. F., Scholle, S. H., Willits, J., Jennings, L. A., & Giovannetti, E. R. (2022). Patient and provider perspectives on using goal attainment scaling in care planning for older adults with complex needs. *Journal of Patient-Reported Outcomes, 6*(1), 37. https://doi.org/10.1186/s41687-022-00445-y

Clark, D. A., Beck, A. T., & Alford, B. A. (1999). *Scientific foundations of cognitive theory and therapy of depression*. John Wiley & Sons.

Clark, D. A., & Oates, T. (1995). Daily hassles, major and minor life events, and their interaction with sociotropy and autonomy. *Behaviour Research and Therapy, 33*(7), 819–823. https://doi.org/10.1016/0005-7967(95)00020-X

Clark, D. A., Steer, R. A., Haslam, N., Beck, A. T., & Brown, G. K. (1997). Personality vulnerability, psychiatric diagnoses, and symptoms: Cluster analyses of the sociotropy–autonomy subscales. *Cognitive Therapy and Research, 21*(3), 267–283. https://doi.org/10.1023/A:1021822431896

Clarke, G., Hops, H., Lewinsohn, P. M., Andrews, J., Seeley, J. R., & Williams, J. (1992). Cognitive-behavioral group treatment of adolescent depression: Prediction of outcome. *Behavior Therapy, 23*(3), 341–354. https://doi.org/10.1016/S0005-7894(05)80162-5

Clarke, G., & Lewinsohn, P. M. (1989). The Coping With Depression Course: A group psychoeducational intervention for unipolar depression. *Behaviour Change, 6*(2), 54–69.

Conner, K. R., Pinquart, M., & Gamble, S. A. (2009). Meta-analysis of depression and substance use among individuals with alcohol use disorders. *Journal of Substance Abuse Treatment, 37*(2), 127–137. https://doi.org/10.1016/j.jsat.2008.11.007

Cook, S. C., Schwartz, A. C., & Kaslow, N. J. (2017). Evidence-based psychotherapy: Advantages and challenges. *Neurotherapeutics, 14*(3), 537–545. https://doi.org/10.1007/s13311-017-0549-4

Crawford, M. J., Thomas, O., Khan, N., & Kulinskaya, E. (2007). Psychosocial interventions following self-harm: Systematic review of their efficacy in preventing suicide. *The British Journal of Psychiatry, 190*(1), 11–17. https://doi.org/10.1192/bjp.bp.106.025437

Cruwys, T., Dingle, G. A., Haslam, C., Haslam, S. A., Jetten, J., & Morton, T. A. (2013). Social group memberships protect against future depression, alleviate depression symptoms and prevent depression relapse. *Social Science & Medicine, 98*, 179–186. https://doi.org/10.1016/j.socscimed.2013.09.013

Cuijpers, P., Berking, M., Andersson, G., Quigley, L., Kleiboer, A., & Dobson, K. S. (2013). A meta-analysis of cognitive-behavioural therapy for adult depression, alone and in comparison with other treatments. *Canadian Journal of Psychiatry, 58*(7), 376–385. Advance online publication. https://doi.org/10.1177/070674371305800702

Cuijpers, P., de Wit, L., Kleiboer, A., Karyotaki, E., & Ebert, D. D. (2018). Problem-solving therapy for adult depression: An updated meta-analysis. *European Psychiatry, 48*(1), 27–37. https://doi.org/10.1016/j.eurpsy.2017.11.006

Cuijpers, P., Karyotaki, E., Weitz, E., Andersson, G., Hollon, S. D., & van Straten, A. (2014). The effects of psychotherapies for major depression in adults on remission, recovery and improvement: A meta-analysis. *Journal of Affective Disorders, 159*, 118–126. https://doi.org/10.1016/j.jad.2014.02.026

Cuijpers, P., Miguel, C., Harrer, M., Plessen, C. Y., Ciharova, M., Ebert, D., & Karyotaki, E. (2023). Cognitive behavior therapy vs. control conditions, other psychotherapies, pharmacotherapies and combined treatment for depression: A comprehensive meta-analysis including 409 trials with 52,702 patients. *World Psychiatry, 22*(1), 105–115. https://doi.org/10.1002/wps.21069

Cuijpers, P., Muñoz, R. F., Clarke, G. N., & Lewinsohn, P. M. (2009). Psychoeducational treatment and prevention of depression: The "Coping with Depression" course thirty years later. *Clinical Psychology Review, 29*(5), 449–458. https://doi.org/10.1016/j.cpr.2009.04.005

Cuijpers, P., van Straten, A., & Warmerdam, L. (2008). Are individual and group treatments equally effective in the treatment of depression in adults? A meta-analysis. *The European Journal of Psychiatry, 22*(1). Advance online publication. https://doi.org/10.4321/S0213-61632008000100005

Culpin, I., Heron, J., Araya, R., Melotti, R., & Joinson, C. (2013). Father absence and depressive symptoms in adolescence: Findings from a UK cohort. *Psychological Medicine, 43*(12), 2615–2626. https://doi.org/10.1017/S0033291713000603

Damschroder, L. J., Aron, D. C., Keith, R. E., Kirsh, S. R., Alexander, J. A., & Lowery, J. C. (2009). Fostering implementation of health services research findings into practice: A consolidated framework for advancing implementation science. *Implementation Science: IS, 4*(1), 50. https://doi.org/10.1186/1748-5908-4-50

David, D., Cristea, I., & Hofmann, S. G. (2018). Why cognitive behavioral therapy is the current gold standard of psychotherapy. *Frontiers in Psychiatry, 9*(4). https://doi.org/10.3389/fpsyt.2018.00004

Davydov, D. M., Stewart, R., Ritchie, K., & Chaudieu, I. (2010). Resilience and mental health. *Clinical Psychology Review, 30*(5), 479–495. https://doi.org/10.1016/j.cpr.2010.03.003

de Oliveira, I. R. (2016). *Trial-based cognitive therapy*. Routledge. https://doi.org/10.4324/9781315725000

DeLongis, A., Folkman, S., & Lazarus, R. S. (1988). The impact of daily stress on health and mood: Psychological and social resources as mediators. *Journal of Personality and Social Psychology, 54*(3), 486–495. https://doi.org/10.1037/0022-3514.54.3.486

Dexter-Mazza, E. T., & Korslund, K. E. (2007). Suicide risk assessment. In M. Hersen & J. C. Thomas (Eds.), *Handbook of clinical interviewing with adults* (pp. 95–113). https://doi.org/10.4135/9781412982733.n8

Dobson, D. J. G., & Dobson, K. S. (2017). *Evidence-based practice of cognitive behavioral therapy* (2nd ed.). Guilford Press.

Dobson, K. S. (2022). Diversity and Canadian psychology: An evolving relationship. *Canadian Psychology, 63*(2), 163–168. https://doi.org/10.1037/cap0000317

Dobson, K. S., Allan, L., Marandola, G., & Pusch, D. (2020). The long shadow of adverse childhood events: 1. Mental health outcomes in an adult community sample. *American Journal of Preventive Medicine and Public Health, 6*(5), 119–129.

Dobson, K. S., & Dozois, D. J. A. (2008). *Risk factors in depression*. Academic Press.

Dobson, K. S., & Dozois, D. J. A. (2019). *Handbook of cognitive behavioral therapies* (4th ed.). Guilford Press.

Dobson, K. S., & Haubert, L. C. (2008). Termination with persons with depressive disorders. In W. T. O'Donohue & M. Cucciare (Eds.), *Terminating psychotherapy: A clinician's guide* (pp. 303–324). Routledge.

Dobson, K. S., Pusch, D., Allan, L., Gonzalez, S., Poole, J., & Marandola, G. (2020). The long shadow of adverse childhood events: 2. Physical health outcomes in an adult community sample. *American Journal of Preventive Medicine and Public Health*, *6*(2), 39–49.

Dobson, K. S., & Scherrer, M. C. (2007). Major depressive disorder. In M. Hersen & J. C. Thomas (Eds.), *Handbook of clinical interviewing with adults* (pp. 134–152). Sage Publications Ltd. https://doi.org/10.4135/9781412982733.n10

Dombrovski, A. Y., Cyranowski, J. M., Mulsant, B. H., Houck, P. R., Buysse, D. J., Andreescu, C., Thase, M. E., Mallinger, A. G., & Frank, E. (2008). Which symptoms predict recurrence of depression in women treated with maintenance interpersonal psychotherapy? *Depression and Anxiety*, *25*(12), 1060–1066. https://doi.org/10.1002/da.20467

Donkin, L., Christensen, H., Naismith, S. L., Neal, B., Hickie, I. B., & Glozier, N. (2011). A systematic review of the impact of adherence on the effectiveness of e-therapies. *Journal of Medical Internet Research*, *13*(3), Article e52. https://doi.org/10.2196/jmir.1772

Dozois, D. J. A., & Dobson, K. S. (Eds.). (2023). *Treatment of psychosocial risk factors in depression*. American Psychological Association. https://doi.org/10.1037/0000332-000

Dozois, D. J. A., Wilde, J. L., & Dobson, K. S. (2020). Depressive disorders. In M. M. Antony & D. H. Barlow (Eds.), *Handbook of assessment and treatment planning for psychological disorders* (pp. 335–378). Guilford Press.

Dupuy, J. M., Ostacher, M. J., Huffman, J., Perlis, R. H., & Nierenberg, A. A. (2011). A critical review of pharmacotherapy for major depressive disorder. *International Journal of Neuropsychopharmacology*, *14*(10), 1417–1431. https://doi.org/10.1017/S1461145711000083

Ebeid, E., Nassif, N., & Sinha, P. (2010). Prenatal depression leading to postpartum psychosis. *Journal of Obstetrics & Gynaecology*, *30*(5), 435–438. https://doi.org/10.3109/01443611003802321

Elkin, I., Shea, M. T., Watkins, J. T., Imber, S. D., Sotsky, S. M., Collins, J. F., Glass, D. R., Pilkonis, P. A., Leber, W. R., Docherty, J. P., Fiester, S. J., & Parloff, M. B. (1989). National Institute of Mental Health Treatment of Depression Collaborative Research Program: General effectiveness of treatments. *Archives of General Psychiatry*, *46*(11), 971–982. https://doi.org/10.1001/archpsyc.1989.01810110013002

Elliott, R., Bohart, A. C., Watson, J. C., & Murphy, D. (2018). Therapist empathy and client outcome: An updated meta-analysis. *Psychotherapy*, *55*(4), 399–410. https://doi.org/10.1037/pst0000175

Engel, G. L. (1977). The need for a new medical model: A challenge for biomedicine. *Science, New Series*, *196*(4286), 129–136. http://www.jstor.org/stable/1743658.

Engel, G. L. (1981). The clinical application of the biopsychosocial model. *The Journal of Medicine and Philosophy*, *6*(2), 101–124. https://doi.org/10.1093/jmp/6.2.101

Engel, R. A., & DeRubeis, R. J. (1993). The role of cognition in depression. In K. S. Dobson & P. C. Kendall (Eds.), *Psychopathology and cognition* (pp. 83–119). Academic Press.

English Study Online. (n.d.). *List of emotions | 275 useful words of feelings & emotions*. https://englishstudyonline.org/list-of-emotions/

Erikson, E. H. (1959). *Identity and the life cycle*. International Universities Press, Inc.

Ettman, C. K., Abdalla, S. M., Cohen, G. H., Sampson, L., Vivier, P. M., & Galea, S. (2020). Prevalence of depression symptoms in US adults before and during the

COVID-19 pandemic. *JAMA Network Open, 3*(9), Article e2019686. https://doi.org/10.1001/jamanetworkopen.2020.19686

Evans, D. R., & Dobson, K. S. (2021). *Law, standards, and ethics in the practice of psychology* (4th ed.). Thomas Reuters.

Eysenbach, G. (2005). The law of attrition. *Journal of Medical Internet Research, 7*(1), Article e11. https://doi.org/10.2196/jmir.7.1.e11

Eysenck, H. J. (1953). *The structure of human personality.* Metheun & Co.

Farb, N., Anderson, A., Ravindran, A., Hawley, L., Irving, J., Mancuso, E., Gulamani, T., Williams, G., Ferguson, A., & Segal, Z. V. (2018). Prevention of relapse/recurrence in major depressive disorder with either mindfulness-based cognitive therapy or cognitive therapy. *Journal of Consulting and Clinical Psychology, 86*(2), 200–204. https://doi.org/10.1037/ccp0000266

Farchione, T. J., Fairholme, C. P., Ellard, K. K., Boisseau, C. L., Thompson-Hollands, J., Carl, J. R., Gallagher, M. W., & Barlow, D. H. (2012). Unified protocol for transdiagnostic treatment of emotional disorders: A randomized controlled trial. *Behavior Therapy, 43*(3), 666–678. https://doi.org/10.1016/j.beth.2012.01.001

Fava, G. A., Grandi, S., Canestrari, R., & Molnar, G. (1990). Prodromal symptoms in primary major depressive disorder. *Journal of Affective Disorders, 19*(2), 149–152. https://doi.org/10.1016/0165-0327(90)90020-9

Feighner, J. P., Robins, E., Guze, S. B., Woodruff, R. A., Jr., Winokur, G., & Munoz, R. (1972). Diagnostic criteria for use in psychiatric research. *Archives of General Psychiatry, 26*(1), 57–63. https://doi.org/10.1001/archpsyc.1972.01750190059011

Fenton, W. S. (2000). Depression, suicide, and suicide prevention in schizophrenia. *Suicide and Life-Threatening Behavior, 30*(1), 34–49. http://www.ncbi.nlm.nih.gov/pubmed/10782717

Ferster, C. B., & Hammer, C. (1965). Variables determining the effects of delay in reinforcement. *Journal of the Experimental Analysis of Behavior, 8*(4), 243–254. https://doi.org/10.1901/jeab.1965.8-243

First, M. B., Williams, J. B. W., Karg, R. S., & Spitzer, R. L. (2015). *Structured Clinical Interview for DSM-5—Research version.* American Psychiatric Association.

Flint, J., & Kendler, K. S. (2014). The genetics of major depression. *Neuron, 81*(3), 484–503. https://doi.org/10.1016/j.neuron.2014.01.027

Ford, D. E., & Cooper-Patrick, L. (2001). Sleep disturbances and mood disorders: An epidemiologic perspective. *Depression and Anxiety, 14*(1), 3–6. https://doi.org/10.1002/da.1041

Fournier, J. C., Forand, N. R., Wang, Z., Li, Z., Iyengar, S., DeRubeis, R. J., Shelton, R., Amsterdam, J., Jarrett, R. B., Vittengl, J. R., Segal, Z., Dimidjian, S., Shea, M. T., Dobson, K. S., & Hollon, S. D. (2022). Initial severity and depressive relapse in cognitive behavioral therapy and antidepressant medications: An individual patient data meta-analysis. *Cognitive Therapy and Research, 46*(3), 517–531. https://doi.org/10.1007/s10608-021-10281-x

Franzen, P. L., & Buysse, D. J. (2008). Sleep disturbances and depression: Risk relationships for subsequent depression and therapeutic implications. *Dialogues in Clinical Neuroscience, 10*(4), 473–481. https://doi.org/10.31887/DCNS.2008.10.4/plfranzen

Fresco, D. M., Frankel, A. N., Mennin, D. S., Turk, C. L., & Heimberg, R. G. (2002). Distinct and overlapping features of rumination and worry: The relationship of cognitive production to negative affective states. *Cognitive Therapy and Research, 26*(2), 179–188. https://doi.org/10.1023/A:1014517718949

Freud, S. (1917). Trauer und melancholie [Mourning and melancholia]. *Internationale Zeitschrift für Ärztliche Psychoanalyse, 4*(6), 288–301. Retrieved July 20, 2023 from https://www.textlog.de/freud/aufsaetze/trauer-und-melancholie

Frey, J., & Hall, A. (2021). *Motivational interviewing for mental health clinicians: A toolkit for skills enhancement.* PESI Publishing.

Gabriel, F. C., de Melo, D. O., Fráguas, R., Leite-Santos, N. C., Mantovani da Silva, R. A., & Ribeiro, E. (2020). Pharmacological treatment of depression: A systematic review comparing clinical practice guideline recommendations. *PLOS One, 15*(4), Article e0231700. https://doi.org/10.1371/journal.pone.0231700

Gardner, J. R., Lipner, L. M., Eubanks, C. F., & Muran, J. C. (2019). A therapist's guide to repairing ruptures in the working alliance. In J. N. Fuertes (Ed.), *Working alliance skills for mental health professionals* (pp. 159–180). Oxford University Press. https://doi.org/10.1093/med-psych/9780190868529.003.0008

Gergen, K. J. (1971). *The concept of self.* Holt, Rinehart & Winston.

Gilbert, P. (2009). *The compassionate mind: A new approach to the challenges of life.* Constable & Robinson.

Gilbert, P. (2010). *Compassion focused therapy: The CBT distinctive features series.* Routledge. https://doi.org/10.4324/9780203851197

Gill, K. E., Quintero, J. M., Poe, S. L., Moreira, A. D., Brucato, G., Corcoran, C. M., & Girgis, R. R. (2015). Assessing suicidal ideation in individuals at clinical high risk for psychosis. *Schizophrenia Research, 165*(2–3), 152–156. https://doi.org/10.1016/j.schres.2015.04.022

Gilman, S. E., Kawachi, I., Fitzmaurice, G. M., & Buka, S. L. (2003). Family disruption in childhood and risk of adult depression. *The American Journal of Psychiatry, 160*(5), 939–946. https://doi.org/10.1176/appi.ajp.160.5.939

Giugliano, D., & Esposito, K. (2008). Mediterranean diet and metabolic diseases. *Current Opinion in Lipidology, 19*(1), 63–68. https://doi.org/10.1097/MOL.0b013e3282f2fa4d

Gladwell, M. (2008). *Outliers: The story of success.* Little, Brown and Company.

Glaser, B., Campbell, L. F., Calhoun, G. B., Bates, J. M., & Petrocelli, J. V. (2002). The Early Maladaptive Schema Questionnaire-Short Form: A construct validity study. *Measurement and Evaluation in Counseling and Development, 35*(1), 2–13. https://doi.org/10.1080/07481756.2002.12069043

Goldfarb, M. R., & Trudel, G. (2019). Marital quality and depression: A review. *Marriage & Family Review, 55*(8), 737–763. https://doi.org/10.1080/01494929.2019.1610136

Goldstone, A., Javitz, H. S., Claudatos, S. A., Buysse, D. J., Hasler, B. P., de Zambotti, M., Clark, D. B., Franzen, P. L., Prouty, D. E., Colrain, I. M., & Baker, F. C. (2020). Sleep disturbance predicts depression symptoms in early adolescence: Initial findings from the Adolescent Brain Cognitive Development Study. *Journal of Adolescent Health, 66*(5), 567–574. https://doi.org/10.1016/j.jadohealth.2019.12.005

Greenberg, L. S., & Watson, J. C. (2006). *Emotion-focused therapy for depression.* American Psychological Association. https://doi.org/10.1037/11286-000

Grencavage, L. M., & Norcross, J. C. (1990). Where are the commonalities among the therapeutic common factors? *Professional Psychology: Research and Practice, 21*(5), 372–378. https://doi.org/10.1037/0735-7028.21.5.372

Grosso, G., Micek, A., Castellano, S., Pajak, A., & Galvano, F. (2016). Coffee, tea, caffeine and risk of depression: A systematic review and dose-response meta-analysis of observational studies. *Molecular Nutrition & Food Research, 60*(1), 223–234. https://doi.org/10.1002/mnfr.201500620

Grosso, G., Micek, A., Marventano, S., Castellano, S., Mistretta, A., Pajak, A., & Galvano, F. (2016). Dietary n-3 PUFA, fish consumption and depression: A systematic review and meta-analysis of observational studies. *Journal of Affective Disorders, 205*, 269–281. https://doi.org/10.1016/j.jad.2016.08.011

Gupta, A., Leong, F., Valentine, J. C., & Canada, D. D. (2013). A meta-analytic study: The relationship between acculturation and depression among Asian Americans. *American Journal of Orthopsychiatry, 83*(2–3), 372–385. https://doi.org/10.1111/ajop.12018

Hadjistavropoulos, H. D., Pugh, N. E., Hesser, H., & Andersson, G. (2016). Predicting response to therapist-assisted internet-delivered cognitive behavior therapy for depression or anxiety within an open dissemination trial. *Behavior Therapy, 47*(2), 155–165. https://doi.org/10.1016/j.beth.2015.10.006

Hadjistavropoulos, H. D., Schneider, L. H., Edmonds, M., Karin, E., Nugent, M. N., Dirkse, D., Dear, B. F., & Titov, N. (2017). Randomized controlled trial of internet-delivered cognitive behaviour therapy comparing standard weekly versus optional weekly therapist support. *Journal of Anxiety Disorders, 52*, 15–24. https://doi.org/10.1016/j.janxdis.2017.09.006

Hamilton, M. (1960). A rating scale for depression. *Journal of Neurology, Neurosurgery & Psychiatry, 23*(1), 56–62. https://doi.org/10.1136/jnnp.23.1.56

Hamilton, M. (1967). Development of a rating scale for primary depressive illness. *British Journal of Social and Clinical Psychology, 6*(4), 278–296. https://doi.org/10.1111/j.2044-8260.1967.tb00530.x

Hammen, C. (1991). Generation of stress in the course of unipolar depression. *Journal of Abnormal Psychology, 100*(4), 555–561. https://doi.org/10.1037/0021-843X.100.4.555

Hammen, C. (2018). Risk factors for depression: An autobiographical review. *Annual Review of Clinical Psychology, 14*(1), 1–28. https://doi.org/10.1146/annurev-clinpsy-050817-084811

Harkness, K. L., Lumley, M. N., & Truss, A. E. (2008). Stress generation in adolescent depression: The moderating role of child abuse and neglect. *Journal of Abnormal Child Psychology, 36*(3), 421–432. https://doi.org/10.1007/s10802-007-9188-2

Hartmann, H. (1958). Ego development and adaptation (D. Rapaport, Trans.). In H. Hartmann & D. Rapaport (Trans.), *Ego psychology and the problem of adaptation* (pp. 48–56). International Universities Press, Inc. https://doi.org/10.1037/13180-004

Harvey, A. G., Lee, J., Smith, R. L., Gumport, N. B., Hollon, S. D., Rabe-Hesketh, S., Hein, K., Dolsen, E. A., Haman, K. L., Kanady, J. C., Thompson, M. A., & Abrons, D. (2016). Improving outcome for mental disorders by enhancing memory for treatment. *Behaviour Research and Therapy, 81*, 35–46. https://doi.org/10.1016/j.brat.2016.03.007

Harvey, B. H., & Slabbert, F. N. (2014). New insights on the antidepressant discontinuation syndrome. *Human Psychopharmacology: Clinical & Experimental, 29*(6), 503–516. https://doi.org/10.1002/hup.2429

Hayes, S. C., & Hofmann, S. G. (Eds.). (2018). *Process-based CBT: The science and core clinical competencies of cognitive behavioral therapy.* New Harbinger Publications, Inc.

Hayes, S. C., Strosahl, K. D., & Wilson, K. G. (2011). *Acceptance and commitment therapy: An experiential approach to behavior change* (2nd ed.). Guilford Press.

Henssler, J., Heinz, A., Brandt, L., & Bschor, T. (2019). Antidepressant withdrawal and rebound phenomena. *Deutsches Ärzteblatt International, 116*(20), 355–361. Advance online publication. https://doi.org/10.3238/arztebl.2019.0355

Hersen, M., & Thomas, J. C. (2007). *Handbook of clinical interviewing with adults.* Sage Publications. https://doi.org/10.4135/9781412982733

Hettema, J., Steele, J., & Miller, W. R. (2005). Motivational interviewing. *Annual Review of Clinical Psychology, 1*(1), 91–111. https://doi.org/10.1146/annurev.clinpsy.1.102803.143833

Heyman, R. E., Sayers, S. L., & Bellack, A. S. (1994). Global marital satisfaction versus marital adjustment: An empirical comparison of three measures. *Journal of Family Psychology, 8*(4), 432–446. https://doi.org/10.1037/0893-3200.8.4.432

Hirschfeld, R. M. A. (2001). The comorbidity of major depression and anxiety disorders: Recognition and management in primary care. *Primary Care Companion to the Journal of Clinical Psychiatry, 3*(6), 244–254. https://doi.org/10.4088/PCC.v03n0609

Hoare, E., Collins, S., Marx, W., Callaly, E., Moxham-Smith, R., Cuijpers, P., Holte, A., Nierenberg, A. A., Reavley, N., Christensen, H., Reynolds, C. F., III, Carvalho, A. F., Jacka, F., & Berk, M. (2021). Universal depression prevention: An umbrella review of meta-analyses. *Journal of Psychiatric Research, 144*, 483–493. https://doi.org/10.1016/j.jpsychires.2021.10.006

Hoberman, H. M., Lewinsohn, P. M., & Tilson, M. (1988). Group treatment of depression: Individual predictors of outcome. *Journal of Consulting and Clinical Psychology, 56*(3), 393–398. https://doi.org/10.1037/0022-006X.56.3.393

Hofstede, G. (2001). *Culture's consequences: Comparing values, behaviors, institutions, and organizations across nations* (2nd ed.). Sage.

Hollon, S. D., DeRubeis, R. J., Andrews, P. W., & Thomson, J. A., Jr. (2021). Cognitive therapy in the treatment and prevention of depression: A fifty-year retrospective with an evolutionary coda. *Cognitive Therapy and Research, 45*(3), 402–417. https://doi.org/10.1007/s10608-020-10132-1

Hollon, S. D., DeRubeis, R. J., Shelton, R. C., Amsterdam, J. D., Salomon, R. M., O'Reardon, J. P., Lovett, M. L., Young, P. R., Haman, K. L., Freeman, B. B., & Gallop, R. (2005). Prevention of relapse following cognitive therapy vs medications in moderate to severe depression. *Archives of General Psychiatry, 62*(4), 417–422. https://doi.org/10.1001/archpsyc.62.4.417

Hollon, S. D., Thase, M. E., & Markowitz, J. C. (2002). Treatment and prevention of depression. *Psychological Science in the Public Interest, 3*(2), 39–77. https://doi.org/10.1111/1529-1006.00008

Holmes, J. (2014). Termination in psychoanalytic psychotherapy: An attachment perspective. *European Journal of Psychoanalysis, 1*(1).

Hong, R. Y., & Cheung, M. W. L. (2015). The structure of cognitive vulnerabilities to depression and anxiety: Evidence for a common core etiologic process based on a meta-analytic review. *Clinical Psychological Science, 3*(6), 892–912. https://doi.org/10.1177/2167702614553789

Horney, K. (1937). *The neurotic personality of our time.* W. W. Norton & Company.

Horowitz, M. J. (1991). *Person schemas and maladaptive interpersonal patterns.* Chicago University Press.

Hu, M. X., Turner, D., Generaal, E., Bos, D., Ikram, M. K., Ikram, M. A., Cuijpers, P., & Penninx, B. W. J. H. (2020). Exercise interventions for the prevention of depression: A systematic review of meta-analyses. *BMC Public Health, 20*(1), 1255. https://doi.org/10.1186/s12889-020-09323-y

Huibers, M. J. H., & Cuijpers, P. (2015). Common (nonspecific) factors in psychotherapy. In R. L. Cautin & S. O. Lilienfeld (Eds.), *The encyclopedia of clinical psychology* (pp. 1–6). John Wiley & Sons, Inc. https://doi.org/10.1002/9781118625392.wbecp272

Hunsley, J., & Mash, E. J. (Eds.). (2018). *A guide to assessments that work* (2nd ed.). Oxford University Press. https://doi.org/10.1093/med-psych/9780190492243.001.0001

Iacoviello, B. M., Alloy, L. B., Abramson, L. Y., Whitehouse, W. G., & Hogan, M. E. (2006). The course of depression in individuals at high and low cognitive risk for depression: A prospective study. *Journal of Affective Disorders, 93*(1–3), 61–69. https://doi.org/10.1016/j.jad.2006.02.012

Iacoviello, B. M., Grant, D. A., Alloy, L. B., & Abramson, L. Y. (2009). Cognitive personality characteristics impact the course of depression: A prospective test of sociotropy, autonomy and domain-specific life events. *Cognitive Therapy and Research, 33*(2), 187–198. https://doi.org/10.1007/s10608-008-9197-7

Ingram, R. E., Miranda, J., & Segal, Z. V. (1998). *Cognitive vulnerability to depression.* Guilford Press.

Israel, J. A. (2010). The impact of residual symptoms in major depression. *Pharmaceuticals, 3*(8), 2426–2440. https://doi.org/10.3390/ph3082426

Jacka, F. N., O'Neil, A., Opie, R., Itsiopoulos, C., Cotton, S., Mohebbi, M., Castle, D., Dash, S., Mihalopoulos, C., Chatterton, M. L., Brazionis, L., Dean, O. M., Hodge, A. M., & Berk, M. (2017). A randomised controlled trial of dietary improvement for adults with major depression (the 'SMILES' trial). *BMC Medicine, 15*(1), 23. https://doi.org/10.1186/s12916-017-0791-y

Jacka, F. N., Pasco, J. A., Mykletun, A., Williams, L. J., Hodge, A. M., O'Reilly, S. L., Nicholson, G. C., Kotowicz, M. A., & Berk, M. (2010). Association of Western and traditional diets with depression and anxiety in women. *The American Journal of Psychiatry, 167*(3), 305–311. https://doi.org/10.1176/appi.ajp.2009.09060881

Jacobson, E. (1964). *The self and the object world.* International Universities Press.

Jacobson, N. S., Dobson, K. S., Truax, P. A., Addis, M. E., Koerner, K., Gollan, J. K., Gortner, E., & Prince, S. E. (1996). A component analysis of cognitive-behavioral treatment for depression. *Journal of Consulting and Clinical Psychology, 64*(2), 295–304. https://doi.org/10.1037//0022-006x.64.2.295

Jacobson, N. S., Martell, C. R., & Dimidjian, S. (2001). Behavioral activation treatment for depression: Returning to context roots. *Clinical Psychology: Science and Practice, 8*(3), 255–270. https://doi.org/10.1093/clipsy.8.3.255

James, I., Todd, H., & Reichelt, F. K. (2009). Schemas defined. *The Cognitive Behaviour Therapist, 2*(1), 1–9. https://doi.org/10.1017/S1754470X08000135

Jank, R., & Pieh, C. (2016). Effektivität und evidenz von gruppenpsychotherapie bei depressiven störungen [Efficacy and evidence base of group psychotherapy for depressive disorders]. *Psychotherapie Forum, 21*(2), 62–71. https://doi.org/10.1007/s00729-015-0059-y

Janssen-Kallenberg, H., Schulz, H., Kluge, U., Strehle, J., Wittchen, H. U., Wolfradt, U., Koch-Gromus, U., Heinz, A., Mösko, M., & Dingoyan, D. (2017). Acculturation and other risk factors of depressive disorders in individuals with Turkish migration backgrounds. *BMC Psychiatry, 17*(1), Article 264. https://doi.org/10.1186/s12888-017-1430-z

Jarrett, R. B., Basco, M. R., Risser, R., Ramanan, J., Marwill, M., Kraft, D., & Rush, A. J. (1998). Is there a role for continuation phase cognitive therapy for depressed outpatients? *Journal of Consulting and Clinical Psychology, 66*(6), 1036–1040. https://doi.org/10.1037/0022-006X.66.6.1036

Jarrett, R. B., Kraft, D., Doyle, J., Foster, B. M., Eaves, G. G., & Silver, P. C. (2001). Preventing recurrent depression using cognitive therapy with and without a continuation phase: A randomized clinical trial. *Archives of General Psychiatry, 58*(4), 381–388. https://doi.org/10.1001/archpsyc.58.4.381

Johnston, A., Kelly, S. E., Hsieh, S. C., Skidmore, B., & Wells, G. A. (2019). Systematic reviews of clinical practice guidelines: A methodological guide. *Journal of Clinical Epidemiology, 108*, 64–76. https://doi.org/10.1016/j.jclinepi.2018.11.030

Joiner, T. (2005). *Why people die by suicide*. Harvard University Press.

Joiner, T. E., Jr., & Metalsky, G. I. (2001). Excessive reassurance seeking: Delineating a risk factor involved in the development of depressive symptoms. *Psychological Science, 12*(5), 371–378. https://doi.org/10.1111/1467-9280.00369

Jongsma, A. E. (2004). *The complete depression treatment and homework planner*. J. Wiley & Sons.

Josefsson, T., Lindwall, M., & Archer, T. (2014). Physical exercise intervention in depressive disorders: Meta-analysis and systematic review. *Scandinavian Journal of Medicine & Science in Sports, 24*(2), 259–272. https://doi.org/10.1111/sms.12050

Kabat-Zinn, J. (1990). *Full catastrophe living: The program of the Stress Reduction Clinic at the University of Massachusetts Medical Center*. Dell Publishing.

Kabat-Zinn, J. (1994). *Wherever you go, there you are: Mindfulness meditation in everyday life*. Hyperion.

Kaplan, B., & Rucklidge, J. (2021). *The better brain: Overcome anxiety, combat depression and reduce ADHD and stress with nutrition*. Houghton Mifflin Harcourt.

Karpiak, C. P., & Norcross, J. C. (2022). Evidence-based therapy relationships. *Neuroscience and Biobehavioural Psychology*, 119–127. https://doi.org/10.1016/B978-0-12-818697-8.00132-1

Kavanagh, D. J., & Wilson, P. H. (1989). Prediction of outcome with group cognitive therapy for depression. *Behaviour Research and Therapy, 27*(4), 333–343. https://doi.org/10.1016/0005-7967(89)90003-X

Kay, D. W. K., Garside, R. F., Roy, J. R., & Beamish, P. (1969). "Endogenous" and "neurotic" syndromes of depression: A 5- to 7-year follow-up of 104 cases. *The British Journal of Psychiatry, 115*(521), 389–399. https://doi.org/10.1192/bjp.115.521.389

Kazantzis, N., Dattilio, F. M., & Dobson, K. S. (2017). *The therapeutic relationship in cognitive-behavioral therapy: A clinician's guide*. Guilford Press.

Keeley, R. D., Brody, D. S., Engel, M., Burke, B. L., Nordstrom, K., Moralez, E., Dickinson, L. M., & Emsermann, C. (2016). Motivational interviewing improves depression outcome in primary care: A cluster randomized trial. *Journal of Consulting and Clinical Psychology, 84*(11), 993–1007. https://doi.org/10.1037/ccp0000124

Kendler, K. S., Gardner, C. O., & Prescott, C. A. (2002). Toward a comprehensive developmental model for major depression in women. *The American Journal of Psychiatry, 159*(7), 1133–1145. https://doi.org/10.1176/appi.ajp.159.7.1133

Kendler, K. S., Gatz, M., Gardner, C. O., & Pedersen, N. L. (2006). A Swedish national twin study of lifetime major depression. *The American Journal of Psychiatry, 163*(1), 109–114. https://doi.org/10.1176/appi.ajp.163.1.109

Kendler, K. S., Karkowski, L. M., & Prescott, C. A. (1999). Causal relationship between stressful life events and the onset of major depression. *The American Journal of Psychiatry, 156*(6), 837–841. https://doi.org/10.1176/ajp.156.6.837

Kendler, K. S., Muñoz, R. A., & Murphy, G. (2010). The development of the Feighner criteria: A historical perspective. *The American Journal of Psychiatry, 167*(2), 134–142. https://doi.org/10.1176/appi.ajp.2009.09081155

Kendler, K. S., Thornton, L. M., & Gardner, C. O. (2000). Stressful life events and previous episodes in the etiology of major depression in women: An evaluation of the "kindling" hypothesis. *The American Journal of Psychiatry, 157*(8), 1243–1251. https://doi.org/10.1176/appi.ajp.157.8.1243

Kenealy, P. M. (1986). The velten mood induction procedure: A methodological review. *Motivation and Emotion, 10*(4), 315–335. https://doi.org/10.1007/BF00992107

Kessler, R. C., & Bromet, E. J. (2013). The epidemiology of depression across cultures. *Annual Review of Public Health, 34*(1), 119–138. https://doi.org/10.1146/annurev-publhealth-031912-114409

Keyes, K., Allel, K., Staudinger, M., Ornstein, K., & Calvo, E. (2019). Alcohol consumption predicts incidence of depressive episodes across 10 years among older adults in 19 countries. *International Review of Neurobiology, 148*, 1–38. https://doi.org/10.1016/bs.irn.2019.09.001

Kim, Y. K. (Ed.). (2019). *Understanding depression: Volume 1. Biomedical and neurobiological background.* Springer.

Kirby, K. R., Gray, R. D., Greenhill, S. J., Jordan, F. M., Gomes-Ng, S., Bibiko, H. J., Blasi, D. E., Botero, C. A., Bowern, C., Ember, C. R., Leehr, D., Low, B. S., McCarter, J., Divale, W., & Gavin, M. C. (2016). D-PLACE: A global database of cultural, linguistic and environmental diversity. *PLOS One, 11*(7), Article e0158391. https://doi.org/10.1371/journal.pone.0158391

Kiresuk, T. J., Smith, A., & Cardillo, J. E. (1994). *Goal attainment scaling: Applications, theory and measurement.* Psychology Press.

Kirkham, J. G., Choi, N., & Seitz, D. P. (2016). Meta-analysis of problem solving therapy for the treatment of major depressive disorder in older adults. *International Journal of Geriatric Psychiatry, 31*(5), 526–535. https://doi.org/10.1002/gps.4358

Klein, D. N., & Allmann, A. E. S. (2014). Course of depression: Persistence and recurrence. In I. H. Gotlib & C. L. Hammen (Eds.), *Handbook of depression* (pp. 64–83). Guilford Press.

Klein, D. N., Schwartz, J. E., Santiago, N. J., Vivian, D., Vocisano, C., Castonguay, L. G., Arnow, B., Blalock, J. A., Manber, R., Markowitz, J. C., Riso, L. P., Rothbaum, B., McCullough, J. P., Thase, M. E., Borian, F. E., Miller, I. W., & Keller, M. B. (2003). Therapeutic alliance in depression treatment: Controlling for prior change and patient characteristics. *Journal of Consulting and Clinical Psychology, 71*(6), 997–1006. https://doi.org/10.1037/0022-006X.71.6.997

Kleinman, A., & Good, B. (1985). *Culture and depression: Studies in the anthropology and cross-cultural psychiatry of affect and disorder.* University of California Press. https://doi.org/10.1525/9780520340923

Klerman, G. L., Weissman, M. M., Rounsaville, B., & Chevron, E. S. (1984). Interpersonal psychotherapy for depression. In J. E. Groves (Ed.), *Essential papers on short-term dynamic therapy* (pp. 134–148). New York University Press. (Reprinted from "Psychiatry Update," 3, 1984, pp. 56–67)

Klocek, J. W., Oliver, J. M., & Ross, M. J. (1997). The role of dysfunctional attitudes, negative life events, and social support in the prediction of depressive dysphoria. *Social Behavior and Personality: An International Journal, 25*(2), 123–136. https://doi.org/10.2224/sbp.1997.25.2.123

Klonsky, E. D., May, A. M., & Saffer, B. Y. (2016). Suicide, suicide attempts, and suicidal ideation. *Annual Review of Clinical Psychology*, *12*(1), 307–330. https://doi.org/10.1146/annurev-clinpsy-021815-093204

Knoll, A. D., & MacLennan, R. N. (2017). Prevalence and correlates of depression in Canada: Findings from the Canadian Community Health Survey. *Canadian Psychology/Psychologie canadienne*, *58*(2), 116–123. https://doi.org/10.1037/cap0000103

Kobak, K. A., & Reynolds, W. M. (1999). Hamilton Depression Inventory. In M. E. Maruish (Ed.), *The use of psychological testing for treatment planning and outcomes assessment* (pp. 935–969). Lawrence Erlbaum Associates Publishers.

Kovacs, M., & Beck, A. T. (1978). Maladaptive cognitive structures in depression. *The American Journal of Psychiatry*, *135*(5), 525–533. https://doi.org/10.1176/ajp.135.5.525

Kraepelin, E. (1906). *Über sprachstörungen im traume*. Engelmann.

Krijnen-de Bruin, E., Scholten, W., Muntingh, A., Maarsingh, O., van Meijel, B., van Straten, A., & Batelaan, N. (2022). Psychological interventions to prevent relapse in anxiety and depression: A systematic review and meta-analysis. *PLoS ONE*, *17*(8), Article e0272200. https://doi.org/10.1371/journal.pone.0272200

Kroenke, K., & Spitzer, R. L. (2002). The PHQ-9: A new depression diagnostic and severity measure. *Psychiatric Annals*, *32*(9), 509–515. https://doi.org/10.3928/0048-5713-20020901-06

Kroenke, K., Spitzer, R. L., & Williams, J. B. W. (2001). The PHQ-9: Validity of a brief depression severity measure. *Journal of General Internal Medicine*, *16*(9), 606–613. https://doi.org/10.1046/j.1525-1497.2001.016009606.x

Krogh, J., Videbech, P., Thomsen, C., Gluud, C., & Nordentoft, M. (2012). DEMO-II trial. Aerobic exercise versus stretching exercise in patients with major depression—A randomised clinical trial. *PLOS One*, *7*(10), Article e48316. https://doi.org/10.1371/journal.pone.0048316

Kuyken, W., Padesky, C. A., & Dudley, R. (2009). *Collaborative case conceptualization: Working effectively with clients in cognitive-behavioral therapy*. Guilford Press.

Kuyken, W., Warren, F. C., Taylor, R. S., Whalley, B., Crane, C., Bondolfi, G., Hayes, R., Huijbers, M., Ma, H., Schweizer, S., Segal, Z., Speckens, A., Teasdale, J. D., Van Heeringen, K., Williams, M., Byford, S., Byng, R., & Dalgleish, T. (2016). Efficacy of mindfulness-based cognitive therapy in prevention of depressive relapse: An individual patient data meta-analysis from randomized trials. *JAMA Psychiatry*, *73*(6), 565–574. https://doi.org/10.1001/jamapsychiatry.2016.0076

Kvam, S., Kleppe, C. L., Nordhus, I. H., & Hovland, A. (2016). Exercise as a treatment for depression: A meta-analysis. *Journal of Affective Disorders*, *202*, 67–86. https://doi.org/10.1016/j.jad.2016.03.063

Lai, J. S., Hiles, S., Bisquera, A., Hure, A. J., McEvoy, M., & Attia, J. (2014). A systematic review and meta-analysis of dietary patterns and depression in community-dwelling adults. *The American Journal of Clinical Nutrition*, *99*(1), 181–197. https://doi.org/10.3945/ajcn.113.069880

Lam, T. C. M., Kolomitro, K., & Alamparambil, F. C. (2011). Empathy training: Methods, evaluation practices, and validity. *Journal of Multidisciplinary Evaluation*, *7*(16), 162–200. https://doi.org/10.56645/jmde.v7i16.314

Lane, M. M., Gamage, E., Travica, N., Dissanayaka, T., Ashtree, D. N., Gauci, S., Lotfaliany, M., O'Nell, A., Jacka, F. N., & Marx, W. (2022). Ultra-processed food consumption and mental health: A systematic review and meta-analysis of observational studies. *Nutrients*, *14*(13), 2568. https://doi.org/10.3390/nu14132568

Leahy, R. L. (2001). Depressive decision making: Validation of the portfolio theory model. *Journal of Cognitive Psychotherapy*, *15*(4), 341–362. https://doi.org/10.1891/0889-8391.15.4.341

Leahy, R. L. (2002). A model of emotional schemas. *Cognitive and Behavioral Practice*, *9*(3), 177–190. https://doi.org/10.1016/S1077-7229(02)80048-7

Leahy, R. L. (2015). *Emotional schema therapy*. Guilford Press.

Leahy, R. L., Holland, S. J. F., & McGinn, L. K. (2012). *Treatment plans and interventions for depression and anxiety disorders* (2nd ed.). Guilford Press.

Lee, E., Cho, H. J., Olmstead, R., Levin, M. J., Oxman, M. N., & Irwin, M. R. (2013). Persistent sleep disturbance: A risk factor for recurrent depression in community-dwelling older adults. *Sleep*, *36*(11), 1685–1691. https://doi.org/10.5665/sleep.3128

Lejuez, C. W., Hopko, D. R., Acierno, R., Daughters, S. B., & Pagoto, S. L. (2011). Ten year revision of the brief behavioral activation treatment for depression: Revised treatment manual. *Behavior Modification*, *35*(2), 111–161. https://doi.org/10.1177/0145445510390929

Lejuez, C. W., Hopko, D. R., Hopko, S. D., & McNeil, D. W. (2001). A brief behavioral activation treatment for depression: Treatment manual. *Behavior Modification*, *25*(2), 255–286. https://doi.org/10.1177/0145445501252005

LeMoult, J., & Gotlib, I. H. (2019). Depression: A cognitive perspective. *Clinical Psychology Review*, *69*, 51–66. https://doi.org/10.1016/j.cpr.2018.06.008

Leventhal, A. M. (2008). Sadness, depression, and avoidance behavior. *Behavior Modification*, *32*(6), 759–779. https://doi.org/10.1177/0145445508317167

Lewinsohn, P. M. (1974). A behavioral approach to depression. In R. J. Friedman & M. M. Katz (Eds.), *The psychology of depression: Contemporary theory and research* (pp. 150–172). John Wiley & Sons.

Lewinsohn, P. M. (1975). The behavioral study and treatment of depression. *Progress in Behavior Modification*, *1*, 19–64. https://doi.org/10.1016/B978-0-12-535601-5.50009-3

Lewinsohn, P. M., Antonuccio, D. O., Steinmetz, J. L., & Teri, L. (1984). *The Coping With Depression Course: A psychoeducational intervention for unipolar depression.* Castalia.

Lewinsohn, P. M., & Clarke, G. N. (1984). Group treatment of depressed individuals: The 'coping with depression' course. *Advances in Behaviour Research and Therapy*, *6*(2), 99–114. https://doi.org/10.1016/0146-6402(84)90005-5

Lewinsohn, P. M., Clarke, G. N., & Hoberman, H. M. (1989). The Coping With Depression Course: Review and future directions. *Canadian Journal of Behavioural Science/Revue canadienne des sciences du comportement*, *21*(4), 470–493. https://doi.org/10.1037/h0079846

Lewinsohn, P. M., Munoz, R. F., Youngren, M. A., & Zeiss, A. M. (1978). *Control your depression.* Prentice-Hall.

Lewinsohn, P. M., Sullivan, J. M., & Grosscup, S. J. (1980). Changing reinforcing events: An approach to the treatment of depression. *Psychotherapy: Theory, Research & Practice*, *17*(3), 322–334. https://doi.org/10.1037/h0085929

Li, Z., Wei, A., Palanivel, V., & Jackson, J. C. (2021). A data-driven analysis of sociocultural, ecological, and economic correlates of depression across nations. *Journal of Cross-Cultural Psychology*, *52*(8–9), 822–843. https://doi.org/10.1177/00220221211040243

Libet, J. M., & Lewinsohn, P. M. (1973). Concept of social skill with special reference to the behavior of depressed persons. *Journal of Consulting and Clinical Psychology*, *40*(2), 304–312. https://doi.org/10.1037/h0034530

Lilienfeld, S. O., Ritschel, L. A., Lynn, S. J., Cautin, R. L., & Latzman, R. D. (2013). Why many clinical psychologists are resistant to evidence-based practice: Root causes and constructive remedies. *Clinical Psychology Review, 33*(7), 883–900. https://doi.org/10.1016/j.cpr.2012.09.008

Limbana, T., Khan, F., & Eskander, N. (2020). Gut microbiome and depression: How microbes affect the way we think. *Cureus, 12*(8), Article e9966. https://doi.org/10.7759/cureus.9966

Linde, K., Kriston, L., Rücker, G., Jamil, S., Schumann, I., Meissner, K., Sigterman, K., & Schneider, A. (2015). Efficacy and acceptability of pharmacological treatments for depressive disorders in primary care: Systematic review and network meta-analysis. *Annals of Family Medicine, 13*(1), 69–79. https://doi.org/10.1370/afm.1687

Liu, Q., He, H., Yang, J., Feng, X., Zhao, F., & Lyu, J. (2020). Changes in the global burden of depression from 1990 to 2017: Findings from the Global Burden of Disease study. *Journal of Psychiatric Research, 126*(June 2019), 134–140. https://doi.org/10.1016/j.jpsychires.2019.08.002

Liu, R. T. (2013). Stress generation: Future directions and clinical implications. *Clinical Psychology Review, 33*(3), 406–416. https://doi.org/10.1016/j.cpr.2013.01.005

Loades, M. E., Chatburn, E., Higson-Sweeney, N., Reynolds, S., Shafran, R., Brigden, A., Linney, C., McManus, M. N., Borwick, C., & Crawley, E. (2020). Rapid systematic review: The impact of social isolation and loneliness on the mental health of children and adolescents in the context of COVID-19. *Journal of the American Academy of Child & Adolescent Psychiatry, 59*(11), 1218–1239.e3. https://doi.org/10.1016/j.jaac.2020.05.009

Lotfaliany, M., Bowe, S. J., Kowal, P., Orellana, L., Berk, M., & Mohebbi, M. (2018). Depression and chronic diseases: Co-occurrence and communality of risk factors. *Journal of Affective Disorders, 241*, 461–468. https://doi.org/10.1016/j.jad.2018.08.011

Lovato, N., & Gradisar, M. (2014). A meta-analysis and model of the relationship between sleep and depression in adolescents: Recommendations for future research and clinical practice. *Sleep Medicine Reviews, 18*(6), 521–529. https://doi.org/10.1016/j.smrv.2014.03.006

Lovibond, P. F., & Lovibond, S. H. (1995). The structure of negative emotional states: Comparison of the Depression Anxiety Stress Scales (DASS) with the Beck Depression and Anxiety Inventories. *Behaviour Research and Therapy, 33*(3), 335–343. https://doi.org/10.1016/0005-7967(94)00075-U

Lovibond, S. H., & Lovibond, P. F. (1995). *Manual for the Depression Anxiety Stress Scales*. Psychology Foundation of Australia.

Lundgren, T., & Larsson, A. (2018). Values choice and clarification. In S. C. Hayes & S. G. Hofmann (Eds.), *Process-based CBT: The science and core clinical competencies of cognitive behavioral therapy* (pp. 375–387). New Harbinger Publications, Inc.

Lundgren, T., Luoma, J. B., Dahl, J. A., Strosahl, K., & Melin, L. (2012). The Bull's-Eye Values Survey: A psychometric evaluation. *Cognitive and Behavioral Practice, 19*(4), 518–526. https://doi.org/10.1016/j.cbpra.2012.01.004

Malcolm, M., Frost, H., & Cowie, J. (2019). Loneliness and social isolation causal association with health-related lifestyle risk in older adults: A systematic review and meta-analysis protocol. *Systematic Reviews, 8*(1), Article 48. https://doi.org/10.1186/s13643-019-0968-x

Malki, K., Keers, R., Tosto, M. G., Lourdusamy, A., Carboni, L., Domenici, E., Uher, R., McGuffin, P., & Schalkwyk, L. C. (2014). The endogenous and reactive depression subtypes revisited: Integrative animal and human studies implicate multiple distinct molecular mechanisms underlying major depressive disorder. *BMC Medicine, 12*(1), Article 73. https://doi.org/10.1186/1741-7015-12-73

Mansell, W., Harvey, A., Watkins, E., & Shafran, R. (2009). Conceptual foundations of the transdiagnostic approach to CBT. *Journal of Cognitive Psychotherapy, 23*(1), 6–19. https://doi.org/10.1891/0889-8391.23.1.6

Martell, C. R., Addis, M. E., & Jacobson, N. S. (2001). *Depression in context: Strategies for guided action.* W. W. Norton & Company.

Martell, C. R., Dimidjian, S., & Herman-Dunn, R. (2010). *Behavioral activation for depression: A clinician's guide.* Guilford Press.

Martell, C. R., Dimidjian, S., & Herman-Dunn, R. (2021). *Behavioral activation for depression: A clinician's guide* (2nd ed.). Guilford Press.

Maske, U. E., Buttery, A. K., Beesdo-Baum, K., Riedel-Heller, S., Hapke, U., & Busch, M. A. (2016). Prevalence and correlates of *DSM-IV-TR* major depressive disorder, self-reported diagnosed depression and current depressive symptoms among adults in Germany. *Journal of Affective Disorders, 190,* 167–177. https://doi.org/10.1016/j.jad.2015.10.006

McCullough, J. P., Jr. (2003). Treatment for chronic depression using Cognitive Behavioral Analysis System of Psychotherapy (CBASP). *Journal of Clinical Psychology, 59*(8), 833–846. https://doi.org/10.1002/jclp.10176

McDermut, W., Miller, I. W., & Brown, R. A. (2001). The efficacy of group psychotherapy for depression: A meta-analysis and review of the empirical research. *Clinical Psychology: Science and Practice, 8*(1), 98–116. https://doi.org/10.1093/clipsy.8.1.98

McGlinchey, J. B., & Dobson, K. S. (2003). Treatment integrity concerns in cognitive therapy for depression. *Journal of Cognitive Psychotherapy, 17*(4), 299–318. https://doi.org/10.1891/jcop.17.4.299.52543

McHugh, R. K., & Weiss, R. D. (2019). Alcohol use disorder and depressive disorders. *Alcohol Research: Current Reviews, 40*(1), 3–10. https://doi.org/10.35946/arcr.v40.1.01

McKay, M., & Fanning, P. (1991). *Prisoners of belief: Exposing and changing beliefs that control your life.* New Harbinger Publications.

McKenzie, G. L., & Harvath, T. A. (2016). Late-life depression. In M. Boltz, E. Capezuti, T. Fulmer, & D. Zwicker (Eds.), *Evidence-based geriatric nursing protocols for best practice* (5th ed., pp. 211–232). Springer Publishing Company LLC. https://doi.org/10.1891/9780826171672.0015

McLaren, N. (1998). A critical review of the biopsychosocial model. *Australian & New Zealand Journal of Psychiatry, 32*(1), 86–92. https://doi.org/10.3109/00048679809062712

McNair, D. M., Lorr, M., & Droppleman, L. F. (1992). *Revised manual for the Profile of Mood States.* Educational and Industrial Testing Services.

McRoberts, C., Burlingame, G. M., & Hoag, M. J. (1998). Comparative efficacy of individual and group psychotherapy: A meta-analytic perspective. *Group Dynamics: Theory, Research, and Practice, 2*(2), 101–117. https://doi.org/10.1037/1089-2699.2.2.101

McWilliams, N. (1999). *Psychoanalytic case formulation.* Guilford Press.

Mendels, J., & Cochrane, C. (1968). The nosology of depression: The endogenous-reactive concept. *The American Journal of Psychiatry, 124*(11S), 1–11. https://doi.org/10.1176/ajp.124.11S.1

Miller, T. R., Waehrer, G. M., Oh, D. L., Purewal Boparai, S., Ohlsson Walker, S., Silverio Marques, S., & Burke Harris, N. (2020). Adult health burden and costs in California during 2013 associated with prior adverse childhood experiences. *PLOS One*, *15*(1), Article e0228019. https://doi.org/10.1371/journal.pone.0228019

Miller, W. R. (1983). Motivational interviewing with problem drinkers. *Behavioural Psychotherapy*, *11*(2), 147–172. https://doi.org/10.1017/S0141347300006583

Miller, W. R., & Rollnick, S. (2013). *Motivational interviewing: Helping people change* (3rd ed.). Guilford Press.

Miller, W. R., & Rose, G. S. (2009). Toward a theory of motivational interviewing. *American Psychologist*, *64*(6), 527–537. https://doi.org/10.1037/a0016830

Minkov, M., Dutt, P., Schachner, M., Morales, O., Sanchez, C., Jandosova, J., Khassenbekov, Y., & Mudd, B. (2017). A revision of Hofstede's individualism–collectivism dimension: A new national index from a 56-country study. *Cross Cultural & Strategic Management*, *24*(3), 386–404. https://doi.org/10.1108/CCSM-11-2016-0197

Mitchell, A. J., Yadegarfar, M., Gill, J., & Stubbs, B. (2016). Case finding and screening clinical utility of the Patient Health Questionnaire (PHQ-9 and PHQ-2) for depression in primary care: A diagnostic meta-analysis of 40 studies. *BJPsych Open*, *2*(2), 127–138. https://doi.org/10.1192/bjpo.bp.115.001685

Mitchell, L. J., Bisdounis, L., Ballesio, A., Omlin, X., & Kyle, S. D. (2019). The impact of cognitive behavioural therapy for insomnia on objective sleep parameters: A meta-analysis and systematic review. *Sleep Medicine Reviews*, *47*, 90–102. https://doi.org/10.1016/j.smrv.2019.06.002

Molino, C. G. R. C., Leite-Santos, N. C., Gabriel, F. C., Wainberg, S. K., Vasconcelos, L. P., Mantovani-Silva, R. A., Ribeiro, E., Romano-Lieber, N. S., Stein, A. T., Melo, D. O., & the Chronic Diseases and Informed Decisions (CHRONIDE) Group. (2019). Factors associated with high-quality guidelines for the pharmacologic management of chronic diseases in primary care: A systematic review. *JAMA Internal Medicine*, *179*(4), 553–560. https://doi.org/10.1001/jamainternmed.2018.7529

Moody, R. (2022). *Screen time statistics: Average screen time in US vs. the rest of the world*. Comparitech. https://www.comparitech.com/tv-streaming/screen-time-statistics/

Moore, R. G., & Blackburn, I.-M. (1994). The relationship of sociotropy and autonomy to symptoms, cognition and personality in depressed patients. *Journal of Affective Disorders*, *32*(4), 239–245. https://doi.org/10.1016/0165-0327(94)90087-6

Morissette, S. B., Lenton-Brym, A. P., & Barlow, D. H. (2020). Panic disorder and agoraphobia. In M. M. Antony & D. H. Barlow (Eds.), *Handbook of assessment and treatment planning for psychological disorders* (3rd ed., pp. 138–179). Guilford Press.

Morris, L., & Bhatnagar, D. (2016). The Mediterranean diet. *Current Opinion in Lipidology*, *27*(1), 89–91. https://doi.org/10.1097/MOL.0000000000000266

Moshe, I., Terhorst, Y., Philippi, P., Domhardt, M., Cuijpers, P., Cristea, I., Pulkki-Råback, L., Baumeister, H., & Sander, L. B. (2021). Digital interventions for the treatment of depression: A meta-analytic review. *Psychological Bulletin*, *147*(8), 749–786. https://doi.org/10.1037/bul0000334

Moussavi, S., Chatterji, S., Verdes, E., Tandon, A., Patel, V., & Ustun, B. (2007). Depression, chronic diseases, and decrements in health: Results from the World Health Surveys. *The Lancet*, *370*(9590), 851–858. https://doi.org/10.1016/S0140-6736(07)61415-9

Muñoz, M.-A., Fíto, M., Marrugat, J., Covas, M.-I., Schröder, H., & the REGICOR and HERMES investigators. (2009). Adherence to the Mediterranean diet is associated with better mental and physical health. *British Journal of Nutrition, 101*(12), 1821–1827. https://doi.org/10.1017/S0007114508143598

Murakami, K., & Sasaki, S. (2010). Dietary intake and depressive symptoms: A systematic review of observational studies. *Molecular Nutrition & Food Research, 54*(4), 471–488. https://doi.org/10.1002/mnfr.200900157

Murri, B. M., Ekkekakis, P., Magagnoli, M., Zampogna, D., Cattedra, S., Capobianco, L., Serafini, G., Calcagno, P., Zanetidou, S., & Amore, M. (2019). Physical exercise in major depression: Reducing the mortality gap while improving clinical outcomes. *Frontiers in Psychiatry, 9,* Article 762. https://doi.org/10.3389/fpsyt.2018.00762

Naar, S., & Flynn, H. (2015). Motivational interviewing and the treatment of depression. In H. Arkowitz, W. R. Miller, & S. Rollnick (Eds.), *Motivational interviewing in the treatment of psychological problems* (2nd ed., pp. 170–192). Guilford Press.

Nandam, L. S., Brazel, M., Zhou, M., & Jhaveri, D. J. (2020). Cortisol and major depressive disorder—Translating findings from humans to animal models and back. *Frontiers in Psychiatry, 10,* Article 974. https://doi.org/10.3389/fpsyt.2019.00974

National Institute for Health and Care Excellence. (2022). *Depression in adults: Treatment and management.* https://www.nice.org.uk/guidance/ng222

National Research Council. (2011). *Toward precision medicine: Building a knowledge network for biomedical research and a new taxonomy of disease.* National Academies Press.

Negt, P., Brakemeier, E. L., Michalak, J., Winter, L., Bleich, S., & Kahl, K. G. (2016). The treatment of chronic depression with cognitive behavioral analysis system of psychotherapy: A systematic review and meta-analysis of randomized-controlled clinical trials. *Brain and Behavior, 6*(8), e00486. Advance online publication. https://doi.org/10.1002/brb3.486

Nelson, E. C., Heath, A. C., Madden, P. A. F., Cooper, M. L., Dinwiddie, S. H., Bucholz, K. K., Glowinski, A., McLaughlin, T., Dunne, M. P., Statham, D. J., & Martin, N. G. (2002). Association between self-reported childhood sexual abuse and adverse psychosocial outcomes: Results from a twin study. *Archives of General Psychiatry, 59*(2), 139–145. https://doi.org/10.1001/archpsyc.59.2.139

Nemeroff, C. B., Schatzberg, A. F., Rasgon, N., & Strakowski, S. M. (2022). *The American Psychiatric Association Publishing textbook of mood disorders* (2nd ed.). American Psychiatric Association.

Nezu, A. M., & Nezu, C. (2018). *Emotion-centered problem-solving therapy: Treatment guidelines.* Springer Publishing. https://doi.org/10.1891/9780826143167

Nezu, A. M., Nezu, C., & D'Zurilla, T. (2013). *Problem-solving therapy: A treatment manual.* Springer Publishing.

Nezu, A. M., Nezu, C., & Hays, A. (2019). Emotion-centered problem-solving therapy. In K. S. Dobson & D. J. A. Dozois (Eds.), *Handbook of cognitive-behavioral therapies* (4th ed., pp. 171–190). Guilford Press.

Nezu, A. M., Nezu, C., & Perri, M. (1989). *Problem-solving therapy for depression: Theory, research and clinical guidelines.* John Wiley.

Nezu, A. M., & Perri, M. G. (1989). Social problem-solving therapy for unipolar depression: An initial dismantling investigation. *Journal of Consulting and Clinical Psychology, 57*(3), 408–413. https://doi.org/10.1037/0022-006X.57.3.408

Nezu, A. M., Ronan, G., Meadows, E., & McClure, K. (2000). *Practitioner's guide to empirically based measures of depression* (AABT clinical assessment series, Vol. 1.) Kluwer Academic/Plenum.

Nierenberg, A. A., Keefe, B. R., Leslie, V. C., Alpert, J. E., Pava, J. A., Worthington, J. J., III, Rosenbaum, J. F., & Fava, M. (1999). Residual symptoms in depressed patients who respond acutely to fluoxetine. *The Journal of Clinical Psychiatry, 60*(4), 221–225. https://doi.org/10.4088/JCP.v60n0403

Nock, M. K., Hwang, I., Sampson, N., Kessler, R. C., Angermeyer, M., Beautrais, A., Borges, G., Bromet, E., Bruffaerts, R., de Girolamo, G., de Graaf, R., Florescu, S., Gureje, O., Haro, J. M., Hu, C., Huang, Y., Karam, E. G., Kawakami, N., Kovess, V., . . . Williams, D. R. (2009). Cross-national analysis of the associations among mental disorders and suicidal behavior: Findings from the WHO World Mental Health Surveys. *PLOS Medicine, 6*(8), Article e1000123. https://doi.org/10.1371/journal.pmed.1000123

Nolen-Hoeksema, S. (2000). The role of rumination in depressive disorders and mixed anxiety/depressive symptoms. *Journal of Abnormal Psychology, 109*(3), 504–511. https://doi.org/10.1037/0021-843X.109.3.504

Nolen-Hoeksema, S., & Watkins, E. R. (2011). A heuristic for developing transdiagnostic models of psychopathology: Explaining multifinality and divergent trajectories. *Perspectives on Psychological Science, 6*(6), 589–609. https://doi.org/10.1177/1745691611419672

Nolen-Hoeksema, S., Wisco, B. E., & Lyubomirsky, S. (2008). Rethinking rumination. *Perspectives on Psychological Science, 3*(5), 400–424. https://doi.org/10.1111/j.1745-6924.2008.00088.x

Norcross, J. C. (2011). *Psychotherapy relationships that work: Therapist contributions and responsiveness to patient needs* (2nd ed.). Oxford University Press. https://doi.org/10.1093/acprof:oso/9780199737208.001.0001

Norcross, J. C., & Lambert, M. J. (2018). Psychotherapy relationships that work III. *Psychotherapy, 55*(4), 303–315. https://doi.org/10.1037/pst0000193

Norcross, J. C., & Wampold, B. E. (2019). *Psychotherapy relationships that work* (3rd ed., Vol. 2). Oxford University Press.

Normann, N., & Morina, N. (2018). The efficacy of metacognitive therapy: A systematic review and meta-analysis. *Frontiers in Psychology, 9*, Article 2211. https://doi.org/10.3389/fpsyg.2018.02211

Nowell, P. D., Buysse, D. J., Reynolds, C. F., III, Hauri, P. J., Roth, T., Stepanski, E. J., Thorpy, M. J., Bixler, E., Kales, A., Manfredi, R. L., Vgontzas, A. N., Stapf, D. M., Houck, P. R., & Kupfer, D. J. (1997). Clinical factors contributing to the differential diagnosis of primary insomnia and insomnia related to mental disorders. *The American Journal of Psychiatry, 154*(10), 1412–1416. https://doi.org/10.1176/ajp.154.10.1412

Nunes, E. V., & Levin, F. R. (2004). Treatment of depression in patients with alcohol or other drug dependence: A meta-analysis. *JAMA, 291*(15), 1887–1896. https://doi.org/10.1001/jama.291.15.1887

Nutt, D., Wilson, S., & Paterson, L. (2008). Sleep disorders as core symptoms of depression. *Dialogues in Clinical Neuroscience, 10*(3), 329–336. https://doi.org/10.31887/DCNS.2008.10.3/dnutt

Nyström, M. B. T., Neely, G., Hassmén, P., & Carlbring, P. (2015). Treating major depression with physical activity: A systematic overview with recommendations. *Cognitive Behaviour Therapy, 44*(4), 341–352. https://doi.org/10.1080/16506073.2015.1015440

O'Donohue, W. T., & Cucciare, M. A. (2008). *Terminating psychotherapy: A clinician's guide*. Routledge.

Oei, T. P. S., & Baranoff, J. (2007). Young Schema Questionnaire: Review of psychometric and measurement issues. *Australian Journal of Psychology, 59*(2), 78–86. https://doi.org/10.1080/00049530601148397

Oei, T. P. S., & Shuttlewood, G. J. (1996). Specific and nonspecific factors in psychotherapy: A case of cognitive therapy for depression. *Clinical Psychology Review, 16*(2), 83–103. https://doi.org/10.1016/0272-7358(96)00009-8

Ohayon, M. M. (1997). Prevalence of *DSM-IV* diagnostic criteria of insomnia: Distinguishing insomnia related to mental disorders from sleep disorders. *Journal of Psychiatric Research, 31*(3), 333–346. https://doi.org/10.1016/S0022-3956(97)00002-2

Okereke, O. I., Reynolds, C. F., III, Mischoulon, D., Chang, G., Vyas, C. M., Cook, N. R., Weinberg, A., Bubes, V., Copeland, T., Friedenberg, G., Lee, I. M., Buring, J. E., & Manson, J. E. (2020). Effect of long-term vitamin D₃ supplementation vs placebo on risk of depression or clinically relevant depressive symptoms and on change in mood scores: A randomized clinical trial. *JAMA, 324*(5), 471–480. https://doi.org/10.1001/jama.2020.10224

Olinger, L. J., Kuiper, N. A., & Shaw, B. F. (1987). Dysfunctional attitudes and stressful life events: An interactive model of depression. *Cognitive Therapy and Research, 11*(1), 25–40. https://doi.org/10.1007/BF01183130

Ottenbreit, N. D., Dobson, K. S., & Quigley, L. (2014). An examination of avoidance in major depression in comparison to social anxiety disorder. *Behaviour Research and Therapy, 56*(1), 82–90. https://doi.org/10.1016/j.brat.2014.03.005

Padesky, C. A., & Greenberger, D. (2021). *The clinician's guide to CBT using mind over mood* (2nd ed.). Guilford Press.

Parent, G. (2006). *Prisoners of our own beliefs*. Network 3000 Publishing.

Pass, L., Brisco, G., & Reynolds, S. (2015). Adapting brief behavioural activation (BA) for adolescent depression: A case example. *The Cognitive Behaviour Therapist, 8*, Article e17. Advance online publication. https://doi.org/10.1017/S1754470X15000446

Paterson, R. J. (2002). *Your depression map*. New Harbinger Press.

Paykel, E. S. (1994). Life events, social support and depression. *Acta Psychiatrica Scandinavica, 89*(s377), 50–58. https://doi.org/10.1111/j.1600-0447.1994.tb05803.x

Paykel, E. S. (2003). Life events and affective disorders. *Acta Psychiatrica Scandinavica, 108*(s418), 61–66. https://doi.org/10.1034/j.1600-0447.108.s418.13.x

Paykel, E. S. (2008). Partial remission, residual symptoms, and relapse in depression. *Dialogues in Clinical Neuroscience, 10*(4), 431–437. https://doi.org/10.31887/DCNS.2008.10.4/espaykel

Paykel, E. S., Myers, J. K., Lindenthal, J. J., & Tanner, J. (1974). Suicidal feelings in the general population: A prevalence study. *The British Journal of Psychiatry, 124*(582), 460–469. https://doi.org/10.1192/bjp.124.5.460

Peale, N. V. (1952). *The power of positive thinking: A practical guide to mastering the problems of everyday living*. Prentice Hall.

Perlis, M. L., Giles, D. E., Mendelson, W. B., Bootzin, R. R., & Wyatt, J. K. (1997). Psychophysiological insomnia: The behavioural model and a neurocognitive perspective. *Journal of Sleep Research, 6*(3), 179–188. https://doi.org/10.1046/j.1365-2869.1997.00045.x

Persons, J. B. (2008). *The case formulation approach to cognitive-behavior therapy*. Guilford Press.

Persons, J. B., Brown, C., & Diamond, A. (2019). Case formulation-driven cognitive-behavioral therapy. In K. S. Dobson & D. J. A. Dozois (Eds.), *Handbook of cognitive-behavioral therapies* (4th ed., pp. 145–168). Guilford Press.

Phillips, W. J., Hine, D. W., & Thorsteinsson, E. B. (2010). Implicit cognition and depression: A meta-analysis. *Clinical Psychology Review, 30*(6), 691–709. https://doi.org/10.1016/j.cpr.2010.05.002

Piaget, J. (1928). *The child's conception of the world.* Routledge & Kegan Paul.

Piaget, J., & Inhelder, B. (1962). *The psychology of the child.* Basic Books.

Posner, K., Brent, D. A., Lucas, C., Gould, M. S., & Stanley, B. H. (2008). *The Columbia Suicide Severity Rating Scale (C-SSRS).* https://cssrs.columbia.edu/

Posner, K., Brown, G. K., Stanley, B., Brent, D. A., Yershova, K. V., Oquendo, M. A., Currier, G. W., Melvin, G. A., Greenhill, L., Shen, S., & Mann, J. J. (2011). The Columbia-Suicide Severity Rating Scale: Initial validity and internal consistency findings from three multisite studies with adolescents and adults. *The American Journal of Psychiatry, 168*(12), 1266–1277. https://doi.org/10.1176/appi.ajp.2011.10111704

Rasmussen, P. R. (2005). *Personality-guided cognitive-behavioral therapy.* American Psychological Association. https://doi.org/10.1037/11159-000

Reangsing, C., Rittiwong, T., & Schneider, J. K. (2021). Effects of mindfulness meditation interventions on depression in older adults: A meta-analysis. *Aging & Mental Health, 25*(7), 1181–1190. https://doi.org/10.1080/13607863.2020.1793901

Rehm, J., & Shield, K. D. (2019). Global burden of disease and the impact of mental and addictive disorders. *Current Psychiatry Reports, 21*(2), Article 10. https://doi.org/10.1007/s11920-019-0997-0

Rehm, L. P. (1977). A self-control model of depression. *Behavior Therapy, 8*(5), 787–804. https://doi.org/10.1016/S0005-7894(77)80150-0

Reich, A. (1950). On the termination of analysis. *The International Journal of Psychoanalysis, 31,* 179–183.

Reising, M. M., Watson, K. H., Hardcastle, E. J., Merchant, M. J., Roberts, L., Forehand, R., & Compas, B. E. (2013). Parental depression and economic disadvantage: The role of parenting in associations with internalizing and externalizing symptoms in children and adolescents. *Journal of Child and Family Studies, 22*(3), 335–343. https://doi.org/10.1007/s10826-012-9582-4

Renner, F., Arntz, A., Leeuw, I., & Huibers, M. (2013). Treatment for chronic depression using schema therapy. *Clinical Psychology: Science and Practice, 20*(2), 166–180. https://doi.org/10.1111/cpsp.12032

Rethorst, C. D., & Trivedi, M. H. (2013). Evidence-based recommendations for the prescription of exercise for major depressive disorder. *Journal of Psychiatric Practice, 19*(3), 204–212. https://doi.org/10.1097/01.pra.0000430504.16952.3e

Reynolds, W. M. (1991). Psychometric characteristics of the Adult Suicidal Ideation Questionnaire in college students. *Journal of Personality Assessment, 56*(2), 289–307. https://doi.org/10.1207/s15327752jpa5602_9

Riso, L. P., du Toit, P. L., Stein, D. J., & Young, J. E. (Eds.). (2007). *Cognitive schemas and core beliefs in psychological problems: A scientist–practitioner guide.* American Psychological Association. https://doi.org/10.1037/11561-000

Robbcrcgt, S. J., Brouwer, M. E., Kooiman, B. E. A. M., Stikkelbroek, Y. A. J., Nauta, M. H., & Bockting, C. L. H. (2022). Meta-analysis: Relapse prevention strategies for depression and anxiety in remitted adolescents and young adults.

Journal of the American Academy of Child & Adolescent Psychiatry. Advance online publication. https://doi.org/10.1016/j.jaac.2022.04.014

Robins, C. J., Block, P., & Peselow, E. D. (1989). Relations of sociotropic and autonomous personality characteristics to specific symptoms in depressed patients. *Journal of Abnormal Psychology, 98*(1), 86–88. https://doi.org/10.1037/0021-843X.98.1.86

Rock, P. L., Roiser, J. P., Riedel, W. J., & Blackwell, A. D. (2014). Cognitive impairment in depression: A systematic review and meta-analysis. *Psychological Medicine, 44*(10), 2029–2040. https://doi.org/10.1017/S0033291713002535

Rogers, C. R. (1957). The necessary and sufficient conditions of therapeutic personality change. *Journal of Consulting Psychology,* 21, 95–103). https://doi.org/10.1037/h0045357

Rush, A. J., Beck, A. T., Kovacs, M., & Hollon, S. (1977). Comparative efficacy of cognitive therapy and pharmacotherapy in the treatment of depressed outpatients. *Cognitive Therapy and Research, 1*(1), 17–37. https://doi.org/10.1007/BF01173502

Rush, A. J., Hollon, S. D., Beck, A. T., & Kovacs, M. (1978). Depression: Must pharmacotherapy fail for cognitive therapy to succeed? *Cognitive Therapy and Research, 2*(2), 199–206. https://doi.org/10.1007/BF01172735

Ruusunen, A., Lehto, S. M., Tolmunen, T., Mursu, J., Kaplan, G. A., & Voutilainen, S. (2010). Coffee, tea and caffeine intake and the risk of severe depression in middle-aged Finnish men: The Kuopio Ischaemic Heart Disease Risk Factor Study. *Public Health Nutrition, 13*(8), 1215–1220. https://doi.org/10.1017/S1368980010000509

Saddichha, S., & Chaturvedi, S. K. (2014). Clinical practice guidelines in psychiatry: More confusion than clarity? A critical review and recommendation of a unified guideline. *ISRN Psychiatry, 2014,* Article 828917. https://doi.org/10.1155/2014/828917

Safran, J. D., & Muran, J. C. (2000). *Negotiating the therapeutic alliance: A relational treatment guide.* Guilford Press.

Sánchez-Villegas, A., Delgado-Rodríguez, M., Alonso, A., Schlatter, J., Lahortiga, F., Serra-Majem, L., & Martínez-González, M. A. (2009). Association of the Mediterranean dietary pattern with the incidence of depression: The Seguimiento Universidad de Navarra/University of Navarra follow-up (SUN) cohort. *Archives of General Psychiatry, 66*(10), 1090–1098. https://doi.org/10.1001/archgenpsychiatry.2009.129

Santini, Z. I., Koyanagi, A., Tyrovolas, S., Mason, C., & Haro, J. M. (2015). The association between social relationships and depression: A systematic review. *Journal of Affective Disorders, 175,* 53–65. https://doi.org/10.1016/j.jad.2014.12.049

Sauer-Zavala, S., Bentley, K. H., Steele, S. J., Tirpak, J. W., Ametaj, A. A., Nauphal, M., Cardona, N., Wang, M., Farchione, T. J., & Barlow, D. H. (2020). Treating depressive disorders with the Unified Protocol: A preliminary randomized evaluation. *Journal of Affective Disorders, 264,* 438–445. https://doi.org/10.1016/j.jad.2019.11.072

Saunders, B. E., Villeponteaux, L. A., Lipovsky, J. A., Kilpatrick, D. G., & Veronen, L. J. (1992). Child sexual assault as a risk factor for mental disorder among women. *Journal of Interpersonal Violence, 7*(2), 189–204. https://doi.org/10.1177/088626092007002005

Schatzberg, A. F., & DeBattista, C. (2019). *Schatzberg's manual of clinical psychopharmacology* (9th ed.). American Psychiatric Association.

Schema Therapy Institute. (n.d.). *Overview of the schema inventories.* https://www.schematherapy.com/id49.htm

Schildkraut, J. J. (1965). The catecholamine hypothesis of affective disorders: A review of supporting evidence. *The American Journal of Psychiatry, 122*(5), 509–522. https://doi.org/10.1176/ajp.122.5.509

Schmidt, N. B., Joiner, T. E., Jr., Young, J. E., & Telch, M. J. (1995). The schema questionnaire: Investigation of psychometric properties and the hierarchical structure of a measure of maladaptive schemas. *Cognitive Therapy and Research, 19*(3), 295–321. https://doi.org/10.1007/BF02230402

Segal, Z. V. (1988). Appraisal of the self-schema construct in cognitive models of depression. *Psychological Bulletin, 103*(2), 147–162. https://doi.org/10.1037/0033-2909.103.2.147

Segal, Z. V., Kennedy, S., Gemar, M., Hood, K., Pedersen, R., & Buis, T. (2006). Cognitive reactivity to sad mood provocation and the prediction of depressive relapse. *Archives of General Psychiatry, 63*(7), 749–755. https://doi.org/10.1001/archpsyc.63.7.749

Segal, Z. V., & Walsh, K. M. (2016). Mindfulness-based cognitive therapy for residual depressive symptoms and relapse prophylaxis. *Current Opinion in Psychiatry, 29*(1), 7–12. https://doi.org/10.1097/YCO.0000000000000216

Segal, Z. V., Williams, J., & Teasdale, J. D. (2013). *Mindfulness-based cognitive therapy for depression* (2nd ed.). Guilford Press.

Segal, Z. V., Williams, J. M., Teasdale, J. D., & Gemar, M. (1996). A cognitive science perspective on kindling and episode sensitization in recurrent affective disorder. *Psychological Medicine, 26*(2), 371–380. https://doi.org/10.1017/S0033291700034760

Segrin, C. (2000). Social skills deficits associated with depression. *Clinical Psychology Review, 20*(3), 379–403. https://doi.org/10.1016/S0272-7358(98)00104-4

Shah, S. M. A., Mohammad, D., Qureshi, M. F. H., Abbas, M. Z., & Aleem, S. (2021). Prevalence, psychological responses and associated correlates of depression, anxiety and stress in a global population, during the coronavirus disease (COVID-19) pandemic. *Community Mental Health Journal, 57*(1), 101–110. https://doi.org/10.1007/s10597-020-00728-y

Shakespeare, W. (1950). *Henry IV, Part 2* (W. G. Clark & W. Aldis Wright, Eds.). Nelson Doubleday. (Original work published 1598)

Sheffield, A. (2003). *Depression fallout: The impact of depression on couples and what you can do to preserve the bond.* William Morrow.

Shirk, S. R., Gudmundsen, G., Kaplinski, H. C., & McMakin, D. L. (2008). Alliance and outcome in cognitive-behavioral therapy for adolescent depression. *Journal of Clinical Child and Adolescent Psychology, 37*(3), 631–639. https://doi.org/10.1080/15374410802148061

Silvani, M. I., Werder, R., & Perret, C. (2022). The influence of blue light on sleep, performance and wellbeing in young adults: A systematic review. *Frontiers in Physiology, 13*, Article 943108. https://doi.org/10.3389/fphys.2022.943108

Sokol, L., & Fox, M. G. (2019). *The comprehensive clinician's guide to cognitive-behavioral therapy.* PESI Publishing and Media.

Spitzer, R. L., & Robins, E. (1978). Research diagnostic criteria: Rationale and reliability. *Archives of General Psychiatry, 35*(6), 773–782. https://doi.org/10.1001/archpsyc.1978.01770300115013

Stanley, B., & Brown, G. (2012). Safety planning intervention: A brief intervention to mitigate suicide risk. *Cognitive and Behavioral Practice, 19*(2), 256–264. https://doi.org/10.1016/j.cbpra.2011.01.001

Stopa, L., Thorne, P., Waters, A., & Preston, J. (2001). Are the short and long forms of the Young Schema Questionnaire comparable and how well does each version predict psychopathology scores? *Journal of Cognitive Psychotherapy, 15*(3), 253–272. https://doi.org/10.1891/0889-8391.15.3.253

Strauss, C., Cavanagh, K., Oliver, A., & Pettman, D. (2014). Mindfulness-based interventions for people diagnosed with a current episode of an anxiety or depressive disorder: A meta-analysis of randomised controlled trials. *PLOS One, 9*(4), Article e96110. Advance online publication. https://doi.org/10.1371/journal.pone.0096110

Sullivan, H. S. (1953). *The interpersonal theory of psychiatry.* W. W. Norton & Co.

Szumilas, M. (2010). Explaining odds ratios. *Journal of the Canadian Academy of Child and Adolescent Psychiatry, 19*(3), 227–229.

Tan, E. J., Raut, T., Le, L. K., Hay, P., Ananthapavan, J., Lee, Y. Y., & Mihalopoulos, C. (2023). The association between eating disorders and mental health: An umbrella review. *Journal of Eating Disorders, 11*(1), 51. https://doi.org/10.1186/s40337-022-00725-4

Tanaka-Matsumi, J. (2019). Culture and psychotherapy: Searching for an empirically-supported relationship. In K. D. Keith (Ed.), *Cross-cultural psychology: Contemporary themes and perspectives* (pp. 482–497). Wiley Blackwell. https://doi.org/10.1002/9781119519348.ch23

Tang, T. Z., & DeRubeis, R. J. (1999). Sudden gains and critical sessions in cognitive-behavioral therapy for depression. *Journal of Consulting and Clinical Psychology, 67*(6), 894–904. https://doi.org/10.1037/0022-006X.67.6.894

Teasdale, J., Williams, M., & Segal, Z. (2014). *The mindful way workbook: An 8-week program to free yourself from depression and emotional distress.* Guilford Press.

Teasdale, J. D. (1988). Cognitive vulnerability to persistent depression. *Cognition and Emotion, 2*(3), 247–274. https://doi.org/10.1080/02699938808410927

Teasdale, J. D., Moore, R. G., Hayhurst, H., Pope, M., Williams, S., & Segal, Z. V. (2002). Metacognitive awareness and prevention of relapse in depression: Empirical evidence. *Journal of Consulting and Clinical Psychology, 70*(2), 275–287. https://doi.org/10.1037/0022-006X.70.2.275

Teasdale, J. D., Segal, Z., & Williams, J. M. G. (1995). How does cognitive therapy prevent depressive relapse and why should attentional control (mindfulness) training help? *Behaviour Research and Therapy, 33*(1), 25–39. https://doi.org/10.1016/0005-7967(94)E0011-7

Teasdale, J. D., Segal, Z. V., Williams, J. M. G., Ridgeway, V. A., Soulsby, J. M., & Lau, M. A. (2000). Prevention of relapse/recurrence in major depression by mindfulness-based cognitive therapy. *Journal of Consulting and Clinical Psychology, 68*(4), 615–623. https://doi.org/10.1037/0022-006X.68.4.615

Terjesen, M. D., & Doyle, K. A. (Eds.). (2022). *Cognitive behavioral therapy in a global context.* Springer Nature. https://doi.org/10.1007/978-3-030-82555-3

Terman, M., Terman, J. S., Quitkin, F. M., McGrath, P. J., Stewart, J. W., & Rafferty, B. (1989). Light therapy for seasonal affective disorder: A review of efficacy. *Neuropsychopharmacology, 2*(1), 1–22. https://doi.org/10.1016/0893-133X(89)90002-X

Thase, M. E. (2003). Therapeutic alternatives for difficult-to-treat depression: What is the state of the evidence? *Psychiatric Annals, 33*(12), 813–821. https://doi.org/10.3928/0048-5713-20031201-08

Thimm, J. C., & Antonsen, L. (2014). Effectiveness of cognitive behavioral group therapy for depression in routine practice. *BMC Psychiatry, 14*(1), 292. https://doi.org/10.1186/s12888-014-0292-x

Thomas-Odenthal. F., Molero, P., Does, W. Van Der, & Molendijk, M. (2020). Diets against depression: Strong conclusions, weak evidence. A systemic review. *The Lancet Psychiatry.* https://papers.ssrn.com/sol3/papers.cfm?abstract_id=3555258

Thompson, C., Kinmonth, A. L., Stevens, L., Pevele, R. C., Stevens, A., Ostler, K. J., Pickering, R. M., Baker, N. G., Henson, A., Preece, J., Cooper, D., & Campbell, M. J. (2000). Effects of a clinical-practice guideline and practice-based education on detection and outcome of depression in primary care: Hampshire Depression Project randomised controlled trial. *The Lancet, 355*(9199), 185–191. https://doi.org/10.1016/S0140-6736(99)03171-2

Trauer, J. M., Qian, M. Y., Doyle, J. S., Rajaratnam, S. M. W., & Cunnington, D. (2015). Cognitive behavioral therapy for chronic insomnia: A systematic review and meta-analysis. *Annals of Internal Medicine, 163*(3), 191–204. https://doi.org/10.7326/M14-2841

Tse, W. S., & Bond, A. J. (2004). The impact of depression on social skills: A review. *Journal of Nervous and Mental Disease, 192*(4), 260–268. https://doi.org/10.1097/01.nmd.0000120884.60002.2b

Turecki, G., & Brent, D. A. (2016). Suicide and suicidal behaviour. *The Lancet, 387*(10024), 1227–1239. https://doi.org/10.1016/S0140-6736(15)00234-2

van der Zweerde, T., Bisdounis, L., Kyle, S. D., Lancee, J., & van Straten, A. (2019). Cognitive behavioral therapy for insomnia: A meta-analysis of long-term effects in controlled studies. *Sleep Medicine Reviews, 48*, 101208. https://doi.org/10.1016/j.smrv.2019.08.002

Van Orden, K. A., Witte, T. K., Cukrowicz, K. C., Braithwaite, S. R., Selby, E. A., & Joiner, T. E., Jr. (2010). The interpersonal theory of suicide. *Psychological Review, 117*(2), 575–600. https://doi.org/10.1037/a0018697

Vanhalst, J., Luyckx, K., Teppers, E., & Goossens, L. (2012). Disentangling the longitudinal relation between loneliness and depressive symptoms: Prospective effects and the intervening role of coping. *Journal of Social and Clinical Psychology, 31*(8), 810–834. https://doi.org/10.1521/jscp.2012.31.8.810

Velicer, W. F., Hughes, S. L., Fava, J. L., Prochaska, J. O., & DiClemente, C. C. (1995). An empirical typology of subjects within stage of change. *Addictive Behaviors, 20*(3), 299–320. https://doi.org/10.1016/0306-4603(94)00069-B

Vellekkatt, F., & Menon, V. (2019). Efficacy of vitamin D supplementation in major depression: A meta-analysis of randomized controlled trials. *Journal of Postgraduate Medicine, 65*(2), 74–80. https://doi.org/10.4103/jpgm.JPGM_571_17

Velten, E., Jr. (1968). A laboratory task for induction of mood states. *Behaviour Research and Therapy, 6*(4), 473–482. https://doi.org/10.1016/0005-7967(68)90028-4

Vieta, E., Alonso, J., Pérez-Sola, V., Roca, M., Hernando, T., Sicras-Mainar, A., Sicras-Navarro, A., Herrera, B., & Gabilondo, A. (2021). Epidemiology and costs of depressive disorder in Spain: The EPICO study. *European Neuropsychopharmacology, 50*, 93–103. https://doi.org/10.1016/j.euroneuro.2021.04.022

Vittengl, J. R., Clark, L. A., & Jarrett, R. B. (2009). Continuation-phase cognitive therapy's effects on remission and recovery from depression. *Journal of Consulting and Clinical Psychology, 77*(2), 367–371. https://doi.org/10.1037/a0015238

Vittengl, J. R., Clark, L. A., & Jarrett, R. B. (2010). Moderators of continuation phase cognitive therapy's effects on relapse, recurrence, remission, and recovery from depression. *Behaviour Research and Therapy, 48*(6), 449–458. https://doi.org/10.1016/j.brat.2010.01.006

Vittorio, L. N., Murphy, S. T., Braun, J. D., & Strunk, D. R. (2022). Using Socratic questioning to promote cognitive change and achieve depressive symptom reduction: Evidence of cognitive change as a mediator. *Behaviour Research and Therapy*, *150*, 104035. https://doi.org/10.1016/j.brat.2022.104035

Wagenaar, B. H., Hammett, W. H., Jackson, C., Atkins, D. L., Belus, J. M., & Kemp, C. G. (2020). Implementation outcomes and strategies for depression interventions in low- and middle-income countries: A systematic review. *Global Mental Health*, *7*, Article e7. https://doi.org/10.1017/gmh.2020.1

Waller, G. (2009). Evidence-based treatment and therapist drift. *Behaviour Research and Therapy*, *47*(2), 119–127. https://doi.org/10.1016/j.brat.2008.10.018

Wampold, B. E. (2001). *The motivational interviewing workbook: Exercises to decide what you want and how to get there*. Lawrence Erlbaum Associates.

Wang, L., Young, L. E., & Miller, L. C. (2021). The structure of social support in confidant networks: Implications for depression. *International Journal of Environmental Research and Public Health*, *18*(16), 8388. https://doi.org/10.3390/ijerph18168388

Wang, Y. Y., Li, X. H., Zheng, W., Xu, Z. Y., Ng, C. H., Ungvari, G. S., Yuan, Z., & Xiang, Y. T. (2018). Mindfulness-based interventions for major depressive disorder: A comprehensive meta-analysis of randomized controlled trials. *Journal of Affective Disorders*, *229*(July 2017), 429–436. https://doi.org/10.1016/j.jad.2017.12.093

Ward, P. J., Lundberg, N. R., Zabriskie, R. B., & Berrett, K. (2009). Measuring marital satisfaction: A comparison of the Revised Dyadic Adjustment Scale and the Satisfaction with Married Life Scale. *Marriage & Family Review*, *45*(4), 412–429. https://doi.org/10.1080/01494920902828219

Watkins, E., & Baracaia, S. (2002). Rumination and social problem-solving in depression. *Behaviour Research and Therapy*, *40*(10), 1179–1189. https://doi.org/10.1016/S0005-7967(01)00098-5

Watkins, E. R. (2008). Constructive and unconstructive repetitive thought. *Psychological Bulletin*, *134*(2), 163–206. https://doi.org/10.1037/0033-2909.134.2.163

Watkins, E. R. (2016). *Rumination-focused cognitive-behavioral therapy for depression*. Guilford Press.

Watkins, E. R. (2022). Rumination-focused cognitive behavioral therapy. In G. Todd & R. Branch (Eds.), *Evidence-based treatment for anxiety disorders and depression: A cognitive behavioral therapy compendium* (pp. 402–417). Cambridge University Press. https://doi.org/10.1017/9781108355605.024

Watkins, E. R., Mullan, E., Wingrove, J., Rimes, K., Steiner, H., Bathurst, N., Eastman, R., & Scott, J. (2011). Rumination-focused cognitive-behavioural therapy for residual depression: Phase II randomised controlled trial. *The British Journal of Psychiatry*, *199*(4), 317–322. https://doi.org/10.1192/bjp.bp.110.090282

Watkins, E. R., & Roberts, H. (2020). Reflecting on rumination: Consequences, causes, mechanisms and treatment of rumination. *Behaviour Research and Therapy*, *127*, 103573. https://doi.org/10.1016/j.brat.2020.103573

Watson, L. C., Amick, H. R., Gaynes, B. N., Brownley, K. A., Thaker, S., Viswanathan, M., & Jonas, D. E. (2013). Practice-based interventions addressing concomitant depression and chronic medical conditions in the primary care setting: A systematic review and meta-analysis. *Journal of Primary Care & Community Health*, *4*(4), 294–306. https://doi.org/10.1177/2150131913484040

Weiner, B. J., Lewis, C. C., & Sherr, K. (2023). *Practical implementation science: Moving evidence into action*. Springer Publishing Company.

Weiss, E. L., Longhurst, J. G., & Mazure, C. M. (1999). Childhood sexual abuse as a risk factor for depression in women: Psychosocial and neurobiological correlates. *The American Journal of Psychiatry, 156*(6), 816–828. https://doi.org/10.1176/ajp.156.6.816

Weissman, M. M. (2001). *Treatment of depression: Bridging the 21st century*. American Psychiatric Press Inc.

Weissman, M. M., Markowitz, J. C., & Klerman, G. L. (2000). *Comprehensive guide to interpersonal psychotherapy*. Basic Books.

Weissman, M. M., Markowitz, J. C., & Klerman, G. L. (2018). *The guide to interpersonal psychotherapy*. Oxford University Press.

Wells, A. (2009). *Metacognitive therapy for anxiety and depression*. Guilford Press.

Wells, A., & Fisher, P. (2006). *Treating depression: MCT, CBT and third wave therapies*. J. Wiley and Sons.

Weziak-Bialowolska, D., Bialowolski, P., Lee, M. T., Chen, Y., VanderWeele, T. J., & McNeely, E. (2022). Prospective associations between social connectedness and mental health: Evidence from a longitudinal survey and health insurance claims data. *International Journal of Public Health, 67,* 1604710. Advance online publication. https://doi.org/10.3389/ijph.2022.1604710

Whisman, M. A., & Beach, S. R. H. (2012). Couple therapy for depression. *Journal of Clinical Psychology, 68*(5), 526–535. https://doi.org/10.1002/jclp.21857

Whisman, M. A., & Bruce, M. L. (1999). Marital dissatisfaction and incidence of major depressive episode in a community sample. *Journal of Abnormal Psychology, 108*(4), 674–678. https://doi.org/10.1037/0021-843X.108.4.674

Whisman, M. A., Sbarra, D. A., & Beach, S. R. H. (2021). Intimate relationships and depression: Searching for causation in the sea of association. *Annual Review of Clinical Psychology, 17*(1), 233–258. https://doi.org/10.1146/annurev-clinpsy-081219-103323

Wiggins, B. J., & Christopherson, C. D. (2019). The replication crisis in psychology: An overview for theoretical and philosophical psychology. *Journal of Theoretical and Philosophical Psychology, 39*(4), 202–217. https://doi.org/10.1037/teo0000137

Wilfley, D., MacKenzie, K., Welch, R., Ayres, V., & Weissman, M. M. (2000). *Interpersonal psychotherapy for group*. Basic Books.

Williams, L. M., & Hack, L. (2022). *Precision psychiatry: Using neuroscience insights to inform personally tailored, measurement-based care*. American Psychiatric Association.

Williams, M., Teasdale, J. D., Segal, Z. V., & Kabat-Zinn, J. (2007). *The mindful way through depression: Freeing yourself from chronic unhappiness*. Guilford Press.

Winnicott, D. W. (1965). *The maturational processes and the facilitating environment: Studies in the theory of emotional development*. International Universities Press.

Witteman, H. O., Ndjaboue, R., Vaisson, G., Dansokho, S. C., Arnold, B., Bridges, J. F. P., Comeau, S., Fagerlin, A., Gavaruzzi, T., Marcoux, M., Pieterse, A., Pignone, M., Provencher, T., Racine, C., Regier, D., Rochefort-Brihay, C., Thokala, P., Weernink, M., White, D. B., . . . Jansen, J. (2021). Clarifying values: An updated and expanded systematic review and meta-analysis. *Medical Decision Making, 41*(7), 801–820. https://doi.org/10.1177/0272989X211037946

Wood, A. (2020). *The motivational interviewing workbook: Exercises to decide what you want and how to get there*. California Rockridge Press.

World Health Organization. (n.d.). *Disability adjusted life years (DALYs)*. https://www.who.int/data/gho/indicator-metadata-registry/imr-details/158

World Health Organization. (1948). *International statistical classification of diseases, injuries, and causes of death* (6th ed.). https://icd.who.int/

World Health Organization. (2014). *Preventing suicide: A global imperative.* https://www.who.int/publications/i/item/9789241564779

World Health Organization. (2019). *International statistical classification of diseases and related health problems* (11th ed.). https://icd.who.int/

World Health Organization. (2023). *ICD-11 for mortality and morbidity statistics.* https://icd.who.int/browse11/l-m/en#/

Wu, J. Q., Appleman, E. R., Salazar, R. D., & Ong, J. C. (2015). Cognitive behavioral therapy for insomnia comorbid with psychiatric and medical conditions: A meta-analysis. *JAMA Internal Medicine, 175*(9), 1461–1472. https://doi.org/10.1001/jamainternmed.2015.3006

Yalcin, O., Lee, C., & Correia, H. (2020). Factor structure of the Young Schema Questionnaire (Long Form-3). *Australian Psychologist, 55*(5), 546–558. https://doi.org/10.1111/ap.12458

Yalom, I. D., & Leszcz, M. (2020). *The theory and practice of group psychotherapy* (6th ed.). Basic Books.

Yanatma, S. (2022). Europe's mental health crisis in data: Which country uses the most antidepressants? *Euronews.* https://www.euronews.com/next/2022/11/27/europes-mental-health-crisis-in-data-which-country-uses-the-most-antidepressants

Yapko, M. D. (1997). *Breaking the patterns of depression.* Doubleday.

Yesavage, J. A., Brink, T. L., Rose, T. L., Lum, O., Huang, V., Adey, M., & Leirer, V. O. (1982). Development and validation of a geriatric depression screening scale: A preliminary report. *Journal of Psychiatric Research, 17*(1), 37–49. https://doi.org/10.1016/0022-3956(82)90033-4

Yoon, E., Chang, C. T., Kim, S., Clawson, A., Cleary, S. E., Hansen, M., Bruner, J. P., Chan, T. K., & Gomes, A. M. (2013). A meta-analysis of acculturation/enculturation and mental health. *Journal of Counseling Psychology, 60*(1), 15–30. https://doi.org/10.1037/a0030652

Young, J. E. (1994). *Cognitive therapy for personality disorders: A schema-focused approach.* Professional Resource Press.

Young, J. E., & Klosko, J. S. (1993). *Reinventing your life: The breakthrough program to end negative behavior and feel great again.* Plume.

Young, J. E., Klosko, J. S., & Weishaar, M. E. (2003). *Schema therapy: A practitioner's guide.* Guilford Press.

Young, L. M., Pipingas, A., White, D. J., Gauci, S., & Scholey, A. (2019). A systematic review and meta-analysis of B vitamin supplementation on depressive symptoms, anxiety, and stress: Effects on healthy and 'at-risk' individuals. *Nutrients, 11*(9), Article 2232. Advance online publication. https://doi.org/10.3390/nu11092232

Zajonc, R. B. (1980). Feeling and thinking: Preferences need no inferences. *American Psychologist, 35*(2), 151–175. https://doi.org/10.1037/0003-066X.35.2.151

Zettle, R. D. (2016). Acceptance and commitment theory of depression. In A. Wells & P. Fisher (Eds.), *Treating depression: MCT, CBT and third wave therapies* (pp. 169–193). Wiley-Blackwell.

Zubernis, L., & Snyder, M. (2016). *Case conceptualization and effective interventions: Assessing and treating mental, emotional and behavioral disorders.* Sage Publications.

INDEX

Cognitive behavior therapy for insomnia
(CBT-I), 138–145
  cognitive and behavioral interventions in,
    139–140
  combining interventions in, 145
  relaxation techniques in, 139
  sleep hygiene in, 140–142
  sleep restriction, 143–145
  stimulus control in, 142–143
Cognitive development, 177
Cognitive distortions, 157–158. *See also*
    Negative thinking
Cognitive interventions, for sleep problems,
    139–140
Cognitive patterns
  associated with depression, 42–43
  as intervention targets, 43–44
  relationship among, 43
Cognitive restructuring, 149–166
  case illustrations of, 164–166
  monitoring cognition in, 151–156
  and power of thoughts, 163
  for rumination, 161–163
  strategies to modify negative thinking in,
    156–161
Cognitive theory, 59–60
Cognitive therapy, 59
Cognitive triad, 178–179
Collaborative empiricism, 101–102
Collectivism, depression and, 47
Columbia-Suicide Severity Rating Scale
    (C-SSRS), 78
Comorbidity(-ies), 219–221
  anxiety, 18, 75
  patterns of, 24
  physical conditions, exercise and, 134
  scales measuring, 75
  sleep disturbance and depression, 38
Compassion training, 163
Concurrent therapies, when ending
    therapy, 207–208
Confidentiality, legal limits of, 72
Confrontation, for belief change, 192
Conner, K. R., 40
Contextualizing client's problems, 84–85
Continuation therapy, 210
Coping With Depression (CWD) *Course*
    (Clarke & Lewinsohn), 57–58
Core beliefs
  advantages and disadvantages of,
    188–189
  assessment of, 182–186
  in cognitive behavior therapy, 59
  in cognitive triad, 178–179
  interaction of life stressors and, 104
  models of, 178–182
  negative, identification and modification
    of, 108. *See also* Modifying core beliefs
    and schemas

"shoulds" attached to, 159
  situations shaped by, 153
Correlational analyses, 236
  of cognitive patterns and depression, 42
  of risk and resilience factors, 30–32
Cossman, E. Joseph, 37
Couples therapy, 222–223
COVID-19 pandemic, 227
CPGs (clinical practice guidelines), for
    biological treatments, 37
Crawford, M. J., 78
C-SSRS (Columbia-Suicide Severity Rating
    Scale), 78
Cuijpers, P., 59, 231–232
Culture
  sense of self as function of, 178
  values embedded in, 190–191
CWD *(Coping With Depression) Course*
    (Clarke & Lewinsohn), 57–58

D

Daily hassles, 45–46
Dairy product consumption, 33, 39–40
Defining the problem (step 1; PST), 169, 170
Delivery models, 223–229
  individual vs. group treatment, 223–225
  in-person vs. distance treatment,
    225–229
Depression (clinical depression; major
    depressive disorder), 3–4, 11–28.
    See also specific topics
  biopsychosocial perspective on, 4.
    See also Biopsychosocial model
  case illustrations of, 26–28
  "classic" vs. manic, 12
  clinical (major depressive disorder), 3
  clinical description of, 12–15
  cognitive model of, 149
  comorbidity patterns in, 24, 134
  course of, 20–21
  developmental pattern of, 206
  diagnosis of, 3
  estimating occurrence of, 21–23
  models of treatment for. *See* Models for
    treating depression
  nature of, 25–26, 103, 178
  possible symptoms of, 3, 13
  presenting as secondary problem, 221
  preventive strategies for, 237
  resilience factors for, 25
  risk factors for, 24–25, 235–236. *See also*
    Risk and resiliency
  stigmatization of, 4
  subtypes of, 17–20, 54
  suicide as response to, 15–16
  as time-bound condition, 4
  varied presentation of, 104
Depressive neurosis, 12–13

modifying. *See* Modifying core beliefs
and schemas
questionnaires assessing, 183–184
Schema therapy, 179–181
Schildkraut, J. J., 36
SCID-5 (Structured Clinical Interview for
DSM-5), 76
Seasonal affective disorder (SAD), 18–19
Selecting best potential solutions
(step 3; PST), 169–171
Self
development of, 54–55
relational aspects of, 178
sense of, 177–178. *See also* Core beliefs;
Schemas
Self-directed treatment, 226–227
Self-efficacy, practices promoting, 194
Self-help, 226
Self-perception of clients, 84
Self-protection, for therapist, 214
Self-report questionnaires, 22, 23, 73
Serotonin, 36, 38
Session gaps, when ending treatment,
209–210
Shakespeare, William, 136
Short-term IPT, 55–56
"Should" statements, 159–160
Significant others, included in treatment
plan, 221–223
Situational analysis, 59–60
Skills
learned in therapy, review of, 205
social. *See* Social skills
10,000-hour rule for improving, 146
Skills deficits
addressed in behavioral activation,
130–132
in managing problems, 168
treatment focusing on, 114
Sleep
needed amounts of, 136
physiology of, 136–137
recording patterns of, 89, 127
and risk of depression, 33, 37–38, 40
Sleep disturbance, residual, 206
Sleep efficiency, 143–145
Sleep hygiene, 61–62, 140–142
Sleep log/diary, 89, 143–144
Sleep problems, 136–145
cognitive behavior therapy for insomnia,
61–62, 138–145
as prodromal sign of depression, 17
sleep medications for, 137–138
Sleep restriction, 143–145
SMILES trial, 135
Social construction of depression, 47
Social contact/engagement
as preventive factor for depression,
45, 221

and risk of depression, 33, 223. *See also*
Social risks
Social events, as risk factors for depression,
45
Social isolation
as consequence of stress generation, 46
and risk of depression, 45, 223
Socialization, sense of self as function of,
178
Social risks, 44–48
adverse childhood experiences, 44–45
culture, 46–47
negative life events, 45–46
stress generation, 46
Social skills
behavioral activation for, 130–132
deficits in, 108
and risk of depression, 41–42, 223
Sociotropy-autonomy models, 178–179
Sociotropy-Autonomy Scale (SAS), 179
Socrates, 102
Socratic questioning and dialogue, 101, 102
in addressing cognitive distortions,
160–161
in addressing thought record, 156
open and genuine inquiry via, 151–152
in rumination-focused interventions,
162
Somatic interventions, integrating
psychosocial treatments and, 229–232
Spitzer, R. L., 13, 74
SSTA (stop, slow down, think, and act)
approach, 173
Stigmatization of depression, 4
Stimulant intake, 140–141
Stimulus control, in cognitive behavior
therapy for insomnia, 142–143
Stop, slow down, think, and act (SSTA)
approach, 173
Strategies to modify negative thinking,
156–161
alternative-based, 159–160
combining evidence- and alternative
based, 160–161
evidence-based, 158–159
Stress
generation of, as risk for depression, 46
in life events. *See* Life stressors
problem solving under, 168
Structured Clinical Interview for *DSM-5*
(SCID-5), 76
Structured interviews, 81
Substance use
and depression, 24, 40–41
depression or depression symptoms with,
221
to sleep better, 138
Subtypes of depression, 17–20, 24, 54

ABOUT THE AUTHOR

Keith S. Dobson, PhD, is professor emeritus of clinical psychology at the University of Calgary, where he has served in roles such as the inaugural director of the clinical psychology program and head of the department of psychology. His research has focused on models and treatment of depression, particularly using cognitive behavior therapies. In addition to his research in depression, Dr. Dobson has examined psychological approaches and the integration of evidence-based treatments in primary care. Further, he has written about developments in professional psychology and ethics and has been actively involved in organized psychology in Canada, including a term as president of the Canadian Psychological Association. Dr. Dobson is a principal investigator for the Opening Minds program of the Mental Health Commission of Canada, which focuses on reducing stigmas related to mental disorders in the workplace. Dr. Dobson's research has resulted in more than 340 published articles and 80 chapters, 18 books, and conference and workshop presentations in many countries. His recent books include *Handbook of Cognitive-Behavioral Therapies* (4th ed., 2019); *Law, Standards, and Ethics in the Practice of Psychology* (4th ed., 2021); *The Stigma of Mental Illness* (2021), and *Treatment of Psychosocial Risk Factors in Depression* (2023). In recognition of his work, he has received numerous awards, including the Canadian Psychological Association Gold Medal for Lifetime Contributions to Psychology, fellow status with several organizations including the Canadian Academy of Health Sciences and the Royal Society of Canada, and officer status with the Order of Canada.